From Bananas to Buttocks

From Bananas to Buttocks

The Latina Body in Popular Film and Culture

EDITED BY MYRA MENDIBLE

University of Texas Press ◆ *Austin*

First edition, 2007

Requests for permission to reproduce material from this work should be sent to:
Permissions
University of Texas Press
P.O. Box 7819
Austin, TX 78713-7819
www.utexas.edu/utpress/about/bpermission.html

♾ The paper used in this book meets the minimum requirements of ANSI/NISO
Z39.48–1992 (R1997) (Permanence of Paper).

Library of Congress Cataloging-in-Publication Data
From bananas to buttocks : the Latina body in popular film and culture /
edited by Myra Mendible. — 1st ed.
     p.   cm.
Includes bibliographical references and index.
     ISBN-13: 978-0-292-71492-2 (cloth : alk. paper)
     ISBN-10: 0-292-71492-0 (alk. paper)
     ISBN-13: 978-0-292-71493-9 (pbk. : alk. paper)
     ISBN-10: 0-292-71493-9 (alk. paper)
     1. Hispanic American women—Public opinion. 2. Hispanic American women—
Ethnic identity. 3. Hispanic American women in mass media. 4. Popular culture—
United States. 5. Body, Human—Social aspects—United States. 6. Femininity—
United States. 7. Stereotypes (Social psychology)—United States. 8. Public
opinion—United States. 9. United States—Ethnic relations. I. Mendible, Myra,
1954–   .
E184.S75F748 2007
305.48′868073009045—dc22
                                                              2007004543

To Ernesto, always; and to Jennie, Ben, and Jonathan, who give me a reason to write . . . and dance.

What do these South American girls have below the Equator that we haven't?

Contents

From Bananas to Buttocks

Embodying Latinidad

An Overview

MYRA MENDIBLE

Miss Lopez's rounded posterior is credited with making curvy bottoms trendy again and is said by American plastic surgeons to have created a demand for silicone buttock implants.

DAILY MAIL (LONDON), FEBRUARY 27, 2003

Despite the promise implicit in the title of this collection of essays, there is no such thing as "the Latina body." While the words evoke a set of predictable responses ("she" is hot-blooded, tempestuous, hypersexual, and in current manifestations has a big butt), "the Latina body" is a convenient fiction—a historically contingent, mass-produced combination of myth, desire, location, marketing, and political expedience. Mediated through various forms of visual representation and discourse, "the Latina body" functions within a social and cultural taxonomy that registers but an echo of the clamor, complexity, and variety of women who embody Latina identities. Building on a feminist assertion that "woman" exists as a social construct subject to renegotiations and mediations, this anthology proceeds from the assumption that "the Latin woman" is a doubly inscribed fantasy—a multiply inflected and variably experienced category. Implicit in this assumption is the understanding that several forces converge in producing acculturated, gendered bodies and that these forces have very real consequences for Latinas in the United States and abroad.

This book explores some of the ways that a shared understanding of Latina sexuality, subjectivity, and difference is constructed and represented. Several related concerns informed its conception, though an overriding objective was to respond critically to the "conspicuous consumption" of Latina bodies realized via marketing and entertainment vectors.

Such a project is especially pertinent in light of recent celebrations of the "Latina body" (buttocks, curves) evidenced in cultural phenomena from the plastic surgery craze cited in my epigraph to an explosion of on-line porn sites promising intimate access to "hot" Latina bodies. Popularized versions of "Latin beauty" have caught on with North Americans to such an extent that an article in the *National Post,* a Canadian paper, posed the question, "Are Latinas the new blond bombshell?"[1]

Such apparent notice of the Latina body (particularly of what plastic surgeons call the "gluteal aesthetic") produces a mixed bag of consequences. On the one hand, I welcome any departure from a dominant aesthetic inherited, as Shohat and Stam have argued, from a colonialist discourse that "exiled people of color from their own bodies" (1994, 322). Latinas are said to be embracing another standard of beauty and reclaiming, along with Jennifer Lopez, "a curvaceous Latin body."[2] Several critics express this optimism, maintaining, like Mary Beltrán, that for Lopez "to declare beautiful and unashamedly display her well-endowed posterior . . . could be viewed as nothing less than positive—a revolutionary act with respect to Anglo beauty ideals" (2000, 73). Frances Aparicio notes that the Latina bodies of Jennifer Lopez and Selena, similarly marked by curvy bottoms, full lips, and dark hair, have become symbols of ethnic pride (2003, 98), while Frances Negrón-Muntaner contends that Latinas' insistent focus on "big butts" is "a response to the pain of being ignored, thought of as ugly, treated as low, yet surviving—even thriving—through a belly-down epistemology" (1997, 192). Josefina Lopez's successful play, *Real Women Have Curves,* builds on this implicit relationship between celebrations of the fuller (presumably "real") Latina body and an affirmative Latina selfhood. As Maria Figueroa puts it, Lopez's text "reclaims and redefines the Latina body from its 'fat,' 'undesirable,' and 'marginal' status, thus rescuing this body from its abject state and transforming it into a body 'that matters'" (2003, 265).

On the other hand, various attendant signs and conditions complicate matters. Although I agree with Figueroa that Latina body images inspired by a "Selena aesthetic" or a J.Lo butt are "more inclusive of diverse physicalities," I also recognize, as she does, the risk that "the Latina body suddenly becomes only a Latina body, racially marked for cultural and commodified circulation" (2003, 271).[3] Leading renditions of "Latin beauty" are performed in harmony with prevailing commercial, political, and cultural repertoires; these are aligned with an epistemology of the body consistently used to justify hierarchies of race, ethnicity, and gender.[4] Latinas' identification with any exclusive set of physical attributes deemed "natural" or "authentic" (in this case, the Latina body as callipygian ideal) performs an unambiguous self-tropicalization, binding Latina femininity to bodily excess, sexuality, or indulgence and imbuing Latinidad with a fixed set of traits, values, and images (Aparicio and Chávez-Silverman 1997).[5] Such acts comply with racialized dualisms of self/other, the very structures that enforce beauty norms and a hierarchy of body types. Most important, if this much-touted validation of "Latin beauty" indeed marks a genuine change in dominant aesthetic patterns—a turn toward what Shohat and Stam (1994, 322) call "an open, non-essentialist approach to looks and identity"—then why are prominent "Latin beauties" still dyeing their hair blonde, slimming their bodies, or wearing blue contact lenses to "whiten" their looks?[6] Why, despite all the hype about Latinas reclaiming a "curvaceous Latin body," are eating disorders increasing rapidly among young Latina females?[7]

Throughout this collection of essays, "the Latina body" refers generally to an amalgam of eroticized, racialized tropes about Latinas that inform U.S. popular culture. A complex history undergirds these imaginings, many of which still evoke familiar caricatures of "Latinness." Thus, a related task of this book is to explore various deployments of Latina identity and sexuality in light of current work in body theory, which has emerged as an investigative field in its own right. Across the humanities, critics foreground the body in analyses that stress the constructed and performative nature of all subjectivities; body theory also informs a range of investigations in history, sociology, psychoanalysis, and legal studies, and there is now a journal devoted exclusively to the subject. Of course, the body has consistently been at the core of much that concerns feminist theorists, many of whom have reformulated the work of thinkers such as Freud, de Beauvoir, Lacan, Merleau-Ponty, and Foucault and paved the way for new directions in film and media analyses.[8] Feminist philosophers in particular have offered powerful critiques of a dualistic tradition that asserted the supremacy of the (masculine) mind over the (feminine) body.[9] While cultural studies extend these conversations to include other layers of differentiation inscribed on the bodies of men and women—the particulars of race, ethnicity, disability, and transgender identity—this anthology situates the Latina body at the center of its analysis, exploring its constitutive role in the production, contestation, and consumption of Latinidad in the United States.

Our project extends Judith Butler's notion of gender performativity (1990, 1993) to the construction of Latinidad, building on the assumption that ethnic groups are constituted through various classificatory, discursive acts and corporeal exchanges.[10] Reconceptualizing identity as an effect that is produced or generated, Butler argues, "opens up possibilities of 'agency' that are insidiously foreclosed by positions that take identity categories as foundational and fixed" (1990, 147). The essays collected here engage Latinidad as a fluid set of cultural boundaries that are consistently reinforced, challenged, or negotiated by and through Latina bodies. Gloria Anzaldúa's conception of the mestiza body as borderland/battleground comes to mind in this regard, for any constitution of ethnic borders is socially mediated and politically contingent.[11] While our collective work seeks to destabilize essentialist notions that frame Latinidad within narrowly prescribed borders—distinguishing, for example, among mediations of "Nuyorican," Cuban, and Chicana identities, it also speaks to the political prospects inherent in group affirmation and participation. We hope to contribute to ongoing debates about what constitutes Latinidad in both national and transnational forms, not with the goal of settling the question but with the aim of affirming the potential for Latina/o self-fashioning and solidarity.

The term "Latinidad," implicated in a history of U.S. marketing and entertainment distortions of Latino/a cultures, has understandably met resistance from many Chicano and Latino critics. They have questioned the usefulness and effect of such labeling, for example, its tendency to homogenize peoples whose histories, language usage, and circumstances may differ significantly or to alienate U.S.-born Latinos, who may not speak Spanish or share other identifying criteria.[12] There are also legitimate reasons to suspect bureaucratic attempts to regulate, profile, and monitor a growing constituency of over 40 million people. Such cataloguing is useful in assessing the special needs of target groups, but it can also bolster stereotypes and misconceptions. As an undifferentiated statistical category, the Hispanic/Latino umbrella masks differences in migration histories, English-language skills, socioeconomic status, and other determinants, often producing data that are inherently flawed or intentionally misleading.[13] Indeed, these taxonomies form part of what Rey Chow in her reading of Foucault recognizes as "mechanisms of regulation and administration" whereby biopower gains momentum "precisely by (repressively) subjugating bodies and controlling populations (through surveillance of birthrate, longevity, public health, housing, and migration" (2002, 13).

Frances Aparicio rightly considers, however, the implications of such opposition for efforts directed at collective resistance, intergroup cooperation, and dialogue. Aparicio suggests that Latino/a critics consider reclaiming Latinidad as a site for exploring "interlatino affinities, desires, and conflicts" and for producing public knowledge about Latino/as (2003, 93). Others have endorsed articulations of Latinidad that are situational and tactical, suggesting that these set the stage for strategic interventions and mobilizations. Suzanne Oboler points out that U.S. Latino/a identity is always already inflected by its internalized others, by the interplay of competing interests that shapes Latinos/as as an ethnic group. Oboler cites Stuart Hall's contention that identity is always in process, reminding us that debates about Latino identity also participate in its discursive formation. She argues that "identifying oneself as Latino/a and participating in a Latino social movement is a *political* decision" that can help Latino advocates "express the strength of *la comunidad* with greater force" (2002, 86). Oboler's assertion tacitly recognizes the challenges posed by an era in which Latinas' symbolic value outweighs their political or material clout. It also echoes the call of Latina and particularly Chicana feminists who have resisted constructs of Latinidad detached from social praxis and embodied experience; many of these critics envision Latinidad as a situated, contingent, and negotiable work-in-progress.[14]

The diverse essays collected here speak to the potential of such an endeavor: we aim to affirm the role of individual agency in the constitution and decoding of our ethnic corporeality, even as we "talk back" to the dominant media that render Latinos/as visible and knowable. In showcasing the Latina body as a site of knowledge production, we claim a space for Latinidad that is invariably gendered, hybrid, and transactional. Our analyses proceed from the assumption that Latinos/as are multifaceted, and that identity is always subject to the vicissitudes of routine encounters, reciprocities, and exchanges. We understand that even when shared contingencies of history, ancestry, language, or material conditions serve to foster the illusion of cohesion, embodied selves rarely comply with the terms or theories that attempt to define them. Our work therefore traces the contours of the Latina body in the interstices where lived reality and public fantasies converge, in those myriad encounters and pleasures that embody the "politics and erotics of culture."[15] This emphasis recognizes that the "ethnic" self is relational, constructed through discursive and bodily mediations that signal its relative status.

Of interest to me in this regard is how ethnic difference, signed and transacted through bodies, visibly connotes the terms and conditions of "Americanness."[16] The ideological construction of "American identity" (and, by extension, "American interests") entails more than assimilation into the particulars of lifestyle or normative cultural values; it has historically involved the foregrounding of physical characteristics said to best represent "Americanness" and register moral and intellectual fitness. From early anthropological debates about the existence of an "American type" (determined by head shape and size and other "scientific" accounts of the body) to contemporary images of "all-American girls" as blonde and blue-eyed, dominant notions of American identity have relied on embodiment for reification.[17] My line of thinking here follows Butler's idea that "to be a woman is to have *become* a woman, to compel the body to conform to an historical idea of 'woman,' to induce the body to become a cultural sign, to materialize oneself in obedience to an historically delimited possibility, and to do this as a sustained and repeated corporeal project" (1990, 404–405).

Similarly, "becoming American" can be said to involve an epistemology of the body: privileged body types function as connotative codes that structure a cultural order. "Americanness" is frequently reified through deployments of what Amy Kaplan refers to as "the 'look' that United States media and advertising industries disseminate as some kind of ideal toward which all people living in America and counted *as* American must aspire" (1997, xx). Through the title of her book, *Latin Looks,* Clara Rodríguez intentionally plays with this notion in terms of how Latina/os are represented, underscoring "the tendency to view Latinos as if they all looked the same"(1997, 6). This binary relationship between body types helps to structure and define the "all-American" self against its others.[18] While this coding process is polysemic in that it engages diverse discourses, it nevertheless functions within a hierarchy of values that relegates certain bodies to prominence and others to relative status. Stuart Hall rightly distinguishes polysemy from pluralism, for connotative codes "are *not* equal among themselves." A society's various classifications constitute its *dominant cultural order,* but these rankings are "neither univocal nor uncontested" (1993b, 98).

Social relations and material conditions reflect the status afforded privileged bodies within a dominant cultural order. Richard Dyer's remark that "white" is not recognized as a particularizing quality (it is "no colour because it is all colours") suggests that this hierarchy of bodies is naturalized to such an extent that it is "invisible." In Dyer's view, the property of white "to be everything and nothing" is the very source of its representational power (1988, 45). The historically privileged subject of American cultural discourse has been forged against this white canvas. Whereas concepts of identity are intangible and elusive, stars are significant for their ability to make such metaphysical notions "a visible show." It is this "visualizing of identity," Dyer notes, "which makes the bodies of stars and the actions performed by those bodies into such a key element of a star's meaning" (1986, 40). To the extent that U.S. Latinas sign in for hybridity, a racial construct between "white" and "black" Americans, the Latina body functions as floating signifier within the American cultural imaginary.[19] Jennifer Lopez recognizes her place within this fluid racial category, commenting about her role in *Money Train:* "They wanted a Latina . . . somebody who could be with Wesley, and with Woody. Apparently in Hollywood, brown is some kind of mediating color between black and white."[20] Of course, as Monique Wittig points out, physical features are neutral in themselves, so that what we perceive as racial difference is only a "mythic construction, an imaginary formation" (1997, 313). Bodies are marked by social systems and reinterpreted through the "network of relationships in which they are perceived. (They are seen as *black,* therefore they *are* black; they are seen as *women,* therefore, they *are* women. But before being *seen* that way, they first had to be *made* that way)."

From Bananas to Buttocks explores some of the ways that certain women's bodies are *seen* and *made* as "Latinas." It is our contention that this public fashioning of "the Latina body" warrants critical scrutiny, and that stakeholders in Latinidad must look to mediations of the Latina body for both a history and a map. In the United States, the Latina body has signed in for somatic differences (body type, coloring, facial features) and differences in culture, class, language, religion, and sexuality. Consistently, its sign value has been linked to ideological currents, economic conditions, and political expediency. Most notably, the Latina body has served as figurative terrain for the nation's defining allegories, a range of which is suggested by this book's title. My ironic reference to bananas and buttocks intentionally conjures images of banana republics and fertile natural resources—literal and figurative "booty." Both have functioned as commodities, and thus by definition as fetishized objects consumed within an economics of desire that obscures the social relationships of its producers. Both connote a history of U.S. tropicalizations vis-à-vis Latin America and evoke the kind of ambivalent desire and disgust that characterizes North-South relations and, by extension, inflects the Latina body as transnational signifier.

The Body Politic: Latin America as Bounty and Booty

The most succulent item of all / the United Fruit Company Incorporated / reserved to itself. . . . the delectable waist of America.

PABLO NERUDA

The "delectable waist" of America is more than a geographical border between North and South: it functions as a critical sign in defining metaphors of nation, difference, and sexuality. While Neruda's lines imagine the body of America as the whole of North and South America,[21] forging a distinct U.S. national identity has involved a dis/membering process—an often violent project of differentiation and exclusion. Throughout this process, America's "delectable waist" has figured as a metaphysical divide, a "torrid zone" between northern mind and southern body. As metonym for Latin America, the Latina body has signaled a permeable racial and national border, a field of diverse oppositions between rationality and sensuality, culture and nature, domestic and foreign. This body metaphor has informed America's defining myths, providing basic themes and motifs for a variety of cultural narratives. Specifically, it has served to justify U.S. corporate exploitation of Latin American labor and resources, invasions and border violations, and the "internal colonization" of U.S. Latino groups.

Narratives of race and gender are crucial vehicles in the production of national identity, and in this sense the Latina body has played a formative role in the defining discourses of "America." Since the early nineteenth century, her racially marked sexuality signaled a threat to the body politic, a foreign other against whom the ideals of the domestic self, particularly its narratives of white femininity and moral virtue, could be defined.[22] At the same time, the Latina body offered a tempting alter/native: an exotic object of imperial and sexual desire. Gendered, raced tropes framed debates about immigration, territorial expansion, and nationhood. More than asserting the United States' difference and independence from Europe, these tropes symbolized its dominant role in the hemisphere.[23] For even as the grand narrative of Anglo-Saxon "manifest destiny" justified the acquisition of land, it complicated myths of racial and national purity. Isolationists argued that territorial expansion threatened to contaminate the national body with inferior races. Both those who favored and those who opposed annexation of Mexico employed erotically charged rhetoric to defend their positions.

In particular, the U.S.-Mexican War (1846–1848) produced political allegories that made their way into popular "story papers" and dime fiction. Shelly Streeby's (2002) comprehensive study of popular fiction during this period shows that the Mexican woman (and, by extension, Mexico itself) figured in numerous imperial romances and sensational novels; these imagined U.S.-Mexico relations as relations between male and female, with U.S. national strength metaphorically aligned with manhood (84). The Mexican woman appeared on the one hand as a suitable marriage partner for the Anglo man and on the other as an unruly and irredeemable other. Streeby contends that questions "about whether 'she' [Mexico] was an appropriate romantic partner for the United States were inseparable from debates about the boundaries of race and the significance of empire for the white republic" (84). Her investigation suggests that these gender metaphors both transmitted and shaped discourses of American nationality and imperialist expansion in ways that would significantly influence early twentieth-century films.[24]

Much of the silent film era's mediation of Latin American identity, for example, reflected the residual hostilities resulting from territorial disputes and clashes with Mexico.[25] As the pretty *señorita* anxious to give herself (and her territory) to the Anglo male or as the hypersexed and treacherous foil to the virtuous Anglo heroine, the Latina body figured prominently in cinematic depictions of U.S. nation building. Film images translated nationalist fantasies and power relations into iconographic and ethnographic shorthand. As signifier, the Latina's erotic sexuality served to affirm the desirability of the Anglo male and, by extension, his national superiority; it also served as moral foil to her more principled feminine counterpart, the wholesome "all-American gal." Yet it is important to note that most roles calling for Latina characters were played by Anglo actresses, whose darkened hair and skin were meant to signal their ethnicity and lend "authenticity" to their portrayals. Latina identity in these films was thus figuratively *disembodied:* present only in familiar metaphorical relation to the imagined national self.[26]

President Franklin Delano Roosevelt's administration turned what had been a dysfunctional relationship at best and a hostile one at worst into a love affair between compatible partners. During this period the United States romanticized its relationship with Latin America through the Latina star body.[27] Both Hoover and Roosevelt sought to improve Latin American relations, but Roosevelt's Pan-American Day speech in April of 1933 openly "repudiated the 'erroneous interpretations' of the Monroe Doctrine that justified U.S. intervention, and extolled 'the principle of consultation' and the 'promotion of commerce' as the bases for improved hemispheric relations" (Roorda 1998, 88). Latin America emerged as an accommodating, inviting movie set, and "South American girls" Dolores del Río, Maria Móntez, Lupe Vélez, and Carmen Miranda enticed American audiences with their exoticism, eroticism, or impish charm. Thus, by April 1945, eighty-four films featuring Latin American stars or locales had been produced.

A primary embodiment of this apolitical, carefree South America was, of course, Carmen Miranda, the "Brazilian Bombshell" in exaggerated headdresses and platform shoes. Familiar to American audiences as the generic "South American girl," Miranda's bared midriff and gyrating hips would provide Americans with frivolous images of an undifferentiated landmass somewhere south of the border. Critics referred to Miranda's exposed midriff as the "torrid zone," thus conflating, as Shari Roberts points out, Miranda's body with Latin America, "equating her 'equator' with that of the planet's, the 'torrid zone' of South America" (1993, 11). Roberts observes that the popular press typically characterized Miranda in terms of her body, like an exotic animal—such as a 1939 *Time* magazine reporter's description of Miranda "swaying and wriggling, chattering macawlike" (quoted in Roberts 1993, 10).

Miranda's ethnic star body served as a synecdoche for Latin America; her banana-laden headpieces in *The Lady in the Tutti-Frutti Hat* enacted the "agricultural reductionism" of Latin America but also functioned as "phallic symbols, here raised by 'voluptuous' Latinas over circular, quasi-vaginal forms" (Shohat and Stam 1994, 158). In Busby Berkeley's *The Gang's All Here* (1943), "Americans" Alice Faye and James Ellison dance the "serious" numbers, whereas "Latin American" characters perform their ethnicity through excessive dance numbers involving "swaying hips, exaggerated facial expressions, caricaturally sexy costumes, and 'think-big' props" (158). Shohat and Stam argue that emblematic character behavior and interaction allegorize North-South relations and reflect ambivalent feelings of attraction and repulsion toward the culturally different (231). The phallic symbolism suggested by such scenes did not escape Brazil's president, Getúlio Vargas, who censored Berkeley's film in Brazil (Woll 1980). Neither did it escape the *New York Times* critic who remarked, "Mr. Berkeley has some sly notions under his busby. One or two of his dance spectacles seem to stem straight from Freud and, if interpreted, might bring a rosy blush to several cheeks in the Hays office."[28] The film's S.S. *Brazil* arrives in New York harbor loaded with a rich cargo ranging from sacks of sugar and coffee to baskets of tropical fruits; Miranda appears beside this staged cornucopia as the very embodiment of Latin American bountifulness.

Born in Portugal and raised in Brazil, Maria do Carmo Miranda da Cunha had achieved considerable popularity in her adopted homeland before her move to Hollywood. Yet Miranda's tremendous success in the United States (she became the highest paid female performer in her day) inspired mixed reactions in Brazil. Many resented what they perceived was a caricature of their folk culture, and others accused Miranda of having sold out to an imperialist North. Miranda's biographer, Martha Gil-Montero, notes that Miranda was most pained by the accusation that she had become "Americanized" and had thus betrayed her "authentic" Brazilian national identity. In 1952, critic David Nassar chastised Miranda in the magazine *O Cruzeiro* for neglecting Brazilian audiences, suggesting that Miranda felt superior to the *bugres* (a pejorative term for savages) who had "always adored her with a passion reserved only to a white goddess" (quoted in Gil-Montero 1989, 225).

At the height of Miranda's U.S. popularity, the largest grower and marketer of bananas, United Fruit Company, created the half-banana, half-woman cartoon character, Chiquita Banana. Modeled on Miranda's lavish reinterpretation of the Brazilian market woman, this feminized banana served as the "friendly face" of the company seen by American housewives.[29] The name itself, ending in the diminutive *-ita*, means "small" and constitutes a literal downsizing of the Latina's potential threat or power. Cynthia Enloe suggests that Miranda's movies helped to make "Latin America safe for American banana companies at a time when American imperialism was coming under wider regional criticism" (2000, 124). Between 1880 and 1930, the United States had colonized or invaded the Hawaiian islands, the Philippines, Puerto Rico, the Dominican Republic, Cuba, and Nicaragua, each valuable for plantation crops. In Enloe's words, "Miranda personified a culture full of zest and charm, unclouded by intense emotion or political ambivalence" (2000, 127). This feminized Latin America, with its subjunctive status and compromised sovereignty, is still reflected in the notion of "banana republics." Here the American self deflects its own involvement in the formation of this corrupt and inept other, disavowing U.S. government complicity and corporate America's own stake in the booty. Despite United Fruit Company's use of the Chiquita cartoon as cheerful façade, the company had been involved in numerous labor disputes with its Latin American workers since 1918.[30] During the 1930s, 1940s, and 1950s, United Fruit exercised its powerful control over the leaders of the republics in which it operated. As historians Stephen Schlesinger and Stephen Kinzer have demonstrated (1999), the United Fruit Company became a "swaggering behemoth" by applying a range of strong-arm tactics including bribery, fraud, extortion, and tax evasion.

Toward the end of her short life, Miranda used a variety of pills to stave off depression and anxiety. While Shari Roberts and others have noted Miranda's complicity in producing her own caricature and have suggested a more subversive reading of Miranda's "ethnic masquerade," there are certainly signs that Miranda became disillusioned with her role. She may have transformed herself into "sheer spectacle" with a wink toward the camera's eye, but it was a difficult role to sustain, and one that seems to have wearied and saddened her. For Miranda's status as ethnic spectacle seems to me less a sign of her self-parody than of her bounded role as perpetual "foreigner." Fixed and contained within these performative boundaries, the Brazilian Bombshell and "scandalous outsider" became, to use Roland Barthes's words in another context, "a pure object, a spectacle, a clown" (1975, 151). Yet in reconsidering Brazil's love-hate relationship with Miranda, composer and singer Caetano Veloso writes, "For the generation of Brazilians who . . . became adults at the height of the Brazilian military dictatorship and the international wave of the counterculture . . . Carmen Miranda was, first, a cause for both pride and shame, and later, a symbol that inspired the merciless gaze we began to cast upon ourselves" (1991, 34). Culling the discomfort that her name inspired among many of his generation, Veloso and other Brazilian intellectuals founded a movement in 1967 known as Tropicalismo. Veloso explains, "We had discovered that she was both our caricature and our X-ray, and we began to take notice of her destiny" (1991, 34).

Miranda's body's function as ethnic commodity — and unwitting marketing rep for U.S. corporate exploitation of Latin American labor and natural resources — does seem strangely prophetic of the relations that would shape not only North-South intercultural economies but also U.S. Latino/as in the age of globalization. In the current climate of post-NAFTA economic policy, U.S. culture is again redefining itself in the context of territorial expansion, admitting Mexico and other Latin American nations into a hemispheric "free trade" zone where commodities can flow unencumbered across borders. Once again, expansion and trade raise questions about the extent to which the U.S. national body will be "invaded" by such transaction and exchange, especially given that Mexico attempted to use NAFTA as a bargaining chip in renegotiating immigration policy with the United States. Again there arises a tension between, on the one hand, a desire on the part of U.S. multinationals to incorporate (and domesticate) Latin America into the U.S. global economic order, and on the other, the fear that the social body will be corrupted or violated by "their" drugs and vices. But given the fresh incentives generated by a global U.S. economy and its increasing interdependency, a crop of so-called "crossover" Latina performers — many born and raised in the United States — now mediates this "new" and decidedly multicultural America, their bodies enticing symbols of equal access, cultural negotiation, and transgression.

Consuming Bodies: In/Corp/orating Latinidad

In today's global economy, the Latina body figures as a kind of negotiable currency, its exchange value fluctuating according to market and political conditions. Latina bodies can help sell America's "new" multicultural image while reaffirming its most enduring defining myths. As a commercial construct, the Latina body is packaged and marketed as an alter/native "type" available for consumption and sale, its design specs, desirability, and visibility held sway to reigning market forces. Here "ethnic" beauty is not negated or assimilated; on the contrary, it is *incorporated*—turned into a spectacle of inclusion and participation. Images of fashionably dressed Latinas with disposable incomes and discriminating tastes add dashes of color to the American dreamscape, affirming the nation's self-image as a meritocracy with opportunity and products for all.

Arlene Dávila's *Latinos, Inc.* (2001) provides a useful analysis of the ways that Latino culture is constituted and popularized through mainstream advertising, where Latina bodies figure as both repositories of traditional "family values" and purveyors of modern consumerism. As Dávila demonstrates, Hispanic-themed marketing campaigns shape images of and for Latino/as; they sell products and lifestyles identified with U.S. consumer society and convey normative ideals of cultural citizenship and belonging.[31] The rise of Hispanic media in the United States, Dávila points out, signals the emergence of an alternative "public sphere" for increasing commercial investment in a minority population and for projecting identity in mass-mediated, multicultural environments. More significantly, it authorizes a field in which to quantify, circumscribe, and standardize "Hispanics" as a constituency, legitimizing their appeal as a viable market for corporate clients and thus "authenticating" the role of Hispanic media professionals in the industry. Dávila's analysis suggests that mutually sustaining interests and alliances structure this transnational commercial enterprise; her interviews with top-level Hispanic media executives, most of whom are Latin American born and highly educated, challenge the assumption that mass-produced Latino/a stereotypes and clichés emerge from a dichotomous and antagonistic relationship between "corporate America" and "authentic" Latinos. Instead, Dávila shows how such representations are "produced in conversation and often complicity with—rather than as a response or challenge to—dominant hierarchies of race, culture, and nationality" (5).

In constructing Latinos as an imagined community of consumers and a viable niche market in the United States, Hispanic media professionals formulate and circulate marketable versions of "Latinness." In doing so, they negotiate the contradictory demands posed by a minority population's need to challenge negative stereotypes ascribed to them and their desire to resist homogenization. Hispanic media professionals are thus engaged in an antithetical process of rejecting and promoting stereotypes. Latina bodies help mediate and reconcile these competing claims. For example, advertising images of the Latin woman as upscale, white, and modern challenge the Carmen Miranda stereotype and evoke more sophisticated views of Hispanics (42). They also promote a generic "Latin look" that reflects existing social hierarchies and narrows the representational field. As Dávila explains, the generic Latina in U.S.-based ads must be both aspirational (beautiful, educated, accomplished) and representative (that is, not too light or too dark). Interestingly, this translates into a Latin look that privileges whiteness and its prevailing beauty myths.

Critical in the production of a nonthreatening, predictable, and generic pan-Latino market and imagined citizenry is the trope of the Latin family, which serves to communicate values associated with Hispanic culture. As vehicles in the production of "positive" cultural role models, Latina bodies mediate a variety of commercially expedient myths and desires. Compared with her Anglo counterpart, the prototypical "Latina consumer" is presumably more family-centered and domesticated. One advertising professional explained that "unlike Anglo women, Hispanic women beautify themselves not for 'selfish, me-oriented purposes,' but in order to please others and obtain their approval and praise" (quoted in Dávila 2001, 95–96). While dominant representations of Latinas in imported Latin American television programming (such as *novelas* or talk shows) consistently feature glamorous, sexualized, and alluringly dressed Latina bodies, the preferred Latina icon in TV ads targeting U.S. Hispanics is "a mom who is young, light-skinned, long-haired, 'soft-featured,' and beautiful . . . [who] is most of all a caretaker and guardian of the family" (131). Dávila notes that the virginal Latinas portrayed in these ads are often predicated on assumptions about "the threatening sexuality that pervades both Anglo and Latino prototypes of Latinas and is always in need of some sort of accommodation" (132). Dávila's study reveals the complex strategies, negotiations, and compromises that constitute the Latina body as both desiring subject of consumer goods and as a carefully crafted product.

Although Dávila is skeptical about the degree to which Hispanic marketing professionals can challenge normative ideals of U.S. cultural citizenship or empower Latinos as a political constituency, Vicki Mayer (2003) offers a more optimistic assessment. Her interviews with San Antonio's Mexican American media producers suggest that many see themselves "as actors in the final stage of a civil rights movement" (20). The Chicano movement provided a shared history of struggle for many of the industry's forerunners, shaping their role as media professionals and binding them to a broader project of social activism. Mayer notes that many of these "envisioned mass media as a space where they could potentially gain respect as Mexican Americans and achieve success" (27). A subsequent generation, more diverse in terms of gender, class, geographic background, and political orientation than its predecessors, does not claim an inherent connection to Chicano activism or to its ethnicity. Interestingly, many in this group attribute their interest in Latino/a culture to their consumption of mass media, which reintroduced them to the language and cultural products of their parents or grandparents. Working from within corporate structures, these younger media professionals have created corporate partnerships with Mexican American communities, initiating industry sponsorships of local literacy campaigns, after-school projects, and hospital fund drives (41). Mayer concludes that this new generation has "gained symbolic capital to construct Mexican Americans as citizens and consumers across cultural and political spheres of life" (43).

Yet this affirmative portrait of upward mobility and increased access is complicated by the limited roles that Latina bodies play as producers. As one Mexican American media worker told Mayer, "It's still a male dominated industry" (38). Mayer's interviewees noted the dearth of female Mexican American media professionals, the near invisibility of Latina writers for mass media, and the scarcity of Mexican American females in directorial positions and on shooting crews. These concerns suggest that Latinas' increased visibility as consumer subjects has yet to empower them as producers or citizens (38). To begin with, Latinas' symbolic value as repositories and emissaries of "Latin culture" concurrently deflects their role as self-directed individualists with desires and interests of their own. Ad campaigns targeting a generic "Latin woman" foreground normative gender roles and behaviors that are not conducive to upward mobility in a highly competitive corporate culture. Furthermore, media kits and ads celebrating the emerging status of Latino/as as affluent consumers and empowered citizens also mask vast economic differences within and across Latino subgroups and between Hispanics and non-Hispanic whites (Dávila 2001, 69).[32] And even as mainstream magazines proclaim the rise of Hispanic entertainment, a recent Screen Actor's Guild survey found that acting roles for Hispanics in Hollywood fell 10.5 percent in 2003.[33]

In the broader social equation, Latinas' signifying power in various consumer tales belies their embodied status as citizens: U.S. Latinas are overrepresented in high school dropout and teen pregnancy rates, while foreign-born Latinas account for a majority share of low-wage factory or domestic jobs. Statistically, U.S. Latinas remain second-class citizens. Clearly, a complex array of competing interests and discursive forces produced the idea of "the Latin woman," and it will take the collective efforts of Latino/a scholars, independent filmmakers, feminist writers, activists, and embodied others to slowly strip the myth of its power to bind or denigrate. For as Judith Ortiz Cofer reminds us, thousands of Latinas without the privilege of an education or the survival skills needed to "belong" in mainstream society continue to "struggle against the misconceptions perpetuated by the myth of the Latina as whore, domestic or criminal" (1995, 107). The diverse essays collected in this volume should also remind us, however, that the complex relationships of domination and resistance in which class, race, gender, and sexuality are so intimately woven make all simplistic dichotomies—self/other, public/private, discursive/material, black/white, exploitation/resistance—vulnerable to recuperation and subversion.

One of the challenges I faced in the selection process for this anthology was the slippery terrain that constitutes "popular culture," particularly as the term is often bound to a reductive set of binary oppositions as well. There is a tendency to imagine the popular in terms of oppositions between high and low, vulgar and elite, center and margin, while ignoring the cross-fertilization that is itself a mark of the popular. Commentators on both the right and the left bemoan the effects of mass-mediated entertainment forms. To the right of the political spectrum, critics object to its vulgar sexual enticements, while to the left, popular culture's pleasures are decried not for their tendency to *incite* but to *placate* the masses. Yet the allures and pleasures of Hollywood films, pop music, and other forms of mass entertainment cut across class, race, ethnicity, gender—and political affiliation. They create a spectacular "peep show" where all of us can catch glimpses of our various others *and* form identificatory bonds and affiliations. The selections in this anthology do not claim popular culture as the terrain of "the people" (conceived either as the "vulgar masses" or as the idealized body of participatory democracy). Neither are they intended to imply a hierarchy of values and aesthetic judgments—say, a preference for Jennifer Lopez over Lupe Ontiveros.

The selections do focus particular attention on star texts that are widely circulated and available. Thus, readers may notice that essays highlight Hollywood stars and divas rather than lesser-known Latina performers or indies. My emphasis on these mass-mediated texts is not based on a set of aesthetic values or judgments about popular tastes but on economic and social realities. As Chon Noriega (1992) points out, "Studios have yet to commit themselves to the grass-roots marketing strategies that ethnic and other specialty films require," opting instead for traditional saturation campaigns that play into stereotypes and alienate potential viewers (147). Writers, scholars, and filmmakers are making strides in promoting and showcasing Latino/a self-representation, and such efforts, combined with increasing economic resources and institutional support, will no doubt widen their reach.[34] But as of this writing, most independent U.S. Latino/a films do not have the wide distribution networks needed to reach mass audiences; many remain accessible primarily in cosmopolitan areas with art house theaters or to students in large urban universities with Latino/a or film studies programs. Highstepping over this material reality ignores a large majority of the U.S. viewing and reading public, who nevertheless form and act on their conceptions of Latino/as founded primarily on Hollywood films and music channels. Patricia Cardoso's critically acclaimed film version of *Real Women Have Curves,* for example, opened in the United States on October 20, 2002, on fifty-five screens. *Maid in Manhattan,* starring Jennifer Lopez, opened December 15, 2002, on over 2,800 screens in the United States alone; it was seen by almost 19 million viewers during its opening weekend alone, and within six months it had been seen by almost 60,000 Argentines, 1.5 million Germans, and over 1 million Spaniards. Aesthetic judgments aside, which of these films is more likely to shape mass perception and knowledge of Latino/as in the United States and abroad?

The good news is that audience reception of these mass-mediated texts is rarely as predictable or as manageable as its producers envision. As several essays in this collection demonstrate, these star texts are co-produced by viewers themselves in various ways. Weblogs, fan clubs, chatrooms, and other "unofficial" forms of discourse engender and circulate meanings. These too form a part of the complex processes through which versions of Latinidad are revised and embodied. While it is true that Latina star bodies serve as emblems of Latinidad in the popular imagination, they also, as Alberto Sandoval-Sánchez contends, "put into question who is Latino/a, what is Latino identity, and which images of Latinidad predominate and circulate" (2003, 16). This cross-fertilization informs "external" views of Latina/o identity and sparks powerful internal censors as well, disabling and enabling various forms of self-identification. In response, Ana Lopez has advocated a shift in Latino/a film criticism away from the analysis of mimetic relationships and toward critical readings of "the historical-political construction of self-other relations—the articulation of forms of difference—sexual and ethnic" structuring Hollywood's power as ethnographer, creator, and translator of otherness (1991, 405).

This collection contributes to such a project. Given the U.S. film industry's global power and significant ethnographic function, the first two sections are weighted in favor of film and star text analyses, while the third traverses a nexus of cultural production and consumption. Our work begins with a retrospective glance at the Latina body, locating founding assumptions about Latina sexuality within broader frameworks of nation building and film spectatorship. Clara Rodríguez's "Film Viewing in Latino Communities, 1896–1934: Puerto Rico as Microcosm" contributes new insights for Latino film scholars, situating Puerto Rico at the inception of transnational film production, distribution, and spectatorship. Rodríguez's research reveals the interplay of identities produced by the U.S. film industry's initial border crossings into post-independence Puerto Rico; her analysis of the reception and influence of silent films during this formative stage in the development of Puerto Rican national identity alerts readers to the surprisingly early advent of U.S. films into Latino international markets.

This case study sets the stage for our bifocal look at Lupe Vélez, whose body, overtly sexualized and uncompromisingly other, registers the birth of a U.S. cinematic "Latina body" that endures to this day. Rosa Linda Fregoso examines Vélez's embodied otherness as a metaphor for shifting, ambiguous social positions, recognizing in the contradictory responses to Vélez the seeds of what would later characterize aspects of Chicana identity. William Nericcio ransacks a history of gossip, cinematic stereotypes, theoretical musings, and racialized imagery to consider their residual effects on Latina embodiment. Nericcio's essay situates Vélez's body—overly determined, reproduced, overly consumed and consuming, within a matrix of desire that both intoxicates and nauseates in its excess. Nericcio and Fregoso both comment on Vélez's suicide, their different approaches speaking not only to their different aims or stylistics but also to the enormously productive and seductive power of star texts.

The second section scans the contemporary entertainment field, focusing on Latina film stars and music divas whose bodies negotiate popular visions of Latinidad and challenge the homogeneity of "Latina" as a category. Reading Celia Cruz's star persona—particularly her wigs, costumes, and shoes—as a marker for class, race, and gender, Frances Negrón-Muntaner offers a fitting tribute to the beloved "Queen of Salsa." Muntaner's engaging analysis of Celia's insistent "Cubanidad" also comments on her unique status in the all-male club of salsa, for as Muntaner argues, Celia was accepted as "one of the boys," unlike La Lupe and La India. Isabel Molina Guzmán explores Salma Hayek's star text as a reconfiguration of exoticism, transgression, and opportunistic entrepreneurship, while Angharad Valdivia analyzes magazine photographs of Penélope Cruz and Jennifer Lopez to locate the representational strategies emerging in the media's "selective differentiations" of Latinidad. Tara Lockhart considers Lopez's ethnic "cross-dressings" both in Lopez's film embodiment of Selena and in circulating for different audiences. Lockhart's inclusion of Web postings and fan club dialogues provides a fascinating glimpse into the ways that diverse ethnic constituencies see and make Lopez as "Latina" within shifting racial categories. Cynthia Fuchs looks at the pop music scene, commenting on Shakira's ability to navigate national and ideological borders. As Fuchs suggests, Shakira's agility in producing and exploiting her own multilayered identities has allowed her to capture and captivate both South American and U.S. markets and fans. Karen Tolchin's essay investigates the challenges posed to conventional notions about Latina femininity by Michelle Rodríguez's character in the film *Girlfight*, offering a refreshing take on the emergent "macho Latina" figure and suggesting both its promise and pitfalls.

The final section expands our focus to explore relevant phenomena in broadcast media, literature, news, and toy production. Charla Ogaz and Isabel Molina Guzmán each look at Latinas whose bodies became the focus of sensational news stories, Lorena Bobbitt and Marisleysis González, respectively. Ogaz's critique considers Lorena's objectification and racialization during and after her trial for the "malicious wounding" of her husband, arguing that media interpolated Lorena's otherness while suppressing the causal role of marital rape and abuse. Molina Guzmán examines press coverage of the Elián González custody battle in relation to broader significations of Latinidad in the national media and specifically Cuban-American political and ethnic positioning. Ana Patricia Rodríguez turns to the detective novel, exploring the best-selling Lupe Solano Mystery series written by Carolina García-Aguilera, a Cuban American former private eye. Rodríguez suggests that Solano's body signs in for the Miami Cuban exile community, which is caught in ambivalent tension between a desire for material success in the United States and for vindication against Castro's "crime." Karen Goldman reviews the literal reconstructions of the Latina body posited by Mattel's versions of Hispanic Barbie and challenged by parodic counterrepresentations. Finally, in "*Chusmas, Chismes, y Escándalos*" (which loosely translates as "Vixens, Gossip, and Scandals"), Viviana Rojas examines Latinas' varied appraisals of Spanish-language television and suggests the effects of class, gender, and social positioning on their assessments of the popular talk shows, *El Show de Cristina* and *Laura en América*. Readers will recognize in these various essays an ongoing struggle among desires, resources, and meanings—a struggle that reminds us that, unlike the categories and labels that fix and tame them, bodies are often messy, unruly, hungering things.

Stuart Hall reminds us that we all "write and speak from a particular place and time, from a history and a culture which is specific" (1993, 68). In the course of editing this collection, the academic in me has sought to denaturalize "the Latina body" as sign and attend to its imagining and inscriptions. In doing so, I have wondered what such a project means for my own embodiment. I am certainly aware of the ways that I celebrate and perform my own versions of Latinidad. As a child growing up in a Cuban enclave in Miami, I delighted in the exuberant physicality I experienced through my parents and their friends. Every Saturday night, long after the age when their bodies were to have submitted to the proverbial rocking chair, my parents joined their compatriots at the local "Centro Marianao"[35] for a *despelote* (figuratively "letting it all out"), an evening of sweaty abandon spent dancing to the bawdy rhythms of Cuban *son* and *guaguancó*. My body still responds to rhythmic beats like a reflex, despite my need to "Americanize" and blend into my colleagues' more reserved social gatherings. For many women of color in the United States, even a simple act—dancing—is loaded with gendered, racialized baggage; in a single butt-shaking instant, this Latina body can resurrect a history of stereotypes, preconceptions, and prejudices.

Gloria Anzaldúa has remarked that the struggle played out on the bicultural body of the mestiza "has always been inner, and is played out in the outer terrains. Awareness of our situation must come before inner changes. . . . Nothing happens in the 'real' world unless it first happens in the images in our heads" (1997, 242). It dawned on me that my concerns had focused on what stereotypes constitute and produce, rather than on what they exclude, repress, or deny—what cannot be made flesh. Yet reclaiming Latinidad involves not just a deconstruction but also an excavation—a disinterment of bodies less docile. For in subduing that other body, the one that too boldly expresses my version of a Latino and familial heritage, I personally reenact a Foucauldian drama of disciplinary power.[36] And so I am reminded of the formative role I play, of the ways that all of us who contributed to this collection are helping to write and rewrite Latina bodies. Most important, I am reminded of Anzaldúa's marvelously simple observation: "For silence to transform into speech, sounds and words, it must first traverse through our female bodies. For the body to give birth to utterance, the human entity must recognize itself as carnal. . . . When she transforms silence into language, a woman transgresses" (1997, 242).

Therein lies the heart of this book, in the bodies of Latinas who dare to speak, to write, or to dance, with abandon.

Notes

1. *National Post* (Canada), March 13, 2003, Arts and Life section, p. AL1.
2. Jennifer Lopez, quoted in "50 Most Beautiful People in the World," *People,* May 12, 1997, 124.
3. Alberto Sandoval-Sánchez (2003) points to the degrading slew of racist, sexist jokes that have accompanied the focus on Lopez's "Latin butt":

Even in major music award shows such as MTV Music Awards and American Music Awards, the male hosts opened the event with vulgar and humiliating jokes about her body shape. VH1 in its Pop-Up Video program overdoes the usage of the preposition "but" to ridicule, and I would accentuate, further humiliate, the rising Latina pop star. It has become such an obsession that this kind of vulgar behavior must be read within the parameters of the Eurocentric imperialist gaze of the Other.

For an astute discussion of the analogous relationship between bodily and moral attributes, see also Tracy Fessenden (1999). For remarks concerning the contemporary celebrations of black women's buttocks, see bell hooks (1997).

4. For the politics of this epistemology in U.S. history, see Wiegman (1995).
5. Self-tropicalizations can be politically subversive, as in Carmelita Tropicana's reappropriation of the signs of Latina sexuality and "Cubanidad." These acts, however, are not an "unambiguous" celebration or embrace of any "fixed" markers of identity; rather, they intentionally complicate potential meanings and responses. Carmelita Tropicana's fruit props, for example, evoke ambivalent reactions in her audiences, who are both disturbed and delighted by this cooptation of the Carmen Miranda stereotype. See Alina Troyano's (2000) *I, Carmelita Tropicana: Performing Between Cultures* (edited by Chon Noriega), especially Noriega's and Troyano's introductions.
6. In a March 10, 2002, article in the *Chicago Tribune,* Teresa Puente commented on the body alterations undergone by Latinas Jennifer Lopez, Shakira, and Spaniard Penélope Cruz *after* achieving fame. Even Selena, celebrated for her full-figured curves, had undergone liposuction on her hips and buttocks shortly before her death. Joe Patoski's biography includes the testimony of one of Selena's school friends, who remembered that "she was so self-conscious about her body—she used to hate her bottom. But she wasn't fat, she just had a big bottom. The only thing she was shy about was thinking her bottom was too big" (1996, 46).
7. See T. N. Robinson et al. (1996).
8. For example, see Susan Bordo (1993), Judith Butler (1990), Teresa de Lauretis (1987), Elizabeth Grosz (1994), Laura Mulvey (1999), and Gail Weiss (1999).

9. See Elizabeth V. Spelman (1982) for an insightful review of this history.

10. For analyses that model ethnicity as a set of socially constructed boundaries, see S. Cornell (1996) and Joanne Nagel (1994).

11. In the humanities, several studies reference the body as border. For examples, see Gloria Anzaldúa (1990), G. Eley (1997), and J. D. Saldivar (1997).

12. In 1987 the *American Journal of Public Health* published a set of essays that marked the onset of this debate and which still provide a useful overview of the issues involved. These writers tended to favor the use of a unifying label: D. E. Hayes-Bautista and J. Chapa, "Latino Terminology: Conceptual Basis for Standardized Terminology"; F. M. Trevino, "Standardized Terminology for Standardized Populations"; and A. Yankauer, "Hispanic/Latino—What's in a Name?" all published in *American Journal of Public Health* 77, 1987. For an opposing view in this period, see Martha E. Gimenez's "Latino/Hispanic—Who Needs a Name? The Case Against a Standardized Terminology," in *The International Journal of Health Services* 19, no. 3 (1989): 557–571.

13. See, for example, "The Criminalization of the Latino Identity Makes Fighting Gangs That Much Harder," David E. Hayes-Bautista and Gregory Rodríguez, online at http://www.azteca.net/aztec/immigrat/crime.html. For case studies, see Mary Romero's "Violation of Latino Civil Rights Resulting From INS and Local Police's Use of Race, Culture and Class Profiling: The Case of the Chandler Roundup in Arizona," with Marwah Serag, *University of Cleveland Law Review* 51 (2004) and "State Violence, and the Social and Legal Construction of Latino Criminality: From El Bandido to Gang Member," in LatCrit V Symposium, *Denver University Law Review* 78, no 4 (2001): 1081–1118. See also Adalberto Aguirre, "Profiling Mexican American Identity: Issues and Concerns," *American Behavioral Scientist* 47 (2004): 928–942.

14. See Ana Castillo Alarcón and Cherríe Moraga (1993), Chéla Sandoval (1995), and María Lugones (1996).

15. See Sherry B. Ortner (1996).

16. I enclose the word "American" in quotation marks to signal its ethnocentric genealogy, which appropriates the whole of the Americas in naming citizens of the United States and often tends to assume a WASP-centered historicity.

17. In the early 1900s, Congress appointed a commission to investigate the effects of immigration on the descendants of foreigners who had immigrated to the United States. As reported in a front-page article in the *Daily Metropolis* on December 21, 1909, the investigation "was conducted in a systematic manner by the comparison of measurements of the bodies of such immigrants and their descendants." The commission reported in its preliminary findings that "racial and physical characteristics do not survive under the new social and climatic environments of America."

18. Buried in the distinguishing word "all" is the discourse of racial purity, which measured degrees of "Americanness" by the absence of even one drop of African blood.

19. I mean here to resist the tendency to theorize Latina identity as "mestiza," which would subsume Afro-Latinas into an overarching ethnic category.

20. Y. Murray, "Jennifer Lopez," *Buzz* 69 (April 1997): 72.

21. In 1950, Chilean Nobel-awarded poet Pablo Neruda published a mock epic

poem about the history of Latin America with a chapter entitled "The United Fruit Company." My epigraph is excerpted from the poem's opening lines:

> Jehovah divided his universe:
> Anaconda, Ford Motors
> Coca-Cola Inc and similar entities
> the most succulent item of all
> The United Fruit Company Incorporated
> reserved to itself: the heartland and coasts of my country
> the delectable waist of America.
> They rechristened their properties:
> the "Banana Republics."

22. See José Limón's (1998) insightful reading of the 1950s films *High Noon* and *Giant*, which Limón situates in relation to the Anglo cowboy's ambivalent desire for the Mexican woman.

23. See Beatriz Urraca (1997) for a fine reading of Richard Harding Davis's *Soldiers of Fortune* in this context.

24. Streeby includes readings of widely popular romances, such as Charles Averill's *The Mexican Ranchero, or The Maid of the Chapparal* (1847), Harry Hazel's *Inez, the Beautiful* (1846), Ned Buntline's *Magdalena, the Beautiful Mexican Maid* (1847), and *The Volunteer, or The Maid of Monterey* (1847). Also, Jose E. Limón offers an astute reading of the early twentieth-century novel *Caballero*, a romance set in this period but written by contemporary Greater Mexican author, Jovita Gonzalez. See "Caballero and the Racial Politics of Marriage" in Limón (1998).

25. For a review of this history, see Charles Ramírez Berg (1997), Blaine P. Lamb (1975), Arthur G. Pettit and Dennis Showalter (1980), and Allan Woll (1974).

26. Actresses Beatriz Michelena and Myrtle Gonzalez were two exceptions, as they were among the first Latina "leading ladies" of the silent screen. Gonzalez, a native Mexican Californian, made her film debut in *Ghosts* in 1911, receiving star billing in more than forty films until her early death in 1918 of influenza. Michelena's first film, *Salomy Jane*, was produced by California Motion Picture Corporation in 1908. See Geoffrey Bell, *The Golden Gate and the Silent Screen: San Francisco in the History of the Cinema* (New York: Cornwall Books, 1984), 67–98.

27. While Hollywood was called on to serve as "goodwill ambassador" to Latin America, a Senate subcommittee in 1941 had investigated Hollywood's allegedly pro-interventionist film propaganda. Testifying before the committee, Senator Gerald Nye of North Dakota claimed that in the movie capital, "one speaks not of the foreign policy of the United States but of the foreign policy of Hollywood" (quoted in Lorence 1993). For the full record, see U.S. Congress, Senate, Committee on Interstate Commerce, *Hearings, Propaganda in Motion Pictures,* 77th Congress, 1st Session, 1941.

28. For the complete text, see "At the Roxy," *New York Times*, December 23, 1943.

29. For an analysis of the economic and social history of the banana and its gender implications, see Cynthia Enloe (2000).

30. In 1928, Colombian banana plantation workers led an unsuccessful strike against United Fruit Company demanding a six-day workweek and eight-hour days. The army responded by firing into the crowd of demonstrators, declaring a state of siege, and ending the strike. This event is referred to as "the Bananera massacre of 1928." In 1998 the *Cincinnati Enquirer* published a series by veteran investigative reporter Michael Gallagher documenting the company's brutal business practices in Central America. A company informant had provided Gallagher access to the company's internal voice-mail archives. Chiquita sued the *Cincinnati Enquirer*, which then fired Gallagher and paid Chiquita $10 million to settle the case. The history of the United Fruit Company also includes (often violent) labor unrest in Honduras, Guatemala, Panama, and Costa Rica. For a discussion of United Fruit's use of harmful biocidal agrochemicals in Central America, see Steve Marquardt (2002). For a description of working conditions in a Latin American banana plantation, see Jeremy Smith (2002).

31. Dávila's use of the term "Hispanic" calls attention to its depoliticized and official status in the United States, as opposed to "Latino," which stems from negotiations between an imposed and a self-generated identity grounded in activism and struggle.

32. For example, in 2000, 63 percent of 25- to 29-year-old Latinos were high school graduates, compared with 87 percent of African Americans and 94 percent of non-Latino whites. U.S. Census (2000, Table A-2) (http://www.census .gov/population/socdemo/education/tableA-2.txt).

33. "Screen Actors Guild Says Hispanics, Asians Losing Acting Roles," Associated Press, October 8, 2003 (http://www.tampabaylive.com/entertainment/ stories/0410/041008guild.shtml).

34. There are several excellent volumes committed to showcasing Latino/a self-representation in a variety of independent and noncommercial venues. See, for example, the collection of essays edited by Michelle Habell-Pallán and Mary Romero (2002). See also Juan Flores (2000) and Alicia Gaspar de Alba (2003).

35. Named after their home province in Cuba, the center was the meeting place for a generation of Cuban exiles longing to recreate versions of home.

36. In *Discipline and Punish* (1995), Michel Foucault details historical efforts to discipline and control bodies. His chapter "Docile Bodies" suggests that modern power relations are manifest in their most concrete form in the body, which self-regulates and controls itself in adherence to social codes.

Bibliography

Alarcón, Norma, Ana Castillo, and Cherríe Moraga, eds. 1993. *The Sexuality of Latinas*. Berkeley, CA: Third Woman.

Anzaldúa, Gloria, ed. 1990. *Making Face, Making Soul: Creative and Critical Perspectives by Women of Color*. San Francisco: Aunt Lute.

Anzaldúa, Gloria. 1997. "*La conciencia de la mestiza:* Towards a New Consciousness." In *Writing on the Body: Female Embodiment and Feminist Theory*, ed. Katie Conboy, Nadia Medina, and Sarah Stanbury, 233-247. New York: Columbia University Press.

Aparicio, Frances. 2003. "Jennifer as Selena: Rethinking Latinidad in Media and Popular Culture." *Latino Studies* 1:90-105.

Aparicio, Frances, and Susana Chávez-Silverman. 1997. Introduction. In *Tropicalizations: Transcultural Representations of Latinidad*. Hanover, NH: Dartmouth College/University Press of New England.

Barthes, Roland. 1975. *Mythologies*, trans. Annette Lavers. New York: Hill and Wang.

Beltrán, Mary. 2002. "The Hollywood Latina Body as Site of Social Struggle: Media Constructions of Stardom and Jennifer Lopez's 'Cross-over Butt.'" *Quarterly Review of Film and Video* 19 (1): 71-86.

Bordo, Susan. 1983. *Unbearable Weight: Feminism, Western Culture, and the Body*. Berkeley and Los Angeles: University of California Press.

Butler, Judith. 1990. *Gender Trouble*. New York: Routledge.

———. 1993. *Bodies That Matter*. New York: Routledge.

Chow, Rey. 2002. *The Protestant Ethnic and the Spirit of Capitalism*. New York: Columbia University Press.

Cornell, S. 1996. "The Variable Ties that Bind: Content and Circumstance in Ethnic Processes." *Ethnic Racial Studies* 19:265-280.

Dávila, Arlene. 2001. *Latinos Inc: The Marketing and Making of a People*. Berkeley and Los Angeles: University of California Press.

———. 2004. *Barrio Dreams: Puerto Ricans, Latinos, and the Neoliberal City*. Berkeley and Los Angeles: University of California Press.

de Lauretis, Teresa. 1987. *Technologies of Gender: Essays on Theory, Film, and Fiction*. Bloomington: Indiana University Press.

Dyer, Richard. 1986. *Heavenly Bodies: Film Stars and Society*. Hampshire, UK: Macmillan.

———. 1988. "White." *Screen* 29, no. 4 (Autumn): 45.

Eley, G., ed. 1996. *Becoming National*. New York: Oxford University Press.

Enloe, Cynthia. 2000. *Bananas, Beaches, and Bases: Making Feminist Sense of International Politics*. Berkeley and Los Angeles: University of California Press.

Fessenden, Tracy. 1999. "The Soul of America: Whiteness and the Disappearing of Bodies in the Progressive Era." In *Perspectives on Embodiment: The Intersections of Nature and Culture*, ed. Gail Weiss and Honi Fern Haber, 23-40. New York: Routledge.

Figueroa, Maria P. 2003. "Resisting 'Beauty' and *Real Women Have Curves*." In *Velvet Barrios: Popular Culture and Chicana/o Sexualities*, ed. Alicia Gaspar de Alba, 265-282. New York: Palgrave Macmillan.

Flores, Juan. 2000. *From Bomba to Hip Hop: Puerto Rican Culture and Latino Identity*. New York: Columbia University Press.

Foucault, Michel. 1995. *Discipline and Punish*, trans. Alan Sheridan. New York: Vintage.

Gaspar de Alba, Alicia, ed. 2003. *Velvet Barrios: Popular Culture and Chicana/o Sexualities*. New York: Palgrave Macmillan.

Gil-Montero, Martha. 1989. *Brazilian Bombshell*. New York: Donald Fine.

Grosz, Elizabeth. 1994. *Volatile Bodies: Toward a Corporeal Feminism.* Bloomington: Indiana University Press.

Habell-Pallán, Michelle, and Mary Romero, eds. 2002. *Latino/a Popular Culture.*
New York: New York University Press.

Hall, Stuart. 1993a. "Cultural Identity and Cinematic Representation." *Framework*
36:68–81.

———. 1993b. "Encoding/Decoding." In *Cultural Studies Reader,* ed. Simon During, 90–103. New York: Routledge.

hooks, bell. 1997. "Selling Hot Pussy: Representations of Black Female Sexuality
in the Cultural Marketplace." In *Writing on the Body: Female Embodiment and
Feminist Theory,* ed. Katie Conboy, Nadia Medina, and Sarah Stanbury, 113–
128. New York: Columbia University Press.

Kaplan, Amy. 1997. *Looking for the Other: Feminism, Film, and the Imperial Gaze.*
New York: Routledge.

———. 1998. "Manifest Domesticity." *American Literature* 70, no. 3 (September):
581–606.

Lamb, Blaine P. 1975. "The Convenient Villain: The Early Cinema Views the
Mexican American." *Journal of the West* 14 (October): 75–81.

Limón, José E. 1998. *American Encounters: Greater Mexico, the United States, and
the Erotics of Culture.* Boston: Beacon Press.

Lopez, Ana. 1991. "Are All Latins from Manhattan? Hollywood, Ethnography, and
Cultural Colonialism." In *Unspeakable Images: Ethnicity and American Cinema,*
ed. Lester D. Friedman, 404–440. Urbana: University of Illinois Press.

Lorence, James J. 1993. " 'The Foreign Policy of Hollywood': Interventionist Senti-
ment in the American Film, 1938–1941." In *Hollywood as Mirror: The Changing
View of "Insiders" and "Enemies" in American Movies,* ed. Robert Brent Toplin.
Westport, CT: Greenwood Press.

Lugones, María. 1996. "Playfulness, World Traveling and Loving Perception." In
Women, Knowledge, and Reality, ed. Ann Garry and Marilyn Pearsall, 419–433.
London: Routledge.

Marquardt, Steve. 2002. "Pesticides, Parakeets, and Unions in the Costa Rican
Banana Industry, 1938–1962." *Latin American Research Review* 37, no 2: 3–36.

Mayer, Vicki. 2003. *Producing Dreams, Consuming Youth: Mexican Americans and
Mass Media.* Piscataway, NJ: Rutgers University Press.

Mulvey, Laura. 1999. "Visual Pleasure and Narrative Cinema." In *Feminist Film
Theory: A Reader.* New York: New York University Press.

Nagel, Joanne. 1994. "Constructing Ethnicity: Creating and Recreating Ethnic
Identity and Culture." *Social Problems* 41, no. 1: 152–176.

Negrón-Muntaner, Frances. 1997. "Jennifer's Butt." *Atzlan* 22, no. 2 (Fall):
181–194.

Noriega, Chon A. 1992. "Between a Weapon and a Formula: Chicano Cinema and
Its Context." In *Chicanos and Film: Representation and Resistance,* ed. Chon A.
Noriega, 141–167. Minneapolis: University of Minnesota Press.

Oboler, Suzanne. 1992. "The Politics of Labeling: Latino/a Cultural Identities of
Self and Others." *Latin American Perspectives* 19, no. 4 (Fall): 18–36.

Ortiz Cofer, Judith. 1995. "The Myth of the Latin Woman: I Just Met a Girl

Named Maria." In *Boricuas: Influential Puerto Rican Writings*, ed. Roberto Santiago. New York: Ballantine.

Ortner, Sherry B. 1996. *Making Gender: The Politics and Erotics of Culture*. Boston: Beacon Press.

Patoski, Joe Nick. 1996. *Selena: Como la flor*. Boston: Little, Brown.

Pettit, Arthur G., and Dennis Showalter. 1980. *Images of Mexican Americans in Film*. College Station: Texas A&M University Press.

Ramírez Berg, Charles. 1997. "Stereotyping in Films in General and of the Hispanic in Particular." In *Latin Looks: Images of Latinas and Latinos in the U.S. Media*, ed. Clara Rodríguez, 104-120. Boulder, CO: Westview Press.

Richard, Alfred Charles, Jr. 1995. *The Hispanic Image on the Silver Screen: An Interpretive Filmography from Silents into Sound, 1898-1935*. Westport, CT: Greenwood Press.

Roberts, Shari. 1993. " 'The Lady in the Tutti-Frutti Hat': Carmen Miranda, a Spectacle of Ethnicity." *Cinema Journal* 32 (Spring): 3-23.

Robinson, T. N., et al. 1996. "Ethnicity and Body Dissatisfaction: Are Hispanic and Asian Girls at Increased Risk for Eating Disorders?" *Journal of Adolescent Health* 19 (December): 384-393.

Rodríguez, Clara E. 1997. *Latin Looks: Images of Latinas and Latinos in the U.S. Media*. Boulder, CO: Westview Press.

Roorda, Eric Paul. 1998. *The Dictator Next Door: The Good Neighbor Policy and the Trujillo Regime in the Dominican Republic, 1930-1945*. Chapel Hill, NC: Duke University Press.

Saldivar, J. D. 1997. *Border Matters: Remapping American Cultural Studies*. Berkeley and Los Angeles: University of California Press.

Sandoval, Chela. 1995. "Feminist Forms of Agency and Oppositional Consciousness: U.S. Third World Feminist Criticism." In *Provoking Agents: Gender and Agency in Theory and Practice*, ed. Judith Kegan Gardiner, 208-228. Urbana: University of Illinois Press.

Sandoval-Sanchez, Alberto. 2003. *Encrucijada/Crossroads* 1, no 1: 13-24.

Schlesinger, Stephen, and Stephen Kinzer. 1999. *Bitter Fruit: The Story of the American Coup in Guatemala*. Cambridge: Harvard University Press.

Shohat, Ella, and Robert Stam. 1994. *Unthinking Eurocentrism: Multiculturalism and the Media*. London: Routledge, 1994.

Smith, Jeremy. 2002. "The Truth about the Banana Trade." *Ecologist* 32, 3 (March 22): 40-42.

Spelman, Elizabeth V. 1982. "Woman as Body: Ancient and Contemporary Views." *Feminist Studies* 8, no. 1: 109-131.

Streeby, Shelley. 2002. *American Sensations: Class, Empire, and the Production of Popular Culture*. Berkeley and Los Angeles: University of California Press.

Troyano, Alina, with Ela Troyano and Uzi Parnes. 2000. *I, Carmelita Tropicana: Performing Between Cultures*, ed. Chon A. Noriega. Boston: Beacon Press.

Urraca, Beatriz. 1997. "A Textbook of Americanism: Richard Harding Davis's *Soldiers of Fortune*." In *Tropicalizations: Transcultural Representations of Latinidad*, ed. Frances Aparicio and Susana Chávez-Silverman. Hanover, NH: University Press of New England.

Veloso, Caetano. 1991. "Caricature and Conqueror, Pride and Shame," trans. Robert Myers. *New York Times,* October 20.

Weiss, Gail. 1999. *Body Images: Embodiment as Intercorporeality.* New York: Routledge.

Wiegman, Robyn. 1995. *American Anatomies: Theorizing Race and Gender.* Durham, NC: Duke University Press.

Wittig, Monique. 1997. "One Is Not Born a Woman." In *Writing on the Body,* ed. Katie Conboy, Nadia Medina, and Sarah Stanbury, 309–317. New York: Columbia University Press.

Woll, Allan. 1974. "Hollywood's Good Neighbor Policy: The Latin Image in American Film, 1939–1946." *Journal of Popular Film* 3 (Fall): 278–293.

———. 1980. *The Latin Image in American Film.* Los Angeles: UCLA Latin American Center Publications.

———. 1987. *Ethnic and Racial Images in American Film and Television: Historical Essays and Bibliography.* New York: Garland.

CASE STUDIES
Silent and Classic Film Era

CHAPTER 1

Film Viewing in Latino Communities, 1896–1934

Puerto Rico as Microcosm

CLARA E. RODRÍGUEZ

If you only knew what I know about life thanks to the movies . . .
YOUNG PUERTO RICAN GIRL, QUOTED BY SERGIO ROMANACCE
IN *PUERTO RICO ILUSTRADO*, SEPTEMBER 18, 1920

Today, the U.S. film industry dominates screens worldwide. This may not come as a surprise to some. What is surprising is the degree of this dominance. According to Segrave (1997, 286), in 1993 the percentage of screen time held by U.S. films abroad was 85 percent. In other words, on average, when someone in the world went to the movies in 1993, in 85 percent of cases that person saw a U.S. movie. This film media dominance continues today and is even more pronounced in some countries. The towering position of the U.S. film industry raises questions about the impact it has had for film viewers in other cultures on several critical dimensions: gender relations, family values, national identity, political leanings. This essay focuses on the earliest period of film in Latino communities, the years between 1896 and 1934, using Puerto Rico as a case study to examine this question within a specific context. The analysis is based on an examination of newspapers, advertisements, and magazines of this era and relevant readings on the period.

When Did Films First Come to Puerto Rican and Other Latino Communities?

Moving pictures arrived in Latin America soon after they were invented and shown in the United States and Europe (Trelles 1991, 5–6). They also spread quickly. In 1896, movies were seen for the first time in Argentina, Brazil, and Mexico. In the following year, 1897, films were showing in Havana, Cuba; in Bogota, Bucaramanga, and Barranquilla, Colombia; and in Maracaibo, Venezuela. By 1900 they had reached Puerto Rico, and by 1902 they had come to Chile. Their arrival and their popularity were closely related to the arrival of European immigrants, who, having been involved in commercial photography, expanded their offerings to include cinematography. In the United States, Latino communities in, for example, California, the Southwest, New York, and Florida were also exposed to film at roughly the same time as other Americans living in the United States. Moreover, Fuller (1996, 196) notes that Hispanic as well as black and Asian entrepreneurs in the North, South, and West opened ethnic movie theaters that brought mainstream white movie culture to disenfranchised groups. Like the spread of cellular phones today, moving pictures moved across national and cultural boundaries quickly and traveled far beyond their points of origin.

An examination of the arrival of films on the island of Puerto Rico provides a fascinating glimpse into when and how films were first seen by Spanish speakers in the Americas. Today we take for granted that Hollywood films can be seen in any part of the world, but when and how did films first come to be distributed on a tiny island in the Caribbean, far from the centers of movie making? What kinds of films were seen? Focusing on Puerto Rico is instructive because it offers details on what was happening all over Latin America and, indeed, much of the world, in countless locales, large and small. Puerto Rico is also a useful place to examine the growth of film viewing and cultural change because it is both part of Latin America and part of the United States. This unique situation allows us to better understand the parameters and boundaries of each America. But during the early period of film watching in Latin countries, Puerto Rico was probably more like its Spanish-speaking Latin American neighbors to the south than the colossus to the north. At the beginning of the twentieth century, Puerto Rico was a country that had been in cultural formation for more than four hundred years, during which time only Spanish had been spoken. Consequently, the impact of U.S. films on its language, culture, and arts may have been quite similar to the impact experienced in other Spanish-speaking Latin American nations.

Given that Puerto Rico entered the U.S. orbit in 1898 as a result of the Spanish-American War, we might expect U.S. films to have predominated in Puerto Rico from the start. We might also expect films to have appeared in Puerto Rico before they appeared elsewhere. However, movies quickly spread to other countries in Latin America before they came to

Puerto Rico, although Puerto Rico was a quick fourth in line, after Cuba, Colombia, and Venezuela. Geographic distance proved not to be a major barrier to importing and enjoying films from the United States. In Chile, for example, which was geographically quite removed from the United States and lacked rapid overland corridors of transportation, films were already an important medium by 1914. By the 1920s, U.S. films accounted for 80-90 percent of all films seen in Chile (Rinke 2002; 2004, 4).

Because the films were silent, they were accessible to all audiences, without regard to language. Latin American countries with fewer economic and political ties to the United States than Puerto Rico had were still able to import and enjoy films. Silent moving pictures fascinated everyone; all could understand them, regardless of the language in which the films were made. Local entrepreneurs took advantage of the fascination with a new medium and moved quickly to bring films to their particular audiences. But even as silent films slipped across cultural and national borders, they began to be felt as a threat to traditional (nationalist) expressions of culture and identities in the countries of reception. As U.S. film companies came increasingly to dominate the market, the Germans, the Chileans, and even the English could be heard complaining that both Europe and Latin America were being "yankified" or "*yanquinizados*" (Rinke 2002; 2004, 1). Puerto Rico shared in both the common fascination with moving pictures and the articulated discontent over the threat U.S. films posed to the established canons of culture.

The Earliest Period in Puerto Rico: A Filmgoing Public by 1909

Soon after the brothers Louis and Aguste Lumiere surprised the world in 1895 with their invention of the *cinématographe* machine and Thomas Alva Edison premiered his kinetoscope, public showings of moving pictures were taking place in Puerto Rico. The first films in Puerto Rico arrived from France, which had taken the lead in film production in the closing years of the nineteenth century (Segrave 1997, 1-20). According to Puttnam (1998, 37), by 1908 the Frenchman Charles Pathé was dominating world cinema. He was selling twice as many films in the United States as all American companies put together, and his firm's subsidiaries were producing films as far afield as Rome and Moscow. Part of the reason for Pathé's success was that he was able to guarantee a consistent supply of films, something his American rivals had not yet been able to do. This was largely due to the fact that he had already adapted the techniques of mass production to filmmaking and so was able to exercise "an almost seamless integrated control over the entire operation" (Puttnam 1998, 35). Pathé manufactured the raw film stock in his factory near Paris, his team shot and edited the films in his studios, and he employed a regular company of actors. Since they were silent films, they could be shown anywhere, and, as Puttnam noted, "the showmen who ran the nickelodeons and traveling shows could not have cared less where their films came from; the only thing that mattered to them was getting their hands on a reliable supply of well-made new titles at the right prices" (Puttnam 1998, 35).

Rafael Colorado, a pioneer of Puerto Rican cinema, related in a 1952 interview an amusing anecdote that reveals the early origins and linguistic impact of film in Puerto Rico.[1] He explained that a Frenchman, a former employee of the Pathé Company, had been the first to bring movies to Puerto Rico; thus the phrase *"apaga musiú"* ("lights out, m'sieur"), which Puerto Rican audiences used in this early period, reflected the "understandable impatience of those first cinéastes," who in this way urged the projectionist to begin the show (Torres 1994).

These early films were probably shown in music halls, magic or drama theaters, or in tents at traveling fairs and circuses, for it was in these venues that the majority of film shows all over the world were seen during the early period (Banco Popular 1994; García 1984; Puttnam 1998, 28–29). In Chile, for example, the first films were shown in "mere shacks with simple banks in working class neighborhoods, which lacked basic hygiene and security and were considered dangerous to public health by contemporary elites" (Rinke 2004, 6). Theaters specifically built or designated for moving pictures did not appear until later. They did not come into existence in the United States until 1905, when nickelodeons, appealing to the urban, often immigrant, poor, first made their appearance. In Puerto Rico, however, theater houses that had been established much earlier for hosting traditional theater were put into service as venues for showing moving pictures. These traditional theaters existed throughout the island, even in small towns. Moving pictures were also shown as part of traveling shows that came from Europe or that Puerto Ricans had developed themselves (García 1984, 13–14). Despite the lack of venues specifically designated for movie viewing, García maintains that by 1909 there was already a filmgoing public in Puerto Rico.

The situation in regard to dedicated venues for movie watching began to improve with the establishment of a reliable supply and distribution system. In the early period of film, there were no film distributors. Those who shot the films often sold them outright to traveling showmen or exhibitors, who took them to the public. According to Puttnam (1998, 29), sales were made by the yard—the longer the picture, the higher the price. This left purchasers with a small number of films (or one) they traveled around with until the film deteriorated or the public tired of viewing the same film. With only a few films to show, purchasers had to continually seek out new audiences. But in 1903, as Puttnam observes, "a number of American film manufacturers simultaneously hit upon a revolutionary idea. They began to buy films from other firms and rent them to individual exhibitors" (1998, 29). New companies emerged specializing in the renting of films, and thus the film distributor was born—a go-between linking producer and exhibitor who secured, delivered, and returned films. The advent of distributors allowed producers to focus on producing films and exhibitors to focus on presenting them. As Puttnam (1998, 29ff.) notes, this move from sales to rentals revolutionized the industry. No longer were purchasers of films obliged to tour with the one or two pictures they had purchased. They could also change their offerings in response to audience demand. This in turn encouraged audiences to return more frequently, thus increasing attendance and revenues. It also contributed to a demand for greater innovation, longer films, and competition. Consequently, higher prices were charged for the best films. In essence, the same film could be rented to several exhibitors at once, who could quickly recover their costs and generate huge profits. Largely as a result of this shift, by 1905, permanent cinemas were springing up all over the United States, and film production soared (Puttnam 1998, 31).

Early Film Distribution in Puerto Rico by 1910

In Puerto Rico, films were already being rented by 1910, just a few years after the rental and distribution model took off in the United States, to change moviegoing forever. In a 1952 interview, Rafael Colorado, one of the earliest distributors in Puerto Rico, described how he came to be a distributor in 1910. He recalled that Manuel Portell and Miguel García had set up a movie theater under a tent in central San Juan, Puerto Rico (Puerta de Tierra),[2] though the public soon tired of their limited collection of films. Colorado noted, "I then made a trip to the U.S. to arrange for the production houses to send me, on a weekly basis, a number of 'cintas' [films] that I would then rent to Portell [and García] and to other exhibitors who were beginning to appear throughout the island" (author's translations throughout unless otherwise noted; quoted in Ortiz Jiménez 1952, 42).

The trips Colorado made were mainly to New York, for Hollywood had not yet emerged as the center of movie making. Consequently, it appears that very early on—indeed, before Hollywood existed as a movie industry center—U.S. films were being imported and distributed in Puerto Rico.

The history of this early period of film distribution in Puerto Rico is sketchy, but apparently women were not involved in the distribution of films, although they were involved as actresses and perhaps as part of the musical accompaniment to early silent films (as pianists) or in managing the early theaters. In the literature on Puerto Rican film, they are also noted as sources for what happened during this early period. As the longer-living survivors of what was often unwritten history, they often functioned as the oral historians of this era (see, for example, Banco Popular 1994, 1–24). Being a distributor may have been an occupation that required up-to-date knowledge of the world, connections, money, and the freedom to travel—advantages that may not have been available to many Puerto Rican women at the time. Although more research is needed, it is very probable that the limited role of women in film distribution was similar throughout Latin America. During this very early period, Puerto Rico was likely an exemplar of film reception among Latin American countries.

Appeals to Morals, Tastes, and the Upper Class

As early as 1912, magazine ads informed the public in metropolitan areas of weekly film showings. One recurring ad in *Gráfico*, a popular weekly magazine, combined notice of the showings at two "salons" and two film theaters in the San Juan area under the heading "Espectaculos" (Spectacles or Spectacular Events) (*Gráfico*, January 21, 1912, and March 3, 1912). Ads in the pre-1920 period reflected the concerns of the times with regard to film viewing. For example, the notices about upcoming films emphasized the newness and distinctiveness of each film, the setting, the public attending, and the selectivity of the films. Although it is hard to imagine today, the names of the films to be shown in each of these four settings were not given in the advertisements. Rather, the advertisements emphasized the popularity and attractiveness of the film showings, and in some cases took note of the morally decent nature of the films. These emphases undoubtedly reflected an attempt by theater owners to attract women, families, and "a higher class of people." The emphasis on the morally decent nature of films likely reflected the public view that women and families needed to be protected from morally indecent displays.

Mentioning the select public that would be in attendance was also an attempt to rescue the filmgoing experience from its unsavory reputation. Film had early been associated with vaudeville, nickelodeons, and urban, immigrant, working-class audiences: entertainment for the masses (Puttnam 1998, 32*ff.*). Also, many of the early theaters were makeshift and uncomfortable. Magazine advertisements had therefore to appeal to the social aspirations of their often elite readership, which, like many Latin American elites today, shared with its class peers in the United States and Europe similar concerns, interests, and habits. Magazine readers also undoubtedly looked to the northerly countries for cues to fast-changing styles, tastes, and pastimes. The ads in these magazines for women's clothing reflected this identification and harmony, even when it may have been unrealistic. For example, some of the advertisements showed heavy, many-layered women's clothing that would have been quite uncomfortable in the perpetual heat of the Caribbean yet evidently were considered fashionable and desirable. These ads appeared in *Gráfico* and *Puerto Rico Ilustrado,* two popular weekly magazines based in Puerto Rico that also circulated elsewhere. (*Puerto Rico Ilustrado,* which was established in 1910, circulated in the Dominican Republic and the United States.) The somewhat high prices of these magazines indicate that they were intended to appeal to the educated, more economically comfortable classes who could afford the annual subscription price. Both magazines were extensively read, existed for a long time, and provided a barometer of upper-class taste.

The language of the movie ads and their positioning in upscale publications suggest an effort to offset earlier impressions of going to the movies as a lower-class pastime and to emphasize the discerning tastes of attendees. Indeed, an ad for a San Juan theater, Cine Luna, added that every night, the ample and comfortable theater was filled with "*una concurrencia distinguida,*" a distinguished gathering of people. Although the popular evening showings were much publicized in magazines, there were also attempts to increase daytime attendance and to lure families with children to matinees. One ad promised gifts for children attending matinees that day and the next (*Puerto Rico Ilustrado,* December 12, 1914).

Foreign Films

Even though Puerto Rico came under U.S. political and economic control with the Spanish-American War, in the first two decades of the twentieth century many of the films shown were made in countries other than the

United States. For example, in December 1914, Cine Luna in San Juan informed the public that it had shown an "interesting film *Espartaco*" (*Spartacus*) to an overflowing house. This was apparently a foreign (non-U.S.-made) film, for it does not appear in the Internet Movie Database (IMDb), the most comprehensive listing of information on and about U.S.-made films to date. The same ad promoting *Spartacus* listed other films as upcoming features—*La mujer es como la sombra* (A Woman Is Like the Shadow) and *El halcon rojo* (The Red Falcon). These films also do not appear in the IMDb listing. The ad also announced that it would celebrate the theater's anniversary by showing a "beautiful and emotional" film entitled *Protea*, which was a 1913 film made in France. A second feature, *Auto Infernal*, also seems to have come from abroad, as it too does not turn up in the IMDb database.[3]

U.S. Serials Arrive

By 1916, more American pictures were being exhibited in Puerto Rico, and U.S. serials had arrived. Serials were an ingenious market creation. They were important in creating audience demand because they allowed cinemagoers to become familiar with particular actors, themes, and settings and to want to return to continue the story. An interesting example of how U.S. serials were marketed to highlight the reputed fame of actors, with a flavoring of sexual innuendo, can be seen in a full-page ad (with photographs) that announced the film series *La moneda rota* (*The Broken Coin*) (*Puerto Rico Ilustrado*, November 4, 1916). The series starred the "ideal, bellisima" Grace Cunard and the incomparable and jovial actor Francis Ford. In 1916, Cunard and Ford were among the most popular stars in Hollywood and were well-known for their serials. Indeed, the success of such films led to Cunard being nicknamed "the Serial Queen" (www.imdb.com). This same 1916 ad also noted that the famous athlete Edee Polo, "whose iron-like muscles are the amazement of all," had a role in the film. (Edee Polo was Eddie Polo, who was known as "the Hercules of the Screen" and made fifty-six movies.) The ad touted the film as the series that had caused the greatest commotion in all the theaters of Europe and boasted the most modern cinematography. (This makes me wonder whether acclaim in Europe, as compared with the United States, had more cachet at this point.) The plot and setting (Gretschoffen) were described, as was the film's message, "the personal effort that goes into achieving an ideal that solves the grave problems of life." (It is hard to imagine how the advertising could have made the message any broader so as to appeal to more people.) The ad ends with a short, perhaps sexually suggestive note from the lead star, Grace Cunard, inviting all to the Tres Banderas Theatre to watch the film so they can see "*qué cosas*" (what things) she does with "The Broken Coin."

Interestingly, in the ad, Grace Cunard ends by inviting viewers to ask the Universal Film Manufacturing Co. for photographs of her. Since the address provided is in San Juan, clearly Puerto Rico was distributing not just films but also photographs of stars. This same address and company appear again in another half-page ad about a film company (Blue Bird Photoplays Inc.) in the same 1916 issue of *Puerto Rico Ilustrado*. This time the ad includes a coupon that can be mailed in to get other actors' photographs. The ad announces the importation of "*los grandes dramas cinematográficos*" (the great dramatic films) of Blue Bird Photoplays Inc. to be shown at Cine Luna, San Juan, on Thursdays. It also highlights the names and fame of many of the actors in the upcoming films. These ads represent the shift that had occurred in films by then. In the earliest period of film, actors were not always credited. Audiences went to see the moving pictures, not the stars. Several factors contributed to this shift. Suffice it to say at this point that the benefits of the star system became more obvious to production companies and distributors. Highlighting star names made for greater audience recognition and identification with actors. This resulted in greater attendance. Also, actors began to demand on-screen credits. The film industry began to include and reinforce the star status of their actors, realizing that these approaches enhanced sales and increased moviegoing. Securing actors' photographs was an adjunct in this process and became a common practice in the United States and elsewhere. It helped to generate and sustain the star system, which in turn contributed to the success of Hollywood movies. By 1916, Puerto Rico was a participant in these developments.

By 1917, Yaguez Films was advertising *Tarzan, the Monkey Man*. This may have been the same movie as the one titled *Tarzan of the Apes* (1918), but it is advertised one year earlier in Puerto Rico. It may have been another earlier movie, or a prerelease of the same movie. The theme is the same, man conquering nature, in particular nature as represented by animals like lions, tigers, leopards, monkeys, and gorillas. For added spice (and perhaps female interest), note is taken of the hero's "precious romance with the first woman he saw." There are also interesting allusions to the world cinema stage in this ad. "Del Cine Mundial" (From the World Cinema) is the caption under the photograph in the ad, suggesting that a European company may have made the film or that it had premiered elsewhere in the world. In contrast to other ads, which by this time emphasized the actors in the film, this ad touted the film for its international fame. For example, it noted the sales of the book on which the film was based (more than 1,700,000 volumes sold), its serialization in 6,000 newspapers in one year, its translation into fourteen different languages, and its box office receipts during eight weeks in New York (*Puerto Rico Ilustrado*, November 4, 1916).

By 1919, Theaters All Over the Island . . .

By 1919, there were numerous theaters throughout Puerto Rico, and movies had become more common. My examination of the newspaper *El Mundo* over three randomly selected, consecutive days in 1919 turned up large and numerous ads for new films by this time.[4] In addition, many of these ads noted that the films advertised would be shown in many theaters outside of the metropolitan area. The theaters mentioned in these 1919 ads included many in San Juan, among them the Rialto, Imperial, Victory Garden, Norma, Ponce, Puerto Rico, Monte Carlo, Real, and Rio Piedras. Also mentioned were theaters in small towns, such as Arecibo, Hatillo, Camuy, Aguadilla, Lares, San Sebastian, Ponce, Ponce-Playa, Guayama, Arroyo, Palmer, Rio Grande, Carolina, Cabo Rojo, and, as the ad noted, "*y demas Cines de la Isla*" (and other theaters on the island) (*El Mundo*, October 2, 1919). As in the States, the theaters in the large metropolitan areas were elaborate, ornate affairs, while those in the smaller towns were more modest. These ads suggest both that movies had become a part of the daily lives of the Spanish-speaking populace of Puerto Rico and the extent to which these Latinos, who were now part of the United States—although as residents of an unincorporated territory—were already consumers of film. They and others throughout Latin America would become major consumers of Hollywood film as Hollywood gained ascendancy in the film world.

By 1919, theaters were also advertising together, suggesting the existence of theater chains with common ownership or distributorships. One quite common ad that appeared on all three days—October 1, 2, and 3—in *El Mundo* listed the showings for eight theaters in San Juan. Each of the theaters had different attractions (or films), and almost all had double features. Interest in U.S. series continued, and large ads indicating where and when a specific film or series could be seen were also evident. For example, there was the *Elmo the Invincible* series with Elmo Lincoln and (again) Grace Cunard, which had very large ads. Significant films—that is, films that had large budgets and big stars—also arrived and made the circuit around the island. For example, Fox Film's *Les misérables* (1917), which cost $1 million to make, received quite a bit of newspaper ink, and it was clear that this movie would debut not just in San Juan but in other theaters throughout the island. Specifically mentioned were "over 20 other theaters," including Humacao, Fajardo, San Lorenzo, Naguabo, Coamo, Santa Isabel, Salinas, Cayey, Aibonito, and Caguas. The star of this movie was William Farnum, who at the time was one of the highest-paid actors in Hollywood, earning $10,000 a week (www.imdb.com).

In 1919, at the now relatively longstanding Cine Luna theater in the capital of San Juan, two daily matinees were shown, one from 2:30 to 4:00 p.m. and the other from 4:00 to 5:30 p.m. This allowed time, the ad said, to attend other movies at night, the theater, retreats, dances, or casinos, to make visits or trips, and so on. This ad gives us an idea of the other evening recreational activities that the Puerto Rican readership engaged in at the time. Children were allowed in for 10 cents and adults for 15 cents. I suspect that these amounts may have varied from theater to theater or town to town for they seem high, especially by 1919 standards. Continuous projections and clear, "fixed" frames were promised. This was obviously a reference to the early complaints of all moviegoers, who grumbled that they had to wait for reels to be changed and who often had to deal with projectors skipping or jumping frames. The ad also indicated there were no commercial interruptions. This was a departure from contemporary moviegoing in Puerto Rico and elsewhere, where local ads and coming attractions took up a considerable amount of time before the advertised film began. By 1919 this theater claimed to have the best pictures first, and its byline had become, "A Step to Progress!" (*Puerto Rico Ilustrado*, March 22, 1919). As in Chile and elsewhere, going to the movies had become "chic" and "modern" (Rinke 2004, 8).

Numerous companies were also now advertising the films they brought into Puerto Rico. These companies included the Liberty Film Co., which brought *Les misérables* to San Juan in 1919; the Universal Film Manufacturing Co. and the Bluebird Photo Plays Inc., which had been advertising films in *Puerto Rico Ilustrado* as early as 1916; Yaguez Films (1917); the San Juan Film Exchange (1918); Corsas and Co. (1918); and the Selection Film Service. Interestingly, one house, Corsas and Co. in San Juan, billed itself as "the company that knows how to select." This company advertised a different type of film. For example, it purchased a one-page ad for a picture entitled *La victima* (*The Victim*, 1917) that included nine reels (lengthy for its day) and was produced by the New York Catholic Association of Art. In the ad, Corsas and Co. pointed out that they had to charge higher prices because of what the film cost them. Although the ad did not specify the film's plot or setting, it emphasized its high moral character and argued that the public "would not tire of viewing it an infinity of times" and would come to see it as "the mother of all pictures" because of its huge success. A peculiar forerunner of films to come, the film was based on a novel (not named) that involved the Catholic Church, drug addiction, false accusations, and the steel industry. It was to be shown in Puerto Rico; Santo Domingo, Cuba; and Venezuela (*Puerto Rico Ilustrado*, June 1918). Clearly, concerns over the morally appropriate nature of films continued: New York Catholics had come together to make the film and export it to these Spanish-speaking countries.

World War I and U.S. Political Influence

It is difficult to interpret the significance of the films advertised during this period in Puerto Rico. Did they reflect the public's tastes, those of the distributor, or just availability, low cost, and the aggressiveness of distribution companies outside Puerto Rico? But it is fairly easy to see the influence of political events and perspectives on what was shown in Puerto Rico's theaters. In 1917 the United States entered World War I; the Jones Act was passed the same year, making Puerto Ricans citizens and obliging them to military service during wartime.

Others have written about the involvement of the U.S. government in films that presented negative views of the enemy and positive views of the United States. Puttnam (1998, 75), for example, says that with the entry of America into the war in 1917, President Wilson began to think seriously about the political value of cinema. That it was popular was undeniable; that it was increasingly associated with the modernity of the United States was equally clear. Why not, argued Wilson, put the movies at the service of a crusade to uphold the values of liberal democracy, which were being put at risk by the Great War?

Consequently, it is not surprising to see a 1918 full-page review of the film *My Four Years in Germany*, which depicted an American ambassador's view of Germany during his stay there between 1913 and 1917 (*Puerto Rico Ilustrado*, July 20, 1918). Writing in 2002, a viewer from Canberra, Australia, described the film this way:

This film, made during World War I, is a fascinating look at the mind-set of wartime America. . . . This is a propaganda piece, with the German leaders portrayed as a bunch of evil lunatics, and German war atrocities toward women and children in Belgium greatly exaggerated. It is also a cry against autocracy and for democracy, with some insights into the way autocrats can manipulate the minds of reasonable patriots into war. Amazing to see how the only German portrayed sympathetically in the film is a socialist, a man who fights for the rights of the people but who is duped into joining the army. His later rebellion against the atrocities he witnesses is both powerful and moving. Of course a few years later no American filmmaker would dare to portray a socialist so positively. (Atfield 2002)

Although it may be seen today as a "truly remarkable window to another age," the review in Puerto Rico at the time accentuated other features of the film. One was that the film cost one and a half million to make—an extremely high cost for a film of that period. Another point emphasized was that the film had the support of the U.S. government. The review in Puerto Rico also noted that the Kaiser appeared in the film and that, after a special showing before the U.S-appointed governor of Puerto Rico, various authorities in San Juan, and other distinguished persons, the film would open at all the principal theaters on the island. Photo stills of the film accompanied the article. A lengthy review such as the one that accompanied this film was a departure from the way other films were discussed in this particular weekly magazine.

Also suggestive of the political context then was a full-page ad for a film entitled *El ojo del aguila* (*The Eagle's Eye*, 1918) in the same magazine during the same year (*Puerto Rico Ilustrado*, July 20, 1918). Written by the retired chief of the U.S. Secret Service, it focused on "how low German diplomacy had sunk" and "on true revelations that cannot be denied concerning the atrocious crimes committed by Germany against the United States." It advertised itself as a complete history of the German spy forces. The IMDb Internet site gives its plot line as follows: "A criminologist and a government agent team up to expose a ring of German spies." Its tagline was "The story of the imperial German government's spies, plots and propaganda in the United States." The San Juan Film Exchange Co. presented it. Other films advertised continued to focus on political issues. For example, in July 1919 an ad for *Bolshevism on Trial* (1919) appeared in *El Mundo*.

In contrast to the earlier period, toward the end of the decade many of the films were U.S. imports. For example, in 1919 there was an ad for

Los que pagan (*Those Who Pay*, 1917), a production of the well-known Thomas H. Ince, who ran the New York Motion Pictures Company (*El Mundo*, October 2, 1919). The film starred Bessie Barriscale, "*la actriz más atrayente de la temporada*" (the most attractive actress of the day). She was indeed recognized as a major attraction in the larger film world at the time. However, some films continued to be imported from Europe. An interesting example is *Fuerza y nobleza* (Strength and Nobility), a film made in Spain in 1917 by the Spanish film pioneer, Ricardo de Baños. The film featured Jack W. Johnson, the first African American to hold the title of World Boxing Champion. He held this title from 1908 to 1915. According to Streible (1996, 170–171), Johnson's bold, confrontational persona radically contradicted prevailing racial stereotypes; however, his "highly publicized feature film presentations showing Johnson pummeling 'white hopes' " raised white anxieties, and many states and cities censored Johnson's films. This Spanish film was shown in Puerto Rico, and the ad for the film included the words "El Negro" (the Black) in parentheses after Johnson's name to clarify who he was (*El Mundo*, October 2, 1919). The ad noted that the film involved four episodes and that it would travel to numerous theaters around the island.

Concern Over the Impact of Movies

By 1920 the public had become used to seeing moving pictures (García 1984, 24). Even in the economically privileged sector, which had earlier rejected moving pictures as lower class, interest had increased such that the Movette home movie camera was being advertised for an approximate cost of $177 in *Puerto Rico Ilustrado* (December 6, 1919). Indeed, movies had become so popular that one news article expressed concern that the longstanding tradition of legitimate theater would be lost to obscurity (*El Mundo*, January 19, 1920) In the same year, another columnist in *Puerto Rico Ilustrado* wrote an article laying out the reasons why he detested the movies. Chief among them was the tendency of movies to corrupt youth, especially young girls. He noted that two months after two movie houses were established in one community, the elementary and high school teachers began to notice that the students' lessons were less well mastered and that young girls' imaginations had been sharpened—for the worse. Moreover, he wrote, young girls who went alone to the movies developed prejudicial relationships. Indeed, one of these responded to her mother who scolded her on this issue: "If you only knew what I know about life thanks to the movies. I know more than you do!" (Romanacce 1920).

Despite the author's perceptions of "corruption," movies continued to grow in popularity. Indeed, a subsequent issue of the same magazine featured on its cover Clara Kimball Young, who was starring in the movie *The Forbidden Woman*, then showing at the Rialto theater in San Juan (*Puerto Rico Ilustrado*, October 2, 1920). An earlier issue had featured Mary Pickford and her new husband, Douglas Fairbanks, on its cover (*Puerto Rico Ilustrado*, June 26, 1920). The caption under the photograph noted that both had arrived in New York to elect the new president of United Artists with whom they, Charlie Chaplin, and D. W. Griffith were involved. Despite Mr. Romanacce's concerns, interest in films and the film community continued to flourish.

The Actual Theaters Then

An interior shot of El Teatro Popular (the Popular Theater) in Cabo Rojo, Puerto Rico, around 1925[5] provides a number of clues to the extent of infiltration of U.S. film culture into Puerto Rico. A truncated poster on the far left of the photograph carries an ad for *le Wives*, which is probably *Single Wives*, a 1924 U.S. film with Corinne Griffith, an acclaimed star of the silent era. The contiguous poster announces *Lady of the Night*, a 1925 U.S. film that reflected the long-term collaboration between well-known director Monta Bell and screen legend Norma Shearer. The film's story was written by Alice D. G. Miller and Adela Rogers St. Johns, the latter a well-known writer of the day whose stories appeared quite often in *Photoplay* and elsewhere. The legendary Joan Crawford was Shearer's double in this movie. Because Crawford had yet to achieve much fame, she was uncredited. The art direction was by the renowned Cedric Gibbons, who five to six years later would become Dolores del Río's second husband. A third poster is unclear; there is the trace of two names, "Walter M." and possibly "Eugenia."

Thus, by 1925, in this small town on an island in the Caribbean, people who are today called Latinos or Hispanics in the United States were viewing the same major movies that brought crowds into New York and other big-city theaters, as well as into the theaters of small-town America.[6] They were all learning who the major stars were, and more subtly, they were learning about "the American way of life." They saw that men drove cars to work and that women not only drove cars but also bobbed their hair, wore makeup, smoked, and acted in a myriad of other ways heretofore not on display. They saw telephones and airplanes as part of everyday life. As Alvarez Curbelo (1994, 5) put it, films conveyed "an energy that molded opinion, language, dress, tastes, behavior and even the physical appearance of more than half of the world's population." According to one Puerto Rican critic in 1923, women's fashion was dramatically influenced by "Mary Pickford's hairdo, Norma Talmadge's hats, Dorothy Gish's sumptuous dresses, Agnes Ayres' shoes, Pola Negri's eyebrows, and Gloria Swanson's large earrings"(*Cinema*, no. 5, 1923, cited in Alvarez Curbelo 1994, 5).

Pre- and Post-Hollywood

What is perhaps most interesting about this early period is that the growth in theaters and in a filmgoing public in Puerto Rico occurred prior to the growth of Hollywood. In 1920, the American film industry had not yet become the strong competitor to the European film industry that it would be by the end of the next decade, and Latin America was not yet making films to any significant degree (Puttnam 1998, 72–73).[7] Indeed, Hollywood was nascent. The first moviemakers had arrived in Hollywood in 1903, but Universal did not begin there until 1912, and Cecil B. De Mille and Lasky did not arrive until 1913–1914 (Puttnam 1998, 65ff.). It was only in 1916–1917 that Hollywood began to gain power and control over the moviemaking business, and it was not until the mid-twenties and early thirties that the Hollywood moguls' "desire to ensure that American movies dominated markets the world over" was fulfilled (Puttnam 1998, 103). By the early 1930s the position of Hollywood as the dominant world player was secured, for Hollywood was producing 75–80 percent of all movies shown around the world. It was also generating $200 million in annual revenues for American distributors, out of a total world gross of $275 million (Puttnam 1998, 122).

The subsequent dominance of Hollywood was also reflected in Puerto Rico's magazines. By 1934 we see extensive coverage of Hollywood film stars in *Puerto Rico Ilustrado*. There was even a regular column, "Cine" (Movies or Film), that covered Hollywood's goings on (see, for example, the issues of January 27, June 30, and July 7, 1934). One article by reporter Miguel de Záreaga included photographs of Hollywood movie stars whose names we recognize today—Carole Lombard, Jean Harlow, Claudette

Colbert, Ida Lupino. It also profiled lesser-known (today) starlets such as Frances Dee, Grace Moore, Verna Hillie, and Mary Carlisle. In addition, it included a photograph and text on the well-known Hollywood star, Lupe Vélez (of Mexico) and her husband, Johnny Weismuller, of Tarzan fame (*Puerto Rico Ilustrado*, September 15, 1934). There were also ads in which Hollywood stars were shown promoting consumer products. For example, ads by both Kay Francis and Raquel Torres advertising Listerine toothpaste appear in several issues of *Puerto Rico Ilustrado* from 1934. Some Hollywood stars—Greta Garbo and Zasu Pitts—received special attention, and Paramount musicals in color were advertised and discussed. Interestingly, there was coverage of *one* Spanish-language film this year. The film, *Una vida por otra* (*One Life for Another*), was referred to in the article as "*el estreno de la superproducción hispanoparlante*" (the debut of the super Spanish-language production). The brief article included a full-page spread with five film stills (*Puerto Rico Ilustrado*, January 3, 1934).[8] Although the Spanish-surnamed actors Nancy Torres, Julio Villarreal, and Gloria Iturbe were listed, the director, John H. Auer, who was born in Budapest and had done a number of Mexican films, was not. Nor was it noted that this was a U.S.-made film known as *One Life for Another* (1933). Very likely this film may have been part of the "Cine Hispano" effort that Hollywood pursued so as to not lose their market share in Latin America after the success of talkies.[9]

Hollywood's rise to world dominance between 1917 and 1935 was aided by a number of factors. World War I curtailed filmmaking in many European countries. Another important factor was the success of the antitrust suit brought by the U.S. government against the Edison Trust, an association of filmmakers that, through strong-arm tactics, controlled distribution, limited the length of films, prohibited the use of actors' names, and kept certain movie companies out of the network. Control of the movie industry by the Edison Trust had kept others from developing their own businesses. The elimination of these industry controls over filmmaking also paved the way for the establishment of new, vertically integrated filmmaking operations that applied industrialist manufacturing principles; in this way films could be produced much as other manufactured products, such as automobiles, were produced. Hollywood's development was further aided by its growing association with the U.S. government, especially during the war, when both government and film studio heads saw the political utility of films to cement or create ideological and cultural alliances and to fill markets that had a limited supply of films.

Nevertheless, the growth of Hollywood would not have occurred without the rise of ambitious entrepreneurs who were poised to become the subsequent movie moguls. Added to this were the growing popularity of films and, finally, the involvement of the financial community that funded the increasingly expensive film ventures (because the expected returns were so great). All of these factors contributed to the growth and development of Hollywood (Puttnam 1998, 1–123). But even as late as the twenties, much of the financial control of Hollywood pictures remained in New York, which had supplanted London as the center of world finance by 1916.

A Summation

Given the subsequent long-term global dominance of Hollywood film-making, this look into the earliest period of film viewing in a somewhat remote part of the world (relative to the centers of filmmaking then) is instructive. The evidence serves to dispel a number of common assumptions. Specifically, it makes clear that despite the U.S. takeover of Puerto Rico in 1898 and the consequent forging of economic ties, the first films to arrive in Puerto Rico in the following decade were not U.S. films but films from France. It also shows that almost a decade before Hollywood began to assert its dominance in film, films and stars' photographs were already being distributed and shown throughout Puerto Rico, as well as in other parts of Latin America and the world. Many of these films were imported from Europe, others from New York. A filmgoing public had already developed throughout the island by 1920.

This overview also suggests how threatening to cultural mores and values the movies were for some, and the magnetism that films held for all classes. It draws attention to the significance of silent films in crossing national as well as economic and political borders, and suggests the influence that political events and the U.S. government had on the movies seen in Puerto Rico during this early period.

Notes

The author would like to thank the following for their help in making this chapter a reality: Sara Ruíz, director of the Collección Puertorriqueña, and Nelly Vásquez-Sotillo, professor in the History Department, both at the University of Puerto Rico, Mayaguez, and the following well-informed residents of Cabo Rojo,

Puerto Rico: Olga Rodríguez Pérez de Conrad, Gerardo Ramírez, Ileana López, Irma and Carlos Ramírez, Dilma Fagundo Montalvo, Margie Montalvo, Luis and Tati Cabrera Miranda, Makiro and Lisette Ortiz, and Chin Ramírez. The epigraph is from Romanacce (1920).

1. Colorado's comments were part of an interview he did in 1952 with journalist Juan Ortiz Jiménez of *Puerto Rico Ilustrado*. These comments were translated and also cited in *Idilio tropical* (1994, 12).

2. The Carnegie Library would subsequently come to occupy this space.

3. Some of these ads were found on microfilmed copies of newspapers. In many cases, page numbers are no longer visible. The archival materials referenced here can be found at the University of Puerto Rico–Mayaguez, in the Collections of the Sala Puertorriqueña, Mayaguez, Puerto Rico.

4. *El Mundo* was one of the largest newspapers on the island in 1919. It is often cited in historical analyses of Puerto Rico.

5. For a local history of the events leading to the establishment of theaters in Cabo Rojo, Puerto Rico, see Ibern Fleytas (1960). For a description of the changing role of movie theaters in the United States, see Putnam (2000).

6. This is an interesting year, for it is also the year that Dolores del Río appeared in her first Hollywood movie, *Joanna* (1925).

7. Some films had been made in Latin American countries (including Puerto Rico) before 1920. On this, see Trelles (1991), García (1984), Rinke (2002, 2004), Banco Popular (1994), and Rodríguez (n.d.).

8. *Puerto Rico Illustrado*, "Cine" column, January 27, June 30, and July 7, 1934; article by Miguel de Záreaga on Hollywood movie stars, September 15, 1934 (vol. 20, no. 1280), p. 14; Listerine toothpaste ads, July 7, 1934, no. 1270, and April 7, 1934, p. 47, vol. 25, no. 1257; Greta Garbo, March 3, 1934; ZaSu Pitts, February 10, 1934; Paramount musicals in color, January 27 and December 1, 1934; Spanish-language film, *Una Vida por Otra* (One Life for Another), January 13, 1934, vol. 25, no. 1245.

9. "Cine Hispano" consisted of Hollywood movies made in the Spanish language. For more on their history, see O'Neil (1998).

Bibliography

Alvarez Curbelo, S. 1994. "Pasion de cine." In *Idilio tropical: La aventura del cine puertorriqueño*, 1–9. Exhibition catalogue. San Juan, PR: Banco Popular.

Atfield, D. 2002. "Truly remarkable window to another age." http://imdb.com/title/tt0009406. Comment posted March 23.

Banco Popular. 1994. *Idilio tropical: La aventura del cine puertorriqueño*. Exhibition catalogue. San Juan, PR: Banco Popular.

El Mundo. El Cine Desorganiza la Produccion de Escenario. January 19, 1920, p. 6.

El Mundo. Issues of October 1–3, 1919, January 19, 1920, and October 25, 1919.

Fuller, K. H. 1996. *At the Picture Show: Small Town Audiences and the Creation of Movie Fan Culture*. Washington, DC: Smithsonian Institution Press.

García, J. 1984. *Breve historia del cine puertorriqueño*. San Juan, PR: Cine-gráfica.

Gráfico. Issues of January 21, 1912, p. 24; March 3, 1912, p. 30.

Ibern Fleytas, R. 1960. *Historia de Cabo Rojo*. Ciudad Trujillo, DR: Editora Montalvo.

Internet Movie Database. http://www.imdb.com/name/nm0192062/bio [Grace Cunard], http://www.imdb.com/name/nm0267912/bio [William Farnum], both accessed August 15, 2006.

O'Neil, B. 1998. "Yankee Invasion of Mexico, or Mexican Invasion of Hollywood? Hollywood's Renewed Spanish-Language Production of 1938–1939." *Studies in Latin American Popular Culture* 17:79–104.

Ortiz Jiménez, J. 1952. "Cuarenta años de cinematografía puertorriqueña." *Puerto Rico Ilustrado*, February 16, 1952, pp. 38–42, 50.

Puerto Rico Ilustrado. 1910–1920. Mayaguez: Archives of the University of Puerto Rico, Sala Puertorriqueña.

Puttnam, D., with N. Watson. 1998. *Movies and Money*. New York: Alfred A. Knopf.

Putnam, M. 2000. *Silent Screens: The Decline and Transformation of the American Movie Theatre*. Baltimore: Johns Hopkins University Press.

Rinke, S. 2002. "Hollywood en Santiago y Berlin, 1916–1930: La nueva historia cultural del triángulo atlántico." In *El triángulo atlántico: América Latina, Europa y los Estados Unidos en el sistema internacional cambiante*, ed. K. Bodmer et al., 271–281. St. Augustin, Germany: KAS (Konrad-Adenaur-Stiftung).

Rinke, S. 2004. "A Splendid Agent of Propaganda: Hollywood in Chile." In *Begegnungen mit dem Yankee: Nordamerikanisierung und soziokultureller Wandel in Chile, 1898–1900*, ed. Stefan Rinke, 196–221. Cologne: Böhlau.

Rodríguez, C. E. n.d. "The Production of Film in Puerto Rico." Manuscript. Available from the author.

Romanacce, S. 1920. "Detesto el cine." *Puerto Rico Ilustrado*, September 18.

Segrave, K. 1997. *American Films Abroad: Hollywood's Domination of the World's Movie Screens from the 1890s to the Present*. Jefferson, NC: McFarland.

Streible, D. 1996. "Race and the Reception of Jack Johnson Fight Films." In *The Birth of Whiteness: Race and the Emergence of U.S. Cinema*, ed. Daniel Bernardi, 170–202. New Brunswick, NJ: Rutgers University Press.

Torres, J. Artemio. 1994. "'Apaga musiú': Los primeros pasos del cine puertorriqueño" [Lights Out, M'sieur: The Beginnings of Puerto Rican Cinema]. In *Idilio tropical: La aventura del cine puertorriqueño*, 10–23. Exhibition catalogue. San Juan, PR: Banco Popular.

Trelles Plazaola, L. 1991. *Cine y mujer en América Latina: Directoras de largometrajes de ficción*. Río Piedras, PR: Editorial de la Universidad de Puerto Rico.

CHAPTER 2

Lupe Vélez

Queen of the B's

ROSA LINDA FREGOSO

She was known as the "Mexican Spitfire," but also as "Whoopee Lupee," "Hot Tamale," and "Tropical Hurricane." She is often dismissed for embodying the "negative" extreme of Mexican femininity: hot-blooded, volatile, sexually promiscuous—the "tragic prototype of the Latina Spitfire stereotype," according to Ríos-Bustamante.[1] Born María Guadalupe Villalobos in San Luis Potosí, Mexico, Lupe Vélez started performing in musical comedies in Mexico City during the 1920s. In 1926, at the age of seventeen, she left for California, joining three thousand other Mexicans with dreams of making it in Hollywood. Initially playing minor parts in two-reel shorts, Velez had her big break the following year, when she co-starred with Douglas Fairbanks in the silent feature *Gaucho* (1927). During the span of her seventeen-year career, Lupe Vélez was one of a handful of actresses who excelled both on the screen and in Broadway musicals. By the time she died, at age thirty-five, Lupe Vélez had starred in forty-five feature films, working in Hollywood, London, and Mexico, though she is best known for her title roles in screwball comedy, the eight feature films known as the Mexican Spitfire series.

One way of studying Lupe Vélez would be to focus on her otherness—her racialized, gendered star persona within the Hollywood industry, which stands in relation to the dominant racial and gender ideology in the United States. Although I recognize this as an important task, my genealogy of Lupe Vélez takes a more circuitous route, one that examines the meaning of her embodied otherness (public persona and star text) as a metaphor for shifting, contradictory, and ambiguous social identities.

In her own time, Vélez's most rancorous critics often positioned her in that shifting social identity of Mexican-ness that today would be characterized as Chicana. At the time, critics in Mexico often measured Vélez against another exotic Mexican star in Hollywood of the period, the "sedate and lady-like" Dolores del Río, who was "carefully crafted" by the industry as a "high class ethnic woman of impeccable morals."[2] They vilified Lupe Vélez as a "commoner" (*populachera*) and "vulgar and unmannerly" (*una chica incorrigiblemente vulgar*), or, as one Mexican critic would write, Vélez had "traces we notice solely in lower class people, without culture, nor ideals, nor patriotism."[3]

These attitudes echo those of the Mexican elite toward the poor workers leaving Mexico for el norte. Like her Mexican compatriots working and living in the United States, Vélez was denounced as "*agringada*" and "*apochada*" (anglicized and assimilated), for "disowning her country"—in sum, for being a *pocha*/Chicana.[4] To a great extent, the construction by the Mexican national elite of Vélez's identity as pocha/Chicana reveals the degree to which her public persona evoked anxieties about the solidity and stability of Mexican national identity during the 1930s. Emerging from decades of social upheavals, postrevolutionary Mexico had embarked on a comprehensive social, political, and cultural project for unifying the nation and defining its "Mexicanidad," or national identity—a unity threatened by the ever-growing exodus of its citizens to the United States. Even though the Mexican diaspora—nearly one-tenth of Mexico's population migrated to the United States between 1910 and 1930, among them Lupe—disrupted Mexican nationalism's imaginary unity, there are also ways in which her otherness raised anxieties about the shifting and contradictory nature of Mexican femininity.[5]

Gabriel Ramírez, Vélez's biographer, characterizes her as a "flapper Azteca," an Aztec flapper of Mexico City's "roaring 1920s." In 1925, at age sixteen, Lupe Vélez bobbed her hair and donned the flapper style, becoming an instant hit with her debut performance of the Charleston at the Teatro Principal.[6] She was part of modernity's revolution in lifestyle in Mexico City, of the modern, "refreshing," "vigorous" new manners and morals that topped the "musty and frivolous European conservativism" dominant in early twentieth-century Mexico.[7] Influenced by jazz, the Charleston, and Hollywood movies, Lupe Vélez was very much a "modern, new woman" of Mexico City, expressing the "new visibility of the erotic in popular culture" through her performances, fashion, and lifestyle.[8] A liberated woman of the twenties, Vélez followed in the footsteps of her mother, who had been an opera singer and her most "enthusiastic" and "unconditional" champion.[9] And when her father prohibited the use of his family name for public performances, she adopted her mother's maiden name, Vélez. Independent and undomesticated, she embodied the new sexual liberalism, the new erotic impulse that surged into the public realm during the 1920s, challenging the existing framework of strict gender roles and providing a new model for Mexican femininity.

At seventeen, Lupe Vélez left Mexico for the United States, where she entered the "youth-centered world" in full swing during the 1920s. She encountered the "new freedoms that post-suffrage women seemed to possess," as well as the new autonomy and mobility of U.S. youth.[10] Arriving in the winter of 1926, unemployed and with a few dollars in her pocket, she would later recall this early resolve: "I was determined to make money and defend myself, because the woman who wants to, doesn't need anyone to defend her"[11] (Figure 2.1).

As Vélez's career flourished, she was adored by fans in the United States and Mexico alike. Mexican critics, in sharp contrast, were threatened by her subversive form of femininity and decried her negative influence on young Mexican women.[12] Her subversion of traditional notions of femininity—especially her newfound sexual freedom—probably also scandalized the parents of a new generation of Mexican American youth. After all, Lupe Vélez openly advocated sex beyond the confines of marriage. In a 1929 article, also translated into Spanish, the columnist Virginia Lane reported, "Lupe can love five men at the same time, with incredible ease, and love them all for five different reasons"—a statement sure to scandalize Catholic Mexican sensibilities.[13]

By 1930, there were "150,000 people of Mexican birth or heritage" residing in Los Angeles. Like adolescents elsewhere, Mexican American teenagers "moved in a youth-centered world" and embraced "the revolution in manners and morals" sweeping the country.[14] In many ways, the social and cultural transformations that were ushered in by the new ethic of capitalist consumerism shook the foundations of Mexican "familial oligarchy," especially its "ideology of control."[15]

Indeed, Los Angeles, the home of Hollywood and Lupe Vélez, was ground zero of the losing battle to discipline and regulate new expressions of sexuality and economic independence among Mexican American youth. They "bobbed their hair like flappers of the screen."[16] "They moved out of their family home and into apartments. . . . They could go out with men unsupervised as was the practice among their Anglo peers."[17] They copied the "models made stylish by movie stars and actresses."[18] And, finally, as Vicki Ruiz observes about these young women of the 1930s: "Sparked by manufactured fantasies and clinging to youthful hopes, many Mexican women teenagers avidly read celebrity gossip columns, attended Saturday matinees, cruised Hollywood and Vine, and nurtured their visions of

Figure 2.1. Lupe Vélez in a dramatic pose from early in her acting career. She was determined to support herself. Courtesy of the Academy of Motion Picture Arts and Sciences.

stardom."[19] The favorite actresses among thirty-seven Mexican teenagers living in a settlement house in 1929 included Greta Garbo, Dolores del Río, Mary Pickford, Clara Bow, and Lupe Vélez.[20]

In Lupe Vélez, Mexican American young women found alternatives to a femininity circumscribed by marriage and masculine authority: "I've always been afraid of marriage," Vélez explained in 1934. "It seems to me like being imprisoned in an iron cage. . . . I do not tolerate anyone telling me what I can and cannot do."[21] Vélez was also a model for female independence and autonomy: "Do you want to know Lupe, the real Lupe? I love freedom. I want to be free to sing and dance always and when I so desire."[22] And through her public persona and movie characters, Lupe Vélez portrayed strong women who were active agents in public spaces both as career women and as players in romance and courtship. In this manner, she provided young women with an alternative model of female behavior and identity. Although she more often symbolized the "new visibility of the erotic," especially the exotic blend of race and sex so stylish in the 1920s, in other ways Lupe Vélez's image worked to undermine the gendered framework of female identity tied exclusively to motherhood. "I have only one solution for whatever difficulties I encounter . . . work, work, work, and more work. . . . My father and mother taught me and my two sisters to work since we were very young. My two sisters are singers and at the age of 15, I was already dancing professionally."[23] The photograph of Vélez holding a pair of turtles she named Lupe and Gary (for Gary Cooper) is a prime example of her trendsetting nature and of the persona of the modern, "new" woman she cultivated (Figure 2.2). Vélez is credited with starting the Hollywood fad (circa 1930) of collecting shelled reptiles.

This model of a modern "new woman" is not the dominant image of Mexican femininity lodged in cultural memory; it is not the image of Mexican female identity that circulated in public discourses, either in Mexico, where the dominant feminine ideal was calcified in self-sacrificing motherhood, or in the United States, with its colonialist investment in an image of premodern Mexican primitivism. In the embrace of sexual liberalism, financial independence, and personal meaning derived from something other than motherhood, Lupe Vélez subverted the prevailing gendered framework and rejected dominant tropes associated with Mexican femininity, especially the ideal of motherhood and passivity made visible in the rebozo-draped Mexicana of Hollywood films. This is not, I should note, the dominant narrative one hears about Lupe Vélez, who is more often maligned in Latino historiography for perpetuating a negative stereotype of Latina identity.[24]

What I find most curious (and unfortunate) about the legacy of Lupe Vélez as the "Mexican Spitfire" is the confusion that exists between the characters she portrayed and her public persona. Vélez's visibility within the star system was predicated on an identity that she herself cultivated,

Figure 2.2. Lupe Vélez with her turtles, Lupe and Gary. Courtesy of the Academy of Motion Picture Arts and Sciences.

as a woman who was "uninhibited," "unpretentious" and "frank," "extravagant" and "unconventional"—a woman who broke with all social conventions. Often this visibility was interpreted differently within Hollywood circles, where she was known for being "impetuous," for her "irreverence" and "heavy-handed pranks," for "a very rich repertoire of bad words," for a "difficult and aggressive personality."

The confusion between Vélez's persona and her characters is nowhere more evident than in the way the term "Mexican Spitfire" is used in Latino historiography today. Initially associated with Lupe's comedic performance in cinema, the term is now interpreted as an insignia for all that masculinist discourse judges as "negative" about Vélez's public persona, as synonymous with the "sexually alluring and available . . . fallen [Latin] woman."[25] In the process, Vélez's talent as a performer—actor, comedian, and dancer, on stage and screen—is erased.

I owe my interest in Lupe Vélez in part to historian Tatcho Mindiola, who characterized Vélez as a "predecessor to Lucille Ball."[26] I now consider Lupe Vélez to be the Chicana Queen of the B's. She is rarely considered as important as Katharine Hepburn or Irene Dunne, but she was one of the most accomplished and popular screwball comedians of the time.[27]

The 1940s were a contradictory period for Mexican Americans in Hollywood: the growing economic crisis in the industry was exacerbating the anti-immigrant xenophobia already under way in the country; then there was the backlash against the sexual liberalism of the 1920s, resulting in a return to gender conservatism, while the introduction of the industry's production codes (sexual and racial) redefined the limits of the "cinematic melting pot," tying restrictions on interracial liaisons to "skin color."[28] In fact, a few years earlier, the dark-skinned Vélez had been explicitly singled out in the media's anti-immigrant campaigns in defense of "U.S.-born" workers during the Great Depression, as this commentator makes evident: "It is time for [Lupe Vélez] and her foreign accent to disappear so that our own American actresses can occupy the space that corresponds to them."[29]

Within this unsettling wartime context, the character Lupe Vélez portrayed in the Mexican Spitfire series seemed to violate all the norms. Carmelita Fuentes, the "spitfire" in the eight films directed by Leslie Goodwins for RKO Studios, was a "new woman" who, though married, maintained her career as a singer and dancer. In spite of Hollywood's unofficial policy imposing limits on the depiction of interracial marriage, Carmelita married a white advertising executive she met in Mexico and later moved with him to an upscale apartment in Manhattan—a characterization that inspired the Mexican critic Emilio García Riera to dub Carmelita a "high-class" Chicana. As he explains, "For once, a Mexican woman is removed from the haciendas, churches, cantinas and cactuses, dressed in fashionable, cosmopolitan clothing, and situated in the most worldly of U.S. urban settings: New York."[30]

The first few films in the series were extremely successful, rekindling

Vélez's popularity among U.S. audiences. *The Mexican Spitfire*, released in 1939, played for three weeks to sold-out crowds at the Rialto in New York. And in Mexico, *The Girl from Mexico* (1939) received high praise from some critics, who described it as a "great comedy" and "an hour of non-stop laughter," and Lupe as a "great actress" and dancer.[31]

Undoubtedly, the plots of the Mexican Spitfire series were simple-minded and formulaic, exploiting, for comedic effect, the deliberate malapropisms and "foreign-ness" of her overblown accent, along with her racialized gender. Throughout her career, Vélez did star mostly in B movies; however, as Ruby Rich reminded me, the revival of B movies as the "true American cinema" during the 1970s makes her contributions as an actress of the forties even more significant today. And whereas in Latin America her status as a star reached mythic proportions, Vélez was marginalized within the Hollywood star system.[32] Despite failing in her aspirations to play the dramatic roles that she believed would launch her into the realm of "true" stardom, however, Vélez was always highly regarded as a performer, receiving mostly favorable reviews throughout her career, especially for her comedic performances in film and Broadway musicals, and, most interestingly, her irreverent camp impersonations of female stars such as Katherine Hepburn, Shirley Temple, Gloria Swanson, Dolores del Río, and Marlene Dietrich (Figure 2.3).

At the Library of Congress I was able to screen Vélez's last U.S. film, *Redhead from Manhattan* (1943), a wartime musical combining the prosaic theme of patriotism with a favorable stance on immigrants from south of the border—a perspective undoubtedly influenced by the Good Neighbor Policy's marketing strategies in Latin America. In *Redhead from Manhattan* Vélez performs multiple roles, including those of Rita, an immigrant from Latin America who has recently arrived illegally, as a stowaway; Rita's cousin, Maria, a star in Broadway musicals who attempts to keep her marriage (and pregnancy) a secret from her manager; and a disturbing, camp performance in blackface of the maid, Mandy Lou.

The plot of the film revolves around Rita's dreams of becoming a star: "In New York I shall be a new discovery. I shall be a great star like Carmen Miranda"—a desire fulfilled when Rita is convinced by her cousin, Maria, to take her place on stage. To the tune of "Somewhere South of Here," Vélez displays her superb talents in camp performance, dancing in front of a chorus line, dressed excessively "ethnic," in tricolor rebozo halters, wearing an outrageous wide-rim hat topped with large antennaed bumblebees—an obvious parody of Carmen Miranda. As Rita, Vélez is able to occupy the place of Carmen Miranda momentarily, intentionally mobilizing a "hyperlatinidad" in her histrionic performance of Carmen

Figure 2.3. Lupe Vélez performing on-stage. Courtesy of the Academy of Motion Picture Arts and Sciences.

Miranda that in many respects parodies not only the Hollywood success of the "Brazilian bombshell" but Vélez's own desire for stardom at any price. *Redhead from Manhattan* was, after all, the final film she made in Hollywood before her death.

In exploring the meaning of Lupe Vélez's embodied otherness as star text I came to realize that this "excess"—her penchant for over-the-top, histrionic impersonations and camp performances—has often been misinterpreted as literal embodiments of Latina otherness (in other words, a stereotype), particularly by a later generation of Latino film historians.

The politics of Latino and Chicano historiography have been unable (or unwilling) to appreciate the subversive humor of Vélez's performances. Vélez is often compared with the other great Mexicana star of the period, Dolores del Río, who, though often idealized for being sedate and "aristocratic," seems trapped in her own seriousness. Vélez, by contrast, was deliberately transgressive, deploying her own image to comment on her position within the industry.

It is thus not surprising that Lupe Vélez gets reclaimed in the world of video art, for one of the basic elements of the genre is appropriation, as well as the refashioning of a space of camp performance and excess. In the recent experimental video, *The Assumption of Lupe Vélez* (1999), Rita Gonzalez examines the "cult of Lupe Vélez" by juxtaposing scenes from two underground films of the 1960s, *Lupe* (1966, Andy Warhol) and *Lupe* (1967, Jose Rodríguez-Soltero) with footage from a performance of "La Lupe" (Bianco Arellano), a Latino drag queen in Echo Park, Los Angeles, who "customizes her/his glamour according to the cult of Vélez," as stated in Gonzalez's publicity flyer.

Gonzalez's video is a poetic memorial to Vélez's transgressive performances, one that opens up a space for the multiple meanings in the word "assumption"—as adoption and appropriation, but also referring to the Assumption (into heaven) of the Virgin Mary—and in the process enshrines her significance in queer performance and avant-garde filmmaking. As Ramon Garcia explains, "The 'assumption' in the title of the piece refers to Lupe Vélez's iconographic status as 'saint' or 'martyr' in a queer hagiography in which movie stars and their drag queen impersonators occupy the Catholic narrative of saints' lives."[33]

The Assumption of Lupe Vélez is itself framed by experimental visual and (non)narrative techniques, yet within its experimental mode, Gonzalez manages to convey a legibly nuanced message about the cultural impact of Vélez beyond the historical context in which the star lived. Gonzalez meditates on the reconstruction of Vélez "as legend of saintly proportions, as Evita Perón or Selena for queer counter-cultural community,"[34] inspiring such avant-garde artists as Andy Warhol, Kenneth Anger, and Jose Rodríguez-Soltero. Throughout the video Gonzalez strategically summons the haunting presence of Lupe Vélez, mainly through visually blurred, surreal images, accompanied by the tormented voice of Mexican experimental artist Ximena Cuevas, who, as Vélez, comments on her own exploitation as stereotype by Hollywood and reads excerpts from her own obituary (written by Heda Hopper).

It was La Lupe's camp performances in *The Assumption of Lupe Vélez* that led me to search for other excesses in the public persona of Lupe Vélez, for transgressions beyond the sexual liberalism and female autonomy I mentioned earlier. In the details of her life I found evidence of what Yvonne Yarbro-Bejarano calls "queer quotes or traces," beginning with the fact that as a child, Vélez played with boys because girls considered her to be too rough.[35] "I used to dress in my brother, Emigdio's, pants and jackets," she told a reporter. "I also imitated the dance steps, walking style, gestures and attitudes of all the boys I played with."[36]

There are further queer traces of the adult Lupe Vélez in drag: a sighting of Lupe wearing a "sports jacket and a cap" in New York city; a commentary on the oil-stained pants she often wore while repairing cars.[37] And then there was Vélez's passion for boxing: "She never missed boxing matches, attending almost every Friday, when she would be spotted in front row seats at the American Legion Stadium, wearing a red wig and standing on her seat, yelling outrageous instructions to the boxers."[38] I often wonder if it is this androgyny in Lupe Vélez's gender identity that scandalized her critics, or perhaps it was the combination of transgressions that made her so unacceptable.

In closing, I would like to return to this question of fantasy. Vélez committed suicide two days after throwing a big bash in honor of her saint's day, Our Lady of Guadalupe, on December 12, 1944. Four months' pregnant, she died of an overdose of Seconal. It does not surprise me that even in death, Lupe Vélez was the source of controversy (her death having been the subject of discrepant accounts) or that a proliferation of other fantasies, including my own, would be animated by this controversy. In his biography of Vélez, Gabriel Ramírez writes, "Her death, a marvel of theatricality and of poor taste, was fitting of Hollywood. And perhaps, even of Lupe Vélez."[39]

As Gonzalez's video reminds us, the major culprit behind the discrepancies surrounding Lupe's death is Kenneth Anger's underground classic, *Hollywood Babylon*. In his gossip-riddled "exposé" of Hollywood scandals, the chapter entitled "Chop-Suicide" describes the sordid details that he claims newspapers refused to publish:

> When Juanita, the chambermaid, had opened the bedroom door at nine, the morning after the suicide, no Lupe was in sight. The bed was empty. The aroma of scented candles, the fragrance of tuberoses almost, but not quite masked a stench recalling that left by Skid-Row derelicts. Juanita traced the vomit trail from the bed, followed the spotty track over to the orchid-tiled bathroom. There she found her mistress, Señorita Vélez, head jammed down in the toilet bowl, drowned.
>
> The huge dose of Seconal had not been fatal in the expected fashion. It

had mixed retch-erously with the Spitfire's Mexi-Spice Last Supper. The gut action, her stomach churning, had revived the dazed Lupe. Violently sick, an ultimate fastidiousness drove her to stagger towards the sanitary sanctum of the *salle de bain* where she slipped on the tiles and plunged head first into her Egyptian Chartreuse Onyx Hush-Flush Model Deluxe.[40]

Initially I found Anger's account of Vélez's death to be mean-spirited and degrading; it constructed her as a figure of abjection. However, reading Matthew Tinkcom's study of the discursive production and context of *Hollywood Babylon* forced me to rethink my initial impulse. Reclaiming the "camp sensibilities" in Anger's writings on Hollywood, Tinkcom characterizes *Hollywood Babylon* as a form of "queer fan textual production," one that employs "the discursive strategies of queer male camp," including "dissemblance, subterfuge and ironic play."[41] From the perspective of queer camp sensibilities, Anger's account of Vélez's death is less demeaning or degrading than irreverent and ironic, deriving from his liberal use of tabloid imagery and gossip. Like his other over-the-top stories of Hollywood celebrities in the book, Anger's version of Vélez's suicide represents a counterhistory to the idealized publicity that animated Hollywood's production of stardom and fandom. According to Tinkcom, a literal reading of the book ignores Anger's "antagonistic stance toward Hollywood," his critique of scandal and tabloid culture, as well as of "Hollywood's own impulse to profit from gossip-driven knowledge."[42]

Anger's irreverent satire would find echoes in the experimental film by Warhol, *Lupe*, featuring Edie Sedgwick as Lupe Vélez. One of Warhol's first experimental films in multiple projection, *Lupe* reenacts "the last evening in the life of Lupe Vélez."[43] Playing on both Warhol and Anger, Gonzalez's video opens with a disturbing toilet-drowning scene. This grotesque framing of Lupe's suicide as excess has nonetheless fueled distortions and confusions about the details surrounding Lupe Vélez's death.

A few things are known, and none substantiates the sensational accounts that were spun from the account given by Anger. For one, Juanita was not the name of her "chambermaid," as Anger referred to the woman who found Lupe Vélez. It was rather Buelah Kinder, Vélez's secretary and companion of ten years (whom Lupe referred to as "mammy") who first discovered her body, as originally recounted, lying on "a soft-feathered cover, between silk sheets, wearing her favorite blue, shimmering silk pajamas, with her blond hair carefully arranged over a pink pillow." "'I thought she was asleep. She looked so peaceful,' Kinder add[ed], 'But when I touched her head, it was cold, so I called the police.'"[44]

Then there are the reasons behind her suicide, given by Vélez herself, in two notes she left on a nightstand by her bed. The first is to Harald Ramond, an aspiring actor she had been involved with during the past few months:

> To Harald,
>   May God forgive you and forgive me, too but I prefer to take my life away and our baby's before I bring him with shame or killin him. Lupe

On the back of the same note she had written:

> How could you, Harald, fake such a great love for me and our baby when all the time you didn't want us? I see no other way out for me so goodbye and good luck to you. Love Lupe

I am skeptical. For the reason even Vélez herself provides is too transparent and patently obvious, too one-faceted, lacking complexity and, just as important, going against the grain of the feminist genealogy I have just constructed. Not that I am looking for a conspiracy or for Mafia-connected perpetrators, as in the "suicide" of Marilyn Monroe. But it does seems uncharacteristic that Lupe Vélez, a survivor of spousal battery at the hands of her ex-husband, the ninth Tarzan, Johnny Weissmuller, would fall victim to unrequited love, or would be unable to resolve the contradictions with her Catholic upbringing.

I find companionship and comfort in the words of Jorge Labra, published in the obituary he wrote for the *Diario del Sureste*:

> Why did Lupe commit suicide? According to the letter she left, because she was having a baby without a father. She wanted to escape the shame and scandal. Then, why would she write it? She could have very well died, taking this secret to her tomb. On the other hand, who would believe that Little Lupe would fear a scandal? It is difficult to believe that a woman who marries, divorces, and lives through various *romances*, as they call them there, would be so easily tormented by the same ups and downs of a "quinceañera" [fifteen-year-old girl] who has slipped lamentably, and decides to hide her offense with death.

Labra explains her suicide in moralistic terms ("She was a young woman living during frivolous times . . . far away from the moral principles designed to guide young women . . . at the mercy of her passions").[45] Yet his comments prompt me to look elsewhere. Perhaps a structural explanation makes more sense: Lupe as victim of modernity, a woman ahead of her times, or belonging to another time, a woman overwhelmed at the cross-roads by contradictions, unable to resolve the conflicts between sexual liberalism and gender equality, on the one hand, and on the other, Mexican Catholicism, familial oligarchy, and gender backlash in the United States.

I look elsewhere, combing the pages of her biography, searching for other meanings to the "Mexican Spitfire": she was "uncontrollably impatient."[46] Then there is the "uncomfortable behavior in which sudden bursts of euphoria and depression emerged constantly."[47] As early as 1932, Frank Cordon of the *Saturday Evening Post* reported that "Lupe could not stay still for more than ten seconds. Sitting on her legs in a chair, she wrapped herself like a Mexican pretzel and while she talked her mouth, hands, eyes and shoulders moved rapidly."[48]

There's more. While filming in Mexico during the last year of her life, she exhibited symptoms of "disequilibrium." "Her angry outbursts became intolerable . . . she progressively became more depressed and exalted; her mood swings left her out of control."[49] Celebrating her saint's day with "a big party on the 12 of December," she invited "many Mexicans in the industry, employed and unemployed, wealthy and poor" to her house on North Rodeo Drive, where "many saw her nervous, confused, and visibly disconcerted."[50]

And then I remember Kay Redfield Jamison's research on moods and madness, her memoir of manic depression, *An Unquiet Mind*, in which she details moods that remind me of Lupe Vélez's: an electrifying bolt of energy, overflowing with laughter, exuberance, and fluctuating tides of emotion. And the photograph I discovered at the Academy of Motion Picture Arts and Sciences in Los Angeles lent credence to my hypothesis. Although the phantasmic multiple image of Vélez is an effect of technical manipulation, I believe its photographer, Ernest A. Bachrach, serendipitously (or perhaps knowingly) captured her oscillating temperament. I recognize that I am veering toward speculative psychobiography, even bordering on pseudo-science, in my attempt to diagnose Lupe Vélez with manic-depressive illness. Yet, like Kay Redfield Jamison, Vélez "lived a life particularly intense in moods" (Figure 2.4).[51]

In an earlier book on the subject, *Touched with Fire*, Jamison explores the controversial claim of the relation between "artistic temperament and manic depressive illness." In the introduction, she writes:

> The fiery aspects of thought and feeling that initially compel the artistic voyage—fiery energy, high mood, and quick intelligence; a sense of the vision-

Figure 2.4. Haunted by an artistic temperament: This composite shot on one negative, entered in the Hollywood studios' still photography show of 1941 by RKO Radio, eerily captures the overlapping moods of Lupe Vélez. Photograph by Ernest A. Bachrach, RKO Studios, courtesy of the Academy of Motion Picture Arts and Sciences.

ary and the grand; a restless and feverish temperament—commonly carry with them the capacity for vastly darker moods, grimmer energies, and, occasionally, bouts of "madness." The opposite moods and energies, often interlaced, can appear to the world as mercurial, intemperate, volatile, brooding, troubled, or stormy. In short, they form the common view of the artistic temperament, and . . . they also form the basis of the manic-depressive temperament.[52]

The Assumption of Lupe Vélez closes with the Mexican *ranchera* singer Chavela Vargas's interpretation of the melancholic tune, "No soy de aquí; ni soy de alla," rolling over the credits. Herself an international figure of lesbian excess, Vargas seems to be guiding us toward an understanding of Lupe Vélez's death. "No soy de aquí; ni soy de alla." Lupe was neither from here nor from there; she embodied an otherness that was too excessive for Mexico and Hollywood. Unlike Dolores del Río, who returned to Mexico after Orson Wells jilted her, the jilted and pregnant Lupe Vélez could not go back. In the mournful lyrics by Chavela Vargas I find a clue to Lupe's final predicament: in the end, she had nowhere to go.

There are scientific arguments "associating the artistic and manic-depressive temperaments," Jamison tells us, scientific studies documenting "the high rate of mood disorders and suicide" in the lives of "eminent poets, artists, and composers."[53] I offer biographical evidence for the possibility of "overlapping natures of artistic and manic depressive temperaments" in the life/body of Lupe Vélez.[54] Perhaps the meaning of the "Mexican Spitfire," of the Mexicana who could spit fire (as the literal translation of her nickname would read), has less to do with sexuality (sexual promiscuity) or cultural temperament (hot-bloodedness) and more to do with moods and emotions. Perhaps to have been a spitfire means more: to have had an artistic temperament "touched with fire."

Notes

1. Antonio Ríos-Bustamante, "Latinos and the Hollywood Film Industry," in *Chicanos and Film*, ed. Chon Noriega (New York: Garland, 1992), 23.

2. Joanne Hershfield, *The Invention of Dolores del Río* (Minneapolis: University of Minnesota Press, 2000), 10.

3. Mexican critic quoted in Gabriel Ramírez, *Lupe Vélez: La mexicana que escupía fuego* (Mexico City: Cineteca Nacional, 1986), 53.

4. Ibid., 114. "*Pocho/pocha*" is a disparaging term used by Mexicans in Mexico to refer to the Mexican diaspora. Throughout the twentieth century,

pocho served to deride Mexicans living in the United States, and especially their U.S.-born children, for losing their culture, customs, and language. Until the Chicano movement reclaimed "Chicano" as a political identity, the term was used interchangeably with pocho.

5. Vicki L. Ruiz, *From Out of the Shadows* (New York: Oxford University Press, 1998), 6.

6. Ramírez, *Lupe Vélez*, 29.

7. Ibid., 28.

8. John D'Emilio and Estelle B. Freedman, *Intimate Matters: A History of Sexuality in America* (New York: Harper and Row, 1988), 241.

9. Ramírez, *Lupe Vélez*, 29.

10. D'Emilio and Freedman, *Intimate Matters*, 265.

11. Ramírez, *Lupe Vélez*, 43.

12. Ibid., 53.

13. Lane, quoted in Ramírez, *Lupe Vélez*, 56. This and subsequent translations of Ramírez are mine.

14. D'Emilio and Freedman, *Intimate Matters*, 240.

15. Ruiz, *From Out of the Shadows*, 65.

16. Douglas Monroy, "'Our Children Get So Different Here': Film, Fashion, Popular Culture, and the Process of Cultural Syncretization in Mexican Los Angeles, 1900–1935," *Aztlan* 19, no. 1 (Spring 1988–1990): 87.

17. Ruiz, *From Out of the Shadows*, 59.

18. Monroy, "'Our Children,'" 90.

19. Ruiz, *From Out of the Shadows*, 58.

20. Monroy, "'Our Children,'" 83.

21. Ramírez, *Lupe Vélez*, 94.

22. Ibid., 62.

23. Ibid., 128.

24. See especially Ríos-Bustamante, "Latinos and the Hollywood Film Industry"; Gary D. Keller, *Hispanics and United States Film* (Tempe, AZ: Bilingual Press, 1994); and Luis Reyes and Peter Rubie, *Hispanics in Hollywood: An Encyclopedia of Film and Television* (New York: Garland, 1994).

25. See especially Reyes and Rubie, *Hispanics in Hollywood*, 20–21.

26. I thank Tatcho Mindiola for sharing his reservations about the critiques of Lupe Vélez by Chicano historiographers and for providing me with copies of Vélez films that he had taped from television.

27. I owe my understanding of "screwball comedy" to the work of Maya Higgins, who wrote an undergraduate thesis under my supervision at the University of California–Davis.

28. Quoted in Hershfield, *The Invention of Dolores del Río*, 18.

29. Published originally in *Continental* (December 1931) and quoted in Ramírez, *Lupe Vélez*, 80.

30. Emilio García Riera, *México visto por el cine extranjero* (Mexico City: Ediciones Era: Universidad de Guadalajara, Centro de Investigaciones y Enseñanzas Cinematográficas, 1987–1988), 231.

31. Ramírez, *Lupe Vélez*, 126–127.

32. Ibid., 124.

33. Ramon Garcia, "New Iconographies: Film Culture in Chicano Cultural Production," in *Decolonial Voices*, ed. Arturo J. Aldama and Naomi Quiñonez (Bloomington: Indiana University Press, 2002), 70.

34. Ibid.

35. See Yvonne Yarbro-Bejarano, "Ironic Framings: A Queer Reading of the Family (Melo)drama in Lourdes Portillo's *The Devil Never Sleeps/El diablo nunca duerme*," in *Lourdes Portillo: "The Devil Never Sleeps" and Other Films*, ed. Rosa Linda Fregoso (Austin: University of Texas Press, 2001), 110.

36. Ramírez, *Lupe Vélez*, 27.

37. Ibid., 85, 100.

38. Ibid., 93.

39. Ibid., 12.

40. Kenneth Anger, *Hollywood Babylon* (New York: Bell, 1975), 339.

41. Matthew Tinkcom, *Working Like a Homosexual* (Durham, NC: Duke University Press, 2002), 141. I thank Ann Cvetkovich for bringing this text to my attention.

42. Ibid., 141, 148.

43. According to the catalogue notes of a recent exhibit of Warhol's films at the Whitney, "Lupe was shown on three screens at its premiere." See Chrissie Isles, *Into the Light: The Projected Image in American Art, 1964-1977* (New York: Whitney Museum of American Art, 2001).

44. Ramírez, *Lupe Vélez*, 15.

45. Labra, quoted in Ramírez, *Lupe Vélez*, 139.

46. Ramírez, *Lupe Vélez*, 35.

47. Ibid., 52.

48. Ibid., 82.

49. Ibid., 133.

50. Ibid., 135.

51. Kay Redfield Jamison, *An Unquiet Mind* (New York: Vintage Books, 1996), 211.

52. Kay Redfield Jamison, *Touched with Fire* (New York: Free Press, 1993), 2.

53. Ibid., 5, 240.

54. Ibid., 6.

CHAPTER 3

Lupe Vélez Regurgitated

Cautionary, Indigestion-Causing Ruminations on "Mexicans" in "American" Toilets Perpetrated While Covetously Screening "Veronica"

WILLIAM A. NERICCIO

Soiled Tile Number One

The Gospel According to Lupe

I n the beginning was the Latina bombshell and *she*, this term, or this Hollywood trope, at any rate, was made flesh: flesh *and* blood flesh *and* blood *and* . . . vomit. More on this "vomit" below.

Stereotypes, or, better put, meta-stereotropes, like that of the sexy, wanton, Latina spitfire Lupe Vélez, live on in the popular print media and the boardrooms of Holly-wood, where actresses and enter-tainers like J.Lo (aka Jennifer Lopez, aka Jennie from d'block), Salma Hayek, Penélope Cruz, Cameron Diaz, and Eva Longoria continue to prosper and profit off the patents made by *hot* Latina mademoiselles of another critical moment (Figure 3.1).

Dolores del Río, Carmen Miranda, and Lupe Vélez writhe across the silver screens of the Americas in the

Figure 3.1. A facsimile publicity photograph of Lupe Vélez by Irving Chidnoff, allegedly signed by the deceased star. In this undated still, Lupe Vélez appears to perform a gloss on Borges's famous "Borges and I" poem. But whom are we looking at? A "Mexican Spitfire"? "Lupe Vélez"? "Maria Guadalupe Vélez de Villalobos"? Or someone, something, else? From the private collection of the author.

1930s and the 1940s with such success that alternatives to the vision of the Latina bombshell—hypersexualized, utterly duplicitous, voraciously self-ish, and relentlessly dissatisfied—will go on and on into time infinitum.[1]

Soiled Tile Number Two

Vomit

We will spill. Together, we will hurl.

Out of the depths will cascade the very things that allow us to be: water, food, nourishment—of course, but image, identity, and ideas as well. The tale of Lupe Vélez offers the anticipated attractions of scandal, gossip, and catastrophe, but it brings as well a cautionary warning regarding the powerful forces of the semiotic as they fuse with those of the existential— *as the waters converge.*

So let us approach the mirror, see the silver screen, seek the self, find the *other*, and let the waters flow. The catty *Oxford English Dictionary*, sensing our need to license our licentious use of *vomit* and *vomitoria* as thematic and rhetorical pipelines, stands ready for her cameo: "vomitorium . . . 1. A passage or opening in an ancient amphitheatre or theatre, leading to or from the seats." Here the *OED* quotes no less a figure than Tobias Smollett, who adds that a vomitorium is a place "entered by avenues, at the end of which were gates, called *vomitoriæ* (1766 SMOLLETT Trav. II. 228)." This is a telling illustration, for in reading and regurgitating the life of Lupe Vélez together, it is as if the pages of this chapter were like the confines of a masterfully appointed and gloriously designed theater—perhaps my footnotes or asides enact *vomitoriæ* of sorts.

What happens next is worthy of Hollywood. The *OED* next hands us, or, better put, *shows* us, what it calls an "erron," or erroneous definition (said *erron*, of course, is both near and dear to the heart of this essay as it is the closest thing the *OED* has that can pass for gossip—"errons" as illegitimate, yet *recorded*, bastard etymologies): "[vomitorium:] 2. Erron. A room in which ancient Romans are alleged to have vomited deliberately during feasts." So the *OED* allows herself to have it both ways: vomitorium as theater portal and *erron*, a Roman space of post-feast purging—a theater and a toilet, or, with specific regard to our inquiry into Lupe Vélez, a star site and a spectacle of expulsion, a proscenium *and* a latrine in the midst of a semiotic and semantic barfing up of a Latina spectacle.

More on the niceties of vomit and subjectivity to follow, because in ask-

ing us to recall the life, career, and death of Lupe Vélez, and in particular
the circumstances of her "sic" death—vomiting owing to an overdose—
the dynamics of said exit fall under our purview.

Soiled Tiles Numbers Three, Four, Five, and, Truly Soiled, Six

Four Epigraphs Make a Late Cameo:
Irigaray, Fanon, Castellanos, Faulkner

SPECULUM IN THE TOILET

*Theoretically there would be no such thing as woman. She would not
exist. The best that can be said is that she does not exist yet. Something
of her a-specificity might be found in the betweens that occur in being,
or beings. These gaps reopen the question of the "void," and thereby
most commonly give rise to vigorous, horrified rejection and a move to
plug the hole with speculative "tissues" and "organs." . . . Woman has,
and will have, no place and thus no existence. This will be true even in
her privation of being, which it is the essential task and ceaseless effort
of dialectic and dialectic's indispensable intermediaries to bring or bring
back to the fullness of the self's possession of substance.*

LUCE IRIGARAY[2]

WAITING FOR MY CAMEO IN THE TOILET

*I am overdetermined from without. I am the slave not of the "idea"
that others have of me but of my own appearance. . . . I cannot go to a
film without seeing myself. I wait for me. In the interval just before the
film starts, I wait for me. The people in the theater are watching me,
examining me, waiting for me. A Negro groom is going to appear. My
heart makes my head swim.*

FRANTZ FANON[3]

PREGNANT IN THE TOILET

*In the maternal cavity, a mysterious event takes place, a kind of miracle
that, like all miracles, arouses astonishment: it is witnessed by the
attendants and experienced by the protagonist "in fear and trembling."
Careful. One sudden move, carelessness, an unsatisfied whim, and the
miracle will not happen. Nine unending months of rest, of dependence
upon others, precautions, rites, taboos. Pregnancy is a sickness whose
outcome is always catastrophic for whomever suffers it.*

ROSARIO CASTELLANOS[4]

CASTRATED IN THE TOILET

. . . they saw that the man was not dead yet, and when they saw what Grimm was doing, one of the men gave a choked cry and stumbled back into the wall and began to vomit. Then Grimm too sprang back, flinging behind him the bloody butcher knife. "Now you'll let white women alone, even in hell," he said. But the man on the floor had not moved. He just lay there, with his eyes open and empty of everything save consciousness, and with something, a shadow, about his mouth. For a long moment he looked up at them with peaceful and unfathomable and unbearable eyes. Then his face, body, all, seemed to collapse, to fall in upon itself, and from out the slashed garments about his hips and loins the pent black blood seemed to rush like a released breath. It seemed to rush out of his pale body like the rush of sparks from a rising rocket; upon that black blast the man seemed to rise soaring into their memories forever and ever. They are not to lose it.

WILLIAM FAULKNER[5]

Our eyes and ears upon the tile, anxious with the chore of vomit exegesis, we pause to greet our visitors—Luce Irigaray, Jacques Lacan's canny, cunning nemesis and psychoanalysis's dazzling French femme fatale; Frantz Fanon, Freud's postcolonial *Doppelgänger* who knew how to probe with style and dramatic flair the psyche of the wretched of the earth; Rosario Castellanos, Mexico's underrated feminist diva, a woman who deserves better recognition for having anticipated by a decade the legendary French feminisms of Irigaray, Kristeva, et al.; and, last but not least, William Faulkner, Southern seer, the Old South's gossip, who revealed to his readers so much about the rich American tapestry of racialized hate.

They, all four, give us so much to mull over and chew on.

Moving slowly, we digest carefully, lest we eat too fast and end up getting sick.

We begin with the last epigraph above. While there may be more famous scenes of vomiting in the history of Western literature (take, for instance, the thirty-third chapter of Gustave Flaubert's singularly lurid *Madame Bovary*, in which a trail of black effluvial retching exits Emma's corpse's mouth, figuring the sins of sex and greed enacted by the other mouth, the other *marge*, that perpetrated if not emblematized these sins—*Il fallut soulever un peu la tête, et alors un flot de liquides noirs sortit, comme un vomissement, de sa bouche. . . .*)

I got carried away, Emma's black flood took me away from Lupe—it's almost as if I owe Vélez an apology. . . .

—As I was saying, while there may be more famous literary feats of throwing up, you would have to read a mountain of books to get close to the scene of racialized puking that Faulkner weaves into *Light in August*, his epic allegorical meditation on the complexities of miscegenation in the American South epitomized in the remarkable and singular figure of Joe Christmas.[6]

The selection from Faulkner that I eviscerated from the tail end of the novel begins with a witness vomiting and ends with a castration—a castration that looses a biblical flood of black blood that symbolizes both Joe Christmas's miscegenated, dark, magic, sinful, violent sexuality (you can almost see Frantz Fanon's eyes roll as you reread this quotation) and the displaced, elided African "darkness" that no volume of white blood can dissipate. Faulkner is useful to us here, as this essay treats with issues that pertain to reproduction, race, ethnicity, and violence. That I will be referencing said categories with regard to the body of a Latina woman involved in a lifelong affair with motion pictures and the entertainment industry explains why Fanon, Castellanos, and Irigaray appeared above before Will Faulkner's none too subtle cue: when a Latina gets in bed with Hollywood, we are going to need more than one psychoanalyst around to help us wade through the mess.

But I am getting ahead of myself again and should stick to the facts, the plain facts and nothing but the facts, at least for a little while, to let you get your fill.

Soiled Tile Number Seven

Pepto-Bismol

This essay is authored in the spirit of a twenty-first-century, Foucault-stained archeology project—some odd farrago of words, images, history, hearsay, gossip, and philosophy that might accurately characterize the figuration of Mexicans in mass culture here in the United States. It concerns moments in the career of Lupe Vélez, or, as she was christened, María Guadalupe Vélez de Villalobos. Her origins were in San Luis Potosí, Mexico; from there she moved north to California and experienced an ascent to the heights of cinematic fame in Hollywood and, of course, exited this world via her eventual suicide in a "fake hacienda on Rodeo

Drive" on December 13, 1944, five months' pregnant with the baby of her jilting lover, Harald Ramond.[7] In a scene that anticipates the denouement of Marilyn Monroe, Kurt Cobain, Hunter Thompson, and others later in the century, Vélez's staged exit comes to define the dynamics of her career and delimit the discourse of her cinematic legacy. But as much as my essay concerns itself with a now forgotten Hollywood tragedy, it is also driven by a curiosity about the material outcome of her success across the United States.

After Vélez, one came to expect a certain type of Latina in film. Perhaps more than any other figure save Dolores del Río and Carmen Miranda, Vélez and her handlers helped concretize an image of Latina "exoticness," sensuality, and silliness that dogs those who have inherited her mantle in film and, most important, those Latinas and Latinos not in film, whose lives unfold in the powerful shadow of Hollywood's convincing confabulations.

Soiled Tile Number Eight

Vomit Exegesis: In and Out of Lupe Vélez's Toilet

With Lupe Vélez we come face to face with the elusive and exhilarating allure of celebrity, a category Richard Burt and Jeffrey Wallen remind us "is all about exclusion—what you can't have." Burt and Wallen's take on icons of fame and glamour are to the point here: "What is desired is something that is not achievable by degrees, by slowly moving up the ladder, or by transmission, by a passing on of what one knows. What one desires, in [a] celebrity, is what one cannot have. Hollywood celebrity is built on distance, on the unbridgeable gap that defines desire—one desires here precisely what has been reproduced, the image" (87).[8] Tag-team critics Burt and Wallen speak here to a kind of existential jump-cut or crosscut, where our fated celebrity evolves overnight from no one to someone. But when that someone is Mexican, and living in the United States, more thought must be sprinkled on our dish.

We need to know more, think about more, take more into account; we must affix to our notion of stereotypes and celebrity a sensitivity to the power of parody in our critical inquests: merely self-righteously outing the damned purveyors of stereotypes will not end their eternal cycle, and acknowledging the unreality of a desire will not in any way diminish the very real pull of that desire. In this regard, the singular rhetorical flourishes of the dynamic Sianne Ngai are useful, especially when she reminds us in her meditation on animated ethnic types that

> racial stereotypes and clichés, cultural images that are perversely both dead and alive, can be critically interrogated not only by making them more dead (say, by attempting to stop their circulation) but also by reanimating them. Thus while animatedness and its affective cousins (liveliness, vigor, and zest) remain ugly categories of feeling reinforcing the historically tenacious construction of racialized subjects as excessively emotional, bodily subjects, they might also be thought of as categories of feeling that highlight animation's status as a nexus of contradictions and as a technology with the capacity to generate unanticipated social meanings and effects—as when the routine manipulation of racialized bodies on screen results in an unsuspected liveliness undermining animation's traditional role in constituting bodies as raced.[9]

When Ngai ends by stating that "animation calls for new ways of understanding the technologizing of the racialized body as well as the uneasy differential between types and stereotypes" (596), she offers a new way to understand Lupe Vélez's over-the-top antics, a new way to see in her and her celebrity a means to ending a circuit of unmediated consumption and vomiting; a cinematic vomitorium where the traces of filmed subjectivities stay behind, the residua we come to know with familiarity as our unconscious.

But stop! one might cry out. *Vélez was a person, not an animated cartoon character. Save your quotes for Speedy Gonzales.*[10]

Perhaps.

But when you are dealing with the seductive hallucination of a "Mexican" in the semiotic and cultural history of the Americas, especially in the United States of America, rigorous lines dividing animated marionette (Vélez) from animated puppet (Speedy) are hallucinations themselves.

More important in the foregoing gloss is the way that Ngai hands us, generous thinker that she is, a way of simultaneously fathoming Vélez as a victim, Vélez as a perpetrator, glammy perp that she was, and Vélez as a hermeneutic prototype. We, cultural critics both in the know and in the dark (most of the time), can use the bitter, lurid history of a fallen star to gauge the very real day-to-day dynamics that drive the figuration of Latina bodies today.

Soiled Tile Number Nine

Taking off the Gloves

Some stills from a fantastic boxing flick directed by Benjamin Stoloff in 1934 called *Palooka*, starring Jimmy Durante and Lupe Vélez, while they cannot be reproduced here, bear "looking at." The movie follows the rise and fall of the titular hero making his way through the surly, gamey world of big-city boxers, and exhibits Vélez's extraordinary range.[11]

The opening credits of *Palooka* set the stage for the flavor of "woman" being featured in the production. Lupe Vélez winks at us in the dark in the audience of the theater, and as she does so, we are let in on her secret, we are part of her secret, and perhaps we will be the target of her secret. All that matters is that we are put into a scenario where Vélez's celebrity and her *Latinness* are part and parcel of the same dialectical wet dream of taunt, desire, and seduction.

Awash with stereotypes, *Palooka* features African American early Hollywood regulars, Louise Beavers and "Snowflake," to wile away the audience's time between shots of Vélez as a hot-blooded, tempestuous, duplicitous floozy. An industry designed to cook up tasty treats for mass consumption, Hollywood regularly dished out more than we can now stomach.

Feature films, especially 1934 United Artists vehicles (this one directed by Benjamin Stoloff, with writers Jack Jevne, Arthur Kober, and Gertrude Purcell, adapted from the comic strip "Joe Palooka" by Ham Fisher), could be counted on to reaffirm any and all racialized worldviews popular in pre–World War II America.

One of the best scenes in *Palooka* is the dance sequence at the nightclub where Nina Madero dances and attempts to woo Joe Palooka, played by the dopey Stuart Erwin; the scene anticipates Rita Hayworth's magnificent turn as Gilda in 1946. Lupe as Nina shields her face, semiotically underscoring her facile, self-interested "play" with dope Palooka, who, having defeated Nina's boyfriend, Al "Mac" McSwatt, played by William "brother of James" Cagney, becomes the coveted new target of Nina's boundless affection.

Enough of *Palooka*. Let us end this pictureless review with a flash from a film featuring Vélez that had appeared four years earlier. In 1930, Vélez played opposite Lew Ayres in *East Is West* for Universal Pictures. A publicity still I found in a box outside a junk shop in Studio City depicts Lupe's voracious and violent Latina diet in a memorable fashion. In the image, Vélez chomps on the hand of a horrified Ayres. Said taste would have consequences for Vélez and Latinas in the ensuing generations. After all, even cannibals vomit sometimes.

Soiled Tile Number Ten

Pinup Muchacha One and Two

Two views of Lupe Vélez: the first, from 1929, on the cover of the April issue of *Movie Classics*, showing leg, bosom and fun promises (Figure 3.2), the second, from 1937, a publicity glossy of Vélez at the height of her stardom, showing less bosom and a knowing adoption of Rita Hayworthy glam (Figure 3.3).[12]

Figure 3.2. Photograph of Lupe Vélez published in 1929 on the cover of the April issue of *Movie Classics*. From the private collection of the author.

Figure 3.3. A 1937 publicity glossy of Vélez at the height of her stardom. *Modern Times, Palace Classic Films* (http://www.moderntimes.com/). The image also appears on page 328 of Kenneth Anger's *Hollywood Babylon*.

Soiled Tile Number Eleven

Listening to Other Critics Talk While Hidden in the Stalls

Critics hurl, at times, as well. And we? We *attend*.

Let's have our first serving from Joanne Hershfield, a sober admonition that contends "representations of race and gender in Hollywood cinema need to be examined not only within the context of public discourse but also *in relation to pressures* of the market during particular historical moments."[13] And, as I have argued elsewhere, one of the reasons Latina stereotypes propagate is that there is remarkable profit in propagation.

(I sometimes wonder if my own fascination with Latina and Latino celebrities is not in some way caught up in a sordid economy wherein I help fuel and drive some peculiar re-reification of these figures.)

In any event, let us return to Joanne Hershfield's findings, to the moment in her piece when she humbly offers that her "argument brings to light some problems with existing studies [not identified, ed.] that are concerned primarily with the relation between ideology and representation" (153). In a piece published years ago and cited above, on Orson Welles and Chicano and Latin American advocacy, I referenced the drive in Hollywood during World War II to befriend Latin American nations. This was part of the war effort for a Washington very, very concerned about the prospect of Germany developing a southern front in Mexico, Central America, Argentina, and Brazil. In this light, Hershfield's reminder about Ella Shohat and Robert Stam's identification of exotic stereotypes in *Unthinking Eurocentrism* (Routledge, 1994) as the "tropes of empire" is of no little use. Hershfield's shorthand gloss of Latina stereotype genotype is also quite good, reminding us how these stereotypes tend to focus on the stars' bodies, with Latin American women most often linked to "verbal epithets evoking tropical heat, violence, passion, and spies." In another recent study, Brian O'Neill offers us a lot to chew on in "The Demands of Authenticity," noting how for Latinas, "lots of eye-rolling, body movement, double entendres, frantic bursts of Spanish dialogue, and fractured English marked by malapropisms" are the name of the game (377).[14]

Other critical treatments of Lupe Vélez include that of Alicia I. Rodríguez-Estrada, who reminds us that in the eight Mexican Spitfire movies, "[s]tereotypes abound, including Carmelita's lack of breeding, her social unacceptability, her refusal to put her show business career aside, [and] her lack of desire to have kids." When Rodríguez-Estrada writes of "Vélez's sexual personification . . . mesh[ing] with her ethnicity," she invokes that odd marriage of geography, politics, eugenics, and aesthetics always at work when one traces the history of ethnicity in Hollywood.[15]

The best piece presently available on Vélez is Henry Jenkins's "'You Can't Say That in English!': The Scandal of Lupe Velez." Allow me to quote a telling movement from Jenkins's Web reverie at length:

> The following is one of the many stories Hollywood told about Lupe Velez. This version appeared in *New Movie* in 1932 and begins when Lupe is 12 years old:
>
>> Even at that tender age, Lupe had sex appeal and no race is as quick to recognize this quality as the Mexican. The house was surrounded by boys of all ages, who whistled in various keys. For Lupe those young swains were simply a means to an end. She had an absorbing curiosity about motion picture stars and she discovered, young as she was, that her kisses were marketable. She would bestow a chaste salute on a masculine cheek in exchange for a picture of a star or a colored ribbon to wind in her dark braids. Thus, men became to her tools to gain the things she wanted, and the house was besieged with them. Her more placid sister, Josephine, carried notes between Lupe and the boys, and Lupe's keen little ears soon learned the different whistles of the young lovers.
>
> This remarkable story links together the origins of Lupe's transgressive female sexuality (her willingness to use men as "tools" for her own ends) with the origins of her desire for film stardom. Lupe, the young Mexican girl, desires glamour photographs of Hollywood stars and is willing to trade her sexual favors to get them, to exchange bronze flesh for glistening celluloid. Underlying this story is a perverse suggestion of child sexuality.[16]

Jenkins's revelation shows how Vélez's overdetermined sexuality evolves with the certainty of DNA—as if Latino spitfireness was an attribute that could be traced at the level of the chromosome (Holy Mengele, Batman!). Even less subtle than *New Movie* is the online bio of Vélez that used to be maintained at the Mr. Showbiz Web site, which heralded Vélez as "born to a streetwalker mother" and claimed Vélez herself plied the "oldest profession" in some of the raunchy burlesque houses of Mexico City in her early teens.

Other Vélezians teach us much, such as Brian O'Neill's testy corrective for those of us that would content ourselves with merely self-righteously indicting the "badness" of stereotypes, their evil dynamics, and the like, which merits rehearing: "I am not interested in simply pointing out the 'errors,' 'distortions,' and 'stereotypes' within these pictures, rather, I suggest that Hollywood Latino/a images . . . reflect two socially powerful discourses: those represented mirror the imagined national identities of Latin American elites[;] second, the resilience of Hollywood's attitudes towards Latin America" (361). I might add something here that testy O'Neill does not: many of these "attitudes" have everything to do with the contiguity of Southern California and Northern Baja in Mexico.

For those of us spelunking in the noxious caves of Hollywood's history with Latinos, O'Neill's findings are quite rich, as when he reminds us how actor Paul Muni devised a special preparation for his Latino roles (in 1935, Muni played Johnny Ramirez in *Bordertown* and spent two weeks "swimming in tequila" in Mexicali [364]) or when he outs Hollywood's prime research resources for Latin American-based action: *National Geographic Magazine* and the racist, elite gossip of Latin American governmental attachés working in Southern California embassies (365). His research schools us in the dynamics of a plotted whitewashing, so that "in the foreground of Hollywood's Pan American productions, only light-skinned good neighbors—like . . . Lupe Vélez—could represent the region."

Soiled Tile Number Twelve

Anger-y Vomit

Time and again in the pages of this chapter I wrestle with facets of stereotypes. How, for instance, am I to approach the career of a woman who helped concretize notions of the female Latina subject for most of the Western world?

Never can I seem to effectively articulate the uncanny, dogged power of stereotypes, those "bloodstains of cultures in conflict," which swim with lyric efficiency through mass culture with an almost libidinal force. Stereotypes imprint themselves upon their purveyor, their projectors, and their witnesses in a way that is hard to characterize without seeming to exaggerate.

By the end of her career, Lupe Vélez is full, so damn full of "her" self, her "spitfire"-ness, her hot-blooded Latinness, her expressionistic spiciness. One might argue optimistically that our Spitfire is filled with lies, untruths, and distortions, but she is full all the same.

One quick premature conclusion at the head of this paragraph: Lupe Vélez is so full of her self or, better put, so full of these carnival mirror others that *she has to purge, has to vomit it all out of herself* in a self-manufactured spectacle that leads to her death (Figure 3.4).

And now we are ready—ready, in the midst of a proto-denouement for our lurid, filthy-tiled exercise, to treat you to Kenneth Anger's written version of Lupe Vélez's suicide, where the salty rhetoric of gay camp fuels the fires of Latina stereotypes to an almost ethereal level. Anger's tongue-in-cheek obituary, or should I say *obitch*uary, aims to chronicle, cheekily and gleefully, the final moments of Lupe Vélez's Hollywood dream-cum-nightmare. A taste? He titles his Vélez chapter "Chop-Suicide," evoking the name of at least one of Vélez's survivors, Chop, one of her darling Chihuahuas.

Now, Anger's anger, or kitschy rage, is not reserved for Latinas alone, and a reading of his legendary *Hollywood Babylon* (an excerpt appears below) will soon disabuse you of any regard you might retain for those pearly denizens of the silver screen. Most, like Anger, speak of Vélez's "regurge-all" denouement as an accident, a mistake born of the unhappy coupling of barbiturates and a taco. Even the mythology seems painfully covered with a Latinesque *mise-en-scène*; all that's missing is the cactus, the tequila, bandoleras—you know the props. Enter Kenneth ANGER, stage right:

> When Juanita the chambermaid had opened the bedroom door at nine, the morning after the suicide, no Lupe was in sight. . . . Juanita traced the vomit trail from the bed, followed the spotty track over to the orchid-tiled bathroom. There she found her mistress, Señorita Vélez, head jammed down in the toilet bowl, drowned.
>
> The huge dose of Seconal had not been fatal in the expected fashion. It had mixed rech-erously [pause and comment on camp chic glib manner] with the Spitfire's Mexi-Spice Last Supper.[17]

Anger's epochal scene enacts in metaphorical glory a regurgitation of epic proportions; again, clinician readers might point out that vomiting is an involuntary act, controlled by the medulla oblongata and not under the direction of the will, of the subject, of the psyche; but let us give credit where credit is due, give the director her credit as the final credits roll again and see in Lupe Vélez's magnificent suicide, in her dramatic regurgitation, her epic upchuck, witness there in all its glory the final eruption, the lucid dismissal, of a raging, contentious bolus of imposed stereotypes that Vé-

Lupe's Deathbed, Beverly Hills

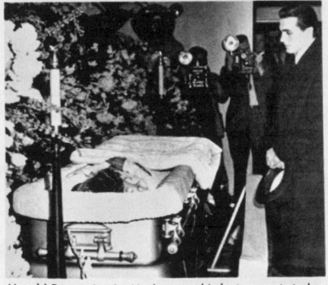

Harald Ramond—the Heel—pays his last respects to Lupe

Figure 3.4. The infamous page 340 from *Hollywood Babylon*, by Kenneth Anger. The longing look of jilting lover Harald Ramond seems almost genuine.

lez just could not stomach. Gaze upon the sexy Latina, not-mother, killing herself and her unborn child; see the living, now dying embodiment of an anti-Mexican mother, a not-*mamacita*, on the stage of her final *toilette* and toilet.

But there is a certain something about Anger's touch here, the pen is slimed with the blood of a certain sword. Whether Vélez's exit was perfect or a perfect nightmare, what matters here is the staging of it all—Vélez's own attempt to frame her finale and Anger's rhetorical staging. These staged scenes, one lived, the other rhetorical, force us to keep in mind an uncanny reminder: that death brings with it the spectacle of an irreversible divorce of body and the soul. Does it take all that much faith to believe that this twin suicide of mother and unwanted child, Hollywood superstar and incipient child star, warrants further inquiry?

Celebrities, our gods on earth, provoke a certain set of uncontrollable emotions—the outpouring of affect for the departed Princess of Wales was sincere (all the more scary, uncanny, and profound because it was so); alluding to Vélez as a goddess, or god on earth, is more than metaphorical—it reminds us of the power that projected, industrially reproduced and distributed bodies have on spying, consuming subjects.

If I linger a tad too long it is owing to the depth, the ubiquity of this most fixed stereotype—the Latina bombshell. Lupe Vélez had a lot to do with the manufacture of this trope, and she profited handsomely from it as well. By the time she made *Palooka* with Jimmy Durante, she had managed, with her handlers, to perfect a loopy, sexy, hot persona that would hold her in good grace with American audiences for decades.

Soiled Tile Number Thirteen

The Past Is the Future Is the Past

In a 2003 interview, Christine Spines of *Premiere Magazine* asks Salma Hayek, "In the beginning you were repeatedly cast as characters dripping with primal sexuality. Was that something you promoted in yourself?" Hayek's response is to the point: "That sexual side is a very small part of me. But those characters were more of a reflection of how other people saw me—it's more about who *they* are" (41). The echo here is pronounced, she is very much swimming through a stream, or, better put, swimming against the stream, swimming against the sewer-borne effluvia of a tainted fetid channel of Lupe Vélez's vomit.

You have your doubts? Take a peek at a couple of publicity stills avail-

Figure 3.5. *After the Sunset*, Studio "Wallpaper" (http://www.afterthesunset.com/).
All images, facsimiles, and reproductions from *After the Sunset* are the property of
© 2004 New Line Production, Inc., and New Line Cinema. All rights reserved.

able via the Internet in October 2005 from Hayek's then-latest vehicle,
After the Sunset (Figure 3.5). You can only swim against the stream so
long.[18]

It gets even more complicated when a Spanish photographer, Penélope
Cruz, who is also an actress, gets in on the art of representing "Mexicans"
by photographing and interviewing Hayek—as in the *Interview Magazine*
splash from 2004 (Figure 3.6).[19] Or when Hayek, promoting her Frida
Kahlo film for *Premiere Magazine* in September 2002, allows herself to
be posed (shades of Speedy?) awkwardly on an old autopsy gurney as
garnish for a curious interview (Figure 3.7). Hayek, a latter-day "Mexican
Spitfire" without Vélez's manic comic timing, is, however, white savvy
about the next-generation sewer-trap she finds herself swimming in, with,
and against: "Well, a week and a half ago they [the U.S. Census Bureau]
officially declared that Latins were the country's largest minority. And
because I spoke up about the lack of Hispanic representation [in Holly-
wood], now everybody always wants me to go into the drama and become

Figure 3.6. Penélope Cruz's interview on Salma Hayek and herself, in the April 2003 issue of *Interview Magazine*. Reproduced by permission.

Figure 3.7. On what looks like an antique operating table or, if you prefer, an autopsy platform, Salma Hayek "assumes the position." In what can be read as a pantomime of Latina objectification, Hayek makes like a twisted mannequin in the pages of *Interview Magazine*. Reproduced by permission.

a victim every time they interview me. It's a cliche. It's like you complain about the cliche, and then you get asked these questions so you can be the cliche of the Latina complaining about the cliche."[20]

Soiled Tile Number Fourteen

Homage

Film knows film. And sometimes the best critical response to a particular medium comes from that medium itself. This is the case with Lupe Vélez, as the most provocative views of her life history have come from the camera of painter, Andy Warhol, who, in December 1965, made one of his perplexing independent movies on Vélez with a piece entitled *Lupe*, starring Edie Sedgwick, from a script by Ronald Tavel. Most recently, Chicana filmmaker Rita Gonzalez has authored a cinematic/sinematic project on Vélez that folds together the life of Vélez and Warhol's odd filmed meditation—all this through the eyes of a Chicano/a drag queen named "La Lupe."[21]

Gonzalez's revelatory short film, entitled *The Assumption of Lupe Vélez* (1999), functions simultaneously as biography, criticism, and fiction in its attempt to disclose a Vélezian cosmography that reveals woman, celebrity, fan, and industry. A media artist and independent curator/writer who lives and works in Los Angeles, where she is finishing her Ph.D. at UCLA, Gonzalez is most interested in the "constructions and elaborations of biography and myth." Her filmed reveries "portray the manufactured transformations of everyday people into cultural icons—Margarita Cansino into Rita Hayworth, Michael Jackson into Peter Pan, and Lupe Vélez, who[m] Rosa Linda Fregoso rightly dubs the 'Queen of the B's' for both her celebrity *and* her legacy, into Hollywood Babylon celebrity."[22]

The opening frames of *The Assumption* are haunting, but, curiously, not out of sync with the rolling waves of our Vélezian pastiche.

Soiled Tile Number Fifteen

Celebrities and Ikons

Let us toy a minute with a notion of twentieth- and twenty-first-century magic—let us play with the idea of reading Hollywood stars as ikons with a decidedly rich history. And to understand the sacred function of celebrities in American mass culture, to learn the oddly moving matrix of desire, repetition, at the heart of our stars, it behooves us to move to the work of medievalists, those experts in the arcane art of archeologically meditating on the dynamics of the sacred and the sign, the magic of the signifier.

Jeffrey Hamburger, writing in his magnificent and beautiful book *The Vision and the Visionary: Art and Female Spirituality in Late Medieval Germany*, spends a chapter, "Vision and the Veronica," documenting the odd medieval history of the Veronica.[23]

The Veronica is the VERA IKON (note: this derives from a false or illicit etymology, as Hamburger notes, yet, as with the *OED* and its tales of "erron," I value it all the same)—the real deal. The Veronica is, as the *OED* herself reminds us, "the cloth or kerchief, alleged to have belonged to St. Veronica, with which, according to legend, the face of Christ was wiped on the way to Calvary, and upon which His features were miraculously impressed. This cloth is preserved at St. Peter's, Rome, and is venerated as a relic." The New Testament records that a miracle occurred on the way to the cross—Jesus Christ's image was imprinted on the proffered hanky. Hamburger, in loving detail, documents the medieval cults (in particular novitiates, young nuns) that built themselves around this special relic. Cue Hamburger on the Veronica:

> For [most fifteenth-century viewers] there existed myriad reproductions of the Veronica, all different, yet all aspiring to authenticity. In the *face* of the Roman relic's inaccessibility [do please note—and it's another thing I love about medievalists—do please note Hamburger's fondness for puns] . . . genuine replicas—a notion fraught with paradox—enhanced and elaborated the image's claim to reflect and reenact an unmediated dialogue with Christ. (317)

We should pause here and linger on this image of an "unmediated dialogue" with an ever-present god. If we were making a film, we would call it a cross-cut, as we fold in here the idea of Hollywood films and our imagined real-life relationship with movie stars because of the time we spend with them in the dark of a movie house or even our semidark bedrooms where our synapses fire (shades of Plato's cave, that lovely precursor of Hollywood movie palaces) or are fired by our eyes' unmediated dialogue with reproduction of these latter-day celebrity gods (Figure 3.8).[24]

Later in the same chapter, Hamburger (whose name alone vies with Toilets in some odd Freudian allegory of anality and orality) aptly notes how Elaine Scarry, following Sartre, observes that (and here I am quoting Hamburger quoting Scarry) "'the face of a beloved friend,' if imagined, 'will be, by comparison with an actually present face, 'thin,' 'dry,' 'two-dimensional,' and 'inert'"—a recollection Hamburger relates to the Veronica relic, "whose images lent life to a face that the viewer longed to see, but had in fact never seen." Jesus's facial fingerprint, his physiognomic signature, some *sacrosanct* and magical great grandfather of the 8-by-10 publicity glossy, is both relic and icon—both an alleged physical link to the son of God *and* a representation of the man, the son of God, himself.[25] This is not the least of the reasons that cults of the Veronica prospered throughout medieval Europe.

And so the telling tale of a leading medievalist holds the key to a cinematic legacy in the twentieth century. This comes as no surprise to me at all; it's always the medievalists who sanction sensitivity to what I call

Figure 3.8. The *vera ikon* or Veronica pictured here is *St. Veronica with the Holy Kerchief*. The painting hangs in the Alte Pinakothek, Munich; origin c. 1420, tempera on oak, 78 × 48 cm. From the Web Gallery of Art, Virtual Museum (http://www.wga .hu/).

Figure 3.9. An unidentified publicity still picked up in a Studio City antique shop, August 2005. From the private collection of the author.

the incestuous progeny, that odd oversexed exchange between image-dominant and word-dominant narrative across the ages.

And now the cat is out of the bag, or the plumber reveals his plunger, or the pipes are really clear, because, dear reader, you can now well imagine where I am going with this. In the odd, disputed death of Lupe Vélez, whether in the whitewashed version, where, like Mary after her death, she rises, godlike, into the ethereal heavens, flanked by her twin Chihuahuas

Chip and Chop, or in the tawdry, camp, queered Kenneth Anger version, where she dies in the reek of a skid-row, vomitorial *mise-en-scène*, we witness the death of an icon, the erasure of a sacred soul. This is the direct result of a purge, of a sacrifice, of a bizarre ritual (Anger lights my fire) in which our beloved Santa Vélez embodies some fusion of Calvary and Hollywood, where the Vatican and Tinsel Town merge as our marvelous spitfire, cum martyr, ends her time on the planet.

Holy Tile

Flushed, or, Communion Time

Let the sacrament unfold, the silver screen turn on; enter, stage left, Julie Kristeva, high priestess, presiding:

> since food is not an "other" for "me," who am only in their desire, I expel *myself*, I spit *myself* out within the same motion through which "I" claim to establish myself. During that course in which "I" become, I give birth to *myself*. That detail, one that they ferret out, emphasize, evaluate, that trifle that turns me inside out, guts sprawling; it is thus that *they* see that "I" am in the process of becoming an other at the expense of my own death. During that course in which "I" become, I give birth to myself amid the violence of sobs, of vomit.[26]

Kristeva's redolent lines, coupled with Vélez's tragic denouement, put me in the mood for some sort of lyric periphrasis: with Vélez, through Kristeva, we are between purging and devouring, some odd, peculiar, and pungent fusion of the bulimic with the vampiric. Sacred icons move us to these acts.

Jeffrey Hamburger, in telling the tale of the Veronica, writes of how the whole industry of medieval reproductions of this bizarre handkerchief-cum-signature of god "functioned as an ersatz body, one that the nun, in her role as *sponsa Christi* [bride of Christ], showered with kisses" (323). In rescuing Lupe Vélez's corpse from the infamous and scandalous discourse of tawdry Hollywood gossip, I am in a sense asking all of us to assist in a closeted ritual, a sacred rite wherein we would conspire together to lift Vélez's body off the floor, move it to another space.

We are cleaning up the mess, shining the tiles, and closing the door on one of the more bizarre chapters in the history of Mexican bodies in the bathroom of American mass culture.

But we are also lifting to *the lips of our watching eyes* the body of Lupe Vélez, worshipping again at the cinematic font, the ceramic fetiche/fetish, of our venerated, voluptuous, departed goddess of the silver screen.

Fin.

Notes

1. Scholarship of late has exploded with regard to these singular Latino icons. If you get the chance, you wouldn't be wasting your time if you perused Joanne Hershfield's *The Invention of Dolores del Río* (Minneapolis: University of Minnesota Press, 2000); her take on movie stars as "signs of other signs" is intriguing, to say the least. Also quite good: Victoria Sturtevant's "Lupe Vélez and the Ambivalent Pleasures of Ethnic Masquerade," in *The Velvet Light Trap* 55 (2005), 19–32. The world of Vélezian exegesis is in full go-go mode these days. I should add here in the warm confines of the footnotes that this chapter appears in this collection owing to the invitation of the one and only Joy James of Brown University. Its first incarnation was as "Lupe Vélez, Cinema, and the Toilet: Tales of the Mexican Spitfire in an American Vomitorium," in which form it was presented at the conference titled Imagination, Imaging and Memory: Racial, Gender and Political Violence, sponsored by Brown's Department of Africana Studies in March 2003.

2. Luce Irigary, "How to Conceive (of) a Woman," in *Speculum of the Other Woman*, trans. Gillian C. Gill (Ithaca, NY: Cornell University Press, 1985), 166.

3. Frantz Fanon, "The Facts of Blackness," in *Black Skins, White Masks*, trans. Charles Lam Markham (New York: Grove Press, 1967), 116, 140.

4. Rosario Castellanos, "Woman and Her Image," in *The Rosario Castellanos Reader*, trans. and ed. Maureen Ahern et al. (Austin: University of Texas Press, 1988), 241.

5. William Faulkner, *Light in August* (New York: Vintage International, 1990), 464–465.

6. A must-read in this vein, pardon the pun, is Joseph R. Urgo's "Menstrual Blood and 'Nigger' Blood: Joe Christmas and the Ideology of Sex and Race," *Mississippi Quarterly* 41, no. 3 (1988): 391–402.

7. Yet to be translated is the best bi-op piece on Lupe Vélez, Gabriel Ramírez's *Lupe Vélez: La mexicana que escupía fuego* [Lupe Vélez: The Mexicana Who Spit Fire] (Mexico City: Cineteca Nacional, 1986).

8. Richard Burt and Jeffrey Wallen, "Knowing Better: Sex, Cultural Criticism, and the Pedagogical Imperative in the 1990s," *Diacritics* 29, no. 1 (1999): 72–91.

9. Sianne Ngai, "'A Foul Lump Started Making Promises in My Voice': Race, Affect, and the Animated Subject," *American Literature* 74, no. 3 (2002): 571–601.

10. For more on Speedy and his ilk, see my *Tex[t]-Mex: Seductive Hallucinations of "Mexicans" in America* (Austin: University of Texas Press, 2007).

11. *Palooka* was released on January 26, 1934, by Edward Small Productions, operating as Reliance Pictures, Inc. Distribution was handled by United Artists. Henwood Cinema of Pennsylvania was responsible for its first release in video format.

12. *Modern Times, Palace Classic Films*, http://www.moderntimes.com/palace/non_image/lupe37.jpg (accessed October 5, 2005).

13. The italics are mine. Joanne Hershfield, "Delores del Río, Uncomfortably Real: The Economics of Race in Hollywood's Latin American Musicals," in *Classic Hollywood, Classic Whiteness*, ed. Daniel Bernardi (Minneapolis: University of Minnesota Press, 2001), 139–156, 153.

14. Brian O'Neill, "The Demands of Authenticity: Addison Durland and Hollywood's Latin Images During World War II," in *Classic Hollywood, Classic Whiteness*, ed. Daniel Bernardi (Minneapolis: University of Minnesota Press, 2001), 359–385.

15. Alicia I. Rodríguez-Estrada, "Dolores del Río and Lupe Vélez: Images On and Off the Screen 1925–1944," in *Writing the Range: Race, Class and Culture in the Women's West*, ed. Elizabeth Jameson and Susan Armitage (Norman: University of Oklahoma Press, 1997), 475–492.

16. Henry Jenkins, "'You Can't Say That in English!': The Scandal of Lupe Velez," http://web.mit.edu/cms/People/henry3/lupe.html (accessed October 5, 2005).

17. Kenneth Anger, *Hollywood Babylon* (New York: Bell, 1981), 238.

18. Figure 3.5 comes from *After the Sunset*, Studio "Wallpaper," http://www.afterthesunset.com/wall_salma_1024.html (accessed October 5, 2005). All images, facsimiles, and reproductions from *After the Sunset* are the property of © 2004 New Line Production, Inc., and New Line Cinema. All rights reserved. While every effort has been made to contact the copyright holders for this and other reproduced images, some identified license-holders did not return the queries of this author. The author is responsible for the materials herein reproduced.

19. Penélope Cruz, "Salma Hayek: A One-of-a-Kind, Behind-the-Scenes Look at the Inner Life of One of Hollywood's Most Daring and Hottest—by a Photographer and Interviewer Who's Not Bad on the Big Screen Herself," *Interview Magazine* (April 2003).

20. Penélope Cruz, "Salma Hayek: A One-of-a-Kind . . . ," http://www.findarticles.com/p/articles/mi_m1285/is_3_33/ai_99165056 (accessed October 5, 2005).

21. Rita Gonzalez, *The Assumption of Lupe Vélez* (1999), 22 min.

22. A more extensive treatment of Gonzalez's outrageous filmed short appears in the one and only Rosa Linda Fregoso's "'Fantasy Heritage': Tracking Latina Bloodlines," in *MeXicana Encounters: The Making of Social Identities on the Borderlands* (Berkeley and Los Angeles: University of California Press, 2003), 103–125.

23. Jeffrey Hamburger, *The Vision and the Visionary: Art and Female Spirituality in Late Medieval Germany* (New York: Zone Books, 1998).

24. The illustration for the vera ikon or Veronica pictured here is reproduced

from the Web Gallery of Art, Virtual Museum, *St. Veronica with the Holy Kerchief*, c. 1420, tempera on oak, 78 × 48 cm, Alte Pinakothek, Munich, http://www.wga.hu/frames-e.html?/html/m/master/veronica (accessed October 5, 2005).

25. Etymology: Sacrosanct comes from Latin *sacrosanctus*, consecrated with religious ceremonies, hence holy, sacred, from *sacrum*, religious rite (from sacer, holy) + *sanctus*, consecrated (from *sancire*, to make sacred by a religious act).

26. Julia Kristeva, *Powers of Horror: An Essay on Abjection*, trans. Leon S. Roudiez (New York: Columbia University Press, 1982), 3.

PERFORMING BODIES

Contemporary Film and Music Media

Figure 4.1. Cuban singer Celia Cruz's shoes. As the photographer recounts, "It was towards the end of our shoot on a glorious South Florida afternoon. . . . We had just been given the honor of having Celia sing for us a capella. . . . I asked her if I could take a photo of her shoes and she said 'Ay, Alexis no, porque yo tengo las piernas muy feas.' I told her que era solamente de sus zapatos y ella me dijo, 'Bueno, está bien.' Se levantó su bata cubana y me dejó fotografiar sus zapaticos. Muchos años después, ella me dijo que yo había sido el único fotógrafo que le había retratado sus zapatos como un bodegón." Photographer Alexis Rodríguez Duarte, photograph and quotation used by permission. ["Oh, no, Alexis, I have ugly legs." I told her that I only wanted a shot of her shoes and she said, "OK." She lifted her Cuban skirt and let me photograph her shoes. Many years later, she told me that I was the only photographer who had taken a picture of her shoes like a bodegón.]

CHAPTER 4

Celia's Shoes

FRANCES NEGRÓN-MUNTANER

Shoes can tell us where a person has been and where she wants to go.
ERIN MACKIE, "RED SHOES AND BLOODY STUMPS"

I held a pair of Cuban singer Celia Cruz's most famous shoes long enough to marvel at the seven-inch, razor-thin platforms that had lifted her solid frame up in the air for decades. I had barely touched the shoes when I felt compelled to put them down as fast as possible, to avoid effacing the awe of the object, the fact that they had belonged to a queen. Hand carved by Mexican artisan Miguel Nieto, *el zapatero de los sueños* (the shoemaker of dreams),[1] the one-of-a-kind shoes also felt heavy, as if in their stage life they had carried not only the memories of salsa music's most important female star in history but also of Cubanness itself.

Because of their iconic status, Celia's shoes are part of the permanent collection of the Smithsonian National Museum of American History. The shoes found their way to the U.S. capital through the initiative of Marvette Pérez, the Smithsonian's Latino history and culture curator. A passionate advocate for the preservation and exhibition of Latino cultural iconography, Pérez had started to acquire Caribbean music memorabilia for the museum, which, despite having a rich collection of objects belonging to African American music greats such as Ella Fitzgerald and The Supremes, had few Latino items. Since coming to rest at the Smithsonian, Celia's shoes have been exhibited four times to large and appreciative audiences. To find them off-season, however, I had to be led through the museum's back rooms by Pérez, a generous if hesitant Virgil, who asked at every step, "Why do you want to see Celia's shoes?"

The year I made the journey into the singer's displaced closet, 1998, I was not entirely sure of the answer. Yet it came to me soon enough.

Shortly after returning home, I mentioned my impulsive visit to a distinguished Cuban who had been a diplomat under Fidel Castro's government
and who still considers himself a socialist. To my surprise, the former
ambassador held only the deepest contempt for what he called the Smithsonian's "pedestrian" taste. Insisting that the museum's exhibition of
Celia's finery was a way of humiliating Cuban exiles in the United States,
he asked acidly, "Couldn't the Smithsonian choose something more elevated to represent the Cuban people? A poem by patriot José Martí? A
portrait of Father Varela, the nineteenth-century priest called 'the first
Cuban'? A uniform worn by pro-independence fighter Antonio Maceo?"

Whereas depending on how you look at it, the difference between
Maceo's pants and Celia's shoes might be only a matter of accessories,
the Cuban diplomat did see one thing straight: the display of the singer's
worn shoes as representative of all Cuban exile experience in the United
States references the lowliest of signs according to elite cultural hierarchies, whether in the Caribbean or on terra firma. For how much lower
can you possibly go, socially speaking, than under the feet of an old, salsa-
dancing, Afro-Cuban woman?

Seen from below, of course, Celia's shoes are much more than footwear.
On their skin and in plain sight, they bear the mark of endless negotiations
with the trappings of upward mobility, Latinidad, and the eternal feminine.
But even further, that some of us may be inexplicably drawn to and others
uneasily repulsed by Celia's shoes implies that they are part of an intricate
signifying net. One which, to paraphrase Jacques Lacan, "catches" Latino
spectators in their desire to be seen and identified in specific ways.[2] This
is why, with (if not entirely in) Celia's shoes it is possible to walk through
her unique career as a Cuban female singer in the nearly all-Puerto-Rican-
male club of salsa, examine how a self-described "ugly woman" became
a pan-Latino icon, and string together the ways that style tells stories of
hardship and triumph differently enjoyed—and sometimes disowned—by
Latinos as part of their public "ethnic" body in the United States.

Oye Como Va

Born Úrsula Hilaria Celia Caridad Cruz Alfonso on October 21, 1924,
the singer began her unlikely rise to stardom in Santos Suárez, one of
Havana's poorest neighborhoods. Although Celia's class origins prompted
official biographer Ana Cristina Raymundo to write that "nothing in her
background gave any indication of the heights she would reach,"[3] a sense

that this young girl had a special gift became evident early on. According to Cruz lore, reproduced in an infinite number of published accounts in the popular press, Celia began to sing to put her siblings to bed. In time, her voice attracted the attention of her neighbors and cousins, one of whom registered her to participate in an amateur singing contest, *La Hora del Té* (The Tea Hour). Already a university student, the twenty-three-year-old Celia won the competition by singing the tango "Nostalgia"—a prophetic choice, in light of her eventual and permanent exile from Cuba.

Before considering a career in music, Celia studied to be a schoolteacher, a relatively low-paying profession that nevertheless carried a certain level of respect for blacks in Cuba, who historically had been excluded from educational opportunity. By 1951, only four years after her debut on the radio, Celia had become the lead singer for La Sonora Matancera, Cuba's most popular orchestra. Even if fans initially rejected Celia because she was virtually unknown and had replaced the wildly popular Puerto Rican singer Myrta Silva, she quickly consolidated her own following, earning the first in a succession of cultural titles: *La guarachera de Cuba*.

In 1959, after years of touring and recording with La Sonora, Celia responded dramatically to the Cuban Revolution's swift restructuring of the entertainment industry. She first moved to Mexico and then settled permanently outside New York City. This last move was to have significant if contradictory effects. On the one hand, Celia experienced exile as a great personal loss; she would never see her parents or set foot in Havana again. On the other hand, exile provided the conditions for her to ascend professionally from the genre-specific and nationally bound musical identity as *la guarachera de Cuba* to a pan-Latino global identification as the Queen of Salsa. Even if Celia rationalized this loss of national identity by arguing that salsa was only a variation of the Cuban *son*—a long and arguably exhausted debate among musicians and scholars—she had little trouble incorporating the new accents that came to define "Latin" music for over the past half-century. True to form, the last major hit of her career, "La negra tiene tumbao," combined elements of salsa, reggae, and hip-hop.

Undoubtedly, Celia's talent in fusing a wide range of sounds played a large role in her ability to retain salsa's royal title for more than fifty years. Yet in an era when bodily image, not vocal ability, often sells more CDs, Celia had to creatively solve another matter to ensure long-term success: that of not "looking good" as a performer. At the height of her global fame, for instance, Celia was not beautiful in a conventional sense, slim, or young. She was also hailed as a "nice" person in a context in which scandal sells newspapers and a racy personal life defines iconicity. "The collective question," recalls television producer Cristina Saralegui after she pitched Celia's story to make a biopic in Hollywood, was "How do you write a compelling screenplay about somebody whose life had no apparent Tina Turner tragedy, no Behind the Music crash and burn, no tabloid-worthy scandal?"[4]

What Hollywood producers may have missed, however, was precisely what her fans saw in her, and I would argue was the secret of the legendary salsera: whatever Celia may have lacked in typical celebrity fashion, she made up for by other means, through what many came to refer to as the "unique and unmistakable Celia Cruz look."[5]

From the start of her career, Celia showed great interest in style, admittedly spending all her money on clothes when she was a starving young singer in Havana.[6] It was in exile, though, living in a racially polarized country where Latinos were socially expendable, that Celia became equally as famous for her distinctive voice as for her wardrobe. Easily recognizable from near or far, Celia's style consisted of dresses "with feathers, spangles, lace, and yards upon yards of multi-colored fabrics."[7] The outfits were often topped with outrageously designed wigs, and complimented by hands "featuring long painted nails and expensive jewelry" that, according to eveningwear designer Julian Asion, made it "quite obvious that she's never had to do the dishes."[8]

But if wigs, gowns, and nail polish constituted an important part of Cruz's public anatomy, shoes were considered "Celia's signature," in Asion's words, and bore a considerable weight in narrating her public persona: "On top of these heels, you have this voluptuous body moving around, dancing around. Those heels are her."[9] And given the many ways that footwear communicates more than one is able or willing to say, this correspondence between Celia, salsa fans, and her shoes could not have been otherwise.

Esa Negrita que va Caminando

As has been noted by journalists and other observers, Celia had a formidable collection of shoes. The collection included thousands of pairs kept at home and in New Jersey warehouses that were worn "for photo shoots and to perform on stage or on the red carpet."[10] Despite the collection's size, the vast majority of these shoes were of only one style: high heels, a type of footwear originally linked to the aristocracy since it was considered to be "highly impractical for women who had to perform menial labor."[11] While Celia may not have been aware of this historical detail, the fact that her shoes were generally made of glittery materials simulating diamonds or rubies, and in colors reminiscent of gold and silver, references the style's origins and appears to insist on her status as a queen—*la reina de la salsa*—at the same level with, if not a cut above, that other voracious collector of high-heel shoes, the French queen Marie Antoinette.[12]

Celia's signature shoes, however, went beyond simply elaborately decorated high heels. They were very high heels, some nine inches up. Perhaps because footwear worn by the poor has traditionally been ill-fitting, due to coarse material and design,[13] Celia's shoes were hand-made, too complex and costly to mass-produce and fitted exclusively for her. Furthermore, the shoes seemed to defy gravity itself, as they did not rest on a conventional heel but on the thinnest of soles. By appearing physically infeasible, Celia's shoes ultimately offered the illusion of walking on air, a magical attribute that again elevated the queen above mere mortals.[14]

Part of the explanation, then, rests on the ways that shoes themselves connote wealth, uniqueness, and even magic. Given the singer's "undistinguished" class origins and membership in a racial and ethnic group rarely afforded the dignity of individuality, Celia's shoes insisted on her distinctiveness as a person and a performer, a one-of-a-kind brand. If shoes are, as Maureen Turim has argued, the "most abject part of the body . . . the body part in direct contact with the dirt and assigned the role of support,"[15] Celia's shoes literally lifted Celia from the ground, away from her lowly social origins and onto a stage where reality appeared to be free and self-fashioned. In this regard, Celia's "wildly stylish"[16] shoes "dressed up" her struggle of upward mobility while insisting that a black woman born in poverty on a small Caribbean island could reach the heights of a transnational singing star.[17]

Fittingly, in the hagiographic story of her upward mobility, Celia's social location is consistently narrated in relation to shoes. For instance, Celia was one of thirteen children "as shoeless as her" who managed to finish her education by going to class with "torn shoes."[18] This state of poverty only began to change when, as a teenager, "Cruz got her first pair of quality shoes singing for a tourist on the street."[19] Toward the end of her career, it was said more than once that no one, including her handpicked successor, La India, could fill her shoes.[20] And still in old age, when her high place in popular music history was completely assured, Cuban journalist Norma Niurka wrote that after finally recording her first album with a major label in 2000, Celia felt like "a girl with new shoes."[21]

Although Celia frequently disputed the anecdote that she sang to tourists for her shoes, saying that "I was very poor but never a beggar,"[22] this tale with *ribetes de leyenda* (streaks of legend)[23] stands as her founding myth. "Not only had my singing made them happy," Celia recalled in her autobiography, "but those white patent-leather shoes, which meant so much to me, initiated my lifelong fascination with fashion."[24] Shoes, then, refer to and reify an "originary event" that, as Erin Mackie has written, "fixes together previously disparate, heterogeneous elements into a novel identity"[25]—in this case, that of an Afro-Cuban female star. Even further, they made Celia not simply a singer of humble origins who became famous but nothing less than a "black Cinderella," a girl who, as if in a fairy tale, went from a "poor neighborhood of Havana to a queen's burial in New York."[26]

De Cuba Vengo

The idea that shoes denote social class is common to many of the globe's cultures. With a simple drawing of wooden shoes, the painter Vincent Van Gogh signified the exploitation endured by Dutch peasants in his native country. Imelda, wife of former Philippine dictator Ferdinand Marcos, infamously signified her wealth and power in a class-polarized country through her vast collection of shoes. At the same time, Celia's choice of shoes as a way to speak to and about poverty has a long tradition in the Caribbean. Since the (shoeless) native peoples on two continents encountered the (well-heeled) Europeans, to have or have not shoes has become a significant social concern for everyone who lives in the Americas. As Maureen Turim reminds us, "The opposition of shoes to bare feet is central . . . to significations of wealth, public space, and civilization itself."[27]

Puerto Rican history, for instance, is full of references to shoes as a means to narrate the particularities and vicissitudes of national life. Starting in the eighteenth century, the Spanish priest and historian Iñigo Abad y Lasierra described criollos as promiscuous and lazy, and also as a group that was prone to going barefoot.[28] More than a century later, an 1899 report requested by President McKinley on the state of Puerto Rico measured the island's poverty in part by the size of its shoeless population: "child labor was common practice, unemployment was widespread, and out of a population of nearly a million people some seven hundred thousand were without shoes."[29] Not surprisingly, the post–World War II industrialization campaign that transformed Puerto Rico from the poorhouse to the economic "miracle" of the Caribbean is generally known in English as Operation Bootstrap. This prompted writer Luis Rafael Sánchez to ironically conclude during the 1980s that despite the increase in consumption levels brought about by pulling themselves up by their own bootstraps, Puerto Ricans still belonged to *la Americá descalza* (barefoot America) of the south, and not the wealthy north signified by the United States.[30]

Among Cubans, shoes are also tied to national narratives, and perhaps with a tighter bow. In his memoir from the 1868 war of independence, *A pie y descalzo—de Trinidad a Cuba (1870/71): Recuerdos de campaña* (1890),[31] historian Ramón Roa measured the *mambíses'* enthusiasm for the war in terms of their willingness to fight without shoes, and urgently defined his own situation—shoeless and horseless, *a pie y descalzo*—as the most abject and dehumanizing of all social conditions.[32] In Roa's words, "[with] my feet cracked and swollen due to the stones and bushes. . . . I began for the first time in life to suffer the moral horrors that can only be suffered when one sees oneself, above all, barefoot and hatless, something like abandoned by mankind and at the enemy's mercy."[33]

Even when writer and pro-independence advocate José Martí harshly criticized Roa's book in his speech "*Los pinos nuevos*" because it would discourage Cubans from embracing the cause, his own texts further elaborated on the relationship between shoes, class, and national struggle. In the 1891 classic "*Nuestra América*," Martí represents U.S. imperial power as a boot (*los gigantes que llevan siete leguas en las botas*)[34] and authentic Latin American as the culture of those who wear not "*charreteras y togas*" (epaulets and professor's gowns) but "*alpargatas en los pies y la vincha en la cabeza*" (hemp sandals and headbands).[35] Martí perhaps uses the shoes as a trope to maximum effect in his broadly anthologized modernist poem, "*Los zapaticos de rosa*" (The Little Pink Shoes), in which a well-off girl offers her pink shoes to another who is ill and poor in order to temper the shame of class privilege.[36]

Far from ending with the nineteenth-century's independence struggles, the allusion to shoes in Cuban cultural production continued well into the twentieth century and without ideological distinctions. In an untitled text published just a year after the Mariel exodus, Cuban exile activist and writer Lourdes Casal defined "democratic normalcy" as "an office full of shoe boxes."[37] From another place, the dissident and *marielito* Reinaldo Arenas, who once called Casal's journal *Areíto* "the official organ of the Cuban state police in New York," uses a pair of torn shoes, "a little bashful because they had holes in their tips," to suggest that someone who lives in material poverty can also enjoy the wealth of country living in a short story titled "*Los zapatos vacíos*" (The Empty Shoes).[38]

In the United States, high heels have also been tied to Latina and Cuban American feminine identity. As feminist scholar Tace Hedrick has observed, "the connection of heels with the exotic beauty of certain Latin America and Hispanic American women has been part of the United States' collective imaginary for decades."[39] For some Cuban American women of the postwar period, high heels were explicitly associated with ethnic difference, autonomous sexuality, and validation of a different body, one often considered to be below "average" height, that is, inferior to (other) Americans. According to Cuban American columnist Liz Balmaseda, during the 1970s "it was the heels that distinguished the Latinas from the Americanitas. We were the chicks in the seven-inch, custom-designed platforms, the ones unconcerned by details such as dwarfing our dates."[40]

Since Celia would never have been confused with the white girls Balmaseda calls "Americanitas," her fashion choices were arguably more intimately coupled to her desire to be seen as a Latina rather than as an "American" black woman, a common response for Afro-Caribbean people living in the United States who reject this country's rigid racial binary and overt exclusion of racialized people as citizens. Stepping up her Latinidad did not, however, imply a denial of her black identifications, evident in her recordings of Afro-Cuban and African diaspora rhythms and lyrics and her display of pan-African style. Yet Celia's "Latin thing" ruled over her "blackness" in public discourse. The success of using style as a means to assert Latinidad rather than "blackness" is evident when designer Julian Asion makes Celia's shoes the litmus test of Latino identity. Referring to a pair of Celia's high-heeled shoes, Asion says, "If you don't know whose shoes these are, you're not Latino."[41]

Celia's shoe fetishism, that is, her tendency to invest shoes with meanings that are not inherent in them, was therefore not an obscure personal or private matter. If for Celia shoes stood in for her success as a black working-classs Latina in gringolandia, for the fans, many of whom were women, black, Latinos, and queers, they offered both the hope of reaching a similar stature and of upsetting the hierarchies that kept them down. This partly explains why, despite the extravagance inherent in Celia's shoes and the affluence implicit in acquiring a sizable collection, her admirers did not resent these displays of wealth. On the contrary, Celia's overt love for shoes struck a chord with many fans (including those in the popular media), who saw in the popular singer a person who, "despite adversity, never allowed her dreams or dignity to be stepped on."[42] The importance of Celia's shoes to telling her story ultimately makes evident that a fetish is, as psychoanalyst Robert J. Stoller once put it, "a story masquerading as an object."[43]

Caballero y Dama

Celia's buying into the stereotype of the high (and well)-heeled Latina helped her to maintain ethnic and national specificity and to underscore a different way to be a black star, not to be confused with other African American divas. Still, to the extent that in Western culture shoe styles are gender coded, and high heels in particular are intimately tied to "universal" femininity and sexuality,[44] Celia's love of shoes is also about standing up for femininity itself. On more than one occasion, in fact, Celia pointed to shoe style as a fundamental marker for gender differentiation, irrespective of ethnicity, nationality, or race. As she vehemently argued with her husband, Pedro Knight, on the subject of stars wearing sneakers with tuxedos during a press interview, "But they're men, Pedro. . . . Women can't do that."[45]

At the same time, while high heels made Celia a woman, she did not want to be just any kind of woman. She wanted to be seen as a Cuban, Latina, and an Afro-Caribbean woman, but also as a decent woman. Celia did not, for instance, fail to tell interviewers about the contrast between her and the woman she replaced at La Sonora Matancera, the Puerto Rican Myrta Silva, who was known for projecting a sexually unconventional and mischievous public persona, captured by nicknames such as "*la gorda de oro*" and "*la vedette que arrolla*" (the vedette that will sweep you away).[46] In Celia's words, "She would come out in *Bohemia* magazine wrapped just in a towel. I was very serious."[47] Celia's need to be perceived as serious and seriously actually reached panic levels in 1949. During an engagement in Venezuela, one of the women dancing in the troupe that accompanied Celia, Las Mulatas del Fuego, became ill. On a whim, Celia offered to replace the fallen dancer on the show. Although Celia dressed in the *mulatas'* customary bikini and made it to the edge of the curtain, she could not go forward. "I froze. I couldn't go on. I just couldn't. . . . I felt naked. There were so many people out there looking at me."[48]

For Celia, the resistance to exposing herself in a certain way was explicitly associated with the shame of being looked upon as an "easy woman." In Celia's narrative, this shame arose from her father's damning gaze as he viewed the singer's entry into show business as tantamount to being a whore. "Since my father wanted all his children to be professionals," recalled Celia, "when he saw the path that I was on as an entertainer, he feared that I would disregard my teaching aspirations and fall prey to the *mujeres de la vida* culture. My father was ashamed of me and he wouldn't even tell anyone I even existed. Fortunately, all of that changed one day." [49] The fear of being taken for a *mujer de la vida* also explains Celia's confessed inability to dance in public before leaving Cuba. Celia's physical rigidity on the stage was so pronounced that her Aunt Ana repeatedly advised her to loosen up and "shake a little: You have to understand that you have to let the public feel everything you're carrying inside through your entire body. Not just your voice." [50]

While Celia's growing success and public avoidance of the fast track eventually resulted in her father's approval and in her loosening up, a more pervasive shame involving her entire body came to constitute her public persona: the shame of being "ugly." In fact, ugliness appears in Celia's story of self as the one major liability that she had to overcome, rather than any of the obstacles commonly associated with race, ethnicity, sexuality, and gender. For example, when things got rocky early on at La Sonora, Celia has said that she compensated by hard work and good values: "God may have not given me a pretty face, but He gave me many gifts." [51] Celia further claims that during her early years she was unable to hire an agent because "I was ugly. Yes, I did have a pretty voice, but I didn't have the look many agents wanted to represent." [52] In a succinct declaration, Celia described herself as *"fea de cara pero bella de alma"* — having an ugly face but beautiful soul — underscoring the highness of spirituality over the lowliness of her racialized and gendered body.

In addition to her facial features, Celia specifically disliked her lower body. As she confided to friends and interviewers, "I have ugly legs." [53] Celia's shoes then carried the burden of a shamed body, one that dared not be seen in the bare flesh and was instead represented through fabric, leather, or glitter. This is why Celia spectacularized her body away from "natural" conceptions of beauty. Most of her wigs, for instance, were dyed with colors not found in nature. While Celia argues that wigs were good because they were "practical" and easy to use since the "natural" hair did not have to be worked on,[54] the kind of hairstyle (straight), color (blue, red) and other features of the majority of her wigs underscore that Celia's general aesthetic was against regimes if representation that signified beauty as part of women's nature. And although it is true that Celia experimented with an "Afro" look during the 1970s and early 1980s, not only was this latter look equally spectacular, but her own hair was rarely seen, and when it was, it was in the chemically relaxed style. Not surprisingly, the wig she donated to the Smithsonian was blonde, and so was the one she was buried in. In this sense, Celia's extreme style, to build further on critic Dick Hebdige's analysis, can be understood as "an expression both of impotence and a kind of power"—the power to disfigure "a body that was considered ugly."[55]

That Celia covered up her lower body did not mean that she did not want to be seen: on the contrary. Celia wanted the audience not just to listen but also to take note of her body, particularly as it aged. In Celia's words, "If I can't call attention on my own, I will do so through my clothes."[56] Given this, it is important to underscore that Celia did not hide as covered up to avoid being perceived in the ways that black women are racially engendered to signify available and "hot" sexuality. This move protected Celia against a certain discriminating look, one that threatened to consume her as a vulnerable object—female and black—and that may not have found her to embody black "beauty" in acceptable terms.

To cover up was then more than a simple matter of accessories. It was, above all, a style of struggle employed by a woman who was aware of the forces that aimed to limit her possibilities as an "ugly" black female singer. Similarly, Celia often threw a protective mantle over all details of her "private" life. She always insisted, for instance, that she had an idyllic sentimental life with her husband and manager Pedro Knight, and avoided the specter of "scandal" at all costs. She characterized her body's hard-fought ability to dance less as a sign of her sexuality than as part of the "joy of singing," an offering and a plea not to be excluded from cultural exchange because of race, class, sexuality, or gender. As Celia observed on more than one occasion, "Music is the only gift that God has given me. Unless he takes it away from me, I will continue to share that gift with the world."[57] Celia protected this gift—and her hard-won social privilege— by always appearing as a "black Latin woman, who achieved greatness through a lot of hardships that she always kept to herself."[58]

Celia's strategy of looking good and covering up of course had a price, that of accepting the stereotype of the maternal and asexual black woman. She has been called charming, generous, affectionate, motherly, and gracious by many musicians, writers, and television personalities, but only rarely sexy or attractive.[59] According to novelist Oscar Hijuelos, "Celia was the kind of gracious lady that we would love to have for an aunt, a fairy godmother whose tender-heartedness works a healing magic on even the most troubled souls."[60] Celia was also frequently represented as a guardian angel, not unlike the matronly black nannies and cooks that populate canonical Hispanic Caribbean and American fiction, characters that exhibit, in Toni Morrison's words, great "benevolence, harmless and servile guardianship and endless love."[61] Celia was ultimately able to become a salsa icon without engaging in the racialized sexual ambiguities of her hand-picked successor Linda Cabellero, better known as La India, or proclaiming the erotic discomformity performed by her contemporary, the Queen of Soul, Guadalupe Yoli Raymond, "La Lupe," who took off her shoes and threw them at the audience.[62]

Ultimately, the twin discourses of *seriedad* and excessive style constituted the enigma of Celia Cruz's public persona, supposedly *seria* in the inside, extravagant on the outside. In the words of friend and colleague Gloria Estefan, "the wild outfits were just an act. . . . There was such a dichotomy between the personality and the clothes."[63] Yet less than a dichotomy the fusion of *seriedad* and extravagance allowed Celia to be seen both as a spectacle worth looking at and as a decent woman, in no way to be confused with the *mujeres de la vida* her father worried about.[64] If Celia was going to sing salsa—that is, black music—and was not deemed beautiful enough to be appreciated by the eyes of strangers, her unique style allowed her to project herself as an illusion of abundance, dignity, talent, Cubanness, beauty, femininity, and, toward the end of her life, eternal youth.

Mi Vida Es Cantar

There is, however, a second important reason why Celia required a style that accentuated her femininity. The kingdom of salsa, like the nation, is almost universally associated with men and male ideologies of sexuality. Salsa's virility is reiterated in multiple ways, including in the fact that, as scholar Wilson Valentín-Escobar has commented, top *salseros* are habitually baptized with names calling attention to their masculinity. In this canon, the mellow Gilberto Santa Rosa is *"el caballero de la salsa"* and the very macho Tito Rojas is *"el gallo de la salsa."* Moreover, the salsa that Celia was part of creating is considered salsa dura (hard), in contrast to more recent incarnations like the salsa monga or sensual, which is characterized by the bolero's "feminine" discourse of courtly love and has a "bland" sound that "contain[s] little or no brass and percussive sounds."[65] In this context, any woman that attempted to crown herself Queen of Salsa had to artistically situate herself on the hard side of the genre without losing her feminine look—which is precisely what Celia did.

From a musical point of view, Celia always succeeded in being perceived in the best of terms, that is, in masculine terms. Celia, for instance, is often represented as a woman who "entered" the salsa world, or, in a Puerto Rican critic's terms, "she has the distinction of being one of the few women who has dared sing salsa . . . [who] has had the gallantry of incurring in this genre."[66] Celia's voice itself was repeatedly described with adjectives that underscore its masculinity: "tough," "raspy,"[67] "a powerful contralto,"[68] and projecting "a mature marimacho punch."[69] Her impressive ability to *sonear*, a skill that separates not only the men from the women but also the boys from the men, earned her the admiration of other singers. As salsero Cheo Feliciano succinctly put it, Celia was different from other female singers because unlike most women, who were confined to singing boleros and ballads—"girl stuff"—she "understood and assimilated the masculine way of singing and feminized it. . . . That is why there will be never be any other woman who can wear her shoes and do what she did."[70]

At the same time that Celia was widely praised for her "masculine" way of singing salsa, her male peers equally valued her feminine "discretion" in personal matters. In Feliciano's words, "Since she was the only woman in the group, she was always very discreet touring. You know . . . men things, she never said a word."[71] More important, Celia never crossed the line that distinguishes singers from true musicians. She followed the "feminine" tradition of interpreter and did not participate in arranging, producing, or distributing her music. A widely available example of the ways that musicianship is gendered in classic salsa can be appreciated in a 1989 Fania concert in Zaire, available on DVD and currently marketed as *Celia Cruz and the Fania Allstars in Africa*.[72] Although Celia opened the concert, sang, and was arguably the most compelling performer to the audience, she was clearly different from the rest of the participants. Unlike every other musical or vocal performer on stage—which number included Santana, Ray Barreto, Hector Lavoe, Johnny Pacheco, and Roberto Roena—the fact that Celia was literally not a boy in the band underscored that the business of salsa music remained not only a Latin but also a male thing.

The importance of successfully manipulating gender codes for women aspiring to stardom in Caribbean music genres can be confirmed by comparing Celia to other major female stars. The Puerto Rican Ivy Queen, otherwise known as "the queen of reggaeton,"[73] has also been able to stay on top of a male-dominated music genre. In contrast to Celia, Ivy Queen initially became famous during the genre's underground period for a hard look that allowed her to be seen as just another *cangri*. As this rhythm has gone global, however, Ivy Queen has been exposed to more discriminating eyes and has nurtured a differently gendered persona with a similar formula to the Cuban queen's. On the one hand, Ivy Queen reminds fans that she is a "real" woman through a "flaming" style that includes high heels, long hair, nails up to four inches long, platinum accessories, and plastic surgery to enhance bust size. On the other hand, given the perception that she is not a conventionally attractive woman, she insists that "in contrast to other divas she does not come to sell her *nalgas* but her lyrics." Ivy Queen's claim that despite her looks she is not seeking to be looked at as a woman is bolstered by how her "raspy" vocals, considered by some as hardly distinguishable from those of men, set her apart from other female singers.[74] In the words of on-line journalist Gavin Mueller, "Ivy Queen is the most notable female MC in reggaeton, which has to be due to her voice. It's strong and throaty and strangely asexual—she sounds less feminine than a lot of male reggaeton MCs."[75]

Celia's and Ivy Queen's successful incorporation into their respective genres contrasts to other female stars in Latin music. Celia's great contemporary, La Lupe, continues to be ignored in the salsa canon due to her excessive "feminine" performance style—desiring, hysterical, impossible to contain—even if, as Frances R. Aparicio argues, she "gave voice to the urban, warlike, and male-gendered modulations of salsa."[76] Similarly, although La India's voice is regularly described in gendered terms as having an "androgynous style rather than a soft, melodious tone,"[77] her ambiguous sexuality has made many see her not as a lady in the midst of a male world but as "the industry's Tomboy, who likes to play with the big boys and knows how to hold the pants better than they ever will."[78] Though La India's women-centered lyrics and self-fashioning have won her some hard-core fans among women and gays, who claim her as the "Princess of Salsa and underground dance music,"[79] the fact that from the inception of her career she has been rumored to be a lesbian marginalizes her in relation to the salsa family. The difference then lies in what kind of masculinity is invoked and to what ends. While La India's imagined sexual masculinity and La Lupe's feminine sensibility make some uncomfortable, Celia's masculine vocal range and feminine sensibility constituted the perfect gendered arrangement.

Given the consequences of a style misstep, Celia's markedly feminine costuming can be understood as a means "to hide anxieties about being perceived as masculine."[80] It is revealing that in some classic studies about salsa and Latin music, such as *The Latin Tinge,* by John Storm Roberts, and *Salsa, sabor y control,* by Angel Quintero Rivera, she is largely ignored. Yet when Celia is addressed at length, the excessive style of her star persona tends to take precedence over her male connections. Perhaps because she was aware that style was an important strategy to hold her place in popular memory, Celia encouraged drag queens to "perform" and never forget her. In doing so, Celia well knew that immortality—a critical concern for any queen—came from being constantly remembered as a public woman, one bound by the "feminine" discourse of fashion while singing "like a man."

Epilogue: *¡Yo Viviré!* (I Will Survive)

The question of how Celia would be remembered came sooner than expected. On July 16, 2003, *la reina de la salsa* passed away at her home in Fort Lee, New Jersey, after a relatively short battle with brain cancer.

News that Celia Cruz had died traveled fast throughout Latino communities in the United States. In Miami, the capital of Cuban exiles and the home of over a million Latinos, emails, phone calls, and street chatter underscored the importance of the singer as a dignified representative of Latino America. For several months before her death, as she struggled with illness yet continued to release hit songs, scribbled messages on cardboard frequently appeared at the front entrances of *cafetines* and other modest gathering places. One I often went by in Coral Gables put it simplest: "*Celia te queremos*" (Celia we love you). But although many fans loved her, Celia's popularity among Latinos, including Cubans, was far from universal. If the donation of her shoes to the Smithsonian had provoked a rumble of discontent from those that felt the shoes did not adequately represent Latin culture, perhaps no other event of her public life brought to light so many tensions between Cubans as her funeral.

Envisioning her memorial service as a grand finale, Celia desired nothing short of making a spectacle of her dead self. In her own words, "I want a wake and a funeral home where a lot of cars can park and everybody attends."[81] And they did—over half a million people stood in interminable lines to see Celia "laid out in a platinum-blonde wig, a sequined gown and flashy jewels, her nails painted white, her lips hot pink."[82] As is often the case, however, the wake revealed as much—if not more—about the mourners than the cadaver. If New York was to be the final resting place in lieu of Cuba, Miami was the showcase, the surface on which Cubans contemplated the state of their national selves.

While in the streets, the grief of the people was displayed and televised by the Spanish-language media, in the pages of Miami's newspapers angry letters to the editor indicated that the bitterness I had originally encountered with the Cuban diplomat was neither idiosyncratic nor isolated. For readers like Efraín Hernandez of the weekly *Street*, Celia Cruz "did nothing useful in this society except jiggle around on stage and scream. She is an embarrassment to all Cubans who are trying not to be the laughing stock of the American community. . . . Did you ever take the time to listen to her talk? She was dumber than two boxes of rocks, and she represents the Cuban people? No way! We have many successful Cuban doctors, educators, politicians, businessmen. . . . Thanks to Celia Cruz, every person in the modern world thinks Cubans are nothing but Salsa dancing, banana eating idiots. . . . Let's move on." [83] It was at this moment, after her death, when it became clear that if Celia had played it safe as a "good" black, a "good" wife, and a "good" exile, she had her reasons. For Efraín was not alone.

In the mail section of Miami's main cultural weekly, the *Miami New Times*, letters poured in in response to an article by Celeste Fraser Delgado in which the journalist underscored how race had played a role in Cruz's life and death. During the first week, two letters expressed "offense" at Delgado's "foolishness": "What an idiot Celeste Fraser Delgado is. . . . As a Cuban woman I was quite offended by her constant mention of Celia Cruz being black. First and foremost, Celia was Cuban." [84] But the real fireworks came a week after the first batch of letters. In the August 14–20 issue, five letters were printed. Of the five, three found the suppression of race and a discussion on racism to be the offensive part. "What I find offensive," wrote Maggie Urrely, "is to hear cries of racism, and once backs are turned, hearing racist remarks blurted out." [85] And from Doris Fernandez, "I know from firsthand experience that white Cubans are just as bigoted as their American counterparts, so they can try that rhetoric on other Cubans because we Americans know better." [86]

The crudeness of the racism of some exiles seemed to contrast with Celia's popularity with the white Cuban elite. In writing about the virtues of the past versus a mediocre present, historian Luis Aguilar León commented that Celia Cruz herself was a symbol of better times. Times of spectacle, "mulatta laughter," "the narrow streets of Havana," "the smell of coffee": "Celia Cruz is living Cuba, present, flaming, seminal and eternal," a performer capable of offering "class, hierarchy, elegance."[87] Significantly, this type of positive assessment was not confined to Cubans of Celia's own generation. For Richard Pérez-Feria, the "generation ñ" editor of *People en Español*, "Celia Cruz . . . always made herself felt in my home . . . her spirit, her energy, her cubanía, which was [what] my parents wanted me and my siblings to emulate."[88]

In addition to her status as one of the most famous bodies of exile— "*estandarte del pueblo cubano y del exilio patriótico,*"[89] "*vibra en ella Cuba entera*"[90]—Celia's acceptance also rests in her having the right line concerning Fidel. According to popular accounts, the only topic that made Celia lose her habitual composure and dignified stance was her hatred of Castro, whom she once allegedly called "*hijo de la gran . . . pura y sincera*" (son of a . . . saintly and sincere).[91] If in private Celia was in constant communication with relatives in Cuba and sent money to them, in public she was represented as a queen who was never seduced by the tyrant and who was made to suffer for her integrity when Fidel did not allow her to return to the island to bury her mother. For influential segments of the exile community, Celia was then an acceptable symbol, one who never embarrassed them politically, cherished presocialist Cuban culture, preached the importance of hard work and success so essential to the myth of Cubans as a model minority, and, although "proud of being black," sang to harmony and good humor in the face of adversity.

In this sense, publicly loving Celia was a way to cover up the pain of exile itself. Not coincidentally, although most of her fashion choices had pan-Latino appeal or origin, some elements of style, such as her dresses inspired by the traditional *bata cubana* and the *rumbera* outfits directly evoked Cuba. An example of the importance of fashion as a stand-in for national space is the much-photographed Cuban flag outfit that Cruz wore in a May 20, 2002, concert in Miami to commemorate Cuban Independence Day. The idea that by dressing up as Cuba one could literally remain there constituted a strategy to minimize the political defeat of Cuban exiles. To live solely for the stage was also a way of never leaving Cuba.

The defense of exile as an in-between space is also evident in that Celia never attempted to cross over into the English-language market. Her famous refusal to speak English because her *inglés* was not "very good-looking"[92] and pretending that she did not understand it articulated a resistance to accept exile as a permanent location and persist in "foreign" ways of fashioning the public self in the United States. If being an exile is to suffer a break between time and space, to be suspended, Celia lived for the stage, a trope for home and a site of memory. By always insisting that she had left her heart in Havana, her feet took her all over the world in a frenzied pilgrimage to assert the present. In Celia's words, "The stage, my performances, and my audience have always been my refuge."[93]

Celia's final crossing, however, which underscored to what extent and in what ways many Latinos have become part of America, also heralded the end of the *Cuba de ayer* that Celia represented to so many and the Cuba of Fidel, its necessary inverse. As Marta Cabrera, a Cuban exile in Washington employed as a domestic worker, put it, "Cuba is leaving us. The good ones are leaving us and Fidel doesn't even fall off the bed."[94] Meantime, Celia's passing in style left all salsa lovers with a complex icon who navigated the treacherous constraints of subalterity with caution, creativity, and intelligence. Perhaps a significant part of Celia's legacy is precisely her particular style of crossing over deep waters, that *taconeo*. For as curator Marvette Pérez once said, "The men, when they have died, have left behind other men who could take their place. But Celia left no woman who could step into her shoes."[95]

Notes

In writing this essay, I was fortunate to receive the support of several colleagues and friends. I would like to thank writers Celeste Fraser Delgado and Kathleen McHugh for their editorial and intellectual acumen, Marvette Pérez for her scholarly generosity, and Kairos Llobrera and Katerina Seligmann for their exceptional research assistance. I would also like to thank Myra Mendible for her editorial suggestions and for the opportunity to publish this essay.

The epigraph is from Erin Mackie, "Red Shoes and Bloody Stumps," in *Footnotes: On Shoes*, ed. Shari Benstock and Suzanne Ferris (New Brunswick, NJ: Rutgers University Press, 2001), 233–247, 233.

1. Juan Soto Meléndez, "Pelucas y vestidos," http://66.45.70.203/prfrogui/caribenet/celiatributo2e.htm.

2. Jacques Lacan, *The Four Fundamental Concepts of Psychoanalysis* (New York: Norton, 1981).

3. Celia Cruz with Ana Cristina Reymundo, *Celia: My Life* (New York: HarperCollins, 2004), 3.

4. Lydia Martin, "Adiós to the Queen of Salsa," *Miami Herald*, July 17, 2003, www.puertorico-herald.org/issues/2003/vol7n29/AdiosQueen-en.shtml.

5. Cruz, *My Life*, 5.

6. Telephone interview with Marvette Pérez, September 25, 2003.

7. Ramiro Burr, "La primera en su clase," *El Nuevo Herald*, December 28, 2000, 39D. Original Spanish: "plumas, lentejuelas, encajes y yardas y más yardas de telas de colores."

8. Julian Asion, "Style by Celia," *Latina*, September 1997, 84–86, 85.

9. Ibid.

10. Darío Méndez, "Celia Cruz, ¡Unica!" http://www.mipunto.com/foros/ foros.jsp?forum=266&start=51.

11. Toby Fischer-Mirkin, *Dress Code: Understanding the Hidden Meanings of Women's Clothes* (New York: Clarkson Potter, 1995), 196.

12. Shari Benstock and Suzanne Ferris, Introduction, *Footnotes: On Shoes*, ed. Shari Benstock and Suzanne Ferris (New Brunswick, NJ: Rutgers University Press, 2001), 1–13, 1.

13. Colin McDowell, *Shoes: Fashion and Fantasy* (New York: Rizzoli, 1989).

14. Ibid., 118.

15. Maureen Turim, "High Angles on Shoes," in *Footnotes: On Shoes*, ed. Shari Benstock and Suzanne Ferris (New Brunswick, NJ: Rutgers University Press, 2001), 58–90, 62.

16. Cruz, *My Life*, 181.

17. Dick Hebdige, *Subculture: The Meaning of Style* (London: Routledge, 2003), 78.

18. *Letralia* (Venezuela), July 21, 2003, http://letralia.com/96/ar02-096.htm.

19. "Adiós Celia," *People*, August 4, 2003, 69–78, 71.

20. Marla Friedler, "India Upon Her Grammy Nomination," http://www .salsaweb.com/features/indianew.htm.

21. Norma Niurka, "Celia Cruz: La armada invencible de la salsa," *El Nuevo Herald*, October 26, 2000, 27D. Original Spanish: "se siente como niña con zapatos nuevos."

22. "Biografía no autorizada de Celia Cruz," November 11, 2003, http:// cronica.com.ar/article/articleprint/1060646710/1/27/.

23. Javier Zerolo, "Adiós a la ceniciente negra," September 27, 2003, http.// diariodeavisos.com/2003-07-28/noticias/cultura/28DA2 . . .

24. Cruz, *My Life*, 19.

25. Mackie, "Red Shoes and Bloody Stumps," 236.

26. Zerolo, "Adiós."

27. Turim, "High Angles on Shoes," 62.

28. Hugo Rodríguez Vecchini, "Foreword: Back and Forward," in *The Commuter Nation: Perspectives on Puerto Rican Migration*, ed. Carlos Torre, Hugo Rodríguez Vecchini, and William Burgos (Rio Piedras: Editorial de la Universidad de Puerto Rico, 1994), 29–102, 75–76.

29. Thomas Aitken, Jr., *Poet in the Fortress* (New York: Annal—World Book, 1994), 38.

30. Luis Rafael Sánchez, *La importancia de llamarse Daniel Santos* (Hanover, NH: Ediciones del Norte, 1988), 3.

31. Ramón Roa, *A pie y descalzo—de Trinidad a Cuba (1870-71): Recuerdos de Campaña* (Havana, Cuba: Establecimiento Tipográfico de O'Reilly, 1890). Reproduced in Ramón Roa, *Pluma y machete* (Instituto del Libro: La Habana, 1969).

32. Roa, *Pluma y machete*, 55. Original Spanish: "se dirigían hambrientos, casi desnudos y descalzos a la ambicionada meta."

33. Ibid., 33. Original Spanish: "agrietados los hinchados pies por las piedras y zoquetes de los arbustos . . . empecé a sufrir por primera vez en la vida los

horrores morales que sólo se experimentan cuando se ve uno, sobre todo, descalzo, y luego sin sombrero, also así como abandonado de los hombres y a merced del enemigo."

34. José Martí, "Nuestra América," in *Nuestra América* (Venezuela: Biblioteca Ayacucho, 1977), 26.

35. Ibid. Jeffrey Belnap, trans., "Headbands, Hemp Sandals, and Headdresses: The Dialectics of Dress and Self-Conception in Martí's 'Our America,'" in *José Martí's 'Our America': From National to Hemispheric Cultural Studies*, ed. Jeffrey Belnap and Raúl Fernández (Durham, NC: Duke University Press, 1998), 198.

36. José Martí, "Los zapaticos de Rosa," in *Páginas escogidas*, ed. Roberto Fernández Retamar (Havana, Cuba: Editorial de Ciencias Sociales, 1971), 124–129.

37. Lourdes Casal, *Palabras juntan revolución* (Havana, Cuba: Ediciones Casa de las Americas, 1981), 25.

38. Reinaldo Arenas, "The Empty Shoes," in *Mona and Other Tales* (New York: Vintage, 2001), 3–4, 3.

39. Tace Hedrick, "Are you a pure Latina? or Menudo Every Day: Tacones and Symbolic Ethnicity," in *Footnotes: On Shoes*, ed. Shari Benstock and Suzanne Ferris (New Brunswick, NJ: Rutgers University Press, 2001), 135–155, 135 .

40. Liz Balmaseda, "Seduction by Spikes," *Latina*, September 1997, 82–83, 82.

41. Asion, "Style by Celia," 85.

42. Méndez, "Celia Cruz."

43. Robert J. Stoller, *Observing the Erotic Imagination* (New Haven: Yale University Press, 1985), 15.

44. Benstock and Ferris, Introduction, *Footnotes: On Shoes*, 5.

45. Lydia Martin, "Salsa queen Celia Cruz is praying for a special heeling," *Miami Herald*, October 31, 2001, 1E–2E, 2E.

46. Frances R. Aparicio, *Listening to Salsa: Gender, Latin Popular Music, and Puerto Rican Cultures* (Hanover, NH: Wesleyan University Press and the University Press of New England, 1998), 177.

47. Martin, "Adiós to the Queen of Salsa."

48. Cruz, *My Life*, 47.

49. Ibid., 50.

50. Ibid., 34.

51. Ibid., 62.

52. Ibid., 67.

53. Alexis Rodriguez Duarte, *Presenting Celia Cruz* (New York: Clarkson Potter, 2004).

54. Leila Cobo, "Azúcar para toda una época," *El Nuevo Herald* (December 28, 2000), 31D.

55. Hebdige, *Subculture*, 3.

56. "Sin Celia," *People en Español*, October 2003, 81. Original Spanish: "Si yo no llamo la atención, que la llame mi vestuario."

57. Cited in "Celia Cruz," September 27, 2003, http://geek.musicasdelmundo.org/staticpages/index.php/celia_cruz?m.

58. Lydia Martin, "Salsa star Celia Cruz is recuperating in N.Y. from 'delicate surgery,'" *The Miami Herald*, December 6, 2002, 4A.

59. One such instance is Ernesto Montaner's song "Un son para Celia," in which he calls Celia *"muñequita de café"* and *"negra linda."* In Cruz, *My Life*, 104.

60. Oscar Hijuelos, "A Song of Love for Celia," *New York Times*, July 23, 2003.

61. Toni Morrison, ed., *Race-ing Justice, En-gendering Power: Essays on Anita Hill, Clarence Thomas, and the Construction of Social Reality* (New York: Pantheon, 1992), 207.

62. Oscar Hijuelos, "A Song of Love for Cuba," *New York Times*, August 23, 2003.

63. *People*, August 4, 2003, 69–78, 75.

64. Martin, "Salsa star Celia Cruz is recuperating."

65. Wilson Valentín-Escobar, "Nothing Connects Us All But Imagined Sound," in *Mambo Montage*, ed. Agustín Laó-Montes and Arlene Dávila (New York: New York University Press, 2001), 207–233.

66. Javier Santiago, "Celia: La perseverante de la salsa," *Claridad en Rojo*, June 22–28 1990, 25. Original Spanish: "se distingue como una de las pocas mujeres que se han atrevido a cantar salsa . . . [que] han tenido la gallardía de incursionar en este género."

67. Jon Pareles, "Celia Cruz, Petite Powerhouse of Latin Music, Dies at 77," *New York Times*, July 17, 2003, www.nytimes.com/2003/07/17/obituaries/17CRUZ.html?th.

68. Martin, "Adiós to the Queen of Salsa."

69. Celeste Fraser Delgado, "Over Her Dead Body," *Miami New Times*, August 24, 2003, miaminewtimes.com/issues/2003-07-24/music.html/l/index.html.

70. Estela Perez, "Celia Cruz triunfó en un mundo de hombres," http://holahoy.com/lunes/internet.nsf/All/pg003798.htm.

71. Ibid.

72. Leon Gast, director, *Celia Cruz and the Fania Allstars in Africa* (2001), 56 min.

73. http://www.musicofpuertorico.com/en/queen_ivy.html.

74. Patricia Meschino, "Ivy Queen," Rotations, http://music.miaminewtimes.com/Issues/2004-11-18/music/rotations3.html.

75. Gavin Mueller, http://www.stylusmagazine.com/feature.php?ID=1326.

76. Frances R. Aparicio, *Listening to Salsa: Gender, Latin Popular Music, and Puerto Rican Cultures* (Hanover, NH: Wesleyan University Press and University Press of New England, 1998), 179.

77. Frances R. Aparicio, "La Lupe, La India, and Celia: Toward a Feminist Genealogy of Salsa Music," in *Situating Salsa: Global Markets and Local Meanings in Latin Popular Music*, ed. Lise Waxer (New York: Routledge, 2002), 135–160, 148.

78. "India," http://www.freestylemusic.com/Interviews/india.htm.

79. Howard Perez, "India Loves the Nightlife: The Princess of Salsa talks about her music and her love for the gay community," *qvMagazine*, www.qvmagazine.com/qv6/latinospotlight.html.

80. Lorraine Gamman, "Self-fashioning, Gender Display, and Sexy Girl Shoes: What's at Stake—Female Fetishism or Narcissism?" in *Footnotes: On Shoes*, ed.

Shari Benstock and Suzanne Ferris (New Brunswick, NJ: Rutgers University Press, 2001), 93–115, 98.

81. Ana Cristina Reymundo, "Celia Cruz: La bella época de una diva," *Nexos* (January–March 2003): 69–73, 73. Original Spanish: "Yo quiero que me velen y quiero una funeraria donde quepan muchos carros y que todo el mundo vaya."

82. "Adiós Celia," *People*, August 4, 2003, 69–78, 70.

83. "Not His Queen," *Street*, August 8, 2003, www.miami.com/mld/ streetmiami/entertainment/6480646.htm.

84. Rebecca Díaz, "We Cubans Found It Offensive," *Miami New Times*, August 7–13, 2003, 7.

85. "Celia: I'll Tell You What's Offensive," *Miami New Times*, August 14–20, 2003, 7.

86. "Celia Racial Rhetoric," *Miami New Times*, August 7–13, 2003, 7.

87. Luis Aguilar León, "Hay que refugiarse en Celia Cruz," *El Nuevo Herald*, October 8, 2000.

88. Richard Pérez-Feria, "Mi tía cubana," *People in Español*, October 2003, 12. Original Spanish: "siempre se hacía sentir en mi hogar. No tanto su música, para serles sincero, sino su espíritu, su energía, su cubanía, que era lo que más mis padres querían que mis hermanos y yo emuláramos."

89. Olga Connor, "Tributo a Celia Cruz: de Santos Suárez para el mundo," *El Nuevo Herald*, July 23, 2003.

90. Ernesto Montaner, "Un son para Celia," in Celia Cruz with Ana Cristina Reymundo, *Celia, My Life: An Autobiography* (New York: HarperCollins, 2004), v.

91. For further analysis concerning Celia Cruz's politics, see Frances R. Aparicio, "The Blackness of Sugar: Celia Cruz and the Performance of (Trans)Nationalism," *Cultural Studies* 13, no. 2 (1999): 223–236, 229.

92. Cruz, *My Life*, 102.

93. Ibid. 211.

94. Francisco Ayala-Silva, "De Celia, Comay, Cuba y otras hierbas," July 19, 2003, http://www.elsalvador.com/noticias/2003/07/19/escenarios/escen1.html.

95. Lydia Martin, "Capital museum mounting show on Celia Cruz," *Miami Herald*, October 30, 2004, www.miami.com/mld/miamiherald/news/10015100 .htm?templ . . .

CHAPTER 5

Salma Hayek's *Frida*

Transnational Latina Bodies in Popular Culture

ISABEL MOLINA GUZMÁN

> *Because of her many ills, history tends to remember Kahlo as a victim. Actually, she was a hellraiser, as is Hayek. Like Kahlo, Hayek is of mixed heritage; she's the daughter of a Lebanese born businessman and a Mexican opera singer. Like Kahlo, Hayek defied family expectations to seek her remarkable destiny.*
>
> ANNE STOCKWELL, *THE ADVOCATE*

Given Hollywood's longstanding and complex cinematic relationship with the Latina other, Salma Hayek's career might have been relegated to the unidimensional terrain of Latina stereotypes (Lopez 1991): one more emotionally unpredictable, sexually voluptuous, thickly accented Latina appearing in Hollywood movies like *Desperado* (1995), *From Dusk Till Dawn* (1996), *Fools Rush In* (1997), *54* (1998,) and *Wild Wild West* (1999). However, with the 2002 release of *Frida*, the artsy biopic about the queer-feminist-marxist-Chicana-Mexicana-Latina icon Frida Kahlo, Hayek recuperated her on-screen image and public Hollywood persona. In this essay I argue that Hayek the subject disrupts gendered, raced, and nationalistic borders, while Hayek the body remains constrained by a history of racialized and sexualized mainstream media representations. Using an ethnicities-in-relation approach[1] (Shohat and Stam 2003), the essay explores the relational construction of gender, sexuality, ethnicity, class, and nation through the commodified representations of Hayek's and Kahlo's identity and physicality. Furthermore, it examines how representations of Latinidad as circulated through public discourses about Hayek, Kahlo, and Hayek's performance of Kahlo connect to broader transformative notions of transnational identities.

Acknowledging the academic and political contestations surrounding the use of Latina as a panethnic label (Oboler 1995; Rodríguez 1997), this project builds on Frances Aparicio's (2003) conceptualization of popular representations of Latinidad as a site for the formation of public knowledge about, and exploration of, shared and distinct Latina subjectivities. Such a framework recognizes that actual and perceived differences and similarities exist among Latinas. Nevertheless, the analytical focus is on how mainstream popular culture frames public understandings of Latinidad and Latina identity and how these representations speak to emerging contemporary Latina identity positions. Thus, rather than elide the cultural distinctions that exist between Hayek and Kahlo or erase the problematic question surrounding the identification of Hayek and Kahlo, both Mexican-born and -raised, as panethnic Latinas, this essay engages public discourses of Latinidad surrounding both women as a method for exploring the complex nature of Latina identity.

Bridging the Transnational Latina Body

Since it is through women's bodies that the imagined nation is biologically reproduced and symbolically maintained, mainstream U.S. representations of sexuality are articulated through a complex matrix of nationality, race, class, and gender, predominantly enacted through women's bodies. More often than not it is the bodies of women of color that are controlled, patrolled, and ideologically disciplined through legal and cultural discourses (Barrera 2002; Hodes 1999). Within U.S. popular culture, Latinas are marginalized through racializing constructions of their sexuality as hyper and as a result transgressive of the dominant social order (Molina Guzmán 2005; Ruiz 2002). Examples include news stories about the U.S. Census that focus on a high birth rate among Latinas as a leading cause of demographic shifts, or the framing of Jennifer Lopez in entertainment coverage as sexually and financially excessive. Nevertheless, this eroticized threat of Latina hypersexuality is also a source of white heterosexual desire, opening a potential ideological space for counterdominant representational strategies.

The dual discourses of desire and transgression provide the context for analyzing the cultural role of popular representations of Hayek and Hayek's performance of *Frida*. Hayek functions as racial, sexual, transnational, and symbolic bridge between the representational politics of an exotic, ethnically ambiguous sexuality and a nationalistic, politicized sexuality that threatens to transgress normative definitions of Latina femininity and sexuality, as performed by Frida Kahlo. The remainder of this essay problematizes and recuperates the representations of Latina identity and sexuality as performed by Hayek and circulated through Hollywood movies and the popular news and entertainment media before and after the release of *Frida*. I focus on how narratives about Hayek's identity and sexuality connect with broader discourses about ethnicity, race, and nation, in particular issues of ethnic hybridity and authenticity. The essay concludes by exploring the tension between the representation of Latina sexuality as transgressive and the cinematic objectification of that sexuality as a commodity in the movie, *Frida*.

Performing Salma

Hayek herself acknowledges that before *Frida*, she was often typecast as Hollywood's twenty-first-century Latina Spitfire, reprising the role in at least three of her more successful films, *54*, *Desperado,* and *Fools Rush In*. In each of these films, Hayek portrays a sexually attractive, emotionally temperamental character who often speaks Spanish at the angry drop of a hat. For example, in the 1997 comedy *Fools Rush In*, Hayek portrays Isabel Fuentes, a character who becomes pregnant from a wild one-night stand with the WASPy Alex Whitman, played by Matthew Perry. A loud, talkative, devotedly Catholic, superstitious woman, Fuentes dresses in bright, colorful, revealing clothing and when angry resorts to rapid-fire Spanish, despite having lived most of her life in the United States. The entire film is a contrast in binary oppositions: high/low, Anglo/Mexican, wealthy/working class, urban/rural, rational/emotional, secular/religious, feminine masculinity/hypermasculinity. Through the binary positioning of the character's ethnicity, Fuentes's identity as a Mexican American woman is stabilized via a homogenizing vision of ethnicity that subverts the economic, religious, and cultural differences between Mexican American communities in the United States and reaffirms longstanding popular stereotypes about U.S. Latinas.

Throughout Hayek's Hollywood career, however, it is her sexuality and physically curvaceous body, rather than the performance of a specific ethnic identity, that have often been foregrounded. The hypersexualization of Hayek's body through the racialized articulation of Latina identity within these Hollywood texts is not surprising. For example, in Hayek's first Hollywood role, in the slasher comedy *From Dusk Till Dawn*, produced by Latino director Roberto Rodríguez, she plays a bikini-clad erotic dancer/vampire demon named Satanico Pandemonium who seduces and then attempts to murder the two Anglo protagonists. In another film, 54, Hayek portrays Anita, a married bisexual swinger/dance girl who works at the famous New York club, Studio 54. In contrast to her prudish Anglo husband, Anita is depicted as a morally wanton woman who openly and unproblematically exchanges her body for the right professional connections. Both of these movies, like others that incorporate secondary Latina characters, position Hayek's character as a sexualized ethnic spectacle. Her body provides a voyeuristic moment of sexual fantasy—a spectacle that freezes the cinematic narrative and titillates the audience.

As ambiguously ethnic characters, they are not explicitly identified by national origin but are still informed by the history of cinematic constructions of Latina hypersexuality. Cinematically, these two films position Hayek as a panethnic Latina who is simultaneously like dominant bodies and different from them. Paula Rothenberg (1992, 43) argues that

> Claims about difference are often difficult to deal with precisely because they are offered under the guise of value-free descriptions yet smuggle in normative consideration that carry with them the stigma of inferiority where white, male, middle-class, European, heterosexuality provides the standards of and the criteria for rationality and morality, difference is always perceived as deviant and deficient.

In Hayek's case, where racial and ethnic identity is cinematically undetermined, difference is usually marked by the performance of a hypersexuality that stands in opposition to white heteronormative definitions of socially appropriate feminine sexuality.

Despite the racialized hypersexuality of Hayek's many roles, she has also played against this type. For example, Hayek's 1998 role as the genderless muse Serendipity in Kevin Smith's *Dogma* provides a satirical perspective on Hollywood's stereotypical portrayal of femininity and female sexuality. We meet Serendipity dancing in a strip club to the song "Candy Girl." Her all-male audience is multiracial but segregated—the Anglo protagonist on one side of the stage and a group of men of color on the other. Serendipity uses her super-natural aura to mesmerize the men by sashaying from one side of the stage to the other as the men engage in a tipping war. She literally functions as racial bridge, moving between whiteness and racial otherness, manipulating the men's desire for her financial gain and eventually causing a brawl to erupt. In this instance, the biologically genderless Serendipity is more than a sexualized spectacle. Hayek plays one of the movie's central characters—a feminist who inspired the Bible and a social constructionist who grabs her breast in order to make the point to the main protagonist, Bethany (Linda Fiorentino), "*You* should know better than anyone that *these* don't make a woman."

Hayek's Spanish-accented English always already marks her ethnic difference, bringing to bear on her body a history of racialized and sexualized Western signifiers about Latinidad. A few examples froam the media of the signifying process at work are the teaser for Hayek's February 2003 *Vanity Fair* interview, titled "The Fire and Passion of Salma Hayek"; the October 2002 *Cleveland Call and Post* footer, "Showtime goes to the canvas with the spicy superstar"; and the July 1999 *InStyle* headline, "Salma Likes It Hot." When profiling the actress, U.S. journalists often emphasize accent as much as they do other characteristics. For example, in a September 2002 *Premier* interview, the reporter repeatedly emphasizes Hayek's accented pronunciations by transcribing them: "[*She starts to speak in her sing-songy voice—vowels are stretching, r's are rolling.*] We work in the *gaaarden*. We have Chai *teeeas* when we're on the phone or working on a script. We have lunch *outsiiiide*, with *sangriiia*" (Spines 2002, 40). Together with descriptions of her curvaceous body and exotic looks, Hayek's accent is foregrounded as part of the sexualization of her identity.

Commenting on the ethnic and sexual typecasting that dominated her early roles, Hayek has said:

> That sexual side is a very small part of me. But those characters were more a reflection of how other people saw me—it's more about who they are. I used to whine and complain about it. And then I said, no more. I was done sitting around complaining that I am the victim of a society that doesn't like my accent because it reminds them of their service people. (Spines 2002, 41)

Linking the hypersexuality of her cinematic roles to stereotypes about Spanish-dominant people with accented English, Hayek recognizes the racializing effect that language carries in the United States. Hayek's response to a column in *Vanity Fair* by Dame Edna satirizing a reader's question regarding the need to learn Spanish not only was featured in the magazine, it was also accompanied by a photograph of an angry Hayek yelling and throwing a punch, presumably at Dame Edna: "A victim of your column was interested in learning Spanish, and your response was 'Who speaks it that you are really desperate to talk to? The help? Your leaf blower?' The great irony is that I am Mexican, I speak Spanish, and I am on the cover of the very same issue" (Hayek 2003, 146). Despite her ability to perform across racial and ethnic types as a result of her unclassifiable physical appearance, Hayek acknowledges that her accented English reifies racial, ethnic, and class boundaries and reinforces the sexual exoticness of Latinidad.

Performing Ethnicity

Language and discourses about ethnic specificity are at the core of Hayek's attempts to recuperate her Hollywood image, starting with her production of the Frida Kahlo biopic. Rather than conforming to Hollywood's standards for Latina archetypes, Hayek redefines archetypes and opens the representational space for Latina/o actors and audiences. Part of the driving force behind Hayek's movie production company, Ventanarosa, is a desire to provide alternative narratives of Latina images and stories, her own included. Among other projects, Hayek directed for Showtime *The Maldonado Miracle*, a story about a young Mexican boy, and co-produced as well as starred in *In the Time of the Butterflies*, the highly acclaimed historical novel about three feminist Dominican revolutionaries written by Julia Alvarez. All the same, it is the role of Frida Kahlo that Hayek staked as hers more than twenty years ago. Not only did *Frida* provide a vehicle for Hayek to establish her credentials as a dramatic actress and producer (Hayek earned an Oscar nomination for best actress), but the media coverage surrounding the movie allowed Hayek to appropriate Kahlo as a nationalistic and feminist symbol.

By rejecting the label Latina in favor of Latin, Hayek chooses to highlight her Latin American heritage and Mexican national identity, including her accent and Spanish fluency, as privileged signs of her authentic identity. Notions of authenticity often elide the complexity of differences that define the postcolonial moment and may be more informative of how we inscribe ourselves through the bodies of others (Griffiths 1995). Hayek proudly markets herself and her production company as authentic by using the argument that only Spanish speakers born in the Spanish Caribbean, Mexico, or Central or South America are ethnically authentic Latinas. In a July 2001 article in *El Andar* on the battle for Kahlo between Hayek and Jennifer Lopez, both of whom sought to portray the artist, Hayek's claim to arbiter of authenticity was very much in evidence: "'Her [Lopez's] Spanish is very bad,' Hayek said, even though both films were in English, and 'now it's very convenient, because when she has to be Latin, she's Latin'" (Reynolds 2001, 39). However, by privileging her own ethnic nationality,

Hayek's representational project is constrained by the very discourse of linguistic purity and physicality that marginalizes her in Hollywood.

Throughout her bid to produce and star in *Frida*, Hayek exploited the nationalistic rhetoric of ethnic purity and homogeneity to argue that as the "true" or "pure" Mexican, she should be the one to portray Kahlo's life. This narrative of ethnic authenticity is circulated throughout Hayek's English and Spanish promotional campaign, such as in this October 2002 article by I. Sauceda in *La Opinión*:

> Con esto, Hayek ve uno de sus máximos anhelos cumplidos: "Como actriz, me gusta ser capaz de tener una voz y poder hablar de algo que me interesa. [Esta cinta] es una convicción. Una historia extraordinaria de una mujer extraordinaria. Valía la pena contar esta historia, que se desarrolla en un tiempo en que mi país era un lugar muy interesente. Aún lo es, pero es una parte de México con la cual la gente no está muy familiarizada. Así que me apasioné por contar la historia de los heroes con los que crecí, quise que el mundo supiera eso," expresó emocionada la bella actriz.
>
> [With this movie, Hayek accomplishes one of her major goals: "As an actress, I would like to be able to have a voice in order to talk about what interests me. [This film] is a conviction about an extraordinary woman with an extraordinary story. It was worth telling this story, which develops during a Mexican era in which my country was a very interesting place. Actually it still is, but this is a part of Mexico that few people know about. So I was very passionate about telling the story of the heroes that I grew up with. I wanted the world to know," the actress says with emotion.]

It is true that few mainstream audiences know about Kahlo or Kahlo's place in Mexican history, and Hayek herself acknowledges that a friend introduced her to Kahlo's work for the first time during her late teenage years and that her first response was one of aesthetic displeasure. Aside from Hayek's minor narrative embellishments, stories about her physical likeness, Mexican identity, and heritage are disseminated through the media as evidence of an ethnically privileged and biological connection to the role. Hayek uses nationality and language as the source of a pure or stable identity and therefore commodifiable authenticity in her production of *Frida*. Here Hayek's linguistic accent translates into a marketable cinematic signifier of ethnicity. Through *Frida*, Hayek ideologically recuperates her accent as a mechanism for establishing the movie's Mexican or ethnic *mise-en-scène* while keeping the movie accessible to English-speaking audiences.

The choice not to use Spanish may have made the movie more attractive to English-speaking audiences, but it infuriated many Mexican journalists and Mexican and Chicana/o activists, who interpreted the practice as a Malinche-style betrayal of an authentic Mexican and Chicana/o nationalist cultural icon. Diego Rivera's daughter publicly decried the movie, as did one of Mexico's most beloved actresses, Ofelia Medina, who portrayed Kahlo in Paul Leduc's rendition of the artist's life (Fein 2003). Despite the problematic nature of ethnic authenticity, these journalists and public figures argued that Kahlo, an authentic Mexican, would never have adapted her work for the sake of increasing sales to U.S. English-speaking audiences.

Nevertheless, Kahlo's signifying role in contemporary popular culture is complex. Representations of Kahlo, the Mexican feminist bisexual artist, and her artwork are among the most popular and commodified mainstream images of Latinidad globally, and in the United States in particular. Kahlo resisted homogenizing constructions of femininity, nationality, and sexuality, often using art as a form of personal intervention against the Western patriarchal gaze (Block and Hoffman-Jeep 1999; Franco, Pratt, and Newman 1999; Lindauer 1999; Volk 2000). Representations of her radical self-representations, such as Hayek's *Frida*, ironically recuperate and stabilize Kahlo's gender and ethnic politics within the contemporary global mainstream. Although Kahlo herself stands in for ethnic authenticity within the transnational space of global commodity culture, inside and across national borders both Hayek and her representation of Kahlo draw into question the political, cultural, and theoretical viability of authenticity.

The ethnic authenticity or nationalistic purity of both women is itself complicated. Hayek's father is Lebanese; Frida herself was half Mexican and half German-Hungarian, and prominently identified herself as Jewish, like her father. Thus, both women problematize notions of ethnic authenticity. Nestor García Canclini (2001) suggests that Latin American hybridity is best characterized as liminality, as the border space where stabilized homogeneous notions of identity and culture are decentered and negotiated. Hayek's privileging of her relationship to Kahlo through biological place of birth homogenizes and stabilizes divergent class, cultural, and political trajectories between both women and within Mexican society. Kahlo, a self-avowed Jewish communist with middle-class roots, never enjoyed her visits to the United States, while Hayek, the daughter of upper-class Catholic parents, continues to live an economically privileged lifestyle in the States. Moreover, the commodified signifiers most often associated with Kahlo, the indigenous skirts and shawls she preferred, represent Kahlo's own political and cultural appropriation of indigenous Mexican culture, a culture that remains marginalized within Mexican society. The unstable nature of Hayek's and Kahlo's identity demonstrates the complex process of hybridity at work.

Given Hollywood's longstanding narratives of Latina hypersexuality and the demand for the commodification of gendered ethnic bodies within global popular culture, it is not surprising that Kahlo's sexuality is privileged over Kahlo's leftist politics in the movie *Frida*. Kahlo's politics become the cinematic background to the spectacle of her sexuality and Hayek's physicality; the private sphere is commodified through the ethnic body for the public sphere. For instance, during the film's historically inaccurate representation of Kahlo's visit to New York City, her communist critique of U.S. conspicuous consumption is overshadowed by her lesbian affairs with Diego Rivera's lovers and the emotional suffering brought about by her miscarriage.

As Jean Franco observes with regard to the use of Kahlo to promote the 1990 exhibit of Mexican artists in the United States, "The private had not only become public, as feminists once claimed, but had become publicity" (Franco 1999, 43). Not surprisingly, Hayek's *Frida* is much more sexualized than Kahlo's own self-representations. Hayek's voluptuous body is highlighted through her performance of Kahlo as much as Kahlo's commodification of indigenous exoticness is foregrounded through Hayek's body. Although signified mostly in terms of traditional and indigenous Mexican dress and hairstyles, Hayek's performance of Kahlo is articulated through her difference in relation to the bodies of Anglo women. The articulation of difference through racialized opposition is a pattern particularly apparent during representations of the couple's time in New York or within their circle of elite political and cultural activists in Mexico. Indeed, the movie's exaggerated emphasis on Kahlo's ubiquitous unibrow, for which she has come to be known in global popular culture, is yet another signifier of this difference. Together, these cinematically contextual clues contribute to the general implicit message of exoticness through the sexualized commodification of ethnic otherness.

Conclusion

Hayek's cinematic and popular representation of Latinas problematizes homogenizing articulations of gender and ethnic identity circulated through the popular media. Such representations about Latinas not only inform contemporary U.S. culture and national identity, they also provide a site for examining postmodern transnational formations of ethnicity, gender and sexuality (Sobchack 1991). This essay has explored the narrative contradictions, oppositions, and continuities in mainstream meaning-making surrounding Hayek and Kahlo, Latinas who have been transformed from the localized construction of the individual to the symbolic arena (Molina Guzmán and Valdivia 2004). Thus the mainstream narratives surrounding them are both located within and transgress broader issues of ethnicity, gender, sexuality, and representation. The commercial strength of Latina bodies reflects an ideological shift in the cultural and economic marketplace, a marketplace driven less by rigid identity binaries than by hybridized narratives of identity (Dávila 2001; Halter 2000).

Nevertheless, the ambivalence surrounding Hayek and Kahlo suggests a potentially emancipatory challenge to, or at least an unsettling intervention in, Eurocentric discourses of authenticity. Representations of Kahlo and Hayek may be engaged in the service of selling products, but they can also vex notions of racial and national purity and therefore authentic ethnicity. Popular discourses surrounding Hayek and Kahlo disrupt some of Hollywood's symbolic boundaries surrounding ethnicity, race, gender, nation, and sexuality. As transnational figures, Hayek and Kahlo exist in the tension between the hybrid and the authentic that many diasporic cultures occupy. Kahlo, a German-Hungarian-Jewish-Mexican-identified individual, recuperates female sexuality and indigenous Mexican culture as a way of challenging the imperialistic Western gaze. Kahlo's exaggerated representations of her facial hair serve as a contemporary contestation of the Western commodification and celebration of prepubescent hairless, formless white bodies. As such, one would expect Kahlo to remain outside the realm of the sensual.

Indeed, for many U.S. journalists, Hayek's decision to don the infamous unibrow and mustache placed both women outside the socially acceptable boundary of desirability; and Hayek, often positioned at the site of glamour, was consistently asked to justify and explain her performance of "ugliness." In an interview with Hayek, Oprah Winfrey repeatedly remarked on the eyebrows: "I mean, I couldn't believe it—is that Salma—really, not a moment—there wasn't a breath—not a breath or an eyebrow . . . where you were not Frida" (Winfrey 2002). Despite Hayek's performance of nontraditional femininity, she ultimately takes Kahlo into the sensual and sexual. By visually highlighting her curvaceous body and Kahlo's bisexual identity as a cinematic narrative strategy, Hayek sexualizes Kahlo's body for the consumption of global audiences. She foregrounds the hypersexual construction of Kahlo's body to challenge mainstream narratives about Latinidad, while using Eurocentric discourses of ethnic purity to authorize and privilege her position relative to other iconic Latinas.

Although the stereotypic construction of Latina sexuality continues, popular representations of Hayek and Kahlo problematize the representations of Latina identity through dominant discourses about gender, ethnicity, and race. As independent, racially undetermined, ethnically hybrid, and transnational women, they rupture and affirm the borders marking contemporary significations of Latinas. The mediated circulation of Latina bodies renders Eurocentric discourses of racial and national purity more difficult to sustain. As such, it challenges us to reflect on the complex ways in which Latinas both disrupt the dominant binary racial order and serve as ambiguous symbols for marketing and selling difference.

Note

1. An ethnicities-in-relation approach analyzes the media narratives surrounding marginalized women across sexual, gender, racial, and ethnic backgrounds. Thus, for example, the narratives of working-class Puerto Rican women are discussed in relation to the narratives of wealthy Puerto Rican women, or the narratives of Haitian women are analyzed in relation to those of Mexican women, and so forth.

Bibliography

Aparicio, F. R. 2003. "Jennifer as Selena: Rethinking Latinidad in Media and Popular Culture." *Latino Studies* 1:90–105.

Barrera, M. 2002. "Hottentot 2000: Jennifer Lopez and Her Butt." In *Sexualities in History: A Reader*, ed. K. Phillips and B. Reay. New York: Routledge.

Block, R., and L. Hoffman-Jeep. 1999. "Fashioning National Identity: Frida Kahlo in 'Gringolandia.'" *Women's Art Journal* 19, no. 2: 8–12.

Dávila, A. M. 2001. *Latinos, Inc.: The Marketing and Making of a People*. Berkeley and Los Angeles: University of California Press.

Fein, S. 2003. "Film Reviews." *American Historical Review* 108, no. 4: 1261–1263.

Franco, J. 1999. "Manhattan Will Be More Exotic This Fall: The Iconization of Frida Kahlo." In *Critical Passions: Selected Essays*, ed. J. Franco, M. L. Pratt, and K. E. Newman, 39–47. Durham, NC: Duke University Press.

Franco, J., M. L. Pratt, and K. E. Newman. 1999. *Critical Passions: Selected Essays*. Durham, NC: Duke University Press.

García Canclini, N. 2001. *Consumers and Citizens: Globalization and Multicultural Conflicts.* Minneapolis: University of Minnesota Press.

Griffiths, G. 1995. "The Myth of Authenticity." In *The Post-Colonial Studies Reader,* ed. B. Ashcroft, G. Griffiths, and H. Tiffin, 237–241. London: Routledge.

Halter, M. 2000. *Shopping for Identity: The Marketing of Ethnicity.* 1st ed. New York: Schocken Books.

Hayek, S. 2003. Letter. *Vanity Fair,* March, 146.

Hodes, M., ed. 1999. *Sex. Love. Race: Crossing Boundaries in North American History.* New York: New York University Press.

Lindauer, M. 1999. *Devouring Frida: The Art History and Popular Celebrity of Frida Kahlo.* Middletown, CT: Wesleyan University Press.

López, A. 1991. "Are All Latins from Manhattan? Hollywood, Ethnography, and Cultural Colonialism." In *Unspeakable Images: Ethnicity and the American Cinema,* ed. L. D. Friedman, 404–424. Urbana-Champaign: University of Illinois Press.

Molina Guzmán, I. 2005. Gendering Latinidad Through the Elián News Discourse about Cuban Women. *Latino Studies* 3:179–204.

Molina Guzmán, I., and A. Valdivia. 2004. "Brain, Brow or Bootie: Iconic Latinas in Contemporary Popular Culture." *Communication Review* 7, no. 2: 203–219.

Oboler, S. 1995. *Ethnic Labels, Latino Lives: Identity and the Politics of (Re) Presentation in the United States.* Minneapolis: University of Minnesota Press.

Reynolds, J. 2001. "Las dos Fridas": Hollywood's Long, Slow Race to Make the Definitive Frida Kahlo Film. *El Andar,* July 31, 38.

Rodríguez, C. E. 1997. *Latin Looks: Images of Latinas and Latinos in the U.S. Media.* Boulder, CO: Westview Press.

Rothenberg, P. 1992. "The Construction, Deconstruction, and Reconstruction of Difference." *Hypatia* 5:43–57.

Ruiz, M. 2002. "Border Narratives: HIV/AIDS, and Latina/o Health in the United States. A Cultural Analysis." *Feminist Media Studies* 2:81–96.

Sauceda, I. 2002. "Salma le dio bienvenida a 'Frida.'" *La Opinion,* October 16, 1.

Shohat, E., and R. Stam. 2003. *Multiculturalism, Postcoloniality, and Transnational Media.* New Brunswick, NJ: Rutgers University Press.

Sobchack, V. 1991. "Postmodern Modes of Ethnicity." In *Unspeakable Images: Ethnicity in the American Cinema,* ed. L. D. Friedman, 329–352. Urbana-Champaign: University of Illinois Press.

Spines, C. 2002. "One from the Heart." *Premiere* 16 (February): 37–43, 85.

Stockwell, A. 2002. "The Velocity of Salma." *The Advocate,* December 10.

Valdivia, A. N. 2000. *A Latina in the Land of Hollywood and Other Essays on Media Culture.* Tucson: University of Arizona Press.

Volk, S. 2000. "Frida Kahlo Remaps the Nation." *Social Identities* 6, no. 2: 165–188.

Winfrey, O. "Movies You Should See." Transcript. *The Oprah Winfrey Show,* December 6.

CHAPTER 6

Is Penélope to J.Lo as Culture Is to Nature?

Eurocentric Approaches to "Latin" Beauties

ANGHARAD VALDIVIA

The disciplinary assumption that some films are "ethnic" whereas others are not is ultimately based on the view that certain groups are ethnic whereas others are not.

ELLA SHOHAT AND ROBERT STAM, *UNTHINKING EUROCENTRISM: MULTICULTURALISM AND THE MEDIA*

[A] critical reading of Hollywood's ethnographic discourse (a meta-ethnography) requires . . . the analysis of the historical-political construction of self-other relations—the articulation of forms of difference—sexual and ethnic—and an inscription of, among other factors, Hollywood's power as ethnographer, as creator, and translator of otherness.

A. M. LÓPEZ, *UNSPEAKABLE IMAGES: ETHNICITY AND THE AMERICAN CINEMA*

Contemporary discussions of Latinidad signal the rising importance of Latina/o studies as an emergent interdiscipline. Foregrounding the role of popular culture, media studies scholars explore the location and representation of Latina/o and Latinidad across a wide range of media. On the one hand, we have the rise of Latina/o-themed broadcasting programming and Hollywood film, Latina/o-focused magazines, and Latina/o media and cultural celebrities, each with a specific if in some cases overlapping history whose complexity and difference are erased in a new version of the so-called Latin boom. Yet we also have enduring tendencies that simplify and flatten difference, as demonstrated by the category of Latina/o that aims at panethnic, pan-national, and pan-American commonalities (Mayer 2003; Molina Guzmán 2005), without enough attention being paid to different historical and lived experiences.

Highlighted in all of this coverage are the bodies of women who stand for, or signify, far more than women.

Spanning many of these discussions is Jennifer Lopez, who is treated by all media, whether mainstream or ethnic, whether news or entertainment, whether national or Latin American and Peninsular—publications such as *InStyle*, *Vanidades*, and *¡Hola!*—as a media celebrity and mogul extraordinaire. J.Lo is the contemporary signifier for Latinidad and stands alone in a nearly iconic position vis-à-vis other mainstream Latina actresses-cum-entertainers. The fact remains, however, that there are other Latina/os who are often discussed in relation to and in concert with Jennifer. Mainstream Latinidad also includes some who are neither from the United States nor from Latin America. Foremost among them are a small number of relatively famous actors from Spain, including Antonio Banderas and Penélope Cruz. Quite often both are lumped into the discussion of Latinidad and categorized alongside the previously mentioned Latina/os, in locations ranging from Web sites and magazines to any kind of generalized Latina/o marketing strategy. In this essay I explore the relational representational strategies that are used for Jennifer Lopez and Penélope Cruz, both of whom sign in as Latinas but who have drastically different public images in the United States and thus in the many forms of U.S.-produced popular media, which often circulate globally.

Such an investigation is aided by the growing body of scholarship on contemporary and historical iconic U.S. Latinas such as Carmen Miranda, Dolores del Río, Lupe Vélez, Rosie Perez, Salma Hayek, and Jennifer Lopez. Scholars, both those represented in this book and others (e.g., Fregoso 1993, 2001, 2003; Hershfield 2000; López 1991, 1998; McLean 1992–1993; Ramírez Berg 2002; Shohat and Stam 1994), have studied their ethnic otherness, as well as the fact that it was no coincidence that they were all women. Women continue to function as a very powerful sign for identity and nation (Rakow and Kranich 1991). As van Zoonen (1994) notes, this is not a new phenomenon. Both France and the United States are symbolized by a woman, the virtuous revolutionary Marianne for the former and the Statue of Liberty for the latter. National differences, usually reduced to stereotypic ethnic characteristics, can also be reduced to relationality between women, as witness the two examples of the revolutionary French woman and the welcoming Lady Liberty, which provide a commentary on the identity of and difference between those two nations. Race, ethnicity, and class compose another layer of differentiation for the sign of woman within and between nations. This signification process can and has to be extended to the U.S. Latina, especially in relation to both

Latin America in general and individual Latin American nations and Spain in particular.

López (1991) forcefully argues that Latin American women, and by extension U.S. Latinas, pose a double threat, sexual and racial, to the dominant popular culture and social and political order of a nation that continues to see itself in terms of a dominant white identity and a black minority. This perceived double threat is problematic on both counts. First, in terms of white dominance, 1970 was the last year that U.S. Anglos reproduced in numbers large enough to replace themselves in the general population (Hacker 2000). Second, the United States is increasingly composed both of other ethnic groups and of hybridities within these. At the same time, the dominant minority in the United States is Latina/o, not black. Moreover, Latinas are also coded as posing a class threat to the middle-class-dominant national imaginary of the United States as threatening and inescapably working class. Issues of ethnicity and class are collapsed into their signification. An example is the Hollywood film actress Rosie Perez, who is Latina in films because she is working class and working class because she is Latina (Valdivia 1998). Accordingly, the sexual and racial threat represented by Latinas is likely to be overrepresented across a spectrum of discourses, ranging from the oversignified freeway signs that prominently depict female border-crossers, discussed by Ruiz (2002), which are now on a best selling T-shirt in Southern California, to the media saturation of images of popular Latinas such as Jennifer Lopez and Penélope Cruz. Latin[1] women continue to prominently sign in for sexual, class, and racial difference and excess, as we did at least once before, during the Good Neighbor Policy years. Latinas once again prominently grace the covers of our magazines, the screens of our theaters, and the many other locations where popular culture highlights particular bodies in a nearly ethnographic manner (López 1991). Finally, given the importance of the sign of woman as representing issues of nation, difference, and sexuality, it is not surprising that in today's market situation of synergy across media and general product domains, the bodies of women would lend themselves better to this diversified process of movie star, fashion spokesperson, and general style maven.

This essay proceeds through two theoretical steps, both undergirded by an exploration of contemporary mainstream popular media ranging from film roles as well as general interest magazine stories, television entertainment news, Web sites, and fashion and beauty industry ads. The first part explores the internally contradictory construction of Latinidad as an ethnic identity and segment of the population and market. Since Latina/os present an instance of hybridity, drawing the boundaries around and differentiating within this ethnic group is most challenging. Second, and building on the first part, this essay investigates the differential representation of these two "Latinas." The easiest way within the mainstream to build difference within difference, as within an already gendered ethnicity, is through class differentiation and national origin. Different nations signify different class valuations in global geopolitics. As usual, the most prominent examples include the bodies of women, and thus this case study focuses on Jennifer Lopez and Penélope Cruz.

Relationality and Ethnicities in Relation

As Latinas, at least according to their mainstream label, Jennifer and Penélope can be partially understood through the construction and deployment of a Latinidad that challenges binary constructions of identity. Binary divisions continue to form the backbone of interpretive strategies in the popular imaginary. Ethnic studies, although providing a necessary corrective to the Eurocentric approach to the study of culture, nonetheless tend to reformulate questions in terms of the white and the ethnic, thus reproducing the binary relation of "the West and the Rest." As many scholars have noted (e.g., Shohat and Stam 1994), this binary is often coupled to other Cartesian binaries, such as rational/irrational, mind/body, and culture/nature. The goal and challenge of ethnic studies as a discipline is to get beyond these binary categories, which artificially divide the world, its population, and its cultures. The binary as a category and a way of thinking, however, has proved particularly difficult to dislodge. Nevertheless, this is exactly what the component of ethnic studies known as Latina/o Studies tries to do, by recognizing the inherently fluid nature of what is comprehended by the elusive categories of Latina/o and Latinidad. Increased media coverage as a result of complex exogenous forces such as demographic data seized upon by both marketers and government officials and endogenous demands from within the various components of Latina/o communities have generated this still unsettled category. Given that prominent Latina/o studies scholars such as Arlene Dávila (2001) and Juan Flores (2000) have underscored the tendency for mainstream popular culture, media, and marketing to lump all difference among Latina/os into an undifferentiated pile, this essay suggests, as does Dávila (2002), that media industries are also beginning to pursue a parallel path of selective differentiation between and within types of Latinidad, often built on stereotype and essentialist national characteristics. Obviously, top-down forces will clash with community-generated demands, so the category is full of tension. At a theoretical level, the addition of Latina/os to the ethnic register complicates binary approaches to race and ethnicity and challenges all categories that proposed not only binary divisions but also purity at both ends of the scale. This course is also unsettling to a Cartesian-influenced intellectual culture that derives much of its explanatory framework from structuralist binary divisions. Both at the popular level and at the intellectual level, the introduction of Latina/os and Latinidad is challenging and unsettling.

There is a resulting tension within Latina/o studies and definitions of Latinidad and Latina/os from the creation of this pan-Latina/o category. Despite early proclamations of the brown or bronze race, contemporary scholars agree that Latina/os and Latinidad are far more complex than the one-toned approach would suggest. Although at the level of mainstream mass media there is the tendency toward a light brown signification strategy in terms of skin color, to be sure, many Latina/os identify with a nation, whereas others identify with the pan-national category that is about far more than national origin, whether in one's generation or in one's ancestry. At the level of representation of culture and family relationships, the flattening of difference is present not only within a particular ethnic category such as Latinidad (Dávila 2001) but also across ethnic categories (Halter 2000). Thus, scholars have begun to map out the implicit recognition of different discourses of Latinidad by both audiences and marketers (Dávila 2002). Especially in the United States, where the discussion, rhetoric, and discourse around race and ethnicity historically have centered and continue to do so around mutually exclusive categories of black and white populations, Latina/os, as well as other ethnic populations such as Asian Americans and Native Americans, have metaphorically and literally fallen through the cracks of political and symbolic discourses. Yet as of January 22, 2003, based on U.S. Census data, CNN reported that Latina/os had become the most numerous "minority" population in the United States, surpassing African Americans in terms of their absolute numbers and proportion of the total population. Nonetheless, despite this undeniable presence, which dates back centuries to the days before the United States became a nation, Latina/os continue to challenge binary and essentialist approaches to race (Chabram-Dernersesian 1997).

Beyond the wake-up call of including another ethnicity in the national imaginary and therefore expanding the ethnic register to a fluid spectrum rather than mutually exclusive categories, Latina/os remind us that there is no purity within Latinidad, or indeed within any ethnic category, and therefore there are no easy borders between ethnicities. The resulting effect is that of an internal contradictory tension. On the one hand, there is the effort to flatten all difference in the brown race. On the other hand, there is the recognition that not all browns are alike or that, indeed, not all Latina/os are brown. This is the terrain occupied by Jennifer and Penélope, whose brownness foregrounds the tension between sameness and difference.

Popular culture, including Hollywood film, is replete with egregious instances of the undifferentiated lumping of all things Latina/o or from south of the border. Pérez-Firmat (1994) includes a delightful and hilarious example in his book *Life on the Hyphen* of the film *Too Many Girls* (RKO, 1940). In the movie, Manuelito Lynch, a U.S. American football player from the Argentine provinces, is offered a sports scholarship to an Ivy League school, and ends up playing the conga drums in the desert in the film's finale. Pérez-Firmat comments:

> The picture of an Argentine Desi, dressed in football uniform, with a tumbadora slung around his neck, leading a conga in the New Mexico desert is a kind of mismash that makes Lucy's Carmen Miranda seem authentic by comparison. . . . *Too Many Girls* is a multiculturalist's nightmare. All of the principal American cultures are there—black, white, Indian, Hispanic; but every one is caricatured and distorted. . . . The town plaza becomes a melting pot. (54)

Pérez-Firmat focuses at once on Cuban American representations and on their relation to other Americanisms and the multicultural spectrum in the United States. As well, the iconic Carmen Miranda can be seen as, and has been studied as, the epitome of the floating Latin signifier, with strong shades of excess and hyperfertility (Shohat and Stam 1994). For example, in the film *Copacabana* (1947), she stars with Groucho Marx in a musical that elides Mexican, Argentine, and Brazilian iconography, to name the three most prominent sets of signifiers in the work. In yet another bit of evidence that all difference, not just Latin American difference, functions in relation to the normalizing discourses of U.S. whiteness, in *Copacabana*, Carmen Miranda portrays a performer who easily fools people by performing both a "Latin" Brazilian bombshell and a "French" persona, Mademoiselle Fifi! More contemporary examples from the movies include Salma Hayek's performance in *Fools Rush In*, where she plays a Mexican American woman whose salsa dancing evokes a much more Caribbean location than her landlocked rural Mexican origin would suggest. Food, too, signifies differences within Latinidad. Fashion spreads as well as food layouts that mix the wide array of colors, settings, and flavors particular to a region into an undifferentiated Southwestern, Latin American, and Spanish flair appear in most contemporary lifestyle magazines. Similarly, visits to most Latin or, worse yet, "world food" restaurants reveal a mishmash of ingredients, decorative details, music, and language that can sometimes be downright scary. As Halter (2000) has written, the marketing of ethnicity seems to be the new U.S. American identity, replacing the melting-pot metaphor. We now have a situation where everyone claims ethnic status and ethnicity is hypercommodified and increasingly undifferentiated.

Similarly, the contemporary Latina/o boom is often treated as if it referred to an undifferentiated and homogeneous group of peoples and cultural traditions. Dávila (2001) begins her book *Latinos Inc.* with a vignette of Telemundo launching its marketing strategy at a trade show, with Antonio Banderas as the spokesperson for Latinos. "Latinos are hot, and we are not the only ones to think so," he says. "Everyone wants to jump on the bandwagon, and why not? We have the greatest art, music, and literature. It's time we tell our stories" (1). That Antonio Banderas is Spanish (and continues to reside in Spain) is not deemed relevant in the launching of Latino marketing. Rather, for marketing purposes Banderas signs in as quintessentially Latin—thus demonstrating both the vexed relationship between Latinidad and peninsular peoples and the fact that, in some warped way, the U.S. Census Bureau's category of Hispanic executes a far broader and insidious cultural elision. As Dávila (2001) correctly notes,

> Following the nationalist underpinnings underlying contemporary representations of culture and identity, in which cultures are seen as bounded and contained entities, tied to a territory, a past, and a heritage, it is Latin America rather that a deterritorialized U.S.-Latino culture that has traditionally been valorized as the source of cultural authenticity in Latino/Hispano culture. (79)

We cannot ignore the enduring Spanish heritage that continues to be treated as a contemporary source of Latinidad, both in the commodified popular culture and in many Latina/o communities. If, as Dávila suggests, Latin America is the origin of authenticity in the United States, Spain bears the mantel of that role for much of Latin America, with some exceptions for an indigenous authenticity (Aztec, Mapuche, Aymará, others).

Thus we have to recognize that the deterritorialization has to include the possibility of Spain, and to a lesser extent Portugal, as sources of authenticity and belonging.

In an essay on Spanish-language media in the U.S., Dávila (2002) notes that Latina/o audiences recognize the marketing effort to acknowledge Latina/o difference yet resist the strategy that essentializes national characteristics, "[leaving] us with the impression that there are no blacks in Mexico, blondes in the Dominican Republic, or brunettes in Argentina" (29). If we trace this racionational essentialism back to colonial times, we can examine the Mexican *casta* paintings (Klor de Alva 1996) as an early colonial instance of the effort to regulate difference within the Spanish colonies (which included portions of what is now known as the United States), as well as to reify the whiteness of the Spanish. However, Spain was, and remains, far from the epitome of religious and racial purity (Menocal 2002). Muslims, Christians, and Jews from diverse national origins coexisted in medieval al-Andalus, and their cultural and population traces can still be found throughout Spain, Portugal, and the Americas. The hybrid mixture of native Americans, Asian, African, and European populations—all of them hybrids of hybrids—resulted in a very diverse Latin America. However, we have to complicate not only the racial diversity within U.S. Latinas/os and Latin Americans but among the Spanish as well—that is, the Spanish are a hybrid population.

Issues of differentiation inevitably run against notions of authenticity, as the latter become a way to police the borders around this newly constructed ethnic category. If there is more than one Latinidad, then there will be efforts to mark one version as more authentic than the others. This will be accomplished partly through appeals to national origin, language, and skin color. Scholars (Dávila 2002; Levine 2001; Valdivia 2003, 2004) have begun mapping differentiation within Latinidad. Positing two competing discourses, and drawing on Hamid Naficy, Levine (2001, 34) explores the tension between the syncretic and the hybrid, with the former a "more stable, longer lasting, less ambivalent" and more marketable, "more livable and more comfortable" identity. The marketplace seeks to resolve tensions of the unstable and ever-shifting hybridity through consumerism in the construction of a syncretic vehicle such as Telemundo, which abandons the traditional discourse of Latinidad. Whereas marketers prefer to trigger pan-Latin and panethnic forms of identification rather than nation-specific ones, Dávila (2001) argues they still reiterate preexisting ethnoracial hierarchies that favor lighter and standard Spanish speakers over darker Spanglish others. As well, there are U.S. regional difference between Western Mexican- and Eastern Caribbean-identified populations. These differences extend far beyond nation into food, Spanish, music, and, in sum, major cultural differences and histories. Piggybacked onto these is the frame of reference, to Latin America, and possibly all the way back to Spain, or to the United States itself as a site of authentic Latina/o culture. Jennifer Lopez and Penélope Cruz bear traces of that complicated genealogy because they are both signified as Latinas but differentiated as Nuyorican or Spanish/Hispanic within Latinidad.

Jennifer and Penélope

Despite two major bombs, *Gigli* (2003), which caused her role in *Jersey Girl* (2004) to be nearly entirely edited out, Lopez continues to appear in movies such as *Shall We Dance?* (2004), *Monster-in-Law* (2005), and *Bordertown* (2006), in which she co stars with major Hollywood talent such as Jane Fonda, Antonio Banderas, Richard Gere, Susan Sarandon, and Robert Redford. The unflattering personal coverage following the dissolution of her engagement to Ben Affleck subsided after her marriage to fellow Nuyorican Marc Anthony. She appears to be charting a much different public persona with this latest marriage, one in which she is less extravagant and more grounded in Latina/o culture. Following her popularity as a recording artist, with a string of music video hits that included "Jenny from the Block" and "Love Don't Cost a Thing," she continues to release music albums such as *Get Right* and *Rebirth* (both in 2005). She is a fashion maven with expanding and highly profitable lines of casual and couture wear, the latest of which she introduced during the 2005 Fashion Week in New York City. In sum, Jennifer Lopez has succeeded in becoming that most coveted form of media personality, a brand that can be marketed across a wide array of goods and services, media and nonmedia (Klein 2001). Accordingly, she continues to grace the covers of magazines from *Bazaar* to *InStyle*, *People*, *Redbook*, *Vanity Fair*, *Elle*, and *Rolling Stone*. Jennifer Lopez is a bona fide star, media mogul, and brand. Moreover, as she has crossed over into mainstream representations, she cannot be contained within an ethnic identity. She graces the covers not only of Latina/o media but of media in general. Her personal life is the stuff of front-page entertainment news. She does not play only Latina/o or even ethnic characters but a wide spectrum of possibilities ranging from the hyper-Latina character in *Selena* to the ethnically ambiguous women in *Wedding Planner* and *Shall We Dance?* She is a crossover success.

Penélope Cruz has yet to achieve that level of fame in the U.S. mainstream, although one could argue that she remains famous in her native Spain,[2] where in 1998 she was voted the most beautiful actress. She played the ingénue in Bigas Lunas's *Jamón Jamón* (1992)—a huge Spanish, Latin American, and European hit—and the pregnant nun with AIDs in the Almodovar film, *Todo sobre mi madre* (*All About My Mother*), which won an Oscar for Best Foreign Film in 1999. She has mounted a full-force attempt to cross over into the U.S. market, with some success. She is the face and body of Ralph Lauren fashions and continues to appear in Hollywood films such as *Blow* (2000), *Captain Corelli's Violin* (2000), *Vanilla Sky* (2001), and *Head in the Clouds* (2004), and *Sahara* (2005). As well, she is developing a charitable reputation through financial contributions to Sister Teresa's children's sanctuary in Calcutta and collaboration with Antonio Banderas and Melanie Griffith on Spanish children charities. Her appearance in Coke ads, à la Cindy Crawford, illustrated her mainstream location.

Despite her considerable success, Penélope Cruz is neither the mogul nor the brand that Jennifer Lopez has become; nonetheless, it is useful to study their relational representations. Although they have followed different career and geographic trajectories, there are some commonalities between these two actresses. To begin with, both are treated as Latinas within the mainstream U.S. imaginary, which includes some scholars.[3] Both trained in dance. Both sought crossover success in the U.S. mainstream, Jennifer from the background of Latina dancer and Penélope from Spanish and European fame. Both share a thinning of their bodies and a straightening of their hair as they get closer to the U.S. mainstream, with older photographs showing much fuller bodies and hair. Both somatically fit the stereotype of Latinas in U.S. popular culture—nearly white, but brown enough to count as different; and in their personal lives, both women have had highly publicized relationships with major Hollywood white male stars that enhanced their access to the limelight. Other differences such as accent or height do not figure prominently in still shots, although in film, the accent has resulted in much more traditional Latina roles for Penélope than for Jennifer—witness Cruz's portrayal of the scheming and eventually drug-addicted and child-abandoning Colombian ex-wife in *Blow*. Neither *Maid in Manhattan* nor *Selena*, the two most stereotypical J.Lo movies so far, played up the sexual and racial double-threat discourse as much as that single role in *Blow*. In those three movies, as well as in three of the four images included in this essay, J.Lo's bootie gets top billing over the more subtle portrayal of Penélope's body.

Jennifer Lopez and Penélope Cruz make sense in relation to each other and to the history of gendered and racialized representation within the popular terrain of U.S. mainstream culture. Whereas "blonde girl dressed in white usually signifies innocence and probity, just as dark haired women tend to signify danger and sexuality" (van Zoonen 1994, 74), the system of meaning for these two actresses has to be analyzed discursively in relation to each other and against the backdrop of both whiteness and blackness as two opposite ends of a spectrum of racial signification, and upper class and working class as two ends of a spectrum of class signification. Although both women have long brown hair, dyed to fit the occasion, and attractive facial features, their body shapes are quite different. Jennifer has a curvaceous body with a butt that has nearly eclipsed the rest of her body in fame; Penélope is a thin beauty whose fame has yet to be reduced to a single body part. Within Latina/o studies, much has been written about Jennifer Lopez (Aparicio 2003; Barrera 2002; Fiol-Matta 2002; Molina Guzmán and Valdivia 2004; Negrón-Muntaner 1997). Foremost among the topics is her butt (Barrera 2002; Negrón-Muntaner 1997). Little or nothing has been written about Penélope's body. Although this is not surprising, insofar as she has not achieved Lopez's level of prominence, it can also be partly explained by the embodied coverage of Jennifer in relation to the disembodied approach to Penélope. Thus we can analyze some of the widely available images of these two actresses to study their relationality within Latinidad.

Scholars explore the relational meaning between ethnicity, whiteness, and blackness that allows Jennifer's butt (the exact name of Negrón-Muntaner's 1997 essay) to sign in for difference. Molina Guzmán and Valdivia (2004) trace the history of the Hottentot Venus through Jennifer's body and her contemporary location as an eroticized and ethnicized body in relation to white normativity and black unacceptability. Other scholars have traced the "homology between the lower bodily stratum and the lower social classes" (Kipnis 2001, 136). Within the context of the control that the bourgeois political project seeks over the body, Kipnis adds that the body thus becomes a "privileged political trope of the lower social classes" (137). Since difference is constructed discursively through the body, the relative attention given to these two women's bodies and their component body parts speaks to their individual location within the terrain of popular culture as representatives of ethnic and class affiliations. While Jennifer Lopez undeniably has received far more media coverage and media participation (such as interviews), we can nonetheless choose more or less characteristic representations of these two so-called Latinas.

Whereas Jennifer Lopez continues to perform her embodied and butted Latinidad, Penélope Cruz's body and butt are represented in a totally different manner. Since Jennifer Lopez is nearly ubiquitous in the popular media, her representations range from the full body shot to the extreme close-up, yet a significant portion of those representations focus on her butt. The images in Figures 6.1 through 6.4 illustrate what I mean. Although the poses are somewhat similar—each model is shown here first in a relaxed, somewhat domestic environment, followed by an upright formal pose with the body three-quarters turned away from the camera—the representations are markedly different, roughly translating as eroticism versus purity. These images, all from popular magazine covers and therefore circulating within popular culture, bear closer analysis.

Many of the themes or discourses surrounding these women that I have discussed in this chapter are exemplified in these advertising photographs in terms of text, practices, and institutions. Among the possible units of analysis, I focus on the body through the face/gaze and the butt. The headline for both *Parade* covers speaks to a third unit of analysis, the text, one that frames these actresses differently. Finally, the implied setting speaks to issues of location, which often speak to issues of class (Valdivia 1997).

The Face/Gaze

Both in her cover shot in *Parade* and the ad for Obsession, Penélope looks at the viewer with a direct and steady gaze, a very different facial expression from Jennifer Lopez's playful, friendly, invitingly subtle smile. As Goffman (1987/1976, 48) has noted, "smiles . . . function as ritualistic mollifiers, signaling that nothing agonistic is intended or invited." Representations of Penélope focus on her face or consist of cropped shots of her upper body, like the *Parade* cover, or less often, as in the Obsession ad, show her face and torso. Her face is usually serious, as in the *Parade* cover, or suggests the most subtle of smiles,[4] an arrangement evoking centuries of classical paintings of women in repose (Berger 1977). She is seldom portrayed smiling. The invitation experienced through Jennifer Lopez's smile and expression can be juxtaposed to Cruz's serious facial expression. If smiles and licensed withdrawal are two components of the feminine ritualization of subordination (Goffman 1987/1976) that have been coded into visual popular culture, including advertising photographs, then a reposeful, serious look into the camera can be said to function as more rational and therefore powerful stance. Although both women pose so as to turn themselves into objects of vision (Berger 1977), Penélope stares at us from

Figure 6.1. In this cover shot from the December 8, 2002, *Parade* magazine, Jennifer sits against an off-white backdrop with the discursive hook of "I know true love is my destiny." She is photographically presented with straightforward emphasis on her body and slightly touseled hair (an exotic wife?).

Figure 6.2. In an image from the September 2001 issue of *Stuff for Men*, coy (non)disclosure has replaced the more "natural" look of the *Parade* cover. Jennifer Lopez's back is facing the viewer, and she is naked but for her butt, which is covered by a ruffled pink panty. The headline reads "J.Lo (Delicious New Photos!) Jennifer Lopez! Officially the galaxy's most beautiful woman." What was covered up in the *Parade* cover is now revealed or alluringly protected by bare arms.

the location of leisure, privilege, and power. The camera invites us to focus on her face, which within Western regimes of representation stands for the brain, culture, and the thinking part of our body.

The Butt

Whereas Penélope is most often represented in terms of her face, Jennifer is undeniably represented in terms of her butt. This is not to say that Jennifer's face is excluded, but rather that the image guides one's vision toward the butt. Figure 6.2, a *Parade* cover, showing Jennifer smiling at us from a seated position, is to be contrasted to Figure 6.4, the Obsession ad, where the viewer is just able to glimpse Penélope's extended body, including her very thin butt. The Obsession ad comes closest to showing Penélope's entire body in general and her bootie in particular. It is im-

Figure 6.3. The representation of Penélope Cruz is much different from that of Jennifer Lopez. The two images chosen for this essay speak to her representation as "beyond beauty," the title of the article about her in the August 2002 issue of *Parade*. In this portrait she is presented as ethereal, abstracted, her dark hair a gestural swoop slicing across the undifferentiated blanc de blanc coverall she wears. Figure 6.4. Penélope Cruz in an ad for Ralph Lauren's Obsession perfume, available in 2002. This photograph is the right-hand side of a diptych. The left side shows a close-up of the bottle of perfume. Although her body is angled away from the camera, similar to Jennifer Lopez's pose on the cover of *Stuff for Men*, the portrayal is much more modest. Her long hair curls in to cover her shoulders rather than revealing them (as in J.Lo's photograph). The angle of the shoulder, almost in dead center of the photograph, points to tight graphic control of the image that renders the body an abstraction, and her eye, the punctum of the photo, aimed directly at the viewer, to the degree that her eyebrow wings away from her direct gaze, is a rifle shot of purity and abstraction.

mediately evident that Penélope's bootie is much smaller than Jennifer's, that being one of the main body differences between the two actresses. In fact, Jennifer's butt is the focus of the *Stuff for Men* cover, a trope that is repeated in many of the images of her that circulate in popular culture. A butt-focused pose is unusual both in traditional artworks and in contemporary advertisements. In fact, it can be said that Jennifer has single-handedly ushered in a butt focus in contemporary U.S. popular culture and therefore has intervened in the codes of beauty and femininity that until quite recently relied exclusively on the nearly buttless look of Penélope's

Obsession pose. We might go so far as to say that Jennifer is represented in terms of her butt, and that her butt represents ethnic difference. Neither the pose nor the color nor the clothing detracts from the focus on her butt. All contribute to its foregrounding and celebration.

The Text

Indeed, Penélope's body recedes into the background of her foregrounded "beauty"—a beauty that is about her entire self and is bigger than she and more than beauty, as the "beyond beauty" title of *Parade* magazine suggests. Should we ask ourselves what is beyond beauty, some of us might reach a nearly Arnoldian space of culture as being "a study of perfection . . . the scientific passion for pure knowledge, but also of the moral and social passion for doing good" (quoted in Giles and Middleton 1999, 11). In fact, that passion is quoted in the subtitle as "the wisdom and compassion that add to her appeal"—quite different from the more tropicalist codes (Aparicio and Chávez Silverman 1997), which are usually anchored by allusions to heat and sexual allure. Added to her location of power, Cruz representationally occupies a position of privilege in relation to discourses of culture. She stands for beauty and perfection—the Arnoldian definition of culture—in contradistinction to the popular terrain occupied by Jennifer Lopez.

In contrast, the headline in *Parade* for Jennifer alludes to the star's "two failed marriages" and her search for "true love" in terms of "destiny." Nothing is mentioned about beauty, wisdom, and compassion, just as nothing is mentioned in Penélope's headline about her desire for true love and her recent participation in the break-up of another marriage and family. Thus the headlines differentially set these two women up as one searching for her destiny "despite" failed marriages and the other embodying beauty and wisdom. Their personal histories are foregrounded for Jennifer and backgrounded for Penélope, and their intrinsic value is set in terms of antihumanist destiny for Jennifer and liberal formulations of high culture and individual agency for Penélope.

The Setting

Another potential basis for analyzing representations is the implied setting of the picture. Here the difference is also striking. Whereas Penélope appears to occupy some undetermined space of high-class leisure—first in a hammock, later on the way to and from an urban and therefore cosmopolitan party—Jennifer sits and stands against an off-white backdrop. Lavish settings function as signifiers for class and leisure, and the lack of a setting is more often used in appeals to or codings of the working class (Kipnis 2001; Valdivia 1997). Jennifer assumes not only an inviting smile but also a more purposeful posture—a "come hither" rather than a "look at me" pose. She does not necessarily call us from a space of leisure but more likely from a position of labor.

Conclusion

As Latina/o bodies compose an ever-growing proportion of the U.S. population and begin to populate the representational terrain of popular culture, we can begin to discern two parallel strategies. First, there is the lumping of all that is Latina/o into an undifferentiated, homogeneous pile. Second, and in response to niche marketing approaches as well as to demands for more culturally sensitive portrayals, there is a growing acknowledgment of the need to differentiate within difference. Through a case study of Latinas in general and Jennifer Lopez and Penélope Cruz in particular, we can see both of these contradictory tendencies. Furthermore, the difference between these two is not value neutral, as they fall into a hierarchy of value and authenticity. First, both actresses, though quite different in origin, are treated as Latinas. Second, their representation differs markedly. Jennifer Lopez's embodied figure foregrounds her excessive butt as a site of both desire and difference, her smile inviting enjoyment and consumption. Penélope Cruz dares us to partake of or reach for her privileged space, in that evanescent imaginary country club she appears to occupy. The relationality between these two actresses speaks not only to their individually represented difference but also to broader discourses of Latinidad, authenticity, and the nature/culture binary. Jennifer Lopez as a Nuyorican, with the signification that that term carries of internal minority and relation to an Afro-Caribbean island, signs closer to the body and nature. Her inauthentic status is cemented both by the fact that she is U.S. referent, a Nuyorican, not a Puerto Rican, and by the fact that her Spanish is not native or perfect. Penélope Cruz, with her Spanish heritage and therefore the ancestry of imaginary whiteness, wins high marks for authenticity because of her grounding in Spain, the origin of authenticity, and because she is a native Spanish speaker. Although both women somatically are light brown and quite similar in color, they are coded as different. The matrix of signification places one of them much closer to bourgeois culture and whiteness and the other closer to nature and blackness, without either explicitly uttering the two outer edges of the racial economy. Whereas both are able to parlay their star status into product endorsements, it is imperative to note that Cruz has become the cover girl for Ralph Lauren, a signifier of upscale consumerism, whereas Lopez has developed her own product lines, usually anchored to her difference, with her high-culture crossover Luis Vuitton deal having been short and temporary. While it is undeniable that Lopez is the more successful entrepreneur of the two, it is also evident that in a hierarchy of value, white, European, upper-middle-class culture signs in higher than brown, U.S. Latina/o, working-class nature. Exogenous mainstream market forces recognize differences within Latinidad, as do internal Latina/o forces. This essay suggests that within Latinidad, Europeanness may very well act much as whiteness does in terms of the general U.S. racial topography—that is, it stands for everything, including that imaginary prevalence of the middle class, and nothingness. As well, it falls into another powerful and familiar binary division of nature/culture, where the European once more signs in for culture, whether within or outside of the West, and the natives, whether Latin American or U.S. Latina/o continue to sign in for nature and the working class.

Notes

I thank Isabel Molina Guzmán, Kumarini Silva, and Susan Harewood for technical help with the images and for their sustained scholarly discussion group, which nourished this essay well before it was begun.

1. I use the term Latin deliberately because it is much broader than Latin American or Latina, being applicable to Italian and even Greek women as a means of denoting some sort of Mediterranean origin and complexion.

2. Penélope's career in Spain, like Salma Hayek's in Mexico, was stellar and spectacular. However, this essay examines the contemporary situation in mainstream U.S. culture.

3. A recent blind review of an essay I wrote on Jennifer Lopez asked why I did not study that other Latina, Penélope Cruz.

4. I showed this image to a number of friends, colleagues, and family, and none of them thought she was smiling.

Bibliography

Aparicio, Frances R. 2003. "Jennifer as Selena: Rethinking Latinidad in Media and Popular Culture." *Latino Studies* 1:90–105.

Aparicio, Frances R., and Susanna Chávez-Silverman, eds. 1997. *Tropicalizations: Transcultural Representations of Latinidad*. Hanover, NH: Dartmouth College/ University Press of New England.

Barrera, Magdalena. 2002. "Hottentot 2000: Jennifer Lopez and Her Butt." In *Sexualities in History: A Reader*, ed. Kim M. Phillips and Barry Reay. New York: Routledge.

Berger, John. 1977. *Ways of Seeing*. New York: Penguin.

Chabram-Dernesesian, Angie. 1997. "On the Social Construction of Whiteness Within Selected Chicana/o Discourses." In *Displacing Whiteness: Essays in Social and Cultural Criticism*, ed. R. Frankenberg, 107–164. Durham, North Carolina: Duke University Press.

Dávila, Arlene. 2001. *Latinos Inc.: The Marketing and Making of a People*. Berkeley and Los Angeles: University of California Press.

———. 2002. "Talking Back: Spanish Media and U.S. Latinidad." In *Latina/o Popular Culture*, ed. M. Habell-Pallán and M. Romero, 25–37. New York: New York University Press.

Fiol-Matta, L. 2002. Pop Latinidad: Puerto Ricans in the Latin Explosion, 1999. *CENTRO Journal* 14, no. 1: 27–51.

Flores, Juan. 2000. *From Bomba to Hip-Hop: Puerto Rican culture and Latino identity*. New York: Columbia University Press.

Fregoso, Rosa Linda. 1993. *The Bronze Screen: Chicana and Chicano Film Culture*. Minneapolis: University of Minnesota Press.

———. 2003 *MeXicana Encounters: The Making of Social Identities in the Borderlands*. Berkeley and Los Angeles: University of California Press.

Fregoso, Rosa Linda, ed. 2001. *Lourdes Portillo:* The Devil Never Sleeps *and Other Films*. Austin: University of Texas Press.

Giles, Judy, and Timothy Middleton. 1999. *Studying Culture: An Introduction*. London: Blackwell.

Goffman, Erving. 1987/1976 *Gender Advertisements*. New York: Harper and Row.

Hacker, A. 2000. "The Case Against Kids." *New York Review of Books*, November 30, 12–17.

Halter, Marilyn. 2000. *Shopping for Identity: The Marketing of Ethnicity*. New York: Schocken Books.

Hershfield, Joanne. 2000. *The Invention of Dolores del Río*. Minneapolis: University of Minnesota Press.

Kipnis, Laura. 2001. "(Male) Desire and (Female) Disgust: Reading *Hustler*." In *Popular Culture: Production and Consumption*, ed. C. Lee Harrington and Denise D. Bielby, 123–132. London: Blackwell.

Klein, Naomi. 2001. *No Logo*. London: Flamingo.

Klor de Alva, Jorge J. 1996. "Mestizaje from New Spain to Aztlán: On the Control and Classification of Collective Identities." In *New World Orders: Casta Paintings and Colonial Latin America*, ed. Ilona Katzew, 58–71. New York: Americas Society.

Levine, E. 2001. "Constructing a Market, Constructing an Ethnicity: U.S. Spanish-Language Media and the Formation of a Syncretic Latino/a Identity." *Studies in Latin American Popular Culture* 20:33–50.

López, A. M. 1991. "Are All Latins from Manhattan? Hollywood, Ethnography, and Cultural Colonialism." In *Unspeakable Images: Ethnicity and the American Cinema*, ed. L. D. Friedman, 404–424. Urbana: University of Illinois Press.

———. 1998. "From Hollywood and Back: Dolores del Río, a Trans(national) Star." *Studies in Latin American Popular Culture* 17:5–33.

Mayer, V. 2003. *Producing Dreams, Consuming Youth: Mexican Americans and Mass Media*. New Brunswick, NJ: Rutgers University Press.

McLean, A. L. 1992–3 "'I'm a Cansino': Transformation, Ethnicity, and Authenticity in the Construction of Rita Hayworth, American Love Goddess." *Journal of Film and Video* 44, no. 3–4 (Fall–Winter).

Menocal, María Rosa. 2002. *The Ornament of the World: How Muslims, Jews, and Christians Created a Culture of Tolerance in Medieval Spain*. Boston: Little, Brown.

Molina Guzmán, Isabel. 2005. "Gendering Latinidad Through the Elián News Discourse about Cuban Women." *Latino Studies* 1:1–26.

Molina Guzmán, Isabel, and Angharad N. Valdivia. 2004. "Brain, Brow or Bootie: Latinas in Contemporary Popular Culture" *Communication Review* 7, no. 2: 205–221

Navarro, Mireya. 2002. "Raquel Welch Is Reinvented as a Latina." *New York Times*, June 11, sec. D1.

Negrón-Muntaner, Frances. 1991. "Jennifer's Butt." *Aztlán* 22, no. 2: 182–195.

Pérez-Firmat, G. 1994. *Life on the Hyphen: The Cuban-American Way*. Austin: University of Texas Press.

Rakow, Lana, and Kimberly Kranich. 1991. "Woman as Sign in Television News." *Journal of Communication* 41, no. 1: 8–23.

Ramírez Berg, Charles. 2002. *Latino Images in Film: Stereotypes, Subversion, Resistance*. Austin: University of Texas Press.

Ruiz, Maria Victoria. 2002. "Border Narratives, HIV/AIDS, and Latina/o Health in the United States: A Cultural Analysis." *Feminist Media Studies* 2, no. 1: 37–62.

Saldivar, José David. 1997. *Border Matters: Remapping American Cultural Studies*. Berkeley and Los Angeles: University of California Press.

Shohat, E. 1991. "Ethnicities-in-Relation: Toward a Multicultural Reading of American Cinema." In *Unspeakable Images: Ethnicity and the American Cinema*, ed. L. D. Friedman, 215–250. Urbana: University of Illinois Press.

Shohat, Ella, and Robert Stam. 1994. *Unthinking Eurocentrism: Multiculturalism and the Media*. New York: Routledge.

Valdivia, Angharad. 1997. "The Secret of My Desire: Gender, Class, and Sexuality in Lingerie Catalogs." In *Undressing the Ad: Reading Culture in Advertising*, ed. K. T. Frith, 225–250. New York: Peter Lang.

———. 1998. "Stereotype or Transgression? Rosie Perez in Hollywood Film." *The Sociological Quarterly* 39, no. 3: 393–408.

———. 2000. *A Latina in the Land of Hollywood*. Tucson: University of Arizona Press.

———. 2001. "Community Building Through Dance and Music: Salsa in the Midwest." In *Double Crossings: Entre Cruzamientos*, ed. M. M. Flores and C. von Son, 153–176. New Jersey: Ediciones Nuevo Espacio.

————. 2003. "Radical Hybridity: Latina/os as the Paradigmatic Transnational Post-Subculture." In *The Post-Subcultures Reader*, ed. D. Muggleton and R. Weinzierl. London: Berg Publishers.

————. 2004. "Latinas as Radical Hybrid: Transnationally Gendered Traces in Mainstream Media." *Global Media Journal* 2:4. http://lass.calumet.purdue.edu/cca/gmj/refereed.htm.

van Zoonen, Liesbet. 1994. *Feminist Media Studies*. London: Sage.

CHAPTER 7

Jennifer Lopez

The New Wave of Border Crossing

TARA LOCKHART

Jennifer Lopez is the only celebrity ever to have a number one movie at the box office and simultaneously a number one record on the billboard charts. She has moved from stage to television, from films to record deals, from videos to her own clothing lines and perfume labels. Lopez's rise to stardom raises interesting questions about crossover status, particularly as it involves crossing ethnic and racial borders. This essay considers the ways that Lopez's ethnic star text is co-produced and adapted by diverse audiences, fans, and Lopez herself. First I consider Lopez's portrayal of Tejana crossover music star Selena, positioning this performance as the catalyst for Lopez's breaking into multiple media markets. I then situate Lopez within broader conversations about crossover stardom to consider the ways that her star text circulates for multiple ethnic and racial populations. Crossover here becomes the ability to move between and among bodily significations, to be both situated in and destabilized by multiple star texts and social discourses.[1]

Crossing Over: The Selena Phenomenon

The music is also who I am. And the music is what it is, it's Latin soul, because of where I'm from. The fact that I grew up in the Bronx. . . . I was influenced by R&B and hip-hop, but on the holidays I would listen to salsa, meringue . . . that's what my music is. It's really who I am and where I'm from.

JENNIFER LOPEZ

Ironically, it was the role that Lopez played in the 1997 film *Selena* that made possible not only Lopez's music but also this characterization of her music. Director Gregory Nava chose Lopez from among over two thousand actresses to play Selena on-screen, a role that launched Lopez's career as an actress and motivated her move to music.

Noted for her charisma and talent, Selena Quintanilla was a true crossover music phenomenon. Killed by her business manager just as her career was beginning to peak, Selena was succeeding in the male-dominated world of Tejano music and crossing over into mainstream American venues as well. Her immense popularity made casting the film's lead a challenge. Initially the Tejano and Mexican communities were outraged that Lopez had been chosen to play their beloved star, because of her Puerto Rican background and upbringing in New York. Following the success of the film and Lopez's "accurate" portrayal, however, the furor died down, and Jennifer Lopez began to fill the void that Selena had left.

The film showcased a Selena re-embodied in Lopez's striking depiction. As *Los Angeles Times* film critic Kenneth Turan remarked, "*Selena* closes with documentary footage of the real singer, and it's a shock to realize that Lopez so much resembles her that for an instant you can't tell one from the other. And it's in fact a melding of the two, of the real story and the actress's ability to convey it, that creates emotional connections destined to outlive the doses of biopic boilerplate that surround it."[2] Similarly, historian David R. Maciel and director-writer Susan Racho praised Lopez's ability to capture Selena's charisma, claiming that her "inspiring, sensitive, and moving performance . . . ably captured the charm, electrifying presence, and talent of Selena."[3] Even the film's cinematographer commented that "Lopez's performance is the key to the picture's success. . . . Jennifer really understood and assimilated who Selena was and what she represented."[4]

Portraying Selena launched Lopez's musical career, as she captured Sony baron Tommy Mottola's attention. When critic Chris Connelly asked, "Did the "Selena" experience influence your decision to launch a singing career?" Lopez responded, "I really, really became inspired, because I started my career in musical theater on stage. So doing the movie just reminded me how much I missed singing, dancing, and the like. . . ."[5] Here Lopez hints at her roots in musical performance. Her on-line biography makes the connection even more explicit: "After I had finished filming *Selena*, I was really feeling my Latin roots. I cut a demo all in Spanish, but the big companies were more interested in doing an English record. So I decided the record would be a blend of all of my influences."[6] Playing Selena served as a way for Lopez to reconnect with her ethnicity as it was first introduced to her, through music. This realization of her ethnic identity through the music and dance of another ethnic star thus has allowed Lopez to perform her own "Latinness."

In his article, "All Over the Map: La Onda Tejana and the Making of Selena," Chicano history scholar Roberto R. Calderon charts the influences of traditional Tejano music on Selena's Spanish- and English-language recordings. As Calderon puts it, Selena was forging new territory before her death, not only in terms of her music but also in terms of Latino identity (re)construction:

> Selena was at the cutting edge of a new and emerging Latino identity in the United States. And it was an identity based in a solid norteño Mexican tradition, however infused it might have been with the soul and rhythm of the American pop music of the seventies and eighties. Selena bridged new and old, Mexican and Puerto Rican, Mexican and Salvadoreño, Mexican and Chicano, Mexican and Anglo, Mexican and black, song and dance, languages and cultures, music and life.[7]

By portraying Selena, and doing so convincingly, Lopez positioned herself as the "new" Selena. From this position, her transition to music seemed natural. Like Selena, Lopez is celebrated in terms of her adeptness and success in bridging ethnic and racial gaps. Whether or not her music accurately represents a Latino heritage and identity as Selena's does, Calderon's description is consistent with the ways in which López represents the music. As is customary for stars who die young, much of the present-day discussion surrounding Selena centers on what could have been. Calderon notes, "[the] response to [Selena's] death was indicative of the success that would have awaited her, whether she sang in English or Spanish or performed different musical styles. Selena's career promised a plethora of possibilities."[8] Jennifer Lopez, by incorporating Selena's music and Selena's life into her own performative body, is poised to fulfill that potential.

The possibility of Lopez "completing" Selena's course is reinforced by the cinematic representation of Selena's death. The film does not show Selena being shot; instead, we see Lopez, draped in a white gown and performing the English crossover number "Dreaming" to a stadium lit by white candles. As she sings, a white rose is thrown toward her. Even as she reaches out to catch it, the rose misses Lopez's outstretched hand, and a look of horror crosses her face. Selena's death is suggested by a sequence in which Lopez's hand releases the ring that Selena's business manager, and killer, had given Selena as a gift. In the final scenes, Selena's voice is heard again, finishing the song she had been singing. The fact that the film does not show either the shooting or the dead body is significant, as is the fact that Selena's voice resurfaces at the end, seemingly where she left off in the performance. Selena can go on living, and singing, in the bodily form of Jennifer Lopez.

Supporting this transferal of stardom from Selena to Jennifer Lopez is the trope of "naturalness." Lopez interpolates this trope when noting the casting similarities between herself and Selena: "We were at the same kind of points in our careers: we were enjoying some success, but we weren't like hugely popular. . . . We had a lot of parallels in our lives, and Selena and I were similar types of personalities."[9] Positioning herself as a star experiencing similar success, Lopez attempts to naturalize and thus authenticate her portrayal of the Mexican American Selena. Further, Lopez adds that she was also a singer before playing the role; thus, she wasn't lip-synching during the shooting of the film but was actually singing, though "of course, they didn't record it." She is also quick to point out that *Selena*, like herself, can have wide appeal: "Some people consider [*Selena*] a Latin movie, which it's not. It's a movie that everyone can enjoy." Here Lopez shies away from the "ethnic" category, paving the way to increased marketability and naturalizing her transition from "Latina" actress to all-purpose pop diva and movie star. When asked at what stage of her acting career she felt ready to parlay her acting into a singing career, Lopez's response is ingenuous: "You know, to me, things happen naturally and I let them happen that way."[10] By constructing herself as someone who simply acts "naturally," Lopez skillfully deflects the notion that she is motivated by opportunism and self-promotion.

The strategy of naturalness is also deployed to create the semblance of a stable star personality that fans can come to know. This personality, which presumably reveals the "real Jennifer," defends her against undesirable publicity and provides an illusion of access to the star:

> Sometimes journalists try to create a persona that's not really there. . . . It used to bother me being portrayed as this bitchy person, but now I feel that the public understands me better than some writer. There are people who know who I really am, and that's good enough for me.[11]

Lopez makes it clear that she relies on her fans, faithful enough to flatter her with the endearment J.Lo, and not on "some writer" who may not be able to see who Lopez "really" is. This presumed affinity facilitates her move from film acting to recording. Lopez remarks that "when you're doing a movie, you're playing different characters. People don't really get to know you. With music, you really get a sense of who people are. So now, when people see me perform, it will be a different thing. They'll be getting more of who I am, who Jennifer is."[12] Music, then, particularly music that is performed (this is primarily through videos, since Lopez does not tour regularly)[13] complements the preexisting template of a natural and knowable Jennifer. It hints at a kinship between herself and her fans, an affinity built on the star's accessible and genuine "nature."

Since Lopez participates so actively in authenticating herself, fans and spectators are unlikely to recognize this strategy as part of the process producing her crossover star text. Throughout this process, however, other qualities emerge in tenuous relationship to naturalness—those of control and ambition. Since the primary discourse of Lopez's circulating text is one of natural ability and authenticity, these sub-discourses can be absorbed without threatening implications. Lopez is construed as hard-working and focused, characteristics that, when joined to her natural talent and charisma, have aided her in realizing not only her own dreams but also a particular version of the ethnic-American Dream. If ambition is mentioned at all, it is in restrained terms. Like Selena before her, Lopez is constructed within the narrative framework of successful ethnics who "know where they want to go and how to get there."[14] Emphasizing traits such as hard work and authenticity, Lopez registers this appeal in her song "Jenny from the Block": "Don't be fooled by the rocks that I got / I'm still, I'm still Jenny from the block / Used to have a little, now I have a lot / No matter where I go, I know where I came from (from the Bronx!)."[15] Here the ethnic-American Dream is both fully realized, in terms of her wealth, and authenticated by her allegiance to home and culture. This balancing act allows Lopez to naturalize her fame even as she maneuvers, from genre to genre and market to market, steadily toward stardom.[16]

Such maneuvers are significant in terms of star text redirection. Particularly important to recording artists is the ability to reshape yourself as a musical performer, to stay fresh and current and thus in the market as long as possible. This trait is probably best represented by artists such as Madonna and Cher. As popular culture and music critic Jason King has argued,

> While many fans may assess an artist's periodic refashioning and re-emergence as "authentic" and naturalized, the industry itself views such reinvention in terms of product differentiation. Successful artists like Janet Jackson differentiate themselves from peer performers—and from their own previous images and discourse—through a variety of strategic methods that

may include perceptible alterations in singing style, musical sound, dating choices, name change, fashion choices, or bodily practice.[17]

Although, as King points out, all celebrities go through this process to some extent, this work is particularly crucial for transatlantic superstars. Making and remaking oneself and one's body (through voice, presentation, fashion, appearance) ensures continuing marketability and fan support; the performer's participation in this process, asserts King, indicates that the "industry of superstardom is a symptom of trends toward economic and cultural globalization." With audience bases continuously widening and shifting,

> Superstars attempting to homogenize their impact—to appeal to the widest possible audience—have no choice but to engage in a process of border crossing that transfigures traditional hallmarks of identity politics such as race, class, gender, and sexuality.[18]

Ironically, border crossing is here portrayed as an act of differentiation that is perceived in terms of homogenization. Appearing to reinvent themselves, superstars only adapt within a continuing narrative that is never really altered.

These combined strategies of naturalness/knowability and adaptation shape Lopez's perceived ethnicities. What results is a balancing act of representations and perceptions. Crossing from television to film to music, Lopez appears capable of performing all roles for all audiences, constantly adapting her star text while still remaining "true to herself." In the next sections, I consider the ways in which both her physical body and her perceived ethnic differences are claimed by competing racial discourses, broadening her reach even further.

Latina Soul, Identity, and the Act of Representing

Jennifer Lopez is now the highest-paid Latina actress in history (although she trails her white counterparts, particularly Julia Roberts and Reese Witherspoon). She attributes her first break to her performance as a "FlyGirl" on Fox's *In Living Color*, where she showcased hip-hop street-inspired dance moves. Her first two films, in 1995—Gregory Nava's *Mi familia* and Joseph Ruben's *Money Train* (also starring Wesley Snipes and Woody Harrelson)—both positioned her, although in different ways, as Latina. In *Mi familia*, Lopez plays a young Mexican, newborn baby in arms, who must cross the river border into the United States to reunite with her husband. Lopez is earnest, innocent, and plaintive as the young María. This is countered by her role in *Money Train* as Grace Santiago, a tough transit cop of New York Puerto Rican (or possibly Cuban) descent. Praised for her work in both films, Lopez herself notes that she was the only actor to emerge from *Money Train* unscathed. Like earlier Latina or Hispanic stars (perhaps most notably Carmen Miranda), Lopez's film roles signify multiple Latin/Spanish populations. Lopez has gone on to play a number of Latin ethnicities, including Gabriella, the illegal Cuban nanny (broken English included) and mistress to Jack Nicholson in *Blood and Wine* (1996), and a Southern California Mexican American in *Anaconda* (1997).

Despite these roles, Lopez represents her Puerto Rican heritage largely in terms of her musical career; she is firmly situated in the "Latin explosion," which claims Marc Anthony, Enrique Iglesias, and Ricky Martin as primary figures. As mentioned earlier, it was her portrayal of Selena Quintanilla that caught Tony Mottola's attention just before the Latin boom. With high-profile backers and a voice coach, Lopez was free to market her own brand of "Latin soul." While Lopez asserts her music's distinctively "Latin flavor," she also vacillates with regard to this claim, even in the same breath. In an MTV interview with Chris Connelly, she said, "I call my music 'Latin soul' because it's not so much dance-oriented. . . . It has R&B flavors with the Latin and the pop and the dance, but it definitely has those R&B bass lines."[19] Although Lopez's music has had transatlantic success in both categories, dance and pop, she is careful here to position "Latin" as a primary influence. She went on to say, in the same interview, "I wanted my stuff to have a Latin flavor to it. My favorite type of music is salsa music . . . and hip-hop music, so I wanted to like mesh those elements somehow. . . . I wanted it to have the heavy groove, but then again, I want it to have that Latin flavor—that passion to it." The Latin influence is described as a flavor, invoking both food and categories of taste, and situating Lopez herself within a Latinness defined as "fiery" and "passionate." In describing her place within the Latin explosion, she related this anecdote: "I was so proud [at the Grammy Awards]. They kept cutting to me [in the audience]. . . . The energy in there was incredible. But that's that Latin flavor, and people, when you feel it, it's undeniable. It doesn't matter where you're from."[20] Lopez builds on the notion of community and a sort of happy kinship through music, stressing an "energy" that cannot be denied.

Yet even during the same interview, Lopez was careful to appeal to broader populations by not entrenching her music too deeply within any category. Although she mentioned the one Spanish song performed as a duet with Marc Anthony, "No Me Ames," she noted that the song was actually an old Italian melody they had translated into Spanish. In nearly every interview, she remarks that the hip-hop that blared from her Bronx neighborhood had a profound effect on her. She also makes certain to note her mother's salsa and meringue music tastes, which included Tito Puente and Celia Cruz, and the R&B roots she acquired by listening to Diana Ross and Stevie Wonder. Recalling her work with Emilio Estefen, Lopez claims to have chastised him, "I don't want it to be straight Latin! I want it to be more like, y'know, dance-y music-y."[21] Lopez's oscillation between and among various music genres reveals her desire to combine genres[22]—and, by extension, ethnic signifiers—and represent her work as a hybrid "new" product.

The resulting tension plays out in Lopez's fan discourses. One particular post to the Web site *Jennifer Lopez Latin Soul Forum* broached the topic of Lopez's ethnicity specifically. "Maria" posted the following query:

> I have a question for all of you.
> Do you think that Jennifer represents and is a good role model for Latinos? She is always talking about her heritage but it is said that if she was so proud of being a Latina, she would take some time to learn to speak Spanish well as this is very important if she is representing Latinos. I would like to know what you all think about this?[23]

Here, Maria directly links the question of ethnic authenticity to language proficiency, and a number of responses suggest the tensions underlying the issue. One respondent, "fannnnnn," wrote

> she does very well and she has latin influences in her songs and even her dancing. I like how shes always representing the latin community. Of course shes representin'! she has the puerto rico flag on some of her clothing in her line and she is always mentioning her herritage. The spanish speaking thing . . . i think she speaks good enough spanish for a hispanic-American. I am hispanic-American and i talk spanish just like her. . . . she represent us because she shows that a latina can be the sexiest woman in the world and be the highest paid latina actress. She also represents all the energy latinos have.

This post characterizes Lopez's energy, sexuality, and dancing as "representing" Latinos. It also assumes that Lopez is "representin'"—signifying a positive image of her community—because she wears the flag and mentions her heritage. For this fan, these two factors seem to indicate Lopez's authentic commitment to her ethnicity. Yet "fannnnnn" also identified with Lopez's limited Spanish proficiency, which compared with her own.

Two other responses to Maria's initial post form an interesting commentary. A respondent named "JLOSuperstar" wrote: "I think she's a GREAT role model for latinos and anyone from any ethnic background, cause she went for her dreams and has achieved alot of success by working hard and believing in herself. Thats what everyone should do." This post seeks not only to applaud Lopez as an ethnic role model but also to universalize this model across ethnic lines, celebrating Lopez through a grand narrative of the American dream. An anonymous poster responded: "oh i didn't know she spoke it poorly because i don't understand what she saying. but it all sounds beautiful coming from her mouth. i hope she takes some lessons or something and improves so she can speak beautiful spanish all the time." Ironically, the only response (of fourteen) that encouraged Lopez to improve her skills in Spanish came from a fan who did not understand the language. Here the Spanish language figures only in relation to López's beauty and exoticism. This poster encouraged Lopez to "take lessons or something" not so that she can communicate better or represent Latino populations more accurately but to increase her exoticism and thus her beauty.

Lopez herself has addressed the issue of her Spanish and of "representing" ethnic communities obliquely, through references to her music. Her comment that "if you inspire [people] to go after something that maybe they wouldn't have done cause they're not used to seeing people of their culture in that position, that's all just icing on the cake for me" renders the issue of minor importance in her own hierarchy of values.[24]

J.Lo's Panethnicity and Questions of the Real

Although the discourses surrounding Lopez do not primarily posit her as "white," a number of films signal a trend in that direction. In two films, *Out of Sight* (1998) and *The Wedding Planner* (2001), Lopez signifies as possibly Italian American. In each case, her mother is dead, removing a partial lineage, and her father is portrayed as Italian American. In the films *Angel Eyes* (2001) and *The Cell* (2000), Lopez is consistently positioned as Anglo within the world of each film. In these two films she is estranged from her family, effectively removing traces of any heritage. In *Enough*

(2002), Lopez's identity is marked only by her given name, Slim, and her deadbeat father's given name, Jupiter. Other aspects of her star text—her poor Spanish, her "Nuyorican" roots, her "token" Spanish songs, the initial charges of inauthenticity made by Selena's fans—all serve to position her as not being Latina enough, as being "too white."

Yet these films work insidiously within ethnic stereotypes and genre conventions. Perhaps because Lopez's visual image cannot be fully assimilated into a white discourse, subtle intricacies arise within particular films. In *Out of Sight* and *Angel Eyes*, Lopez plays tough cops who excel at their jobs. This character type loosely follows the Hispanic avenger genre character that works against still earlier stereotypical characters of the Latino/Hispanic druggie/greaser/malcontent.[25] But Lopez's characters also recall another Latina prototype—the sweet señorita/cantina girl who renounces, as Gary Keller explains, "her previous formation" in deference to an Anglo man.[26] This familiar narrative appears in all of the above-referenced films. In *Angel Eyes*, Sharon remains true to the mysterious drifter, played by Jim Caviezel, becoming more vulnerable to him in the process. In *The Wedding Planner*, she remains true to McConaughey despite his plans to marry another woman, in the end revoking her own arranged marriage for McConaughey. In *Out of Sight*, she is faithful to George Clooney's character, Jack, even though he is a bank robber and she is a federal marshal. At the end of the film, she provides Jack with a way to escape en route to prison, although this goes against her moral code. Finally, in *The Cell*, psychologist Catherine Deane relinquishes her authority through a process of reversal, allowing both a young white boy in a coma and a white serial killer to enter *her* mind instead. These films, which generally attempt within the diegesis to register Lopez as Anglo, still register an otherness or tension, figuratively and visually, that is not resolved. Genre conventions and disavowal seem to seep in, even as the films struggle to anchor her.

[Although Lopez is frequently positioned within whiteness, she is also situated in relation to or within blackness. Sometimes she does this herself by foregrounding the hip-hop influences in her life and in her music, a result of growing up in the Bronx.]Her close ties with a number of prominent black producers, rappers, and deejays are cited as avenues through which she is connected to blackness. Some of her earlier dating choices also served to align her with the black community. After divorcing her first husband, Ojani Noa, Lopez began dating infamous rap star Sean "Puffy" Combs. The courtship and ensuing break-up were much publicized over the course of the two-year association, especially after she was arrested with Puff Daddy (now known as P. Diddy) for possessing a weapon. When MTV's Kurt Loder asked Lopez whether she recognized herself in the media's portrayals of the incident, Lopez responded, "I have just come to the realization and accepted totally that nobody is ever going to understand who I am."[27] Confronted with a negative representation, Lopez opted to posit her "true" self as unknowable and inaccessible.

One specific instance is useful for examining the ways in which Lopez's star text negotiates discourses surrounding blackness. With the release of her collaborative remix "I'm Real" with Ja Rule, Lopez was blasted for using the word "nigga" in the song. Alona Wartofsky, a columnist for the *Washington Post,* traced the event, arguing that the line, "People be screamin' what's the deal with you and so-and-so/I tell them niggas mind their biz but they don't hear me, though," is a comment about Lopez's break-up with Puff Daddy.[28] When the song was released, two New York deejays encouraged fans to protest the use of the word "nigga" to Lopez's label, Epic. One of the deejays responded with ethnic epithets of his own, threatening to show up at Lopez's performance on the *Today Show* and throw rice and beans at her. Arguing that "the tempest over Lopez is clearly an illustration of how public reaction to the word continues to depend very much on who uses it," *Post* writer Wartofsky noted a range of public reactions. A more nuanced response in the article noted the "double standard at work here. Dr. Dre uses it. Snoop Dogg uses it. What are they going to do? They should come up with a list of who can say it and who can't." Ironically, it was this respondent's self-declared position as the son of a "black-skinned Puerto Rican" that allowed him to claim that he could "see both sides." Another interviewee accused Lopez of using the word to "stir controversy because controversy sells . . . and to compensate for her lack of talent." A final respondent considered Lopez's target audience and moralized, "When your music is geared toward . . . suburbanites, there's a certain way you should carry yourself. Using a word like that when less than a third of her audience is African American or Latino is inappropriate."[29] This respondent positioned Lopez outside black discourse, as well as outside access to this discourse, because of a perceived lack of ethnic or racial substance in her music (it is geared to "suburbanites"). Clearly, the respondent's perception of Lopez's audience influenced where she situated Lopez's discourse. A Web commentary entitled "Race Relations with Kimberly Hohman" argues that

> Lopez's past relationship with rapper Sean "Puffy" Combs, should serve as a
> clear indication that she herself does not have ill or hateful intentions in her

use of the word. In fact, one could argue that her level of comfort with black people is exactly what led her to feel at ease about using the word in the first place.[30]

These reactions reveal the conflicts underlying Lopez's position both in terms of her own ethnicity and of the discursive identities she is authorized to perform. Because Lopez is not black, she is seen as wanting to capitalize (financially) on controversy, yet she is also identified through her relationships with black men, in which case her use of the word is seen as "affectionate" or as a sign of her "comfortableness" with a demographic to which she at least partially belongs.

To explore this topic from another angle, let me turn now to a message-board exchange posted on the *Jennifer Lopez Latin Soul Forum*.[31] Poster "Meeow" wrote:

> I think it is sick that all of you are supporting J-Lo on this one. I know all of you are fans etc but to say the word "Nigger" in her music being in her affluential position is disgusting. On a street level it is a different story. I agree that the point should be pumped up because say it was a white middle class anglo saxon who made that remark everyone would go crazy. I am not balck [sic] but I know that tension with Black African americans are very sensitive in America and with all their pain and history it is not a good idea that a jumped up Hispanic girl who 'uses' black people as her audience by going on BET, dating Puff Daddy and generally acting like she is down with the balck [sic] community and uses words like Nigga because she want to be down with the black community.
>
> And it is sad that all balck guys are looking at Jl O and drooling over her just because he [sic] is alrightish looking and has big bottom, she know that black guys love her and he [sic] is just pandering to that market . . . she wants to be the be all to all the markets and is clever in doing that she always releases one R'NB track, one dance and one latino track off her album she wants to be britney spears, Maddona and Lil Kim all in one, whatever sells she will do, and I think finally the black market aswell [sic] as other intelligent people are waking up to the fact that she is just very nice to look at with ok songs but using and abusing them . . . she is just making the balck [sic] market resent her. . . .
>
> It is time that Black african americans stopped looking upto her as this wonderful sex symbol when she is doing nothing but degrading and using the black african americans. When she was with Puff Daddy I used to see pics of her and she never looked proud of him the way she with her new boyfriend

and eventually she never would settle down with a black guy and have kids because she into use and abuse. ON top of that Cory Rooney and all the other producers and rappers are black e.g. Ja Rule, Dark Child, I can imagine her fluttering her eyelashes and the[y] come running because they think they may have a chance . . . she has got a niche in the USA industry that I do not see any one else having that is why she is so successful she has the white, black and Hispanic market and she play on all of them. Thi[s] why she so succesful but I think the backlash is here and lets just see.

There are many issues at work here. In the first paragraph, the respondent points out that because of a number of factors, López should not use the word "nigga." Among these are her "affluential" (an interesting amalgamation of affluent and influential) and her "jumped up" ethnic quality, which seemingly connotes an ethnicity that is hyperethnic or aggressively deployed. The idea that Lopez is also "using" black audiences through BET and discourses surrounding Puff Daddy is also raised in the first paragraph, as well as a tension between whether Lopez "is down" or merely desires to "be down" with the black community. All of these anxieties point to confusion concerning where Lopez positions herself and how others view this positioning.

In the second paragraph, the respondent moves to criticize the way that the black community privileges Lopez, largely in terms of her body, and more specifically in terms of her "big bottom." Again, the issue of arousing controversy in order to sell records surfaces, as the respondent remarks that Lopez cleverly releases singles to appeal to different markets, while implying that it is not her talent that audiences find appealing, but her looks. The poster then attacks fans for not recognizing the way that artists "use and abuse" them; here, the writer seems to differentiate herself from most fans by challenging Lopez's star text.

In the third paragraph, the poster intimates that Lopez does not care about the black community, as evidenced by her relationship with Puff Daddy and the way she "never looked proud of him." This assertion alleges not only that Lopez's connection to the black community is a false one but also that her face is a legible marker of this artificiality. She further alleges that Lopez would "never settle down with a black guy and have kids because she into use and abuse." She adds Lopez's producers and rappers to the list of those whom Lopez manipulates through her sexual appeal. These claims rest on Lopez's perceived ability to exploit her body (eyelashes, bottom, etc.) to gain desired ends. The poster ends by suggesting that the backlash against Lopez's niche market is already on the way.

This post reflects a bevy of concerns regarding Lopez's star text and her relationship with the black community. The poster positions Lopez as distinctly different from both the "black" and "ethnic" populations that she presumably uses and abuses. Two of the fourteen responses to this post evoke other ways of understanding the ambivalence surrounding Lopez. "SEXC101" responded:

> . . . all these other artist can say nigga, but if "J-LO" says it it's a big deal. STOP HATING!!!!! i always use that word andf [sic] im hispanic aint no biggy sh@t, and cut all that stuff out about saying black people are more sensetive to americans sh@t hispanic are still slaves to american we get the shitty jobs getting paid almost nothing picking fruits out of filds [sic], maids, cooks, janiters, nanies, body shop or cleaning up after everybody's sh@t in restaurants and you dont see us complaining.

"SEXC101" comments on an issue of "double standards" that also arises in the *Washington Post*'s piece. This writer seems protective of Lopez and her star text, positioning herself as Hispanic and a user of the word in order to redeem Lopez's use of the word. The respondent also makes a case for Hispanics being "slaves to America," a parallel to what "Meeow" writes when referring to the African American population's "pain and history." By doing so, this poster repositions Lopez securely within Hispanic culture and experience. "Fannnnnnn" writes in response to the initial post: "what about @#%$ Eminem! hes not black but hes a wannabe. First of all Jennifer is not racist cuz first of all shes got some black blood in her and she was with a black man and @#%$ Ja Rule wrote the song! i swear this is so stupid." This writer creates a spectrum ranging from "real" to "wannabe black," positioning Eminem at the furthest end from "authentic" blackness. Lopez, however, seems squarely positioned at the "black" end of the spectrum: Lopez cannot possibly be racist because she has "black blood in her" and because she "was with a black man." This second point implies that even if Lopez is not "really" black, she somehow becomes black through her sexual relationships with black men. A final, less powerful point for this writer is that the song was not written by Lopez but by Ja Rule.

This debate over Lopez's intentions in using the word "nigga" speaks to the public's confusion over what Lopez "is" in terms of race and ethnicity. Although some position her as Hispanic, others judge Lopez's "whiteness" or "blackness" relative to her perceived audience. In each case her body is seen as the index of both her appeal and authenticity, with Lopez's butt as primary signifier. In an article for *Vanity Fair* Ned Zeman points to the status her butt has achieved in this discourse:

> The dress [made by Versace and worn to the 2000 Grammy Awards], coupled with Lopez's posterior-intensive music videos, created a phenomenon in which a pair of buttocks became, in and of themselves, a cultural icon. Entire news articles would focus on The Lopez Ass, as if it were a separate life-form; Chris Rock even does a gag in his stand-up routine where her butt is going to break off and get its own agent.[32]

Zeman points to the ways in which Lopez's body, and a somewhat dis-membered body at that, has come to reside in discursive spaces of its own. Zeman attributes this iconography in part to Lopez herself, implying that her videos help perpetuate this image. Comments range from the crass (she "needs more legal trouble 'like an extra inch on her derriere' ") to the sub-lime ("[Lopez's clothing] line grows out of a desire to help other women like her find clothes that fit their curves") to the ridiculous ("Jennifer Lopez has definitely sent demand for [butt-implant] surgery sky-high").[33] Lopez is dissected at the level of anatomy, and this anatomy is intimately connected to her perceived ability to succeed as a star.

Lopez herself, often asked to comment on her own posterior, has remarked,

> if you watch the films I've been in, you can see what my figure's like. It's not like you can hide it. But when I get in with the wardrobe designer, they're thinking, "Let's see, she's looking a little hippy, she's got a big butt, what should we do?" They're always trying to minimize—put it that way—and it's because we see all those actresses who are so thin and white. Latinas have a certain body type. Even the thin ones, we are curvy.[34]

Lopez here posits an "essential" Latina body, situating herself (and her butt) comfortably within a normative cultural stereotype.

Yet Lopez's "big bottom" also connects her to recent hip-hop cul-ture where "booty" is a central topic. Perhaps the rapper that pinpoints and generates this relationship most clearly is Sir Mix-A-Lot, author of the 1992 song (more recently re-released on the 2000 *Charlie's Angels* Soundtrack) "Baby Got Back":

> I like big butts and I can not lie
> You other brothers can't deny

> . . . She gotta pack much back
> . . . So ladies! (Yeah!) Ladies! (Yeah!)
> If you wanna roll in my Mercedes (Yeah!)
> Then turn around! Stick it out!
> Even the white boys got to shout
> Baby got back![35]

Sir Mix-A-Lot situates the fondness for a "big butt" squarely within the black community. Connoting "health" and desirability, in opposition to the "flat butt" rejected in the song, Lopez's ass seems the aspect of her star text most clearly anchored in discourses of blackness and black sexuality.

Conclusion

Jennifer Lopez's star text suggests various levels of concern over how ethnic bodies should be interpreted and categorized. What to make, for instance, of Lopez's own claim that *The Wedding Planner* was the "perfect vehicle for me"?[36] What does this claim, which intersects with the most conservative, most deracializing diegesis of all of Lopez's films, work to produce? Can films such as *Money Train*, *Anaconda*, or *Out of Sight*, in which structures of dominant authority are questioned or reworked, be read as counternarratives? What to make of the fact that in *Anaconda*, Lopez and Ice Cube are left to save the day (after all of the "white" characters have been eaten)? Lopez's success has been considered mainly in terms of her onscreen charisma and sexualized body, but how much of her success is intimately bound to the incongruities of her ethnic star text?

Fan discourse, star interviews, on-line chat rooms, and radio talk shows provide rich ground on which to build more complex understandings of stars and their particular functions within cultures. As Homi Bhabha suggests, such "interstitial moments or processes" can help us interrogate how "subjects are formed 'in-between,' or in excess of, the sum of the 'parts' of difference (usually intoned as race/class/gender); 'What collective identifications become possible in the overlapping, or displacing, of domains of difference?'"[37] Lopez's formations are always in flux, contingent on the star herself, who can choose how and where to align and represent herself; on her marketers, who must make sure that she appeals to the broadest audience possible; and on her fans, who struggle to maintain some kind of coherent narrative in order to participate in her text. Thus Lopez's star text allows points of access to "alternative or oppositional" ways of being in the world, despite dominant representations.[38] Exploring star texts like Lopez's which negotiate so many different terrains is crucial in coming to understand our positions—ethnic, racial, gendered, sexual— in a world where everything, including your butt, is topic for discussion and the conversation includes (potentially) everyone.

Notes

1. Henry Jenkins, *Textual Poachers* (New York: Routledge, 1992).

2. Kenneth Turran, "In the authorized 'Selena,' she's seen in the best light." *Los Angeles Times*, March 21, 1997.

3. David R. Maciel and Susan Racho, "Chicanas/os in Cinema and Television," in *Chicano Renaissance: Contemporary Cultural Trends*, ed. David R. Maciel (Tucson: University of Arizona Press, 2000), 120.

4. David E. Williams, "A Life of Color and Light," *Cinematographer* 78, no. 5 (May 1997): 60.

5. Jennifer Lopez, interview with Chris Connelly, "Jennifer Lopez," http:// www.mtv.com/bands/archive/l/lopezfeature99_1.jtml.

6. From the section of Jennifer Lopez's official Web site titled "Biography," http://www.aclasscelebs.com/jenniferl/biocontact.htm.

7. Roberto R. Calderon, "All Over the Map: La Onda Tejana and the Making of Selena," in *Chicano Renaissance: Contemporary Cultural Trends*, ed. David R. Maciel (Tucson: University of Arizona Press, 2000), 32.

8. Ibid., 37.

9. "Jennifer Lopez: Mr. Showbiz Interview," http://www.aclasscelebs.com/ jennifer/mrshowbiz.htm.

10. Ibid.

11. "Biography."

12. Lopez, interview with Chris Connelly.

13. Lopez's only "tour" to date has been two dates played in Roberto Clemente Stadium in Puerto Rico, which she recorded for DVD distribution and which aired partially on NBC. I do not address Lopez's video productions or the "tour" footage here, although both would help illuminate her star text and concepts of her performativity and charisma. I am working here with the assumption that generally, "music videos predominantly work to support star texts" (Jason King, "Form and Function: Superstardom and Aesthetics in the Music Videos of Michael and Janet Jackson," *The Velvet Light Trap* 44 (Fall 1999): 80–96, 83).

14. Calderon, "All Over the Map," 23.

15. "Jenny from the Block," http://www.lyricstop.com/j/jennyfromtheblock jenniferlopez.html.

16. An interesting question is raised here concerning López's pronounced interest in completing a full circle in terms of crossover modeled by Selena. By releasing a record entirely in Spanish, Lopez will have recrossed over.

17. Jason King, "Form and Function: Superstardom and Aesthetics in the

Music Videos of Michael and Janet Jackson," *The Velvet Light Trap* 44 (Fall 1999): 90–96, 81.

18. Ibid.

19. Lopez, interview with Chris Connelly.

20. Ibid.

21. Ibid.

22. Whether Lopez has achieved this is another matter. Her albums have few representative songs in Spanish, and her latest album (*Rebirth*) has received negative reviews; somewhat characteristically, *On the 6* was described by one reviewer as "full of hackneyed urban beats and very little Latin flair" (www.mtv.com.)

23. Thread titled "Representing Latinos," on the Web site *Jennifer Lopez Latin Soul Forum*, http://pub52.exboard.com/fjenniferlopezlatinsoulforumfrm3.show Message?topicID+243topic. I have reproduced message-board posts directly as they appeared on the Web site, without altering capitalization, spelling, or grammar irregularities. Only in extreme cases have I called attention to a particular error with [sic], to clarify the post.

24. Lopez, interview with Chris Connelly.

25. Gary D. Keller, *Hispanics and United States Film: An Overview and Handbook* (Tempe, AZ: Bilingual Review / Press, 1994).

26. Ibid., 39.

27. Jennifer Lopez, interview with Kurt Loder, "Jennifer Lopez: j.lo's lowdown," *MTV Online*, http://www.mtv.com/bands/archive/j/jloo1/index.3.jhtml.

28. Alona Wartofsky, "No Halo for J. Lo as Fans React to Lyrics," *Washington Post*, July 14, 2001, sec. C01.

29. Ibid.

30. *Race Relations with Kimberly Hohman*, "J-Lo's Uh-Oh," http://racerelations.about.com/library/weekly/aa071601a.htm.

31. "Racist," thread on Web site, *Jennifer Lopez Latin Soul Forum*, http://pub52.exboard.com/fjenniferlopezlatinsoulforumfrm3.showMessage?topicID+9 9topic. I quote extensively from the post that initiated the discussion, as it is rich in material for textual analysis.

32. Ned Zeman, "Every Move She Makes," *Vanity Fair*, June 2001, 172, 234.

33. The sources for the comments are as follow: more legal trouble (http://www.hollywoodgossip.com/current/stories/jenniferlopezbodyguards.shtml); clothing line (http://www.allstarz.org/jenniferlopez/news007.htm); demand for surgery (http://www.jlzone.com/cache/jl_news_jl_news_show_10_.phtml).

34. Jennifer Lopez, interview with *iCast*, http://www.aclasscelebs.com/jennifer/icast.htm.

35. "Baby Got Back," http://www.stlyrics.com/lyrics/charliesangels/babygotback.htm.

36. Lopez, interview with Kurt Loder.

37. Homi Bhabha, "Frontlines/Borderposts," in *Displacements: Cultural Identities in Question*, ed. Angelika Bammer (Bloomington: Indiana University Press, 1994), 269.

38. Richard Dyer, *Stars* (London: BFI Publishing, 1998), 2.

CHAPTER 8

"There's My Territory"

Shakira Crossing Over

CYNTHIA FUCHS

Don't get me wrong. Shaking my butt is fun—it's part of the whole thing. But I wouldn't feel satisfied if my life only had that use.

SHAKIRA, ELLE

Shakira—multilingual, half-Latin, and half-Arabic—is the embodiment of globalization, the digital-age demolition of national boundaries author Thomas Friedman calls the "One Big Thing" now guiding politics and economics.

ROB TANNENBAUM, BLENDER

The commodification of ethnicity . . . presupposes that there is a "right" way of being an "ethnic."

ARLENE DÁVILA, LATINOS, INC.

Shakira won me over when she complained about her designer boots. Dressed to shoot the video (2002) for "Underneath Your Clothes," she sat down for a moment with the *Making the Video* "confessional" camera when lunch was announced. Tossing her tangled bleached-blonde mane, she announced, "My feet hurt!" As proof, she held up a frighteningly stylish boot, spanning what looked like five-inch heels with her perfectly manicured fingers, and asked, "Pretty high, no?" Pretty high, definitely. That boot looked like a weapon. Still, she smiled as she added, "It's fun. It's been very fun . . . so far."

Most obviously, Shakira here appears yet another pop star performing candidness—whether melancholy or optimism—for yet another MTV camera. But at the same time, she's winningly arch about that performance, visibly cognizant of the ways she presents her extraordinary body as a desirable object while simultaneously asserting its subjectivity in the form of her vulnerable, distressed feet. In this instant, she acts her understanding of her role and obligation, as well as her privilege and its attendant excesses. Being a pop star is at once work and "fun," and she can handle all with poise, wit, and an unfailing sense of responsibility.

Shakira Isabel Mebarak Ripoll, working since the age of thirteen, famously resists attempts to label her as "the Latin Britney" or "the next Madonna." Instead, she declares her difference from those who have come before, citing diverse influences (Iggy Pop, Led Zeppelin, the Police, Nirvana, Billie Holiday, Janis Joplin), composing music on her guitar, and playing drums during her live shows. She describes her position as liminal and potential. In a 2003 interview with Nick Duerden of *Blender* magazine, she says,

> There is a bridge between me and my new audience at the moment, and I want to cross it. I want to show them who the real Shakira is. I want to inspire thoughts and ideas. Pop music is the most effective vehicle to reach the masses, and I have always seen myself in this kind of role—a messenger. (122)

Yet for all her aspirations to challenge and inform, Shakira is also surely a pop star in the fullest and most complex sense, reaching the masses with both formulaic and unusual appeals, accommodating as much as she is reshaping consumer tastes and existing markets. This essay examines her career thus far, focusing on her effects on U.S. popular culture and the ways her image and performance adjust to this framework. Like many entrepreneurs and some notorious artists (again, Madonna comes to mind), she sees self-expression as a means to "conquer," to claim turf and make her presence known. In Shakira's work, such geographical metaphors proclaim not a standard desire to exploit resources but a challenge to business as usual—in gender relations, in the music industry, in global politics.

This challenge takes multiple forms, some overt, others subtle and even subversive. Her jokey self-description in an interview with Rob Tannenbaum for *Blender*—"Trouble is my middle name"—points up the dilemma she represents and embraces, in terms simultaneously poetic and banal (Tannenbaum 2005, 76). Even as Tannenbaum describes her as an "embodiment of globalization," her songs and videos insist on tensions and ambiguities, explorations and engagements. "Underneath your clothes," goes the chorus of her popular English-language love ballad (2002), "There's an endless story, / There's the man I chose, / There's my territory, / And all the things I deserve / For being such a good girl, honey." It's possible, as Shakira notes, to read "Underneath Your Clothes" as just another sexy ballad. But look again, and you see one of the more inventively self-assertive pop songs to come along in some time. This good girl reframes nationalistic sagas of masculine dominance, colonialism, and subjugation. Shakira offers multiply layered performances as object and subject, rock artist and pop star, as she works borders between masculine and feminine or national and ethnic identities, deploying conventions defining the pop and "Latin" body to discover and attain new territories.

An overnight sensation who has been years in the making, Shakira— whose name in Arabic means "woman full of grace"—is possessed of obvious commercial appeal, with a powerful voice, remarkable range, and considerable talents as producer and songwriter (taking into account the seductive peculiarity of her English lyrics). It's likely that her self-awareness, self-confidence, and self-confessed "stubbornness" are as much a function of her dedicated public relations team as her celebrated hips. But as commercial images go, Shakira's blend of tough-minded frankness, ambition, and independence is as refreshing as it is admirable. Her emergence as part of the latest "Latin explosion" (along with Jennifer Lopez, Marc Anthony, Enrique Iglesias, Ricky Martin, Paulina Rubio, Carlos Santana *again*, et al.) seems calculated, but that's to be expected. She's a product with a contract.

At twenty-nine (in 2006), Shakira has considerable experience as a product, working across cultures and languages since she was a child. Born and raised in Barranquilla, Colombia (her father is American born, of Lebanese descent, her mother Colombian), she signed with Sony Discos and released her first album, *Magia* (Magic), in 1990, when she was only thirteen, followed by *Peligro* (Danger) at sixteen. She did some acting (on the Colombian soap opera *El Oasis* between 1994 and 1997), but ended up focusing most of her energy on making two more records, *Pies descalzos* (Bare Feet, 1996) and *The Remixes* (1997). (Pies Descalzos is also the name she gave to her foundation for providing educational funding and supplies for children in Colombia.) Under the auspices of manager Emilio Estefan, she recorded her last Spanish-language studio album, *Dónde están los ladrones?* (Where Are the Thieves?, 1998), as well as 2000's *MTV Unplugged*, winner of that year's Grammy for Best Latin Pop Album. Her star was ascending and headed Stateside. As Shakira, still dark-haired at this point, appeared on increasing numbers of Latin and Spanish-language magazines, she was also tapped to represent what Latin American *Time*, in August 1999, called the new "era of the Rockera."

As the marketing machine took wider aim, it conjured still more familiar categories and comparisons for Shakira. During her pre-blonde period, she was compared repeatedly to Alanis Morissette, and since the switch to blonde hair, Shakira has been serially compared to Britney Spears, Christina Aguilera, and fellow Pepsi pitchperson Beyoncé Knowles. Toward the end of this period of lucrative homogenizing, she promoted her first "mostly English language" album, *Laundry Service* (2001), by appearing on many typical U.S. and European media venues: *TRL, Rosie O'Donnell, Today, Tonight, Saturday Night Live*, and *Mad TV* in the States, *Top of the Pops, Abbey Road*, and Radio 1 in the United Kingdom ("I feel like I'm on an anthropological mission," she told the London *Observer Magazine* [Kassler 2002, 14].) *Laundry Service* evolved as part of a plan. Shakira changed managers, with Estefan's blessing, to Freddy DeMann (perhaps most famous for his work with Michael Jackson and Madonna). The album burst into U.S. public consciousness via an astounding Francis Lawrence-directed video for the first single, "Whenever, Wherever." Circulating in English-language and Spanish-language versions, the video has Shakira emerging like a goddess from the ocean, whereupon she strides across a desert, dances among digitized wild horses, crawls in wrestling-ready mud, and stands atop a snowy mountain as the computer-effected camera appears to crane around her—a green-screened woman for all seasons.

The resulting numbers were impressive: the video retired from *TRL* in February 2002, meaning that it made the countdown for sixty-five days. Boosted by such incessant video airplay, *Laundry Service* (so named, Shakira says, because "I went through a stage when I felt cleansed, renewed, thanks to love and music, which are like soap and water") entered the Billboard chart at number 3 in November 2001, and has since gone well past double-platinum sales. Such vigorous (and exhausting) campaigning adapts to expectations for mainstream celebrity, addressing multiple markets, but Shakira is careful to maintain connections with her Spanish-language and multicultural bases.

She doesn't reject the comparisons to U.S. stars but politely accepts their limitations, for now. As she told Matt Lauer on *Today* (May 31, 2002), "I don't think those comparisons are offensive at all because Alanis and Britney, they are great artists, and they're very talented people. But," she added, registering the discomfort of her first fan base, "I think these types of comparisons in countries—in Latin American countries—are a little bit out of order, like, they don't understand why they compare me with these artists because they know me for, you know, such a long time."

Indeed, Shakira's estimable career before *Laundry Service* makes her seeming "newness" now something of a joke for longtime fans. More to the point, perhaps, she doesn't measure herself by her similarities to anyone else; as she told *Blender* in 2001, "I don't feel that I'm artistically similar to anybody right now. I have a unique musical proposal" (Tannenbaum 2001/2002). To some extent, that proposal is a function of her voice. As Frank Kogan wrote in the *Village Voice*, *Laundry Service*, though front-loaded with love songs, is unlike most such albums because of Shakira's athletic vocals. "She has no soft songs," he observed, "Even the ones that are soft in volume are loud in feel, have a hardness or a brightness or a push that says, 'Notice me.' And most of the soft ones don't stay soft even in volume—her voice is a showstopper, and she writes power-ballad choruses in order to show it" (Kogan 2002, 64).

Still, her insistence on her personal and political set of identities defies typical U.S. "ethnic marketing," which, according to Arlene Dávila, "responds to and reflects the fears and anxieties of mainstream U.S. society about its 'others,' thus reiterating the demands for an idealized, good, all-American citizenship in their constructed commercial images and discourses" (Dávila 2001, 218). In other words, the usual way to promote a "foreign" product in the United States is to display its conformity to traditional, unthreatening "American" values (Shakira is family-oriented, hardworking, and engaged to a nice boy, Antonio de la Rua, son of former Argentine president Fernando de la Rua) while also titillating potential consumers with sexy innuendo and exoticism (she belly-dances, she sings in Spanish, she trills). As Shakira reveals in her comments to Lauer, she resists the usual containment of "ethnic marketing," in part by going along with normative U.S. expectations and in part by pointing out such expectations' pathetic lack of perspective. As an international star, she says, "I just feel that my playground is larger now. I now talk to different cultures and I hope that I can bridge those gaps and differences between us. It's an adventure, a dream" (Kassler 2002, 14).

Though MTV and VH1, and her label, Sony, have worked overtime to make Shakira fit an identifiable type, she repeatedly maneuvers just beyond their reach. Knowing well the history of U.S. commercial and political relations to Colombia and other South American nations, Shakira performs her nationality alongside her increasingly international stardom. She makes her appearances bilingual whenever she can, and—however consciously or unconsciously—uses her celebrity to showcase her diverse background. Indeed, her 2005 album, *Fijación Oral Volumen 1* (the first of two CDs, released in June), was entirely in Spanish, while the second CD, released in the fall, was in English and titled *Oral Fixation 2*. (She describes the title as "provocative," but adds, "The word 'oral' is very vast, and that's what I like about it. Through our mouths we discover and explore the world. Our mouth is the first source of pleasure, right?" [Tannenbaum 2005, 80].)

Again and again, Shakira's difference shape-shifts, eludes definition. While the hair color issue has come up frequently, she typically dismisses this concern, refocusing discussion on the more potent matter of national identity. In an interview with Siobhan Grogan of the *Guardian*, she said, "I'm not pretending to be American. How could I? I am Colombian. Everyone knows and nothing could change that. I would never abandon the Latin community. The Latin fans know me and tolerate me, and forgive my mistakes. That's the type of relationship I want to build with my Anglo fans now" (Grogan 2002, 10). Indeed, she represents her work as a kind of relationship building. It's no secret that Shakira remade herself to cross over from Latin and South American to U.S. stardom. Quite beyond dyeing her hair, she learned English and adapted her music to suit rock and pop frameworks, with twists from reggae and traditional Latin sounds. Such a combinatory tactic works in manifold ways. Her self-representation exploits presumed principles of "globalization," or, more precisely, the principles of the U.S. pop production and distribution system. Her stardom in Latino and Spanish markets is in large part based on her understanding of U.S. consumer demands long before she decided to learn English; as she told Alona Wartofksy of the *Washington Post*, "To me, writing, expressing my emotions in English was an adventure. I can think in English, true, but I feel in Spanish" (Wartofsky 2002, G01).

Shakira's enthusiastic embrace of her linguistic "otherness" is well known, as she uses her unfamiliarity with English, for instance, to phrase her thoughts more precisely (and, some might argue, poetically) than most pop lyrics tend to do. While many interviewers and critics have noted the phrase "Lucky that my breasts are small and humble / So you don't confuse them with mountains," in "Whenever, Wherever," she always answers the inevitable question with poise and generosity, as if it's the first time she's heard the question, and even as it does indeed appear to confuse the breasts with mountains (for the broadest, most self-knowing version of this exchange, see Rusty's [Michael McDonald] March 16, 2002, interview with Shakira on *Mad TV*, during which he can barely remain seated, he's so thrilled to be looking at her curvaceous body).

Shakira accommodates the marketing process with finesse and assurance. Working her image as a magazine cover girl, she can appear traditionally "sultry," like a "rock goddess," for *Blender*, *FHM*, *Maxim*, or *Rolling Stone*; self-assertive for *Latina*, *Estylo*, and *Complete Woman*; and vivaciously role-modelish for kids' magazines like *Teen*, *YM*, and *Faze*. When *Maxim*'s Paul Young raunchily asked if she'd ever used the drug for which Colombia is best known, she turned the question into an op- portunity for instruction: "Colombia is a beautiful country. There are 40 million people there and only a small number are dedicated to the business of drugs. . . . And remember, Colombia and the United States are involved in the same business, because who's the biggest importer of drugs? The United States, of course" (Young 2002, 94). Ever audience-appropriate, she tells *Teen Magazine* that her parents travel with her on the road be- cause "I feel that they are my best friends and I can talk to them about anything at all. Of course, I fight with them all the time because we're so close. They're opinionated and so am I" (Wiederhorn 2002, 60). She admits to insecurity and observes that success encourages her to redouble efforts to "build new bridges" (Wiederhorn 2002, 115).

One instance of bridge building comes in the form of her contract with Pepsi. Initially signed as a Spanish-language delegate, she has recently made English-language television ads that underscore her self-consciousness as icon and representative. Consider the first ad's clever deployment of, alter- nately, her "exotic" rock-star energy and her "exotic" sexiness. As the spot begins, she's about to perform on-stage when a small boy comes rushing to her, a large security guard hot on his heels. Though the guard apologizes for the intrusion, she's fine with it; there's no diva-esque pro- priety about her, just friendly close-ups as she leans down to invite the eager interloper to participate: "Do you want to hear some music?" she asks the child. And boom, she launches into a full-on performance of the Pepsi anthem, the transgressive boy invited to feel part of her cagey corpo- rate fluency.

Perhaps more to the point, in another Pepsi ad Shakira initially appears as a cardboard standup in a convenience store. A nerdish clerk approaches her to the tune of "Objection (Tango)," the early accordion strains sug- gesting and parodying his boyish lust. As he embraces the standup, the camera cuts to reveal that it has become flash-and-blood Shakira, leaning slightly back, ready to dance. As Hillary Frey observes in *Salon*, "[W]hen she gets body to body with the clerk and smiles in the most mischievous way, it's clear she's in on the joke. Who cares about the fucking Pepsi? These 30 seconds are owned by Shakira" (Frey 2003). This ad—much like the 2005 Verizon commercial in which multiple, different-bodied cell- phone users shake their hips to match Shakira's in her *La Tortura* video—

markets Shakira's simultaneous mystical and corporeal appeals, as well as her sense of humor. She is ever "in on the joke," a step ahead of the designs to co-opt and coerce consumers, and visibly conscious of selling product in order to make contact, to cross between commercial flippancy and cross-cultural connections.

Shakira's appreciation for the commercial process (and her good sportsmanship with regard to its incessant prying) is perhaps best exemplified in her television "adventures"—VH1's *Being* (March 4, 2002), two episodes of MTV's *Making the Video*, for "Underneath Your Clothes" and "Objection (Tango)," and her 2005 *MTV: Diary*. All these performances indicate her ongoing thinking about celebrity, her efforts to articulate that thinking, and her willingness to explore her relationships with fans, as an object of desire and ineluctable performance. More compellingly, she is able to name and perform her body's relationship with her public, reflecting this relationship in projections and reflections.

Shakira was the first star to appear in VH1's short-lived series, *Being*, in which said star walks around (for days, apparently) wearing a pair of sunglasses mounted with a tiny camera, so that the resulting footage allows "you, the fans" to experience what it's like to be said star. In addition to the point-of-view camerawork, the show also involves, of course, being filmed from every which-angle, at all hours, with all her friends, stylists, and even her parents. In the episode, you are invited to "be" Shakira while she and her band are appearing at the 2001 Jingle Ball in Miami: she rides in a limo from the hotel to the arena and back again (where she looks at her recent spread in a magazine), gets her hair styled (and although she works with many people during the makeup and costuming process, she laughs, "At the end, I'm a dictator"), and sound-checks the arena ("I love it when it sounds like this!" she exults, swaying with her hands in the air, on the floor in front of the stage, as her own music surrounds her, engulfs her). She insists that she is an "artist," as opposed to an "entertainer," and even though she laughs sweetly as she says this, you get the feeling that she means it. The camera in her glasses turns with her, sweeping you up in her enthusiasm.

One of the more effective sunglasses-shots has you stepping into a veritable herd of reporters, many of whom are Latino, asking her "how it feels" to "cross over." "How does it feel to conquer America?" one young man asks, mic thrust toward that camera on her sunglasses, as her blonde hair falls across the lens in lovely wisps. The camera cuts from the point-of-view shot to show her smiling graciously, her eyes hidden behind the sunglasses. "Bueno," she says, then continues in Spanish that's translated in English subtitles, "Little by little, I am stepping on this new territory." Indeed, this is an image Shakira uses repeatedly to describe her experience in "America," that she understands her relationship as one premised on power and property, commerce and conversation. Significantly, Shakira is doing the stepping, moving onto new land, traversing borders. A few minutes later she's in a backstage hallway, greeting fans and signing autographs. When one young English-speaking fan tries out his Spanish, awkwardly asking her to pose for a snapshot, she encourages him, while her voice-over (addressed to you, who are simultaneously being and revering Shakira) observes wryly, "I'm conquering my first American fans."

For all the silliness of the glasses gimmick, *Being* does suggest that Shakira has a solid and self-preserving sense of how all this celebrity stuff works. During one of several intercut on-the-couch "confessional" moments, she poses perfectly, her hair arranged and the lights aimed just so. "I'm hoping," she says, choosing her words carefully, "At some point, I'm going to be considered like an artist and not like an alien." The *Being* camera imagines embodiment as a matter of vision, that you might experience stardom—giddy fans, jostling bodyguards, rides in elevators and limos, preparations for performance, larger-than-life self-consciousness—if you can share the limited vision that characterizes a star's daily activities, the imperative to perform for everyone who comes near you. Shakira makes no bones about the relentless pressures of performance: "You have to be clever, and you have to smile, and you have to, you have to, have to, have to, have to . . . you must always look good!"

It is this imperative to look good that Shakira both fulfills and challenges in her performances. She uses her time in front of cameras to assert her ideas about relationships—between people, and between artists and their consumers, and increasingly, between cultures. Asked to describe her inspiration for the video for "Underneath Your Clothes" during *Making the Video*, Shakira put it this way: "I think in every artist's life, when, right after a performance, we get to feel a certain loneliness and solitude; after receiving so much attention and love from your fans, suddenly everything stops." The video investigates this dilemma, reframed within the context of a love ballad. The video compares, by metaphor and literal imagery, the difficulties of being on the road, separated from a lover and an adoring crowd. Directed by the late Herb Ritts, it includes grainily sincere black-and-white footage, energetic handheld camerawork, and colorful on-stage imagery, tumbled together to emulate what Shakira calls a "documentary feel." She says that it was "destiny" that she and Ritts had a similar approach to the video, in wanting to show the "life of an artist on tour."

The video for "Underneath Your Clothes" opens with Shakira's encounter with a "local reporter" (the meaning of this term is not entirely clear, though the connotation is "minor" and "unsophisticated," perhaps "ignorant"). The scene is shot in black-and-white video, with the grain enlarged to exacerbate the friction of the moment: finding her in an alley behind whatever venue she's just played (she has her guitar with her), he sticks out his microphone and asks her to comment on her "crossing over" to English-language stardom. She doesn't pause, but keeps on striding while answering the question—in Spanish, untranslated by subtitles—as the exasperated local reporter follows along with his tape recorder bouncing on his hip. She reports to the MTV camera that she was especially keen to get this scene into the video, though it has little to do with the love story per se, because it sets the context for her loneliness and her desires, the persistent, unnervingly unself-reflective business of the press, probing her emotional state, reading her body as if it's always already available to them.

And at this point in the video, Shakira, appearing the very picture of loneliness, leaves the local reporter behind and boards the tour bus. As her band plays in the background (apparently being on the road with Shakira means you're ready with instrumentation 24-7), she gazes sadly out the window and begins to sing:

> You're a song
> Written by the hands of God.
> Don't get me wrong cause
> This might sound to you a bit odd.
> But you own the place
> Where all my thoughts go hiding.
> And right under your clothes
> Is where I'll find them.

Here the somewhat awkward translation of her "feelings" into English makes the sentiment all the more poignant. In this song and others on *Laundry Service*, the strangeness is not so much inelegant as it is weird and endearing, making profound sense. As Shakira leans into her tour bus sofa, a series of cuts between the black-and-white, harsh-grain shots and those in soft color suggests her sense of dislocation and puts the viewer nearly inside her fatigued and yearning body, envisioning her desire and also her cozy satisfaction, alone with the band, on the road again. This as her lyrics focus on the energy of intimacy and embodiment: "written by the hands of God" lays down the thematic focus on creation and physicality. The lyrics go on to conceive the relationship in terms of property and territory, but here such terms are not greedy or exploitative but rather exhilaratingly possessive, an assertion of craving and devotion. Given traditional male attitudes toward female bodies, not to mention historical Euro-U.S. attitudes toward Latin American resources, Shakira's declaration of her "territory" in this instance is not a little compelling.

"This might sound to you a bit odd," she sings, "But you own the place / Where all my thoughts go hiding. / And right under your clothes / Is where I find them." As she describes her relationship, the visual register cuts across time, back and forth between her good-bye to her lover and their reunion (the lover is played in the video by Antonio de la Rua), as well as a few more scenes showing Shakira and the band (backstage and on-stage) and her alone, facing herself as mirror image.

The video reinforces her self-affirmation by never quite showing the sorely missed lover's face. He's surely very pretty, but he's also (1) incidental and (2) hers. For most of the video, the boyfriend is actually off-screen altogether, alluded to when Shakira gets his phone call and joyfully rolls around on her bed, happy just to hear his voice (which you don't hear); and she looks simultaneously delicate and vital in her pink sundress, as the camera caresses her bare foot (no painful boots here). When the boyfriend does appear, gazing prettily out the window or embracing her sensuously, his face remains hidden, so that he becomes a body only, a function of her longing as much as her man's, essentially without an identity of his own, visible only as he comforts or aches for her.

By contrast, the video for "Objection (Tango)" situates Shakira in relation to man who is disloyal and deserving of punishment, specifically by the extraordinary power of combined cultures, as rock-meets-Argentine music, with a grinding guitar up blending into rowdy accordion. As Shakira explains in this *Making the Video* episode, she's especially fond of this song, because it's "the first English song I ever wrote in my whole life," and she imagined it as combining "Argentinean instruments and tango choreography." Appropriately, for a song so engaged in the tango as metaphor and structuring device, the video is focused on bodies—dancing, fighting, contorting, and morphing into cartoon images. As Shakira describes the concept (her own, helped along by indefatigably inventive director Dave Meyers), she is betrayed by her boyfriend (played here by tango dancer Rudy Sanchez) and tracks him from a tango dance floor to a bar where he's meeting his mistress (Tabitha Taylor). Here she fights the couple (with help from a pair of costumed superheroes) and ties them up for transport in the trunk of her car to a warehouse (the old Herald Examiner Building, affording terrific deep space and grimy industrial effects), where she and her band quite literally rock out the deceitful duo, sending them spinning into space on giant wheels that resemble, in Shakira's words, "those torture toys on *Batman*."

As the plot suggests, the video involves any number of physical antics, and the camera attends carefully to Shakira's shaking hips, in particular in the first scene, where she expresses her disappointment in her partner's weakness and infidelity. "It's not her fault that she's so irresistible," she sings of the other woman, "But all the damage she's caused isn't fixable. / Every twenty seconds you repeat her name, / But when it comes to me you don't care / If I'm alive or dead, so / Objection!" The tango lasts mere seconds, as the boyfriend pulls her close and Shakira resists falling back into his arms. The dance takes place on a dance floor, where other patrons fade into the background, audience members who highlight the performance, the artifice and the tension of the relationship.

The second setting, at the bar, brings out the cartoon version of Shakira, whom she calls her "alter ego," a ferocious incarnation who leaps into crazed action at the sight of the other woman. "Next to her cheap silicone, I look minimal, / That's why in front of your eyes, I'm invisible." The idea that Shakira might be "invisible" to anyone is ludicrous, but the lyric speaks to the fear of loss that a relationship entails, as it contests the notion that she would be defined by the gaze of her partner. The video underlines the lyrics by printing them out under the animated images, as Shakira fights the girlfriend, and indeed, punctures her silicone breasts. This triumphant moment is a fantasy, however, and the bad boyfriend pushes Shakira away so that she falls rather spectacularly through a glass table (Shakira does her own stunts here, and *Making the Video* emphasizes her physical derring do, with shots of her working with the stunt choreographer Philip Tan, smashing through the table—actually made of sugar—and getting rubbed down afterward by Meyers). When at video's end, she and the band start making noise in the warehouse, she's wearing jeans and working her guitar, as well as taking a moment to rap out her rage ("This is pathetic / And sardonic / And sadistic / And psychotic / Tango is not for three"), playing the vengeful superhero whose self-expressive art—not her relationship with a man or his dishonesty—affirms an identity beyond any observer's adjudication.

In this video, much like the video for "Underneath Your Clothes," variations of Shakira's body—passionate and desiring, subjective and vulnerable, objectified and seductive—challenge conventional representations of women, and, especially, reframe conventional representations of Latina "otherness." In large part she manages such resistance by means that seem ordinary and conformist: she swivels her hips, she parts her lips and runs her hand through her hair, she juts her chin as if in jaunty allure. But in Shakira's self-representation, such routine seductions are also signs of warning: part teasing, part self-protective, and part she's not so available as she seems. She has her own story to tell, her own interests extending beyond those of any possible spectator.

Consistently contextualizing that story, she has made clear her feelings clear about international hostilities—in Colombia, in the Middle East, in Iraq, even at a time when such a stand invited censure from pop consumers fearful of seeming "unpatriotic." In doing so she draws again on her Colombian-Lebanese heritage, which surfaces as much in her repeated references to lessons learned from her war-torn homeland as in her crowd-thrilling hip shaking. Consider her remarkable Tour of the Mongoose, which drew attention for its antiwar imagery and her own pro-peace statements between songs. Asked by Corey Moss of MTV in 2003 what inspired the name for the tour, she explained,

Every time I turn the TV on, I don't see anything else than conversations about war, images of war, war in Colombia, war in the Middle East. I think that little word has invaded our lives. I think this is a moment, we have to awaken, you know, before it's too late. To me, the existence of the mongoose is like the existence of hope, you know. There is on earth an animal that can defeat the snake with a bite. I think that maybe it's not impossible that someday we can bite the neck of hatred and prejudices and resentment. This symbol was very inspirational for the whole concept of the show.

Her protest took the form of background videos and her own on-stage patter, inviting fans to participate in peace activist movements. Before singing "Octavio Dia," she asked fans to support a peace movement, because, she told Moss of *MTV News*, the song "talks about God when he created the world, the eighth day he went for a walk to outer space and when he came back he found our world in an infernal mess. And he found that we were being controlled and manipulated by just a few leaders and that we were like pieces of a chess game." The stage show included a video screen showing a chess game played by two giant puppets modeled after George Bush and Saddam Hussein, presumed to be moving the pieces but revealed as manipulated by the Grim Reaper. She told MTV, "Not always do the governments represent their people. Not always do the governments make the right decisions, because the governments are controlled by just a few, and those few do not always represent faithfully the ideals of the people" (Moss 2003).

Shakira claims her concern is engendered by her childhood experiences in a nation wracked by war, poverty, and political and social unrest. Again, she places her body on the border between ostensible sides—not Iraq and the United States or even the United States and "Old Europe," but between war and peace, situating Bush alongside Hussein as equally culpable, naming as her targets lack of leadership and vision rather than ostensible "sides." In this, she again delineated her differences from other pop stars (perhaps especially when she criticized Madonna for pulling the antiwar video for "American Life," calling her "spineless" and asserting, "Good pop music is always political in times of crisis").

Perhaps most instructive in this instance is the fact that Shakira never drew fire from conservative or pro-U.S.A. groups as did Madonna or the Dixie Chicks. While Madonna was criticized for her ostensible commercial concerns and the Dixie Chicks for Natalie Maines's observation that she was embarrassed to be from the same state as George Bush, Shakira's pointed and persistent protests appeared on music news outlets, but never generated mainstream controversy. In part, this had to do with differences between her audience and those for Madonna and the Dixie Chicks. But it also had to do with public expectations for an artist from Colombia, who sings in Spanish and English, performs like a rock star and looks like a pop girl, and resists categories, fixed identifications, and any "right" way to be "ethnic."

Shakira's most recent television appearances have focused on her continued wrestling with such identifications, in personal and performative senses. These include two videos for singles off *Fijación*, "La Tortura," which she sings with Alejandro Sanz (the video featuring her very provocative black-oily, still astoundingly supple body) and the dark, industrial-backgrounded "No" (sample lyrics: "No, no me mires como antes / No hables en plural / La retórica es tu arma más letal" [No, don't look at me as before / Don't talk in plural / Rhetoric is your most lethal weapon]). Aside from her own tour for *Fijación*, she also appeared at Live 8 concerts on July 2, 2005, and Fashion Rocks (in support of Hurricane Katrina relief), on September 9, 2005, where she shook her hips and sang in Spanish for the express purpose of raising political awareness as well as money.

In 2005's *MTV Diary*, she appears without makeup as she begins the *Fijación* promotional tour, spending a few days in Turkey and then Colombia ("It's always emotional to step in your own land," she says, as young school children swarm around her), and holding a series of press-day interviews. The camera catches her in an elevator with mirrored walls, revealing two Shakiras, as she leans wearily. "My second name is 'chaos,'" she smiles. Remarkably, MTV aired the *Diary* in both English (with her voice-over) and, in her interactions with fans and co-workers, Spanish with English subtitles, a first for the network and an indication that Shakira's crossing over continues.

Bibliography

Bensimon, Gilles. 2003. "Destiny's Child." *Elle*, February, 154–161.
Dávila, Arlene. 2001. *Latinos. Inc.: The Marketing of and Making of a People*. Berkeley and Los Angeles: University of California Press.
Duerden, Nick. 2003. "The Sexiest Woman in Music Today." *Blender*, March, 116–124.
Frey, Hillary. 2003. "Shakira's Pop." *Salon*, April 19.
Grogan, Siobhan. 2002. "Don't be fooled by the pictures." *London Guardian*, December 2, 10.
Kassler, Ted. 2002. "I was born to do this." *Observer Magazine*, July 14, 14.
Kogan, Frank. 2002. "River Deep, Freckle High." *Village Voice*, January 1, 64.
Larmer, Brook. 1999. "Latino America," *Newsweek*, July 12.
Moss, Corey. 2003. "Shakira calls for peace, explains mongoose mystery." *MTV News*, May 2.
Tannenbaum, Rob. 2001/2002 "Who Does Shakira Think She Is?" *Blender*, December–January.
———. 2005. "Miss Universe." *Blender*, July, 72–80.
Wartofsky, Alona. 2002. "Pop's Fluent Asset." *Washington Post*, March 10, G01.
Wiederhorn, Jon. 2002. "The Diva Shakira." *Teen Magazine*, May, 58–61, 115.
Young, Paul. 2002. "Shakira Rocks." *Maxim*, July, 90–96.

CHAPTER 9

"Hey, Killer"

The Construction of a Macho Latina, or the Perils and Enticements of *Girlfight*

KAREN R. TOLCHIN

> *Since when has a man not beaten his wife? If he doesn't beat her, it's either because he doesn't love her or because he isn't a real man. . . . Since when has a woman ever done the same things as a man? Besides, she was born with a wound between her legs and without balls. . . .*
>
> ISABEL ALLENDE, *THE HOUSE OF THE SPIRITS*

It's like, you're all you've got," muses protagonist Diana Guzmán (played by Michelle Rodríguez) in Karyn Kusama's award-winning directorial debut, *Girlfight* (2000). In a rare moment when words take precedence over bodies, the unconventional Latina character attempts to explain her great passion for testing her mettle in the male-dominated sport of boxing. Words have become necessary only because Diana feels pressure to account for her long absences from her friend Marisol, a peripheral character who lives for romance and exists as a vehemently average "control" to Diana's experiment. "You let guys hit you in the face?" Marisol asks in horror, unable to square Diana's obsession with her own more typical agenda of makeup and shopping. Diana has departed from the sort of macho conventional wisdom Isabel Allende anthologizes in her fiction, but without it, she finds it difficult to express herself. She casts about for the appropriate language to convey her dedication, infusing each word with rapture: "You're all alone in there. You know?" Language fails.

Marisol craves solidarity with the same fervor her boxing friend reserves for solitude, routinely practicing self-deprecation in order to accommodate a motley assortment of companions. When Diana utters the phrase "I need to get to his body more," it is to her coach Hector in the context of winning an amateur fight, solidifying her status as "other."

Marisol promptly deems Diana "my crazy friend," joining a large coterie of characters and critics alike who seek to construct, define, and contextualize a new figure in the American film canon, the Macho Latina.

Girlfight stands as a curious fusion of bleak snapshot and wish fulfillment, more eloquent for its contradictions than its legibility. In mainstream reviews, interviews, and scholarly criticism, Diana Guzmán seems to signify progress for a population hitherto consigned to reductive, parodic spaces in mainstream American cinema, spaces dictated almost exclusively by the white male taste for so-called exotic pleasures. If women's options for representation in twentieth-century film were limited, the Latina's were downright paltry. In his history of the Hispanic presence in American cinema, scholar Gary Keller notes that during Hollywood's first few decades, a Latina actress could choose between three sexualized personas, and no other roles: cantina girl, self-sacrificing señorita, or vamp (Keller, 40). Because it reverses normal gender codes and centers on the journey of a Latina protagonist, *Girlfight* serves as a useful yardstick with which to measure how far both the American filmic imagination and Hollywood's financial machinery (if the two may be distinguished) have progressed since these modest beginnings; writers mine films like Kusama's feverishly for signs of change. Yet reports of the death of the cantina girl may be premature, a product of the impulse to provide optimistic *Newsweek* covers.

In this essay I argue that Latina filmic representation remains entrenched in the suffocating realm of dominant cultural ideology. Kusama's film provides tremendous entertainment and satisfaction, but it does so largely by constructing a mythical creature—one chained to the patriarchal rock as surely as her sultry predecessors were. Furthermore, the myth may have negative political consequences for the real-life American Latinas who live and work beneath the silver screen: by the end of this decade, Latinos will make up nearly 13 percent of the U.S. population (Heyck, xviii).

Writer-director Karyn Kusama struggled for three years to accumulate the funding for *Girlfight* and took a substantial risk when she cast an unknown Latina as the lead out of an open call that drew two thousand applicants (Rich). Michelle Rodríguez read the stage directions by mistake during her audition, so new was she to both acting and boxing (Gordon). A protégé of John Sayles, Kusama actively sought a novice for the role, one with "a sort of unschooled sensibility that often, once actors have been trained, they no longer have. . . . For this role you need to see someone working purely on their nerve endings" (Gordon). Kusama, a New Yorker and boxing novice herself, offers the authenticity of the Latin

American presence in New York as rationale for her cultural preference, along with her personal admiration for Latina fighters. For years, potential financial backers questioned the director's vision of an unapologetic, pugilistic, non-Caucasian heroine and pressed her to explain the character's fury: "Part of me just wanted to say, 'Why don't you just pick up a paper in any American city and read it?' You might find several reasons" (Johnston). When she finally acquired support (roughly $1 million, a pittance for a feature film), she and cinematographer Patrick Cady had to shoot all of the footage in a mere twenty-four days, an exercise that proved the importance of storyboarding every moment. As a result, all of *Girlfight*'s narrative choices were planned meticulously and tested before the first roll of discounted, old Fuji 500 stock emerged from the can (Mirchevsky).

One of two dozen women to submit entries to the Sundance Film Festival, Kusama was the first in history to win Sundance's prizes for both best picture and best director, and she would have won a third prize if the festival had given one for "Best Buzz," as *American Cinematographer* notes in its brief synopsis of the "two-fisted tale of a feisty Latina" (Mirchevsky). The character Diana Guzmán finds solace from the grim realities of her existence in a sport that would have rejected her: along the way, she falls in love with a fighter, beats him in a championship duel without losing him, exacts a measure of revenge against a brutal father with impunity, and finds a reason to live. This toppling of the status quo results in tremendous audience satisfaction. *Newsweek,* which subscribes to the notion that the macho Latina marks progress, somewhat gleefully described *Girlfight* as follows: "Karyn Kusama's delightfully unladylike *Girlfight* is a potent mixture of Old Hollywood boy-meets-girl formula and indie grit. It introduced the strikingly sultry Michelle Rodríguez as the macho heroine Diana Guzmán, a pugnacious Brooklyn high-school student. . . ." (Ansen 2000).

The portrait that emerges of Diana's creator in interviews suggests that Kusama may have more grit and anger about the society she encounters than her protagonist: "My character lives to fight. I don't. My fight is a different kind of fight" (Johnston). Kusama takes care to distinguish herself from her heroine but underscores her dedication to a political battle, political on account of its setting: Hollywood. As one critic noted, Kusama's fight "was to take place in a far more vicious arena: the movie business" (Johnston). The director tangled with Sony over the marketing and distribution of the film: "The critic's quote they used was 'better than all the *Rocky*s combined.' There was a fundamental fear of selling it for what it was" (Johnston). (It is worth noting that Kusama gives Diana a love interest with the name of Adrian, tweaking *Rocky* and perhaps inviting such comparisons.) Kusama fumes at the suggestion that she displayed unusually good timing with the release of her film in 2000, years of frustration bubbling to the surface: "To me, three years ago was the right time to make this movie because there will always be a shortage of physically powerful and emotionally complicated women on screen. . . . I was itching to make it a long time ago" (Baker, 69). Kusama and her character reveal exasperation with a crowd that is a few paces behind them intellectually, sharing a fundamental unwillingness to pull a punch. They reflect each other's fortitude and courage and produce a surprising narrative.

Before we turn to the details and differences represented by a female boxer's tale, we should consider the sport's masculine origins, widespread allure, and sociopolitical content. In *The Culture of Bruising: Essays on Prizefighting, Literature, and Modern American Culture*, Gerald Early offers a succinct yet comprehensive and personal history of the sport:

> Modern prizefighting is a remarkable metaphor for the philosophical and social condition of men (and, sometimes, women) in modern mass society. Launched in eighteenth-century England, largely as a way of upper-class betting men to amuse themselves at the expense of lower-class ruffians, prizefighting was created in anticipation of mass industrialized society, where it has flourished as a sport and, even more startlingly, as an aesthetic: namely, to watch without seeing. The prizefighter enacts a drama of poor taste (but not of absurdity, as the modern professional wrestler does) that is in truth nothing more than an expression of resentment or a pantomime of rebellion totally devoid of any political context except ritualized male anger turned into a voyeuristic fetish. (xiv)

The performative quality of the fight will afford a certain type of spectator—one who likes to "watch without seeing" and enjoys "pantomimes of rebellion"—a catharsis. Until recently, as Early notes, the spectator was male and upper class, a point perhaps best dramatized by Ralph Ellison in *Invisible Man*. Most striking about the body of commentary generated by *Girlfight* is the picture that emerges of the opening of that particular boys' club: women have warmed to the sport and its potential as both spectator and agent. *Sight & Sound*'s Ruby Rich discusses a personal introduction to boxing that filled her with a sensation of empowerment, acquired at a birthday party held in a Brooklyn gym by a mutual friend of Karyn Kusama, Sande Zeig: "God, I loved it." In Early-esque fashion, Kusama tries to explain the sport's immediacy and appeal for those who haven't experienced it firsthand: "It's so visceral and aggressive, and it's a great way to sort of blow off steam. Also, I think I wanted to change my life a little bit and experience new things" (Mirchevsky). Critic Monica J. Casper shares the boxing rapture, cued when she viewed *Girlfight*:

> As I sat in a dark theater this past weekend, enjoying Karyn Kusama's excellent *Girlfight* (1999), my shoulder muscles itched, and I fidgeted in my seat with the urge to box, to feel that familiar painful rawness in my knuckles. . . . Watching Michelle Rodríguez, the film's dynamic star, reshape her body and identity, learning to throw punches and throw down in equal measure, I was astounded, inspired, and moved.

Kusama, Rich, and Casper describe a passion for a sport and its representation on-screen shared by a growing segment of women. The sport of boxing seems to hold imaginative power, in large part because of its pathos: "Boxing has a built-in arc of triumph and tragedy. It's more than a sport—it's a narrative" (Rich). The narrative seems to offer redemption, possibility, and wish fulfillment, particularly in Kusama's reversal of gender norms, giving us a female victor. The rewriting of unfair battles waged and lost is a central animating feature of *Girlfight*. In interviews, Kusama often uses the word *pure* to describe the appeal of boxing, which suggests her tendency to idealize the sport and its potential for women's empowerment.

Rich gives *Girlfight* the nod for both its aesthetics and its politics and attempts to situate Kusama's contribution within a subgenre:

> Women's boxing offers the movie screen all the enticements male boxing has always provided, but with something more than the mere novelty of seeing gals take over a boys' game. Finally there's a reason other than sex for looking at women's bodies in the movies, a way for women to show off their forms free of degradation and powerlessness. Near-naked female characters in the movies who aren't hookers or strippers, exotic dancers or girls in love; some place other than the bedroom or the beach or the Vegas club where female flesh can strut its stuff. Finally the guys are out of the picture and women are left alone on screen to claim a primordial power other than that of seduction.

Rich heralds the advent of a gritty, alternative showcase for women's assets on-screen; indeed, the bedroom, the beach, and the Vegas club constitute an accurate list of the meager settings available to women in twentieth-century film, particularly women of color, despite a brief heyday between the world wars for female filmmakers and a slight loosening of the grip by the century's end (Sklar). One of the greatest pleasures of *Girlfight* is that the viewer becomes fascinated with the eyes and demeanor of its heroine, "whose jutting jaw and 10 mile stare hold the viewer's attention like a clamp," as opposed to her ability to conform to traditional notions of women's beauty (Felperin, 48). The emphasis may still be on the body of the lead actress, but the audience grows mesmerized not by the classic parts of breasts and buttocks but by eyes, brow, jaw, and fists. The character's mirror—long a torture device for women—becomes a tool for gauging punching technique, not physical imperfection. She is still the object of the male gaze, but there is a subtle difference.

Some critics and interviewers attempt to sexualize the heroine by focusing on the carnality of boxing, "the intimate nature of a sport where two nearly naked opponents have agreed to fight each other—focusing on a physicality that is so intense as to be hypersensual" (Gordon). In such cases, Kusama often retrains their attention away from the sexual to the emotional: "It's physical, of course, but it's also emotional. There's this agreement between two boxers, this sense of, 'We could hurt each other very badly.' That, to me, is like love; you agree to be in a situation where somebody could get hurt" (Gordon). Diana Guzmán is a sexual person, but she is defined by her almost mystical calling to a sport, not her sexuality. Her agency within the masculine-feminine dialectic comes to the fore, in stark contrast to the convention of a woman's capacity to mirror and perform male desire. Her power stems in large part from her ability to see both the powerlessness in a life devoted exclusively to heterosexual romantic paradigms (although she does fall in love with a young male character) and the steadier rewards of a life devoted to pursuing a different sort of passion and developing her own skills. Kusama takes great pains to clarify the source of Diana's satisfaction, working to situate the film's love plot within the larger goals of the narrative: "In *Girlfight* the sport itself is the journey that changes her life, and I felt it was important to address other things about her life, but also to remain honest about where her emotional transformation was coming from" (Baker). The filmmakers strive for honesty, but the "truth" that gets told seems fraught with contradictions.

Rich gives voice to genuine satisfaction at the righting/rewriting of wrongs, when "guys are out of the picture," leaving women to swill a "primordial" power divorced from their seduction. Yet this sensation seems more a product of fantasy than reality. Housing projects populated largely by disenfranchised minorities seem to manufacture far more girls like Marisol, in thrall to her desire for acceptance in a brutal, sexist culture, than Diana, who refuses to participate in her own degradation. Rich concedes that the newness of the women's boxing film genre poses attendant difficulties for interpretation: "What does it mean for women to enter the sacred masculine zone of boxing? Now that the sport's signifiers are scrambled and its old messages altered, the new meanings are not yet clear." The feminist viewer feels the twofold frisson of excitement that comes with traversing hermetically sealed borders and the promise of equal access, pleasure, and treatment. When greeted in the gym with the taunt "Hey, Killer" by those amused by her actions, chauvinists who assume her interest in boxing must be a front for a desire to trim her figure to make it more palatable to men, Diana Guzmán refuses to slink off in search of aerobics classes designed for toning buttocks. Nevertheless, the "guys" first painted and sustained the picture of competitive boxing; in *Girlfight*, Diana usually shares the ring with them, a girl testing her mettle in an arena populated by boys, no metaphors needed. When she exceeds expectations, they are the expectations of men. In fact, the entire paradigm balances on a patriarchal axis.

Diana Guzmán departs radically from type, particularly in her determination to focus on quantifiable power, not the elusive kind peddled in such venues as bedrooms and Vegas clubs. She distinguishes herself by showing courage in the face of immediate, physical danger in the ring. Yet even more astonishing is her moral courage as she sidesteps and dodges society's restrictions, to her own detriment. At various points in the film, her friends, family members, principal, and love interest all voice objections to her independent stance. Forget positive reinforcement, validation, and other buzzwords: she makes herself an open target for derision. Diana refuses to play the part others seem to conspire to script for her, that of docile, dutiful, obedient creature who defers to authority, paints her face, and smiles, no matter what her inner climate.

Our first glimpse of the young Latina symbolizes her steadfast refusal to comply, her personal signature. The viewer first sees her in military fatigues against a blood-red backdrop of school lockers, her eyes downcast until she trains an unflinching, murderous gaze on the camera, poised for an attack against a female classmate. In the background, the staccato force of a flamenco beat lends a martial quality to the image, the sound of the pounding of heels into stone, as if the reader hadn't already been well cued for a battle. The score seems almost superfluous: only a killer could look into those eyes without experiencing a shot of adrenaline. As filmmaker and writer Bette Gordon notes, "It's refreshing to have a coming-of-age story from a girl's point of view, and to see her as tough and as stubborn as John Travolta in *Saturday Night Fever*, Marlon Brando in *On the Waterfront*, or even Sylvester Stallone in *Rocky*." We note the character's determination before we hear her speak, and she seems every bit as strong as the characters Gordon mentions, if not stronger, or at least more willing to trade her life for the proverbial kill, if necessary. *The Nation*'s Stuart Klawans voices strong criticisms of the film but takes care to praise Michelle Rodríguez's performance as its most redeeming feature, describing the film's opening sequence as follows:

> At last, when she's in close-up, she lifts her face and glares straight into the camera, her eyes steady and dangerous beneath the parapet of her brow. The expression is reminiscent of the young Muhammad Ali; and the framing of the shot, from chin to forehead, brings out the resemblance between one pretty, roundfaced, pouty-lipped fighter and another. . . . Chronically enraged by her beer-guzzling father, chronically furious at the world's flouncy women, Diana doesn't need the Board of Regents curriculum. What she wants is a school for her anger—and she finds one at last when an errand takes her to a local gym, where Hector (Jaime Tirelli) trains young men to box. (37)

Klawans gives an apt description of Rodríguez and the optimizing effect of direction and editing on her violent facial expressions. There is nothing casual or accidental about the errand that lands Diana in the gym: she gets sent by her father specifically to pay a trainer for the boxing lessons he foists upon her artistic, passive brother, Tiny. Diana sees something readily given to men, even to those who would spurn the gift, and decides to take it for herself, stealing when necessary. As one critic notes, she finds not merely a hobby in boxing but a vocation (Segal). Most critics seem to consider the brawl that launches *Girlfight* proof that the protagonist has an anger management problem, a "pugilistic" girl who lacks sufficient outlets and skills to manage her feelings. Critics describe her as "surly" and "bad-tempered," a "trouble-prone Latina teen" (respectively Strauss, Landesman, and Travers). These descriptors may suit, but they obscure vital information: in the film's opening fight sequence, Diana is extracting a measure of justice for Marisol for the duplicitous and hurtful actions of a girl named Veronica (involving Marisol's male love interest). Kusama's heroine is most emphatically *not* a rebel without a cause; in fact, she displays honor, loyalty, courage, and selflessness, since the fight jeopardizes her ability to remain in school. Diana Guzmán must enter a formal, male-constructed ring—and win—before her battles are accorded respect by (some) others, but they were serious from the start.

Diana's high school principal suggests that she needs help, but the sort of help the administrator envisions—one of politely enduring the confines of her existence—seems lethal for Diana, as reductive as a world confined to bedroom, beach, and Vegas club. Her father suggests a similar course of action: he admonishes her to shower at one point, more disgusted with her lack of characteristically feminine pride than with her post-gym odor, and suggests she wear a skirt and find a receptionist position in some office somewhere. Diana routinely rejects these ideas and ridicules them and the women who orbit within them.

At school, Diana performs a pithy and vulgar parody of her adversary Veronica's existence: "Always with that damn mirror of hers. 'Ooooh, just a second, let me get made up just perfect, so I can suck your dick which is all I'm good for anyway!'" Diana rejects both the lipstick and the role, although she does pursue her male love interest avidly. In fact, she becomes the aggressor, telling the object of her affection in an athletic (as opposed to romantic) clinch: "I love you—I really do." She lets go of his body only when she is ready, a sharp departure from the likes of Marisol and Veronica, and Adrian's former girlfriend, who is cut from the same mold. To his credit (and perhaps to the detriment of the film's authenticity), Adrian assuages her fears about her own appeal, insisting that she tastes sweet when she speculates that she must taste salty. "You still like me with my black eye?" she asks him at one point. "I think I like you more," he replies.

Kusama routinely voices her desire to craft an authentic character and story, but her desire to decimate claustrophobic boundaries imposed on girls like Diana Guzmán comes to the fore with equal ferocity. "Most people's lives are more like Diana Guzmán's than they are like anyone on *Dynasty*. I think that's what really ought to upset people," Kusama discloses (Baker). Most people's lives *are* like Guzmán's, but they don't seem to emerge from the same circumstances with the same sense of agency. In fact, Diana's existence comes to take on a *Dynasty*-like sheen as soon as she enters the ring. What confounds about *Girlfight* is not that it offers its protagonist an alternative to the status quo but that it strives to offer the resulting narrative as authentic. Diana's struggles seem common enough, and her skills and talents entirely plausible to this particular viewer, but her triumphs seem to belong to another realm, that of fantasy. We may detect a dual/dueling impulse in the director, between representing reality, with all of its flaws and ambiguities, and rewriting it, since reality tends to be so disappointing for girls like Diana. *Girlfight* fulfills wishes via the medium of mainstream cinema, long a purveyor of wish fulfillment in the traditional, patriarchal mold. It gives a classic fight with a new victor.

Kusama has fielded numerous questions that fall under the rubric of what the film is fighting for, or the politics of *Girlfight*:

> I've had a lot of interviews about *Girlfight*. "Is this character angry? Is this a feminist movie?" All these questions answer themselves or don't ultimately matter. What happened here in New York, with women being accosted by a mob of men in Central Park, is why I made this movie. Sooner or later these types of men are going to run into a woman who's as unenlightened as they are. And it is not going to be a pretty picture. She'll be armed and dangerous. And I don't mean this to sound like angry rhetoric. I'm just shocked that all we see are women running through the streets in fear. (Gordon)

Kusama's comment seems ambiguous, since women run with fear both in real life, as in the New York incident, and in mainstream narrative films, locked in the role of damsel in distress or victim in perpetuity. The film pulls in two directions simultaneously, striving to depict the harsh, reductive reality for Latina women, on the one hand, and on the other trying to furnish a corrective, in the form of a crusading, vindicating Macho Latina. For this reason, Klawans suggests that the film fails, suffering from a didactic, predictable quality and pandering to the politics of its intended audience: "All of the viewer's presumed wishes are fulfilled: Diana gets to be a warrior, her brother Tiny gets to be an artist, the brutal father gets his comeuppance and the sensitive hunk gets to prove himself a better kind of man. Had Kusama done any more to flatter a liberal audience, *Girlfight* would have ended with a November victory rally for Nader." Put starkly, Kusama has written a valentine to the disenfranchised and given audiences a liberal avenging angel in Diana Guzmán, not an authentic character.

Critic Rand Richards Cooper shares Klawans' interpretation of the film's politics but suggests that it does nothing to detract from its success as an entertainment: "Every time she unleashes an uppercut in the ring, it's a blow against horizons that have been set too narrowly for her." In Cooper's estimation, Diana manifests a new cinematic experience, appealing for its catharsis. For others, difference alone makes the film entertaining: "The gender tweak reconfigures all the genre's lines of perspective, like seeing *Othello* with the races reversed or an all-male *Swan Lake*" (Felperin, 48). It is important to remember that most people buy movie tickets not for ideology but for entertainment.

Girlfight poses a veritable gordian knot about how best to represent a Latina in film. In *Reconstructing Womanhood: The Emergence of the Afro-American Woman Novelist*, Hazel Carby examines the disappointing history of minority women's representation in the United States, riddled in the nineteenth century with such prevailing notions as the "cult of true womanhood." She focuses on the African American woman's solitary struggle to gain a voice in American society given "the dominant ideologies and literary conventions of womanhood which excluded them from the definition 'woman'" (6). Countless nineteenth-century novels and beauty manuals underscore the importance of whiteness in American womanhood. As Carby writes, "the struggle of black women to achieve adequate representation within the women's suffrage and temperance movements had been continually undermined by a pernicious and persistent racism" (4). Indeed, African-American women were only allowed to speak at the Columbian Exposition of 1893, which billed itself as a kind of gateway to the future, because of the culture's preoccupation with freaks and the carnivalesque: "The fact that six black women eventually addressed the World's Congress was not the result of sisterhood or evidence of a concern to provide a black political presence but part of a discourse of exoticism that pervaded the fair" (5). *Girlfight* came to light because a woman writer-director could see beyond the confines of her own culture and could imagine a more complex definition of the feminine. Diana challenges the assumptions of those around her as surely as Kusama challenges prevailing attitudes about what mainstream American audiences want to see made manifest in the multiplex. The question is whether Diana Guzmán gets embraced because of her exoticism or because of a culture's boredom with the limited scope of its own vision.

Guzmán seems most dangerously like a total work of fiction when she stands immune to the implied criticisms of others, a feat difficult enough for autonomous adults but exquisitely rare for young women. In the world beyond the silver screen, most teenage girls who subject themselves to harm do so not under the aegis of competition but in the form of "cutting," eating disorders, and sexually pleasuring young men at the risk of their own health, as in the case of Veronica and her infamous blowjobs. If this holds true for mainstream teenagers living in a socioeconomically advantaged environment, how much more so for women who, like Diana's character, dream of a place where "I won't get shot doing my laundry" or "raped in [my] own stairway"? Diana seems unique for a girl of her circumstances in her relative fearlessness and self-assurance, attacked for her choices on all fronts. Struggling to foster peace between Diana and Veronica, Marisol voices her desire to "be friends with everybody"; Diana responds, "yeah, well I hate her, and that's just the way I am." She remains immune to the traditional dictate that women should be likable and pleasing, having replaced it with her liberating gym teachings, which include "don't ever be sorry" and "no personal business in the gym."

Diana rejects her father's advice without trepidation. "Don't front like I'm some girly-girl when you know I'm not," she hurls at him, evenly. One of the most powerful yet improbable fight scenes in the film involves her extraction of justice from her father for his mistreatment of his family, in a brutal beating in the family's kitchen. Every scene of domestic abuse involving a father and daughter seems to locate the daughter as victim, but Diana triumphs over her father. Rand Richards Cooper locates a flaw in the scene's authenticity: "Kusama wants to subvert our conventional expectations, but what gets subverted instead is reality." There is truth to the criticism—the force of her anger is credible, but few daughters of abusive fathers have the sense of self to retrain the violence in the home against the classic perpetrators. The most surprising element of the scene may be its reception by mainstream audiences. Sherrie Inness argues that "toughness has been used to control women throughout America's history, especially in the twentieth century" (1999, 7). One would therefore expect some ambivalence at the theft of toughness by a young woman, but one finds instead unabashed celebration. A Screen Gems series of test screenings found that audience members across demographic lines prized that scene above all others (Gordon). As Kusama put it, "I think people find it extremely satisfying" (Gordon). This enjoyment seems subversive and illicit—sound foundations for pleasure—and thwarts the more typical course charted by films, as illustrated by scholar Rikki Morgan in an article about "the mechanics of masculinity" in Almodovar: "The patriarchal order has created mechanisms for dealing with its own inherent contradictions and vulnerability, however. These are largely based on notions of male moral superiority and a corresponding female inferiority and, consequently, guilt" (123–124). The reasons why an audience containing both men and women of all ages and cultural backgrounds might cheer Diana's humiliation of a patriarch are manifold, including plenty of choices for both the optimist and his/her counterpart.

In many respects, *Girlfight* seems a retelling of the classic fish-out-of-water story. Diana seems not pathological for her difference but out of place, a champion without a ring—until the film provides her with both ring and championship battle. At some point, we must concede the fictitious nature of a narrative that introduces a woman as a creature capable of violence: "Violence is not just the province of men and never has been. It's just been more acceptable to some degree for men to make that kind of trouble" (*"Culture"*). It's only novel because it's "delightfully unladylike" behavior. For what "ails" Diana, the film suggests, only a Panamanian boxing trainer can provide a balm—and Diana is the one who is forced to figure that out, steal and then work to pay for sessions, and finally deal with the consequences of turning her back on the prescribed parameters of her life. Her trainer emerges as a patient, kind revision of her violent father, a redeemed parent given a second chance by an eager surrogate daughter. When Hector prepares her for her ultimate battle, the repetitive cadences of the dialogue give it a religious, sagelike patina, as rich in balance as her exchanges with her father were rife with discord. "Inside, you know him?" he asks her, and she lists her opponent's strengths and weaknesses. "Inside, you know yourself?" he pursues. "Yeah, I do," she replies, and we believe her. "Then that's all you need," Hector decrees, blessing his star pupil before she enters the ring to be pummeled (and win).

When Karyn Kusama discusses the points of intersection between the actress Michelle and character Diana, she uses the language of idealizing or constructing a pure essence: "They both have tremendous raw gifts and native intelligence" ("Culture"). Ironically, the actress poses one of the most significant threats to the work's authenticity, as a young Latina who openly rejects the occupation and stance of her character. Michelle Rodríguez was born in Texas, the daughter of Puerto Rican parents. She spent time in the Caribbean en route to New Jersey. Both the film's countercultural impulse and the director's casting a nonprofessional were recognized and rewarded when Rodríguez won Best Debut Performer in the Independent Spirit Awards, or the Indies (Ebert).

In an interview conducted shortly after the film's release, Rodríguez indicated that she had stopped training as a boxer after the film because of the negative psychological impact: "Actually, I've stopped training. I was walking out of the gym with a, like, 'I-dare-you-to-try-to-rape-me' look on my face, a bit too cocky. I needed to chill out. I think your eyes give a lot away, but if you intimidate the wrong person on the street, forget about it" (Strauss). In other words, Diana Guzmán may emerge victorious within the parameters of *Girlfight*, but she cannot sustain life as an independent, fearless presence in the streets of New York without sustaining harm. Rodríguez goes on to share her mother's opinion of her role in the film: "she thinks it's kind of dykey to be so masculine in a film, where you're punching people" (Strauss). Diana Guzmán does not allow others' perceptions of her activities to alter her choices, and neither does Michelle Rodríguez, who did the film—but they matter enough to her to feature largely in her statements to the media. Ironically, in real life, the cost of being Diana Guzmán seems too steep to the Latina who brought her to life. The character may scorn those perceptions, but a young, heterosexual Latina ignores them at her own peril. A citizen of the United States bound by its laws faces similar obstacles to carrying on the sort of extracurricular battles Diana initiates at the film's start, as Rodríguez may realize after her own brush with the law: "Assault charges against Michelle Rodríguez were dropped Thursday after her roommate told a judge that she didn't want to pursue the case" (Soriano). Fighting and standing apart from society more often yield punishment than reward.

In *Tough Girls*, Sherrie A. Inness considers the cultural capital of Jodie Foster, Xena, Charlie's Angels, and other complex creatures from American popular culture who might make room for Karyn Kusama's new addition. Inness notes the potential uses of the "tough girl" and concludes that she exists in a realm defined largely by its limitations: "Thus, the tough girl might help to radicalize how women view femininity, but she is still very much an outsider in a culture that assumes that the smiling model on the cover of *Ladies' Home Journal* is somehow a more 'normal' woman" (181). Most alarming is the potential for her toughness to backfire:

> Tough women can offer women new role models, but their toughness may also bind women more tightly to traditional feminine roles—especially when the tough woman is portrayed as a pretender to male power and authority, and someone who is not tough enough to escape being punished for her gender-bending behavior. (Inness, 5)

Throwing punches may speak power in a patriarchal lexicon, but it does not necessarily follow that a woman's acquired facility with the language undermines its dissemination. Instead of loosening constraints and opening borders, the tough girl may inadvertently reinforce the very false binary oppositions she seeks to obliterate. When the tough girl is also a member of a minority, the spectacle of her toughness may pose additional complications. To repaint a patriarchal scene with a Latina victor, hard where once she was soft, may have the effect of a Homi Bhaba-esque, postcolonial act of mimicry in which the former colonial subject becomes entangled in a grotesque and painful masquerade. A facsimile of power may only trumpet powerlessness at a higher pitch, underscoring the centrality of the dominant force. Most disturbing of all is the possibility that a filmgoer might watch Diana Guzmán stand alone and dispatch the injustices in her life with relative ease, and deduce that no one need stand alongside the real-life Latina in her social and political battles. After all, her salvation may lie not in the collective righting of social wrongs but in her individual commitment to developing strength and agility in her local gym.

Girlfight does seem to represent some breed of progress for American cinema, but it reminds us with equal force that the process of accurate representation for minority women like the Latina is still in its infancy, perhaps because so much political work remains to be done in the society it strives to reflect. In *The New Latin American Cinema: A Continental Project*, Zuzana M. Pick reports that the case is no different in that arena:

> Although women are still underrepresented within the New Latin American Cinema, their practices represent a broad challenge to a movement that has generally overlooked women's issues. In terms of representation, the films of the movement have perpetuated if not explicitly endorsed traditional images of women. By underscoring class as a primary instance of social relations, the films of the New Latin American Cinema have rarely taken into account gender-specific forms of social and political oppression. The emergence of a new generation of women film- and video-makers in the last decade is only a first step in the attempt to integrate women's concerns into the movement. (66)

In short, we welcome the addition of the Macho Latina—or Macha Latina—to the stable of characters that formerly housed only the cantina girl, self-sacrificing señorita, and vamp, but we hope for a quick maturation process for narrative cinema produced in the Americas and beyond. Authentic wish fulfillment would dictate choices that run the gamut not merely from A to B, to paraphrase Edna St. Vincent Millay, but several alphabets-worth. As long as we're wishing, we should dream and work for a moment in history when a tale of an independent Latina's triumphs would not seem like wish fulfillment at all but a documentary of life so common as to seem banal.

Bibliography

Allende, Isabel. *The House of the Spirits*. New York: Bantam, 1993.

Ansen, David. "Any Given Sundance." *Newsweek*, June 14, 2000, 69.

Baker, Aaron. "A New Combination: Women and the Boxing Film. An Interview with Karyn Kusama." *Cineaste* 25, no.4 (2000): 22–26.

Carby, Hazel. *Reconstructing Womanhood: The Emergence of the Afro-American Woman Novelist*. New York: Oxford University Press, 1987.

Casper, Monica J. "Knockout Women: A Review of Karyn Kusama's *Girlfight*." *Journal of Sport and Social Issues* 25, no.1 (2001): 104–110.

Cooper, Rand Richards. "Girlfight." *Commonweal* 127, no. 20 (2000): 18–19.

"Culture: Giving women a little more punch Karyn Kusama steps into the ring with Alison Jones to talk about a women's sport that dare not speak its name." *Birmingham Post* (UK), April 23, 2001, 12.

Early, Gerald. *The Culture of Bruising: Essays on Prize-Fighting, Literature, and Modern American Culture*. Hopewell, NJ: Ecco, 1994.

Ebert, Roger. "Anti-Oscars Honor Indies." *Chicago Sun-Times*, March 26, 2001, 42.

"Films explore feminism, gender, sexuality: Third women's filmfest." *Korea Herald* (Seoul), April 3, 2001, 1.

Felperin, Leslie. "Girlfight." *Sight & Sound* 11, no. 4 (2001): 48.

Girlfight. Directed by Karyn Kusama, performers Michelle Rodríguez, Jaime Tirelli, and Paul Calderon. Columbia Tri-Star, 2001.

Gordon, Bette. "Karyn Kusama." *Bomb* 73 (Fall 2000). http://www.bombsitc .com/kusama/kusama2.html.

Heyck, Denis Lynn Daly. *Barrios and Borderlands: Cultures of Latinos and Latinas in the United States*. New York: Routledge, 1994.

Inness, Sherrie. *Tough Girls: Women Warriors and Wonder Women in Popular Culture*. Philadelphia: University of Pennsylvania Press, 1999.

Johnston, Sheila. "Film: Beaten black and blue on the rocky road to success 'Girlfight' was a huge hit at Sundance. But its director wasn't impressed as Sony tried to plug it to the masses. She tells Sheila Johnston why." *The Independent* (UK), April 8, 2001.

Keller, Gary D. *Hispanics and United States Film: An Overview and Handbook*. Tempe, AZ: Bilingual Review/Press, 1994.

Klawans, Stuart. "Girlfight." *The Nation*, October 30, 2000, 37.

Landesman, Cosmo. "Girlfight." *Sunday Times* (UK), April 22, 2001, 8.

Mirchevsky, Marie, et al. "Sundance 2000: Variety Is the Spice." *American Cinematographer* 81, no. 4 (2000): 84–115.

Morgan, Rikki. "Pedro Almodovar's *Tie Me Up! Tie Me Down!* The Mechanics of Masculinity." In *Me Jane: Masculinity, Movies and Women*, ed. Pat Kirkam and Janet Thumim. New York: St. Martin's Press, 1995.

Pearce, Garth. "She's a Knockout." *Sunday Times* (UK), April 22, 2001, 6.

Pick, Zuzana M. *The New Latin American Cinema: A Continental Project*. Austin: University of Texas Press, 1993.

Rich, B. Ruby. "Take it Like a Girl." *Sight & Sound* 11, no. 2 (2001): 16–18.

Segal, Victoria. "Choice: *Girlfight*." *The Times* (London), October 13, 2001.

Sklar, Robert. *Movie-Trade America: A Cultural History of American Movies*. New York: Vintage, 1994.

Soriano, Cesar G. "Roomie drops gloves in 'girl fight' case." *USA Today*, April 8, 2002, sec. C.08.

Strauss, Bob. "The Guide: Film: Worthy of the title: Newcomer Michelle Rodríguez trained for her role in *Girlfight* so well, she could have been a professional boxer. Fortunately, Hollywood wanted her more." *The Observer* (London), April 21, 2001, 15.

Travers, Peter. "Dancer in the Dark/Girlfight." *Rolling Stone* 12 (October 2000): 99–100.

SENSATIONAL BODIES
Discourses of Latina Femininity

CHAPTER 10

On the Semiotics of *Lorena Bobbitt*

CHARLA OGAZ

[S]ubversiveness is the kind of effect that resists calculation. *If one thinks of the effects of discursive productions, they do not conclude at the terminus of a given statement or utterance, the passing legislation, the announcement of a birth. The reach of their signifiability cannot be controlled by the one who utters or writes, since such productions are not owned by the one who utters them. They continue to signify in spite of their authors, and sometimes against their authors' most precious intentions.*

JUDITH BUTLER

limitrophe adj [F, *fr*. LL *limitrophus* bordering upon, fr. *L limit-*, *limes* limit + Gk *trophos* feeder, fr. *trephein* to nourish — more at ATROPHY] (1763) : situated on a border or frontier: ADJACENT

(*Webster's*, 661)

After severing her husband's penis in the early morning of June 23, 1993, Lorena Bobbitt was taken up by the media. The trial of Lorena Bobbitt on charges of "maliciously wounding her husband" was televised on CNN with full-day coverage. She entered a plea of not guilty by reason of temporary insanity, the defense arguing that she had "an impulse which she could not resist." In addition to the televised trial, the print media went into full spin to formulate its own characterizations. This essay considers some of this media spin under the trope of what I call a *limit-situation*, a cultural scenario of extreme liminality. I am concerned with understanding the ways in which Lorena Bobbitt is "othered" by and through mass-mediated representations. Given this focus on representations, I italicize *Lorena Bobbitt* to distinguish the cultural construction from the embodied and living Lorena Bobbitt.[1] Through the media's representations, we experienced only the mediated and projected images of Lorena Bobbitt, and in this way we witnessed only the mass cultural production of *Lorena Bobbitt*.

The Long and the Short of It

Newsweek's 1993 article, "Hanging by a Thread," announced John Wayne Bobbitt's acquittal on charges of raping his wife Lorena Bobbitt, as well as Lorena's upcoming trial on charges of "maliciously wounding" her husband.[2] The headline proclaimed, "Justice: A Virginia Jury lets John walk like a man. Lorena still faces her day in court. Rest assured, America, that the Bobbitt saga continues" (Adler et al., 50). The article includes a photo spread: on the left, we see what appears to be a post-trial smile on John Wayne Bobbitt's face; on the right we are shown Lorena Bobbitt, pre-trial, with her eyes averted and her pose suggesting an evasive movement away from the camera. Below the dyptich is another photograph, of the knife that Lorena used in severing John Wayne Bobbitt's penis.

Most interesting, however, is the inset text that serves to frame the photo of Lorena Bobbitt. It reads: "The Long and the Short: Length of the knife . . . Length of the penis that remained on his body . . . Distance Mrs. Bobbitt drove with penis in hand . . . Length of time the penis was separated from Bobbitt's body . . . Length of his recovery." The final line in the article's opening paragraph then remarks, "A hundred million American men will say, but none more fervently than Bobbitt himself, *let the healing begin*." Simultaneously addressing and constructing—that is, interpellating—a (white male) viewer, the article is framed by the promise of a social and physical rehabilitation for John Wayne Bobbitt. While mute on the issue of domestic violence, the narrative does point toward Lorena Bobbitt's upcoming trial and potential punishment. In the case of Lorena Bobbitt, the news media apparatus had swung into full effect.

Other scholars have written about the cultural production of *Lorena Bobbitt*. Feminist scholars, including myself, agree that both in the media coverage and in the trial itself, the representation of *Lorena Bobbitt* was fictionalized not just through interpretive extrapolation but also through social and cultural decontextualization. In a 1996 essay by Patricia J. Priest, Cindy Jenefsky, and Jill D. Swenson entitled "Phallocentric Slicing: 20/20's Reporting of Lorena and John Bobbitt," the authors argue that "[i]solating events from larger societal dynamics obscures the systemic and widespread character of sexual violence by presenting rape stories as unusual, deviant acts by deviant people" (103). The authors also draw on Helen Benedict's conclusions in *Virgin and Vamp: How the Press Covers Sex Crimes:*

> In addition to the overt use of rape myths, other more subtle and structural press practices function to minimize rape and domestic violence: the decontextualization and individualization of sexual/domestic violence stories, and the reliance upon press routines that privilege "the unusual" as news topics. Benedict describes the propensity of the press to focus exclusively on the individual traits of the perpetrator and the victim: "Rape as a societal problem has lost interest for the public and the press, and the press is reverting to its pre-1970 focus on sex crimes as individual, bizarre, or sensational case histories." (quoted in Priest et al., 102)

After their reading of 20/20's coverage, the authors conclude that

> the elision of the larger social context amplifies Bobbitt's behavior as "abhorrent" and renders it inexplicable—in short, "beyond belief." This structurally situates John's injuries at the center of the narrative and, in turn, effectively minimizes marital rape, normalizes male violence, positions him as the most aggrieved party, and constructs Lorena's actions alone as extreme and inhumane. (Priest et al., 103)

This decontextualization of events renders them more available for imaginary play and performative formation. By ignoring the context of patriarchy and its various forms of violent masculinity, the ritual abuse of women and other misogynist acts are perpetuated. Though I disagree with Jean S. Filetti's reading that "Lorena Bobbitt, too, fulfilled society's expectations of the damsel in distress" (475), I do think that domestic violence is about gender performance. However, rather than reading images of *Lorena Bobbitt* for how they define femininity, I argue that *Lorena Bobbitt* was raced/colored, sexualized, and classed (read: othered) in ways that make traditional paradigms of "femininity" unavailable. Instead, we see sexualizations and exotifications that result in a different engendering than that of white women.

To situate my analysis, I consider *Lorena Bobbitt* as a news object and figuration, treating various mass-mediated news texts as a national literature that emplots and characterizes. I assume that *Lorena Bobbitt* functions similarly to what Toni Morrison in her book, *Playing in the Dark*

(1992), calls "a dark, abiding, signing Africanist presence" (5). Morrison suggests that national literatures, like writers, "seem to end up describing and inscribing what is really on the national mind" (14). If we understand national news reporting as a national literature, what becomes transparent for Morrison in her work and also for me in mine is "the self-evident ways that Americans choose to talk about themselves through and within a sometimes allegorical, sometimes metaphorical, but always choked representation of an African presence" (17) and, in this case, of Lorena Bobbitt as other.

Popular cultural texts serve to entertain at the same time that they mediate and represent contemporary social relations. For the purpose of entertaining, they often employ cultural and social liminality to produce their sensation. Often, this liminality is achieved by reproducing social stratification practices in representation. Applying a theory of "multiple subjectivity" to read these texts, we might better understand how liminality is achieved through the performance of a politics of identity and difference in the mass media. As Lynda Nead points out, images of powerful or threatening women simultaneously summon up and visually control their power. Thus the "power of these images cannot be said to lie simply in their subjects, but rather in the complex overlayerings of meaning and desire that run across them" (14).

Like mediated women of color, Lorena Bobbitt contains complex overlayerings of meaning and desire; a theory of multiple subjectivity shows how this complexity produces a liminal zone of entertainment for a dominant gaze. The bifurcations sustaining these representations are legacies of colonialism that persist in contemporary cultural production. While disrupting binaries is part of a postcolonial project, Stuart Hall (1996) warns that

> holding fast to differentiation and specificity, we cannot afford to forget the over-determining effects of the colonial moment, the "work" which its binaries were constantly required to do to re-present the proliferation of cultural difference and forms of life, which were always there, within the sutured and over-determined unity of that simplifying, over-arching binary, "the West and the Rest." (249)

A postcolonial cultural critique must consistently address these colonial legacies as present and persistent. Speaking of the process of colonialism, Hall notes that "[t]his process was organized by those shifting mechanisms of 'otherness', alterity and exclusion and the tropes of fetishism and pathologisation, which were required if 'difference' was ever to be fixed and consolidated within a 'unified' discourse of *civilization*" (252). Thus, "civilization" in the West continues to stabilize its boundaries through primitivist tactics. Mark Antliff and Patricia Leighten define the concept of the primitive as "the product of the historical experience of the West and more specifically as an ideological construct of colonial conquest and exploitation." Its importance "can be best grasped from the standpoint of a related set of oppositions mapped out in terms of time/space, gender, race, and class" (170). A feminist history of primitivism in the depiction of women of color must therefore work to show how they are simultaneously sexed and sexualized, raced, classed and gendered in negating ways in society.

limit *vt* (14c) **1** : to assign certain limits to : PRESCRIBE **2 a** : to restrict to set bounds or limits **b** : to curtail or reduce in quantity or extent

limit *n* [ME, fr. MF *limite*, fr. L *limit-*, *limes* boundary—more at LIMB] (15c) **1 a** : a geographical or political boundary **b** *pl* : the place enclosed within a boundary : BOUNDS **2 a** : something that bounds, restrains, or confines **b** : the utmost extent **3** : LIMITATION **4** : a determining feature or differentia in logic **5** : a prescribed maximum or minimum amount, quantity, or number . . . **7** : something that is exasperating or intolerable
(*Webster's*, 661)

In the Spotlight

An illustration of *Lorena Bobbitt* captioned "In the Spotlight" appeared in the January 24, 1994, edition of *Time*.[3] Eyes bulging and slanted, she is pictured with knife in hand: caricatured. The image portrays derangement and insanity. Her mouth is figured into a gasp, and a shadow looms over her head and behind her. Her skin is darkened. She stares at her husband, who is asleep in the background. The moment just prior to castration is thus imagined, with *Lorena Bobbitt* caught "in the spotlight." At the same time that "intent" is depicted, so is "insanity," the only plea available to victims of domestic violence who self-defend and resist their assailants' violence with violence. Self-defense, however, is not suggested by this caricature, as his only misdeed appears to be defenseless sleep.

Through the mass media, the everyday and the extraordinary are conflated in the cultural construction of *Lorena Bobbitt*. The level and significance she assumes partially reside in her simple everydayishness. To many of us, she is, indeed, familiar. To others, however, she espouses the peculiarity of either gross or tantalizing spectacle. Priest, Jenefsky, and Swenson (1996) argue that the decontextualization of sex crimes is made possible by individualizing these crimes and making them seem unusual:

> The systematic nature of the bias described here . . . further calcifies persistent stereotypes and reinforces public denial about the magnitude of violence against women. Sociologist Herbert Gans claims in his book, *Deciding What's News*, that news stories about "the unusual" are often about threats to the reigning "white male social order." (112)

On most levels, however, the descriptions of her "everyday" materiality are the tantalizing, determining factors. And this, I would say, is determined by the media's representations and creation of objectified others.

Part of the way in which *Lorena Bobbitt* has been othered is connected to her immigrant status and her dispersed/displaced worker status within a global economy. Some references note that Lorena Bobbitt is from Ecuador, others claim she is from Venezuela. Such inexactitude in reporting suggests that it doesn't matter where she's from. Rather, the point seems to be to mark her as immigrant or alien/other. She is also marked as Other via discursive practices that relegate her to U.S. "trash" culture: comedic notations of her *Spandex* shorts and post-trial trips to *McDonald's* and *Disneyworld* mock her working-class status, as do amused references to her job as a manicurist. Yet another immigrant woman of color worker performing domestic labor and serving the leisure status of middle-class U.S. American women, *Lorena Bobbitt* inhabits a discursive space where cultural and liminal artifacts and issues are (re)produced, signified, and (de)valued. That is, *Lorena Bobbitt* is a complex discursive site where U.S. cultural symbols, interpretations, and meanings collide and work to resolve resulting anxieties.

With control over what is to be seen and therefore (consciously) witnessed, the mass-mediated press corps constructs both meaning and literal realities. This opportunity to "perform" (understood as the process of bringing into being) is often guarded with unending racisms, sexisms, heterosexisms, and classisms. Performativity is understood as language having the ability to create reality, as in "I pronounce you man and wife." Historically, performatives are a grammatical and practical realm of public privilege and progress, power and consequence. They have a peculiar relationship to both embodiment and the maintenance of private/public distinctions. The public realm stages and performs subjectivities and embodiments; the private realm must house them. Performatives are used to linguistically (re)construct and repeat boundaries or real-life structures across axes of identity and difference. These spaces where reality is supposedly only re-presented but is actually constructed are what I refer to as limit-situations. I do so in order to focus attention on the axes of identity and difference that get created, imposed, and enforced through limits, that is, through bifurcations between self and other that make self different from other. In performing these limit-situations, the mass media interpellate their market audience, getting people to identify with the dominant subjectivity and to dis-identify with the "butt of the joke," so to speak.

To move toward an examination of performatives, resulting "embodiments," and their role in maintaining the public/private binary in media representations of Lorena Bobbitt, it is helpful to consider Robert Gooding-Williams's (1993) argument in "'Look, a Negro!'" Gooding-Williams (re)posits, through the work of Frantz Fanon, a distinction between what is called an individual's "corporeal schema" and a "racial, epidermal schema":

> By "corporeal schema" Fanon means the image each of us has of him or herself as a body located somewhere in physical space. It is an image that each of us ordinarily constructs and needs repeatedly to reconstruct as he or she moves about the world. Reminiscent of Jean Lhermitte, who situates the corporeal schema or 'body image' on the 'fringe' of consciousness, Fanon himself describes it as the source of an "implicit knowledge" that each of us possesses of the position of his or her body in relation to other physical objects. (164)

Fanon suggests that a "racial epidermal schema" is performed differently than the "corporeal schema." The racial epidermal schema is constructed and enacted in, for example, the performative "Look! A Negro!" that may differentiate and socially construct one's body via "the look." Following Judith Butler (1990), the performative, in its strictest sense, "serves to effect a transition or constitutes the performance of the specified act by virtue of its utterance" (27). Thus, "race" is performed and enacted.

As in Lorena Bobbitt's case, one's "corporeal schema" can be quite violently changed and simultaneously socially (re)constructed to enact "race" itself. With this (re)construction and insertion of a racialized stereo/archetype, one's social, public, visual body becomes an *interpreted image*. Thus I argue that the continual work of imposed, interpreted, racialized, and otherwise oppressive images functions to create a public version (and disavowal) of many bodies. This is, of course, the extent to which bodies are the site of struggle for categories of gender, sexuality, class, race, and other social oppressions and identities.

Because many of us do not have control of the interpreted images that are supposedly representative and performative of our bodies—and with our bodies, our lived experiences—the bodies and corporeal schemas of marginalized peoples and their first-hand experiences are not usually present in the public realm. There are innumerable interpreted images of our embodied experiences, but these acts of signification work via control and maintenance of the public realm, that is, of what can be seen and therefore legitimated. Gooding-Williams credits Fanon with showing how "prejudices are linked to interpreted images, and that these images have a narrative significance" (166). To this end, racisms, (hetero)sexisms, and classisms are used, though used differently, to construct elaborate narratives and judicial truths—not to mention "closets" of subjugated and privatized, invisibilized bodies.

These axes of social and cultural power dynamics are functions of identity and difference: inclusion and exclusion, sameness and otherness. They are constituted through subjectivity and objectivity. Because these ideologies work most dominantly through bifurcation and then hierarchization, there are borders that act as absolute distinctions between the opposites. Culturally, then, it seems reasonable to suggest that politics that are based on and function by bifurcation must also create borders—and then social and cultural limit-situations—through identification and differentiation. The results are absolutist, static, and often oppressive articulations of self and other that resist internal differences within the categories and similarities between the two polar positions.

In his explanation of social conflicts, Victor Turner in *The Anthropology of Performance* (1987) describes a stage characterized by crisis:

> Members of a group . . . remember, when crisis strikes, previous crises—
> where they stood then, how they felt about the positions adopted by other
> group members; and nonrational considerations become prominent—temperamental hostilities, unconscious sexual attractions, reanimated infantile anxieties, and the like. The cleavage is thus likely to deepen by including more and
> more grounds of opposition. (103–104)

Thus, Gooding-Williams refers to his project as one of "demythification":

> The point of such an investigation would not be to *demystify* black bodies
> (that is, the point would not be to identify the social causes of their actions

and attributes), but to *demythify* them, that is, to subject to critical scrutiny the allegories of American social and political life intimated in characterizing them. (158)

Although he is speaking to the Rodney King beating, it is also possible to apply these terms to the discursive production of *Lorena Bobbitt*. In the limits constructed by the mass-mediated construction of *Lorena Bobbitt*, we can locate cleavages and gaps that are then resutured even prior to the trial or verdict. The *Newsweek* article mentioned earlier is one example of this attempt at reconciliation in the narrative. The mythification of *Lorena Bobbitt* incorporates a politics of identity and difference, for, as Gooding-Williams remarks, "in contemporary American society, where all individuals and groups are subject to racial classification, the concept of racial ideology applies in fact to all representations of social activity" (158).

liminal *adj* [L *limin-, limen* threshold] **1** : of or relating to a sensory threshold **2** : barely perceptible

(*Webster's*, 661)

In a more extended example of this mass-mediated performativity of identity and difference, I will now consider an ambivalent though anxious representation of Lorena Bobbitt as an othered body. The invisibility of Latinos in popular culture has left a sort of unknowability, an uncertain categorizability in their social and racial formation. Nevertheless, Latinos experience and suffer racializations and racism. Those outside of the dominant black/white bifurcation are often invisibilized or racialized ambivalently within a continuum of black to white. Elizabeth Martinez (1993) hints at a lack of understanding concerning the ways in which racism is manifested against Latino people. She argues that "a semi-contemptuous indifference toward Latinos . . . has emanated from institutions in the dominant society for decades. . . . we find them somewhat more likely to be invisibilized—rendered 'unseen'—than problematized" (25).

The problem of speaking to this invisibility and exclusion lies in how Latinos remain outside of and behind the dominant oppositions structuring meaning. Understanding particular and localized racisms in nonblack, nonwhite subjectivities is thus challenging. In tandem with this, we must also remember the inherent/inherited hybridity of most Latino subjectivities. Some Latinas, like myself, are regularly able to "pass" in a dominant white culture, while others suffer oppressive exclusion and racial denigration, like my mother, a Mexican-American, who was called "Nigger" in the 1960s South. Nevertheless, a different "racism" can be identified in its matrices of race, ethnicity, culture—and especially for Latinos—nationality. In this regard, Martinez comments,

> More often than not, [Latino/as] are rendered additionally vulnerable by their skin color and other physical features. Nationality then combines with a nonwhite (though not Black) physical appearance to subject them to an oppression that is a form of racism. Even if a nonwhite appearance is lacking, however, nationality and culture create a separate peoplehood as the basis for oppression. (32)

This (in)visibility is strangely linguistic to the extent that it lacks social and popular categories for its conceptualization. Given this, a racialization emerges that is confused and uncertain.

Interestingly, one of the more imaginative attempts to "resuture" *Lorena Bobbitt* into a recognizable cultural paradigm appeared in the liberal news journal, *The Nation*. Entitled "Phallus Interruptus: Culture Watch," John Leonard's (1993) commentary offers a lucid example of the media's ambivalent racialization of *Lorena Bobbitt*. Leonard opens his article with the facts: "Briefly, Lorena, a 24-year-old, 5-foot-2-inch, 95-pound Venezuelan immigrant, says that she was sexually assaulted and raped by her husband, who forced her to have an abortion and, incidentally, never waited for her to come to orgasm: 'I just wanted him to disappear . . .' " (617–620). With these "facts," Lorena Bobbitt is embodied through her height, weight, nationality, and age. Simultaneously, she is sexualized by contempt for her sexual desire.

John Leonard's satirical diatribe works to build a visual impression/ schema of Lorena: "When Lorena made her escape at 4 AM, with the organ and the knife, in a 1991 Mercury Capri, was it some weird form of mourning for her unborn child that made her toss Columbus out the window onto the lawn of the Party-Kake Daycare Center?" He (re)creates the scene for us and makes certain to elaborate the "hidden" facts, the names of the places, the identification of the "get-away car," the point at which we enter as spectators. Leonard slowly motions us away from the presumed certainty of facts, however, and beckons us toward a more ambiguous inquiry:

> Was it altogether necessary that Lorena work in a nail salon, even if she embezzled $7,200 from her employer, and even though that employer, Janna Bisutti, nevertheless stands by her? . . . And I haven't even mentioned the

tape recorder, the satellite dish or the plastic Christmas tree; the Kentucky
Fried Chicken, the spandex shorts or the wedding breakfast at Bob's Big Boy.
(617–620)

The questioning continues as he invokes the implausibility of *Lorena*'s
situation. His assumptions about the "lower class" lead him to wonder
why she needed to work after she embezzled $7,200 from her employer.
The list of kitsch locations speaks contemptuously of the lowly. And yet,
in the same breath, Leonard manages both to condemn *and* problematize
Lorena's circumstances. His signifiers move us out of the realm of the
understandable, and therefore rational, and into the alliteration of the extraordinary. For his purposes, the everyday tape recorder and Kentucky
Fried Chicken become sensationalized as extraordinary. Through the
spectacle of his authorship, the social (re)construction and performativity
of *Lorena Bobbitt* has begun. Simultaneously, within and because of all
of this, the dis-identification of the audience is achieved. The reader is by
now voyeuristically well distanced from this character, ready to imagine
the extraordinary narrative that follows.

Robert Gooding-Williams suggests that one way of analyzing racial ideology is through the use of literary genealogy. In taking up Toni Morrison's analytical strategies in *Playing in the Dark*, he comments,

> How does literary utterance arrange itself when it tries to imagine the Afri-
> canist other? What are the signs, the codes, the literary strategies designed to
> accommodate this encounter? What does the inclusion of Africans or African-
> Americans do to and for the work? . . . they pertain explicitly to the functions
> which literary works assign to racially classified individuals (what the inclu-
> sion of such individuals does to and for a work), and to the ways in which
> literary works "arrange" themselves so as to "accommodate" these functions.
> (160)

In reading Leonard's characterizations, we might ask similar questions to
understand how he racializes *Lorena Bobbitt*. Leonard's literary utterance
has arranged itself as a figurative extrapolation with distance from *Lorena
Bobbitt*. Yet how does his ambivalent racialization perform this?

> None of this would happen at the Royalton, where Conde Nasties dine. But
> out there in the Trash Culture, Lorena Bobbitt is more like Mary Beth than
> she in any way resembles Kali, the Black Mother of the Indian subconti-
> nent, with her girdle of fingers and necklace of skulls. Or Aramaic Atargatis,

Fish Mother of the Syrians, who insisted on castration as a prerequisite for priesthood. Or Dorago, the Volcano Goddess of the Philippines, demanding a male sacrifice once a year, like a magazine subscription renewal. Or Cybele, the Great Mother of the old Near East, who did permanent damage to her lover/grandson Attis. Or Gaea, who fashioned from "gray adamant" the saw-toothed sickle with which Cronus hacked off his father's sex. Or Janet of Reno, the Mesopotamian/Banca Nazionale del Lavoro Cover-Up Girl, who diets on the eyes and wallets of Burbank television executives. (6)

Leonard surveys the world's cultures to find a (mythological) place for *Lorena Bobbitt*. There is a simultaneous distancing and objectification, as she "is more like Mary Beth than . . ." the mythically other. Nevertheless, he outlines comparisons that spell out (his own) anxiety by displaying figures of torturing women who assail and assault men's genitalia. Is *Lorena* to be identified with Black Kali, as Leonard describes mutilation of fingers and heads for self-adornment? Or Ataragatis, who requires worship through loss of virility? Or Dorago the mankiller, if not man-eater? Or Cybele, who incestuously marks her kin? Or Gaea, who fulfills the Oedipal resolution? Or Janet of Reno, who figures similarly and preys on contemporary, powerful men of the kingdom of Burbank? Leonard searches his mythic globe to find a reference to classify and racially identify the new woman (of color) assailant he intends to figure.

Leonard's narrative can be read as one of castration anxiety, or at least of anxiety that the phallus might be interruptus, and through his attempt to master this anxiety, he performs an ambivalent racialization in the course of a ruthless, mythic, and criminalizing sexualization of *Lorena Bobbitt*. Class trashing runs throughout. She is located next to Mary Beth in U.S. trash culture, but just as quickly he "darkens" his suspicions, globalizing his narrative and tapping a multitude of mythological (male) terrors. This narrative works various performatives across lines of sex/gender, sexuality, class, and race in order to resolve a crisis of meaning. Leonard structures his grammar into interrogatives, and in this way, each sentence rests in frustrated uncertainty and ambivalence. He scans the mythic globe to explain and so to categorize and stratify Lorena Bobbitt.

Gooding-Williams's work uses Frantz Fanon to understand the conceptual consequences of these racialized performatives, which encode objectified bodies with cultural meaning: "Fanon interprets such identifications as performative utterances that assail the Negro, destroying his or her 'corporeal schema' and imposing on him or her a 'racial epidermal schema'" (164). For Fanon, the "corporeal schema" is the concept we have of our own bodies that resides in the fringes of consciousness. Gooding-Williams explains that Fanon links

> the experience of being seen by another human being to the experience of being the object of a linguistically performed act of racial identification. Fanon's emphasis on the way in which the experience of being seen is linguistically mediated . . . suggests that the experience of the look of the other always has a specific and historically constituted cultural dimension. (174)

The "specific and historically constituted cultural dimension" of Leonard's work is mythic, though predictable. His performatives work to sexualize Lorena, engender her, and cast her into the lowly. He darkens his image of her through the use and repetition of transcultural myths, and in this way he draws on and narratively performs an ambivalent categorization of *Lorena*. Yet the citations that he makes continue a history of (racially) sexualizing and (sexually) racializing assailants of the phallus. She is engendered with malice and resolved as "trash." Though his citations appear to contextualize Lorena's self-defensive violence, they displace violent patriarchy as the real social and cultural context.

Leonard continually struggles to locate *Lorena* within U.S. racial/class dichotomies. "Waif-thin, keen-eyed Lorena, in fact, lacks even the pluck and perk of those TV heroines from Farrah Fawcett in 1984 to Melissa Gilbert just last week who have made Abuse of the Month movies a redress-of-grievance network genre. As if dreaming instead of Caracas, she did the deed in some sort of fugue state." Our character reappears as a waif, a piece of property found washed up, a stray animal. Her eyes are "keened," a reference to the mourning and wailing practices of women around the world who have historically and anthropologically been described as "hysterical." And rather than call attention to the need for some sort of social meditation on the prevalence of domestic violence in U.S. society, he cites made-for-TV movies where grievances are redressed. But after searching in the "dark" to find a cultural identification, *Lorena* appears stereotypically juxtaposed to the white, "pluck and perky" beauty queens of Hollywood TV who have portrayed, and presumably sold, retaliatory "husband killing" as entertainment.

Leonard travels his mythic globe to find many of the dark women who appear in allegories of castration anxiety. A peculiar (in)visibility is what remains: he performs a racial epidermal schema that adds to the media construction of *Lorena Bobbitt*. Again, a Latina is constructed in the absence of clear historical markers to reference her. Despite Leonard's seeming ambivalence, *Lorena Bobbitt* and the castration liminality which she represents are performed through an extraordinarily raced, sexed, classed, and gendered mythology.

Leonard moves from U.S. trash culture to survey the "Third World," ending up back at the perilous pitfalls of substitution with Farrah Fawcett as cultural marker. Where can Lorena fit in? Leonard manages to (re)construct a sexist and racist history of "dark" Third World women, and in this way take readers on an exotic tour. And still he can only fit *Lorena* into trash culture in the end — which he cannot decide how to race. Gooding-Williams explains that "once the representations of these black characters have been genealogically exposed, the assignment of these characters to particular roles can be read allegorically as commenting on the social and political status of blacks in America" (174). But there is no allegory or fixed racial, epidermal schema for Leonard to use as performative to signify *Lorena* as Latina. Instead, she sits at the bottom of his hierarchy, incomprehensible through his inability to fix her culturally. And yet, while she cannot be precisely located on his cultural and historical map, her "sexuality" — outlined by her threatening ability to self-defend — is clearly marked as perverse. Like the *Time* magazine caricature cited earlier, Leonard's piece ignores the domestic violence she and witnesses described, details that might have offered a more realistic, though less sensational, tale.

In the same sense that Leonard performs *Lorena*'s racially sexualized femininity for his readership in *The Nation*, John Bobbitt abusively performed Lorena's racially sexualized femininity for her in their marriage. The testimony of Susan Feister (SF), the defense's psychiatric expert witness, is quoted at length (Lisa Kemler is LK, defense attorney for Lorena Bobbitt):

> LK: (Can you elaborate) on what John would say to her?
> SF: She described that he began an intermittent barrage of verbal abuse. He would taunt her with repeated degrading and demeaning comments. He told her she was ugly, that she had a bad figure, that she was small, dark, Spanish, a number of them were comments that had racial overtones . . . that she had small breasts, that she was too skinny, that she couldn't speak English, and he would also threaten and taunt her that he was going to have her deported back to South America.
> LK: What effect did that have on Lorena?
> SF: Lorena started to believe a lot of the things that John was telling

her and it started to have a negative impact on how she was feeling about herself. She began to have a very poor self-esteem, have a very bad image of herself, feeling rejected, worthless, unattractive, that no one would want her.[4]

Butler's explanation of the imposed character of femininity is helpful in this context: "femininity is thus not the product of a choice, but the forcible citation of a norm, one whose complex historicity is indissociable from relations of discipline, regulation, punishment" (23). *Lorena Bobbitt* is repeatedly made to perform inferiorized, racist, and sexist versions of femininity. Thus my analysis implicates both Leonard and John Wayne Bobbitt in histories of colonization practices.

Eventually, Leonard cannot contain the real function of his literary and journalistic performance. His admission that "the idea that several hundred years of Anglo-American jurisprudence can be jettisoned when ideological fashion insists on it" (16) is the only honest social contextualization he gives. Notice he racializes jurisprudence or the legal system in general, as White. In order to resolve his own anxiety, Leonard's narrative needed to work through myths, which are instruments of (psychic) survival. The "phallus interruptus" becomes the effect of yet another feminized "dark" alien, not of violent patriarchy.

In response to a cultural crisis, *Lorena Bobbitt* is represented through powerful performatives that construct an "epidermal schema" by imagining and situating her within a body of patriarchal mythology. Lorena Bobbitt's own body posits the limits of John Leonard's and John Wayne Bobbitt's anxious, hierarchic bifurcations. Yet the performativity, journalistic and spousal, that created *Lorena Bobbitt* is made possible only through a decontextualization that refuses to see the epidemic of violence against women. As Priest and colleagues write,

> Lorena's actions become inexplicable and pathological only in the absence of knowledge about systematic sexual violence against women. FBI statistics for 1993 indicate that four women are killed *every day* in the U.S. by current or former husbands or lovers or by prospective suitors. Tragically, too, one in every four women is raped in her lifetime. In light of such systematic abuse and terrorization of women, is it not more surprising that so few women have lopped off penises than that Lorena Bobbitt did so. (107)

The responses to the Lorena Bobbitt affair were widespread and varied, yet always highly invested. Public surveys were taken; talk shows interrogated every person possibly tied to the crime and every person remotely tied to the lives the crime reaches; protests in Ecuador were shown via satellite; individuals, collectives and institutions entered the public discussion. Much of this spin can legitimately be tied to media frenzy and sensationalism. And yet the content also showcases a social and cultural rupture: symbolically, the retaliation against the phallus. The "severing of a penis" as signifier is seen as a cultural but extremely liminal social crisis which demands a symbolic re-suturing to and categorization within the discursive boundaries of a (still) male-dominated U.S. society.

This process of recovery and categorization is liminal, troubling, and significant. These hegemonic narratives are disciplining norms, which in this case, are (re)performed in dramatic ways because of a transgression of the Law of the Father on the body of the white man. In this way, a limit-situation is saturated with cultural vexation and agitation. The situation and location that I point to as/at the center of this project is a third, in-between site of obscured and opaque meaning. That is, I do not point to the guilt or innocence of her crime but to ways that domestic violence is still a very liminal issue in U.S. culture—newsworthy mostly when a man is injured. And it is liminal because it represents a crossroads and a potential crisis in meaning. Unconscious, repressed, and invisibilized cultural material is pushed into the light of day. Its contents capture our attention and stimulate us through repetitive, primary narrative construction. It is a space of disturbance that expresses irresolution, indecision, fragmentation, and loss of order. Characterizing *Lorena Bobbitt* as lowly and extraordinary is one way to discredit the logic of retaliatory violence and the right to self-defend in an environment of consistent and perpetual physical, emotional, and psychic abuse.

But the reporting of this crime didn't have to happen this way. Popular culture is full of sites laden with cultural struggle over meaning. By paying critical attention to mass-mediated texts, we can learn to mark social stratification and oppression. Insisting that cultural critique is part of the exploration and production of meaning can work to further the development of skills for a postcolonial education. However, one must remember that as participants in culture, we all have stakes and emotional investments that must be explored. The liminality of entertainment can touch the identities of people in ways that critique makes conscious, and the work of cultural critique is best served by an affirmation of the important knowledge contained in one's own experience of these forms. Curricular change to include the study of mass and popular culture, the study of women of color and all people who are usually rendered complexly (in)visible in entertainment and history is also a necessity. Only through such critical education will we continue to move US dominant culture beyond its colonial investments.

Notes

1. I make this move in relation to the distinction Kathleen K. Rowe (1994) makes in her article, "Roseanne: Unruly Woman as Domestic Goddess"(*Television: The Critical View*, Oxford: Oxford University Press, 1994, p. 202). Rowe uses the name "Roseanne" in her analysis "to refer to Roseanne Barr-as-sign, a person we know only through her various roles and performances in the popular discourse."

2. In 1993, Lorena Bobbitt severed part of her husband's penis with a kitchen knife as he slept, alleging years of emotional and physical abuse. She was acquitted in 1997.

3. No artist cited. The illustration is signed "c." "In the Spotlight," *Time*, January 24, 1994, 21.

4. Transcribed from a video recording of the "Lorena Bobbitt Trial," Cable News Network, January 17, 1994.

Bibliography

Adler, Jerry, Ellen Ladowsky, and Melinda Liu. "Hanging by a Thread." *Newsweek*, November 22, 1993, 50–51.

Antliff, Mark, and Patricia Leighten. "Primitive." In *Critical Terms for Art History*. Chicago: University of Chicago Press, 1996.

Anzaldúa, Gloria, and Cherríe Moraga, eds. *This Bridge Called My Back: Writings by Radical Women of Color*. Latham, New York: Kitchen Table/Women of Color Press, 1982.

Butler, Judith. *Gender Trouble: Feminism and the Subversion of Identity*. New York: Routledge, 1990.

Filetti, Jean S. "From Lizzie Borden to Lorena Bobbitt: Violent Women and Gendered Justice." *Journal of American Studies* 35, no.3 (2001): 471–484.

Gooding-Williams, Robert. " 'Look, a Negro!' " In *Reading Rodney King, Reading Urban Uprising*. New York: Routledge, 1993.

Hall, Stuart. "When Was 'the Post-colonial'? Thinking at the Limit." In *The Post-Colonial Question: Common Skies: Divided Horizons*, ed. Iain Chambers and Lidia Curti. London: Routledge, 1996.

"In the Spotlight." *Time*, January 24, 1994, 21.

Leonard, John. "Phallus Interruptus: Culture Watch." *The Nation*, November 22, 1993, 617–620.

"Lorena Bobbitt Trial." Cable News Network, January 17, 1994.

Martinez, Elizabeth. "Beyond Black/White: The Racisms of Our Time." *Social Justice* 20 (1993): 22–34.

Morrison, Toni. *Playing in the Dark*. Cambridge, MA: Harvard University Press, 1992.

Nead, Lynda. *Myths of Sexuality*. Malden, MA: Blackwell, 1988.

Priest, Patricia J., Cindy Jenefsky, and Jill D. Swenson. "Phallocentric Slicing: 20/20's Reporting of Lorena and John Bobbitt." In *No Angels: Women Who Commit Violence*. New York: HarperCollins, 1996.

Rowe, Kathleen K. "Roseanne: Unruly Woman as Domestic Goddess." In *Television: The Critical View*. Oxford: Oxford University Press, 1994.

Turner, Victor. *The Anthropology of Performance*. New York: PAJ Publications, 1987.

Webster's New Collegiate Dictionary. Springfield, MA: G.&C. Merriam Company, 1980.

CHAPTER 11

Disorderly Bodies and Discourses of Latinidad in the Elián González Story

ISABEL MOLINA GUZMÁN

In the spring of 2000, at the height of the news coverage surrounding Elián González, the young Cuban refugee found floating in international waters off the Florida coast, 78 percent of the U.S. population was actively and regularly following the story (*Gallup Poll Reports*, April 28, 2000). According to a report by the Center for Media and Public Affairs (2000), the Elián story was the second most reported story in the history of the contemporary general media. (The most reported story was the O. J. Simpson trial.) Few stories in recent U.S. history have so captured the popular imagination and media interest as did the dramatic and sometimes surreal events pertaining to the international custody battle over Elián, a photogenic Cuban boy who watched his mother die as she struggled to bring him to the United States.

Underlying the general news coverage of Elián's saga is a story ideologically driven by symbolic constructions of family, home, and nation, a story ultimately framed by the media as a transnational family conflict (Banet-Weiser 1999).[1] Since "motherhood" is one of the central signs associated with family and domesticity, it is not surprising that the news coverage of the Elián conflict foregrounded the lives, voices, and bodies of Cuban women. Consequently, it was informed by a gendered discourse, a set of textual and visual practices in which the female body and women's ideological position within the private sphere of home and family became central. The goal of this essay is to identify and critique the narrative practices that produced this gendered discourse by examining the politics of signification surrounding Elián's mother, Elisabet Brotons, and his second cousin, the U.S.-born Marisleysis González.[2]

In particular, this essay focuses on Marisleysis, Elián's media-dubbed surrogate mother. The representational politics that surround Marisleysis, however, cannot be understood in isolation from but rather in relation to those surrounding the story's other main woman, Elisabet Brotons, Elián's mother.[3] Thus, my analysis begins by examining the symbolic role of Elisabet as structured through the narrative practice of gendered disembodiment. This practice positioned Elisabet as a hyperinvisible body, while the narrative structure of tropicalized gendering marked Marisleysis as a hypervisible sexualized and racialized body. The essay concludes with a discussion of the performance of Latina bodies as nationalized bodies in the U.S. media.

This project is grounded theoretically in a multicultural feminist framework that interrogates the intersecting identity vectors of gender, sexuality, race, class, and nation (Shohat 1998; Shohat and Stam 2003). As such, it contextualizes the hyperbolized images of Elisabet and Marisleysis within a broader system of signification that generally elides the diverse transnational trajectories of Latina women and specifically erases the racial, economic, and political diversity of U.S. Cubans. As a result, the argument moves beyond an empirical concern with positive and negative stereotypes to an analysis of the ideological strategies and practices that construct gendered representations of Latinidad, in order to characterize how these representations function within the culture at large (Aparicio and Chávez-Silverman 1997; Ganguli 1992). Such an analysis explores how U.S.-mediated images and texts produce gendered and racial signifiers of difference that contribute to dominant constructions of ethnic communities (Molina Guzmán 2005; Molina Guzmán and Valdivia 2004).

Methodology

A discursive approach to the study of mediated representations is centrally concerned with how language produces social meaning (Hall 1997). Building on Lucila Vargas's (2000) work on the genderization of news, this essay examines three main discursive practices: (1) the situational privileging of the voices of Cuban women, (2) the visual foregrounding of Cuban women's bodies, and (3) the narrative positioning of Cuban women as objects rather than subjects of information. Specifically, I examine the language and visuals used to frame the narrative of the story through the voices and bodies of Cuban women. Such a focus of discussion clarifies the social and political role that language plays by connecting the use of mass-mediated language to the exercise of power (Bell and Garrett 1998; Dijk 1993; Fairclough 2001). Media production, media texts, and the reception of media texts are interconnected through ideological processes that contribute to the social construction of knowledge, identity, and social status (Bird and Dardenne 1988; Thorburn 1988; Tuchman 1976; Zelizer 1990). In brief, I examine how the production of mediated verbal and visual narratives contributes to cultural understandings of Cuban and Latina identity and Latinidad.

Because popular media such as personal Internet Web sites are as ideologically informative as elite sources of information like the *New York Times* (Bell and Garrett 1998; Bird and Dardenne 1988), the analysis draws on three kinds of sources. First, the primary data came from the national television news coverage. A total of 166 news segments representing about 6.5 hours of news coverage for the period from late November 1999, when Elián was plucked out of the sea by fishermen on Thanksgiving Day, to June 2000, when Elián returned to Cuba with his father, were collected from the archives of the national evening news networks (ABC, CBS, CNN, NBC). The news scripts were located by searching under the key term "Elián González" in the LexisNexis News database. The broadcast news segments were collected from the Vanderbilt University Evening News Archive. Next, I looked at elite and popular print and cybertext sources. For this I searched the LexisNexis News database for articles from the same period, November 1999 to June 2000, using the terms "Marisleysis" and "Elián's mother." Because of the large number of stories about Elián that had been published, I limited the search to the magazines and periodicals index, the *New York Times*, and the *Miami Herald*. This search turned up 237 stories. Finally, I used the Google, Yahoo, and Netscape search engines to look for Web articles on Marisleysis González. Because a total of 2,230 sites referencing Marisleysis were identified, I chose to examine only the top ten most relevant sites identified by the three search engines. The Web sites varied from personal blogs to the official pages of politically oriented organizations.

Contextualizing Cuban and U.S. Cuban Women in U.S. Popular Culture

Before the Elián controversy, the Miami Cuban exile community occupied a privileged if problematic space within the imaginary of national U.S. popular culture, in part because of the representational dominance of personalities such as Desi Arnaz, Gloria Estefan, and Andy Garcia (Peréz Firmat 1994). Historically, popular representations of Cuban immigrants have not proven as problematic as those of other Latina/o populations. For instance, while contemporary representations of Puerto Ricans remain confined to the urban terrain of poverty, crime, and hypersexuality, dominant constructions of Cubans are located within narratives of prosperity and conservative sexual and social politics. Similarly, unlike the representation of Dominicans, Mexicans, and other Latin American immigrants, inscribed through the popular rhetoric of illegal immigration and migrant poverty, the representation of Cubans and Cuban migration was until recently deracialized and indeed politically romanticized (Kanellos 1998; Ramírez-Berg 2002; Santa Ana 2002). Distinct from popular representations of Latinas/os from the Spanish Caribbean, Mexico, and Central and South America, popular representations of U.S. Cubans typically occur within the discourse of the model Latina/o minority—capitalist entrepreneurs, politically and socially conservative. However, the model-minority role is double-edged. Cuban immigrants are simultaneously seen as ethnic and racial outsiders and as privileged through dominant narratives of Cubanidad that inscribe them as "honorary whites" (Fusco 1995).

Even as the face and the politics of the Cuban exile community have changed,[4] popular representations remain grounded in homogenizing stereotypes of the Cuban exile community as politically conservative, law abiding, religious, predominantly white and middle to upper class, and staunchly anti-Castro. For instance, Constance Marie's second-generation Cuban character on the *George Lopez Show* is often the target of jokes that poke fun at her privileged class background and virulently anti-Castro father by placing her in a contrastive relation to George Lopez, who came from an impoverished background without parental figures. The intergenerational, political, racial, and economic diversity that defines the contemporary Miami Cuban community is often missing from national entertainment and news texts. As one U.S. Cuban observed in the wake of the Elián González coverage:

> Long before the shipwreck survivor landed in America, cigars, music, and antique cars in Havana got more ink than the innumerable human rights abuses of Cuba's repressive government. Coverage of Cuban exiles, meanwhile, would lead you to believe that we are all rich entrepreneurs and fire breathing right-wingers. (Barciela 2000, 128)

Within the U.S. cultural landscape, Cubans are constructed as better educated, more wealthy, and more industrious than African Americans and other Latina/o groups, an image often propagated by U.S. Cubans themselves (Soruco 1996). Although it is true that U.S. Cubans are more likely to complete high school, attend some college, and earn a higher income than other Latina/o groups, the demographic data also demonstrate that compared with Mexican and Central and South American populations living in the United States, a higher percentage of the Cuban population is living in poverty (U.S. Census Bureau 2000). Indeed, Cuban studies scholars have documented the shifts in the racial, political, and economic status of Cuban émigrés from the 1980s and 1990s (Mirabal 2003; Rumbaut 1994; Stepick 2003). Over the past twenty years, Cuban immigration has primarily been driven by working-class laborers from predominantly Afro-Cuban backgrounds (Pedraza 1991; Portes and Jensen 1989; Portes and Stepick 1985).

Nevertheless, the historical symbolic status of Cuban immigrants as temporary political exiles in the U.S. war against communism insulates them from the racializing media discourses of poverty and immigration faced by other Latin American and Caribbean groups. Instead, Cuban immigrants' strong ties to their native culture, religion, and language and their political opposition to Fidel Castro are celebrated and, until recently, went relatively unchallenged by the U.S. media. It is in relation to this longstanding popular narrative of U.S. Cuban identity, or Cubanidad, that the gendered and racialized discourses surrounding Cuban and U.S. Cuban women within the news coverage of the Elián story must be analyzed.

The Gendered Disembodiment of Elisabet Brotons

One of the most provocative figures in the Elián González saga is that of Elisabet Brotons, the tragic maternal figure, whom U.S. journalists subtextually position against Marisleysis González. Brotons's life is rarely the focus of the Elián coverage, but the symbolism of her death plays a pivotal role in the ideological contestation over family, home, and nation (Cacho 2005; Tapia 2001). More than her actions in life, Brotons's silenced voice and missing body inform the narrative discourse circulated through the television news. Representational disembodiment as a thematic structure subverts the voices and bodies of Latinas but does not erase them from the dominant imaginary. Disembodied women are the semiotic shadows casting their flickering shapes on public discourses. While these women may be unwilling or, as in the case of Elisabet, unable to speak on their own behalf, their invisibility in the media text informs how interpretive communities make sense of these events. In turn, how interpretative communities invoke these hyperinvisible bodies acts to discipline the missing or the dead. The media coverage of Elisabet functions on two fronts of signification: as emotional spectacle demanding discipline, and as a contested but disciplined site of national ideologies.

Although a majority of the more than 17,000 Cubans immigrating to the United States each year arrive safely and legally by airplane, it is the life-and-death drama of the fewer than two thousand Cubans who make the illegal journey by sea that most provocatively captures the media's imagination and compels emotional support for the United States' decades-old cold war policies. Elisabet's journey to the United States on an overloaded makeshift boat and her subsequent drowning in the shark-infested waters of the Florida Straits effectively reify the dominant yet inaccurate popular representation of Cuban immigration. For mainstream U.S. journalists, Elisabet's death was a key element in the story's emotionally dramatic background, a background that in the United States is subtly informed by the conservative political discourses of the anti-Castro U.S. Cuban community. While conservative U.S. Cuban politicians gain little from news coverage of the U.S.-Cuba visa program, viewed by some as the first step toward normalization of U.S.-Cuban relations, they benefit from the media storm over a boy whose mother died while attempting the dangerous illegal journey by sea. Popular representations of desperate Cubans fleeing an oppressive regime reinforce constructions of Cubans as deracialized political refugees.

Elisabet's hyperinvisible body is a central but textually subverted element in the media texts. When journalists allude to her, she is consistently nameless and subjectless, identified only through her maternal relation to Elián. For example, in early coverage of the story on *ABC World News Tonight*, the only reference to Elisabet came during Peter Jennings's introduction of Elián as the six-year-old boy "whose mother died at sea as she was bringing him to Florida" (December 8, 1999). Months later, *U.S. News and World Report*'s John Leo described Elián as the boy "whose mother has perished at sea" (May 8, 2000). By invoking Elisabet as a descriptor for Elián, as the nameless mother who sacrificed herself to bring her son to a better life in the United States, the general media position her within long-established Latina archetypes of socially acceptable femininity and domesticity: the self-sacrificing, almost virginal, ethnic mother who gives up her happiness, in this instance her own life, so that her child may achieve the American dream of upward mobility. Brotons remains visually disconnected from all other familial associations except her dutiful relationship to her son. The visual images of Elisabet that circulated

Figure 11.1. Photograph provided by Elisabet Brotons's Cuban family and broadcast in U.S. television news reports.

through the general U.S. media foregrounded her close relationship to Elián (Figure 11.1). She is exclusively located within an asexual, virginal construction of motherhood. The scarcity of references to her personal, romantic, or sexual life sustains the aura of maternal innocence. Not coincidentally, information about the man she was living with and possibly married to, Lazaro Muñero, one of the organizers of the illegal journey, or the birth of Elián years after her official divorce from Juan González, is often missing from media narratives.

Ironically, it is the spectacle of her death—her hyperinvisibility—that makes it possible to contest and discipline her body as a site of competing national ideologies. If as Foucault suggests the discursive functions as a mechanism for power, then the discourses that circulate through Elisabet are central to understanding the productive nature of her elided body (Foucault and Rabinow 1984). For instance, narratives that construct Elisabet's life through the gendered discourse of the selfless, sacrificing single mother foreground the emotional drama surrounding her illegal sea journey and reinforce already existing popular discourses about Cuban immigration. Without personal knowledge of the events that might have motivated Elisabet's departure from Cuba, journalists assume Brotons's unquestioned intentions to provide Elián with political freedom and economic prosperity. With the exception of a column by Gabriel García Márquez published in the *New York Times*, Elisabet's maternal judgment in risking Elián's life is rarely questioned. Throughout the general media coverage, Elisabet is nameless, voiceless, and, with the exception of a few family photographs provided to journalists by her family, faceless. Indeed, in researching this essay, finding the name of Elián's mother, much less the correct spelling of her name, proved difficult. When her name, body, and death are invoked, they are politically, economically, and socially decontextualized, repoliticized, and disciplined by those compelled to speak on her behalf.

Speaking for the Dead: The Tropicalized Embodiment of Marisleysis

If Elisabet is defined through her hyperinvisibility, Marisleysis is characterized through her hypervisibility. Dubbed Elián's surrogate mother by the media, Marisleysis González became the primary voice and body through which Elisabet and the U.S. Cuban community were embodied. However, while Elisabet's invisibility signs in as sacred, Marisleysis's hypervisibility signifies the threat of the Latina other—too emotional to be rational, too sexy to be a maternal figure, and too vociferous to be appropriately feminine. In other words, general media representations of Marisleysis's body are filtered and disciplined through the discourses of gendered tropicalization. Tropicalized bodies are "variously encoded as tropical, exotic, hypereroticized sexuality, or elided, or textualized as a site of productive and complex mestiza hybridity" (Chávez-Silverman 1997, 101). More often than not it is the bodies of women of color that are controlled, patrolled, and ideologically disciplined through legal or cultural discourses, such as that of tropicalization (Barrera 2002; Hodes 1999).

Surrogate Politics

From the story's beginning, Marisleysis assumed the roles of Elisabet's surrogate voice and Elián's surrogate mother. Her English-language fluency, youthfulness, and mutual attachment to Elián from the first day of his arrival in the United States positioned González as a suitable informal and formal spokeswoman for both her Miami family and the Cuban American National Foundation (CANF), the anti-Castro organization that provided the family with legal and financial assistance throughout the lawsuit and one of the most powerful political lobbying groups in Washington, D.C. Nevertheless, as a news source Marisleysis articulated and redefined the longstanding conservative discourses of U.S. Cuban politics. Marisleysis's physicality as both a woman and a second-generation U.S. Cuban countered popular perceptions that anti-Castro Cuban exile politics belong only to the male-dominated Old Guard (the first-generation and one-and-a-half-generation immigrants born in Cuba). Simultaneously, she also affirmed homogenizing constructions of the Cuban exile community as conservative. Indeed, CANF routinely sponsored Marisleysis and her twenty-seven-year-old cousin Georgina Cid Cruz to lobby the U.S. Congress, recognizing the symbolic value of communicating their nostalgic political message through the voices and bodies of young Cuban women. Marisleysis served as a bridge connecting the glorious political past to the tumultuous present and the idealized future.

Marisleysis provided a political voice for her ethnic community by evoking the symbolism surrounding Elián's dead mother. As is standard journalistic practice in reporting on people who are deceased, U.S. journalists often seek out alternative sources of information to speak for or about the dead. Marisleysis's willingness, desire, and political motivation to speak for Elisabet fulfilled U.S. journalism's demand for establishing objectivity and credibility and positioned Marisleysis as a discursive surrogate for the mother and the U.S. Cuban community. Owing in part to Cuba's careful management of the U.S. media and perhaps the reticence of Elián's Cuban family, Marisleysis visually displaced the biological parents by articulating in their stead the political interests of the conservative Cuban exile community. The following excerpted segment from *ABC World News Tonight* (November 28, 1999) is representative of this displacement:

> Ron Claiborne, voice-over images of Juan Miguel González speaking in Spanish: He (Juan Miguel González) told us, "I can offer him, best of all, the love that he needs. That's the most important thing."

But Elián's cousins in Miami say he should remain in the U.S. as his mother wanted.

Marisleysis, on-camera outside the hospital: I think the only reason that she brought him here was to have a better opportunity, a better life, a better career, a better everything, that he's not going to have over there.

The father's love for his son is countered by the promise of economic prosperity, a contrast that suggests that Elián's Cuban father is unable to provide financially for his son but that Marisleysis is more than capable of fulfilling the emotional role of a parent. Language ability further cements the contrast. Unlike Juan Miguel, whose voice is replaced by that of an English-speaking translator, Marisleysis is allowed to speak for herself. As a linguistic code-switcher, she is a news subject who is able to speak for multiple communities to multiple audiences. Marisleysis functions as a linguistic and cultural bridge between her U.S. Cuban community and English-speaking audiences (Goffman 1961). Finally, by concluding the news segment with a reference to the U.S. policy granting Cuban refugees who reach the U.S. shore political asylum, the journalistic narrative implicitly introduces that Elián is yet another political Cuban refugee whose surrogate mother must speak on his behalf.

Once established as a legitimate emotional and political surrogate, Marisleysis consistently and vocally articulated the interest of the deceased mother through the ideological discourse of the conservative Cuban community. For example, in a January 5, 2000, *NBC Nightly News* segment, she is quoted on-camera as saying, "But his mom risked her life for him to get liberty, and I hope that this country gives him an opportunity of knowing what liberty is all about." With slight variations, this became Marisleysis's most circulated sound bite and quote, as illustrated in this *Newsweek* story about her testimony before the U.S. Senate:

To Marisleysis, Elian's 21-year-old cousin, who became a kind of surrogate parent after Elian's mother died in the ill-fated journey, the just outcome is equally clear. "[God] made a miracle to bring this boy to us," said Marisleysis, choking back tears. "I am here to make his mother's dream come true to stay in this country." (Contreras 2000, 31)

Marisleysis's statements are rearticulated through the voices of other U.S. Cuban women, such as Republican Congresswoman Ileana Ros-Lehiten. Together, U.S. Cuban sources constructed a cohesive narrative of Cuban exile politics embodied in the youthful body of Marisleysis but still grounded in the nostalgic cold war rhetoric of freedom, democracy, and capitalism.

As CANF soon discovered, however, the U.S. Cuban community's traditional rhetorical strategies are growing increasingly dissonant with the U.S. public, for two reasons. First, the documented presence of more than one million Cuban immigrants (the fifth largest immigrant population in the United States) contradicts the popular construction of Cubans as temporary political exiles. Second, as a result of their permanent status, U.S. Cubans are equally vulnerable to the resurgence of anti-immigration politics facing Latinos in the South, Southwest, and California (Ono and Sloop 2002). Given the rise of nativist sentiments and the anti-immigration backlash, the Cuban exile is less politically insulated by the fear-based cold war rhetoric of the communist threat—a threat that has diminished even further in the post-9/11 context. At the same time, throughout the 1990s, the Cuban exile community was more identified with the Afro-Cuban *balseros* and with popular Afro-Cuban figures such as music diva Celia Cruz and baseball player Orlando "El Duque" Hernandez, further drawing into question the racialized privilege of Cuban whiteness. Consequently, the conservative leaders of the Cuban exile community found it difficult to reinforce their ethnic privilege. The more conservative discourses of the Cuban community embodied in Marisleysis ultimately fail and are disciplined through the racializing visual excess surrounding her body.

Visual Excess

From the beginning, Marisleysis was visually part of the media narrative. She was shown entering the hospital, wiping tears off her face, and speaking to journalists during an impromptu news conference at Elián's hospital. News audiences were introduced to images of Marisleysis holding Elian's hand as he left the hospital, escorting him through the throngs of cameras outside their Little Havana home, playing with him in the yard, helping him with a piñata, hovering over him as he opened birthday gifts. More often than not, she was also seen wearing makeup, heels, and designer sweaters or black suits—a carefully constructed appearance that made Marisleysis initially appear more maternal, mature, and middle class, more like the socially acceptable image of U.S. Cuban women the public expects.

Competing with Marisleysis's image of middle-class acceptability and feminine appropriateness is another set of images. The excess of her youthful body, associated sexuality, light brown skin, and dark eyes and hair is represented through visuals of Marisleysis in tight-fitting clothes and daringly short skirts that highlight her curvaceous body. By the end of Elián's story, it is this set of images that dominates visual representations of Marisleysis. The same woman who at first appeared to be a model of middle-class femininity eventually becomes another hypersexualized working-class Latina. Because television news is image driven, reporters often edit in previously broadcast footage over the journalistic text or voice-over, a practice known as running file footage. As a result, even when Marisleysis did not speak, her body remained constantly available to news audiences. She became a visual synecdoche for the Miami family and the Cuban exile community. Unlike Elisabet, who is always present in the news coverage through her absence, González circulates through her visual excess.

As U.S. political and popular support for Elián asylum case declined, it was Marisleysis's hyperbolized image that was disciplined. Marisleysis's body became a site of political and cultural contestation, a site where she was transformed from the politically protected voice of a surrogate mother to the sexualized and racialized spectacle of a community on the margins, a community defined by the media's images of working-class neighborhoods and unruly "brown" people floating across the Florida Straits. Transformed from the political spokeswoman of the next generation of U.S. Cuban activists into a tropicalized spectacle no longer protected by the privileged rhetoric of cold war politics, Marisleysis was repositioned as the object rather than the subject of news. Tropes of tropicalism, defined by Frances Aparicio and Susanna Chávez-Silverman (1997, 1) as "the system of ideological fictions with which the dominant (Anglo European) cultures trope Latin American and U.S. Latino/a identities and culture," have a long history in popular representations of Latinas/os. Tropicalism erases specificity and lumps all that is Latin and Latina/o into one homogeneous racialized heap (Lopez 1991; Pérez Firmat 1994). Under this trope, attributes such as brown or olive skin, religiosity, hyperemotional displays, the Spanish language, accented English, and heat metaphors comprise some of the most enduring stereotypes about Latina/os. For Latina bodies in U.S. popular culture, tropicalism often constrains representations of their bodies between virginal religiosity (Elisabet) and hot-tempered sexuality (Marisleysis) (Molina Guzmán and Valdivia 2004).

Through Marisleysis's hypervisibility, the Miami Cuban community was implicitly gendered through the tropicalized discourse of outsiders, of difference, of ethnic and racial Others. Butler (1993, x) argues that gender is constructed through relations of power, through "normative constraints that not only produce but also regulate various bodily beings." In other words, bodies only come to mean or signify as they function through specific gendered, classed, and racialized schemas. Marisleysis is rearticulated through the racialized and sexualized discourse of Latinidad, in particular the archetype of the Latina Spitfire.

As public support dwindled, the U.S. media consistently framed Marisleysis and the Miami Cuban community as hotheaded, lawless, and ethically questionable, tropicalized signifiers that work in opposition to the model-minority discourse. For example, reporting on the protests following the INS decision to repatriate Elián, Byron Pitts, a "CBS Evening News" journalist, interviewed a blind Cuban exile participating in a sit-in. The man argues that he must "fight for the rights of his little Cuban brother and his dead mami." The story concludes with Marisleysis in front of her Little Havana home surrounded by Cuban exile activists, "We'll fight to the end, but we're not returning this child to the father" (January 6, 2000). Not so veiled threats and visuals of demonstrators burning tires and overturning police barricades—the images, selected quotes, and structure of the journalistic story construct Marisleysis and the Miami Cuban community as boiling over with heat, hostility, and violence. Miami, at the hands of Cuban émigrés, becomes another south-of-the-border tropics. It is a place where Marisleysis and her youthful body and associated sexuality are marked as threatening and destabilizing to the U.S. social order already under demographic contestation.

The strength and stability of Marisleysis's surrogate motherhood are replaced by the vulnerability and instability of a woman's misplaced desire. That is, her desire for Elián is eventually coded as physically and psychologically aberrant. For instance, on the *ABC Nightly News* Web site, Marisleysis is characterized in the following manner: "Often tearful, she has acted as a surrogate mother to Elián and has frequently appeared before the news media, pleading for the boy to be allowed to stay in the U.S. . . . But the struggle has affected her health, and has caused her to be hospitalized four times since the custody began."[5] Marisleysis's emotional instability—indeed, apparent neurosis—is increasingly used in the media to undercut her symbolic power as surrogate mother and community spokeswoman. A feature article published in March on the life of Marisleysis González concluded with this observation:

> But signs that the strain of the fight for Elián was getting to be too much for Marisleysis emerged recently, when she made a rambling, tearful speech at

a congressional hearing in Washington. She spoke of how the child wants to stay here with her.

"At night, when he wakes up scared, he says, 'I love you mucho, my cousin,' " Marisleysis told the politicians. Then she broke down and cried. (Yañez 2000)

Two months later, the *Miami Herald* published a report that prior to the Elián case, Marisleysis had a history of stress-related disorders, leading to more than twelve hospitalizations. Visuals of Marisleysis stretched on an ambulance gurney with an oxygen mask strapped to her face circulated through the media. It is precisely these hyperbolized displays of emotions that are central to the visual coverage.

By the end of the story, Marisleysis has shifted from speaking for the dead to speaking for her racialized community, a community depicted as extreme, lawless, and confrontational. Rather than the fully assimilated model minority, the media representations of the conservative Cuban exile community during the Elián case break with dominant constructions of U.S. Cubans as racially privileged political exiles who share an affinity for the U.S. rule of law. Marisleysis's vulnerability and confrontational rhetoric are disciplined through the media's constructions of the U.S. Cuban community as ethnic and racial outsiders. The Cuban other, in this case Marisleysis González, becomes the foreground, the text on which the story is written.

Not only is Marisleysis constructed as vulnerable, she is also hypersexualized in ways that draw into question her relationship with Elián. For instance, on a Web site devoted to psychological coverage of the case, many of the media experts question Elián's attachment to her:

> Elian described "Mary," apparently meaning Marisleysis, as a "secret love." The cousin "may be an idealized love, rather than a maternal figure," Kernberg said. "His feelings for Marisleysis are similar to the romantic feelings of a schoolboy for his teacher or a wished-for girlfriend."[6]

Unlike Elisabet, who performs the role of the virginal, sacrificial mother, Marisleysis is marked as a hypersexualized figure, the sexual object of a schoolboy crush.

Elián's attachment to Marisleysis is no longer coded as innocent. Her love for Elián is characterized as inappropriate. Experts question whether Elián and Marisleysis should be sharing a room, much less a bed. Other Web sites more explicitly raise the question of Marisleysis's sexuality:

And you have to wonder, as you've wondered more and more during this whole sorry saga, whether there isn't something just a bit . . . off, a bit troubling about this 21-year-old, largely self-appointed "surrogate mother" clinging so tightly to the 6-year-old child the fates temporarily tossed her way.[7]

Ironically, U.S. members of the conservative public, usually virulent anticommunist themselves, were among those who used Marisleysis's youthful sexuality to discredit her politics, such as in this story from a conservative Web forum:

> In Cuba, where she's been vilified by the Castro regime for her often-agonized pleas to keep her young cousin here—many men think of her as a sex symbol, as well as a capitalist symbol.
> "Whenever she comes on TV everyone says, 'Man, is she hot,'" said a Cuban immigrant in Miami who recently returned from a visit to the island. "Here, it's the same."[8]

Thus, Marisleysis's sexuality is used to problematize her political voice and the legitimacy of maternal claims to Elián. She is discursively disciplined through the gendered tropicalization of her body.

Perhaps the most infamous example of this gendered and ethnic objectification is the widely circulated visual of Marisleysis accusing the U.S. government of child abuse after the federal raid on her family's home in the working-class neighborhood of Little Havana (Figure 11.2). Marisleysis is depicted sobbing and wide-mouthed. The weight she has gained during the ordeal is visible, and her one-inch-long false nails are clearly noticeable. Despite the respectable black suit she is wearing, she no longer performs to the socially acceptable standards of white Cuban femininity. Instead, Marisleysis is the uncontrollable Latina other—too vociferous to be credible, too brown to be white.

Conclusion

The Elián story documents how the demographically changing face of the United States as an imagined nation is shifting the privileged symbolic, political, and social status of U.S. Cubans from that of deracialized political exiles to racialized ethnic others. Racial formation theory (Omi and Winant 1994) suggests that the meanings assigned to race and racial groups are part of a historically unstable, continuous process intricately

Figure 11.2. In an emotional news conference held after the federal raid on her family's home, Marisleysis González stands next to Donato Dalrymple, one of the recreational fishermen who helped rescue Elián and attempted to hide him from federal officers. The transformation of Marisleysis's media representation from one cliché, the sleek, exotic, well-turned-out Latina, to another, the screaming, hyperemotional, semicrazy Cubanista, was complete by the end of the Elián saga. Photograph and caption courtesy of AP.

connected to political and social structures. An example is the shift in the federal racial designation of U.S. Mexican nationals from "white," following the Treaty of Guadalupe Hidalgo, to the current federal ethnic designation as "Hispanic" or "Latina/o" (Haney-López 1996). In the case of conservative U.S. Cubans, the post-cold war politics of the federal government, along with demographic data documenting the permanent status of three generations of Cubans living in the United States, have moved them from a deracialized, political ethnic enclave associated with whiteness to racialized ethnic exiles associated with the brownness of Latinidad. U.S. Cubans, who once occupied a position of privilege within the U.S. imaginary, now find themselves outside the border of whiteness and within the terrain of panethnic Latinidad. The gendered structuring of Elisabet and Marisleysis in the U.S. media coverage is an example of how popular culture both records and contributes to the dynamic and relational process of U.S. racial formation.

Cuban women, like women in general, serve as a semiotic sign (Rakow and Kranich 1991), a complex symbolic structure of meanings simultaneously positioned within a stabilized set of dominant gendered and racialized constructs of Latina identity, femininity, and sexuality (Aparicio and Chavéz-Silverman 1997; López 1991; Molina Guzmán 2005; Peréz-Firmat 1994; Ramírez Berg 2002; Shohat and Stam 1994; Valdivia 2000). The signification of Cuban and U.S. Cuban women exists through and against Western constructions of Latina femininity, Latina sexuality, white feminine purity, and nonerotic sexuality, such as motherhood, and simultaneously as dangerously impure racialized bodies with uncontrollable emotions and sexual desires, such as the Latina Spitfire (Barrerra 2002; Lopéz 1991; Negrón-Muntaner 1999; Shohat 1998). Within U.S. narratives about family, home, and nation, such as those that attend the Elián saga, Cuban women symbolically function within this domain of signification and its intersecting trajectories of gender, race, ethnicity, and class—made more complicated by the hybridized status of Latina subjects.

Thus, the media coverage of Elian González is not an impartial reflection of the reality of U.S. Latina/os generally or the Cuban exile community specifically, but rather what Stuart Allan (2000) defines as an "ideological construction of reality" or what John Fiske (1991) describes as a "sense of reality that is ideological." As such, it positions Cuban women as localized transnational signifiers of contemporary Latinidad whose intersecting vectors of gender, ethnicity, race, and class resist linear constructions. More important, the gendered discourses surrounding news coverage of Elisabet and Marisleysis are informative of the social status of Latinidad, Latina and Cuban women and their ideological location within the imagined nation.

While Elisabet represents the politics of a nation and transnational diaspora deeply divided from each other, the elision of the social, political, and historical context surrounding Elisabet's journey opens a space for her to simultaneously sign in as emotive spectacle, political subject and disembodied other. She is a floating signifier, a part of the contested terrain of Latina signification (Hall 1997). Because Elisabet cannot speak on her behalf, others, primarily women sources, are asked or compelled to speak for her. Subsequently she is textually embodied in the coverage through the voice of women who are sometimes ideologically opposed to one another. In Elisabet's case, she is caught in the contradictory discourse between Cuban women, who want to recuperate her as a lost daughter, and U.S. Cuban women, who want to symbolically locate her as the sacrificial mother of the contemporary anti-Castro exile movement. While family and neighbors in Cuba construct Brotons as a happy woman with few economic or social problems, U.S. Cuban sources are invested in narratives that frame Elisabet as an anti-Castro patriot with a singular vision. Rather than the melody of a linear narrative, we hear a cacophony of multiple realities, experiences, and stories. Elisabet becomes part of the framework within which meaning is socially contested and constructed. Even if explicitly disembodied from the text, she remains intrinsically part of the gendered discourses that circulate through it.

Unlike the media coverage of other Caribbean and Latina immigrants, that surrounding Elisabet is devoid of racial and class-based language or images. Little mention is made of the U.S. immigration policy that grants more than 15,000 visas to Cubans each year, or the more than 5,000 visas that the United States can grant but often withholds, or of the informal INS policy that would have granted Elisabet asylum had she successfully made it onto U.S. land—policies that some argue encourage the emotionally charged and politically laden spectacle of rickety boats filled with Cuban émigrés "desperate for a free American life."

Even though it is likely that she made the journey for economic or even emotional reasons, as the honorary white sacrificial mother, Brotons's actions are located within the domain of the political and as such are isolated from the racialized discourse in which other Caribbean and Latina women who illegally journey to the United States are often inscribed (Ruiz 2002; Santa Ana 2002; Vargas 2000). Had Elisabet been Haitian, Dominican, Mexican, or Afro-Cuban, we might never have learned her story; had Elisabet lived, we certainly would not have. Indeed, the story of Arianne Horta, one of Elián's fellow shipwreck survivors who left her five-year-old daughter in Cuba because the journey was too dangerous, is known by few and championed by less. It is Elisabet's disembodied voice and racially privileged body that give her agency, even though her agency is disciplined through the voices of others.

Marisleysis González's position within the media is equally complex. Initially invited into the coverage as the family's unofficial spokeswoman, she occupies a space filled with the potential for political activism. However, when the U.S. public and the U.S. government withdraw their support from Elián's asylum claim, so do the media, which increasingly present the conservative Cuban exile community and its most entertaining representative, Marisleysis, as outside the boundaries of lawfulness, social acceptability, and whiteness, as outside the borders of the United States as imagined nation. Consequently, González is defined by her willingness to fight for her political and personal beliefs, an untraditional Cuban woman motivated to enter the political discourse of the public sphere; but her political strength is disciplined by the gendered and racialized discourses of tropicalized Latina femininity that she embodies through her hypervisible excess—her working-class roots, desire for children (yet not her own), youthful sexuality, and emotional passion. Like Elisabet, Marisleysis is a body through which culture and nation are contested. In the case of the Elián coverage, both women are sites through which the representational politics of the conservative Cuban exile community are challenged and eventually recuperated by dominant discourses of gender, ethnicity, and nation circulated through the media. The tropicalization of Marisleysis's body contributes to a rupturing of the discourses of U.S. Cuban political enfranchisement and the mythology of Cubans as the model minority. More important, the gendered structures that surround both women function as signposts of the dynamic relationality of U.S. racial formations.

Notes

1. This article focuses specifically on the national English-language media targeted primarily at English-speaking audiences. The terms "general news" and "general media" are used interchangeably to describe news and media texts produced by U.S. English-language organizations for U.S. English-dominant audiences. The author recognizes that while not the primary target, this general audience is also composed of Spanish-speaking and English-Spanish bilingual audience members. Reports by the National Association of Hispanic Journalists released in 2002 and 2003 show that stories featuring Latina/o issues or communities make up less than 0.62 percent of general television news (Méndez-Méndez and Alverio 2002).

2. Since several of the figures in the Elián story share the last name of González, I use first names to avoid confusion.

3. The spelling Elisabet rather than Elisabeth was used most often by the English- and Spanish-language media and is retained here.

4. Cuban studies scholars have documented the negative media representation and political backlash surrounding the April-October 1980 Mariel boatlift that brought 125,000 Cubans to Miami, and the Balseros boatlift of the early 1990s. Although most of the refugees were working-class laborers, media images focused attention on black Cubans, homosexual Cubans, and the small percentage of refugees with criminal records. For an in-depth discussion of race and the Mariel and Balsero exiles, see Mirabal (2003) and Rumbaut (1994). For an in-depth discussion of the political and economic impact of the Mariel exiles, see Portes and Jensen (1989), Portes and Stepick (1985), Pedraza-Bailey (1985), and Stepick, Grenier, Castro, and Dunn (2003).

5. *ABC Nightly News*, http://more.abcnews.go.com/sections/us/DailyNews/elian_subindex.html (accessed March 5, 2004).

6. Schaler, J. "In the News." Personal Web site, entry dated April 27, 2000, http://schaler.net/inthenews/elian2.htm (accessed September 15, 2005).
7. Horowitz, R. "She Knows Things." http://www.yesrick.com/042500.htm (accessed September 15, 2005).
8. Free Republic. "Forums." Free Republic Web site, http://www.freerepublic.com/forum/a38fc1fe53563.htm (accessed September 15, 2005).

Bibliography

Allan, S. 1998. "News from NowHere: Televisual News Discourses and the Constructrion of Hegemony." In *Approaches to Media Discourse*, ed. A. Bell and P. Garrett, 105–141. London: Blackwell.

Aparicio, F. R., and S. Chávez-Silverman. 1997. *Tropicalizations: Transcultural Representations of Latinidad*. Hanover, NH: Dartmouth College and University Press of New England.

Banet-Weiser, S. 1999. *The Most Beautiful Girl in the World: Beauty Pageants and National Identity*. Berkeley and Los Angeles: University of California Press.

Barciela, S. 2000. Bashing the Cubans: The Elián Saga Prompted Open Season on Exiles. *Hispanic*, July-August, 128.

Barrera, M. 2002. "Hottentot 2000: Jennifer López and Her Butt." In *Sexualities in History: A Reader*, ed K. Phillips and B. Reay, 411–417. New York: Routledge.

Bell, A., and P. Garrett. 1998. *Approaches to Media Discourse*. Oxford: Blackwell.

Bird, E., and R. Dardenne. 1988. "Myth, Chronicle and Story: Exploring the Narrative Qualities of News." In *Media, Myths and Narratives: Television and the Press*, ed. J. Carey, 67–86. Newbury Park, CA: Sage.

Butler, J. 1993. *Bodies That Matter: On the Discursive Limits of "Sex."* New York: Routledge.

Cacho, L. M. 2005. "'You Just Don't Know How Much He Meant': Deviancy, Death and Devaluation." Unpublished manuscript, University of Illinois at Urbana-Champaign.

Center for Media and Public Affairs. 2000. "Elián Story Makes the Biggest Splash." Report by the Center for Media and Public Affairs, Washington, D.C., June, 1–2.

Chávez-Silverman, S. 1997. "Tropicolada: Inside the U.S. Latino/a Gender B(l)ender." In *Tropicalizations: Transcultural Representations of Latinidad*, ed. F. Aparicio and S. Chávez-Silverman, 101–118. Hanover, NH: Dartmouth College Press.

Contreras, J. 2000. "The Elián Family Feud." *Newsweek*, March 11, 2000, 31.

Dijk, T. A. v. 1993. *Elite Discourse and Racism*. Newbury Park, CA: Sage.

Fairclough, N. 2001. *Language and Power* (2nd ed.). Harlow, UK: Longman.

Fiske, J. 1991. "Postmodernism and Television." In *Mass Media and Society*, ed. J. Curran and M. Gurevitch, 55–67. London: Edward Arnold.

Foucault, M., and P. Rabinow. 1984. *The Foucault Reader* (1st ed.). New York: Pantheon Books.

Fusco, C. 1995. *English Is Broken Here: Notes on Cultural Fusion in the Americas.* New York: New Press.

Goffman, E. 1961. *Encounters: Two Studies in the Sociology of Interaction.* Indianapolis: Bobbs-Merrill.

Ganguli, K. 1992. "Accounting for Others: Feminism and Representation." In *Women Making Meaning: New Feminist Directions in Communication,* ed. L. Rakow, 60–79. New York: Routledge.

Hall, S. 1997. *Representation: Cultural Representations and Signifying Practices.* Thousand Oaks, CA: Sage, in association with the Open University, London.

Haney-López, I. 1996. *White by Law: The Legal Construction of Race.* New York: New York University Press.

Hodes, M., ed. 1999. *Sex. Love. Race: Crossing Boundaries in North American History.* New York: New York University Press.

Kanellos, Nicolás. 1998. *Thirty Million Strong: Reclaiming the Hispanic Image in American Culture.* Golden, CO: Fulcrum.

Kramarae, Cheris, and Paula Treichler. 1992. *Amazons, Bluestockings and Crones: A Feminist Dictionary.* London: Pandora.

Lopez, A. 1991. "Are All Latins from Manhattan? Hollywood, Ethnography, and Cultural Colonialism." In *Unspeakable images: Ethnicity and the American Cinema,* ed. L. D. Friedman, 404–424. Urbana-Champaign: University of Illinois.

Mirabal, N. R. 2003. "'Ser de aqui': Beyond the Cuban Exile Model." *Latino Studies* 1:366–382.

Molina Guzmán, I. 2005. Gendering Latinidad Through the Elián News Discourse about Cuban Women. *Latino Studies* 3:179–204.

Molina Guzmán, I., and A. Valdivia. 2004. "Brain, Brow or Bootie: Iconic Latinas in Contemporary Popular Culture." *Communication Review* 7, no. 2: 203–219.

Negrón-Mutaner, F. 2002. "Jennifer's Butt." *Atzlan* 22, no. 2: 182–195.

Newport, F. 2000. "Americans Say It Is Elián González's Best Interest to Return to Cuba With His Father." *Gallup Poll Reports,* April, 26–28.

Omi, M., and H. Winant. 1994. *Racial Formation in the United States: From the 1960s to the 1990s* (2nd ed.). New York: Routledge.

Ono, K. A., and J. M. Sloop. 2002. *Shifting Borders: Rhetoric, Immigration, and California's Proposition 187.* Philadelphia: Temple University Press.

Pedraza, S. 1991. "Women and Migration: The Social Consequences of Gender." *Annual Review of Sociology* 17:303–325.

Pedraza-Bailey, S. 1985. "Cuba's Exile: Portrait of Refugee Migration." *International Migration Review* 19:4–34.

Pérez Firmat, G. 1994. *Life on the Hyphen: The Cuban-American way* (1st ed.). Austin: University of Texas Press.

Portes, A., and L. Jensen. 1989. "The Enclave and the Entrants: Patterns of Ethnic Enterprise in Miami Before and After Mariel." *American Sociological Review* 54:929–949.

Portes, A., and A. Stepick. 1985. "Unwelcome Immigrants: The Labor Market Experience of 1980 (Mariel) Cuban and Haitian Refugees in South Florida." *American Sociological Review* 50, no. 4: 493–514.

Rakow, L., and K. Kranich. 1991. "Woman as Sign." *Journal of Communication* 41, no. 1: 8–23.

Ramírez Berg, C. 2000. *Latino Images in Film: Stereotypes, Subversion, Resistance.* Austin: University of Texas Press.

Rodríguez, C., ed. 1997. *Latin Looks: Images of Latinas and Latinos in the U.S. Media.* Boulder, CO: Westview Press.

Ruiz, M. 2002. "Border Narratives, HIV/AIDS, and Latina/o Health in the United States: A Cultural Analysis." *Feminist Media Studies* 2:81–96.

Rumbaut, R. N. 1994. "Origins and Destinies: Immigration to the United States since World War II." *Sociological Forum* 9, no. 4: 583–617.

Santa Ana, O. 2002. *Brown Tide Rising: Metaphors of Latinos in Contemporary American Public Discourse.* Austin: University of Texas Press.

Schudson, M. 2001. "The Objectivity Norm in American Journalism." *Journalism: Theory, Practice and Criticism* 2, no. 2: 149–170.

Shohat, E. 1998. *Talking Visions: Multicultural Feminism in a Transnational Age.* New York: New Museum of Contemporary Art; Cambridge, MA: MIT Press.

Shohat, E., and R. Stam. 1994. *Unthinking Eurocentrism: Multiculturalism and the Media.* London: Routledge.

Shohat, E., and R. Stam. 2003. *Multiculturalism, Postcoloniality, and Transnational Media.* New Brunswick, NJ: Rutgers University Press.

Stack, J. F., and C. L. Warren. 1990. "Ethnicity and the Politics of Symbolism in Miami's Cuban Community." *Cuban Studies* 20:11–28.

Stepick, A. 2003. *This Land Is Our Land: Immigrants and Power in Miami.* Berkeley and Los Angeles: University of California Press.

Stepick, A., G. Grenier, M. Castro, and M. Dunn. 2003. *This Land Is Our Land: Immigrants and Power in Miami.* Berkeley and Los Angeles: University of California Press.

Soruco, G. R. 1996. *Cubans and the Mass Media in South Florida.* Gainsville: University of Florida Press.

Tapia, R. 2001. "Un(di)ing Legacies: White Matters of Memory in Portraits of Our Princess Cultural Values." *Cultural Values* 5, no. 2: 261–287.

Thorburn, D. 1988. "Television as an Aesthetic Media." In *Media, Myths and Narratives: Television and the Press*, ed. J. Carey, 48–66. Newbury Park, CA: Sage.

Torres, M. 1998. "*Encuentros y encontronazos*: Homeland in the Politics and Identity of the Cuban Diaspora." In *The Latino Studies Reader: Culture, Economy and Society*, ed. Antonia Darder and Rodolfo D. Torres, 43–62. London: Blackwell.

Tuchman, G. 1972. "Objectivity as Strategic Ritual: An Examination of Newsmen's Notions of Objectivity." *American Journal of Sociology* 77:660–679.

Tuchman, G. 1976. "Telling Stories." *Journal of Communication* 3:93–97.

U.S. Census Bureau. 2000. Hispanic Population of the U.S. Current Population Survey. On-line report: http://www.census.gov/population/www.socdemo/hispanic/h000-09.html. Retrieved 10/02/2002.

Valdivia, A. N. 2000. *"A Latina in the Land of Hollywood" and Other Essays on Media Culture.* Tucson: University of Arizona Press.

Vargas, L. 2000. "Genderizing Latino News: An Analysis of a Local Newspaper's

Coverage of Latino Current Affairs." *Critical Studies in Media Communication* 17, no. 3: 261–293.

Yañez, L. "Cousin in Spotlight Has Bond with Elián." Detroit Free Press. http:// www.freep.com (accessed October 2, 2002).

Zelizer, B. 1990. "Achieving Journalistic Authority Through Narrative." *Critical Studies in Mass Communication* 7:336–376.

CHAPTER 12

The Body in Question

The Latina Detective in the Lupe Solano Mystery Series

ANA PATRICIA RODRÍGUEZ

> *Not many women today display their appetites in public.*
> CAROLINA GARCÍA-AGUILERA, *BLOODY WATERS*

In her six-novel mystery series, Cuban American writer and former Miami–Dade County private investigator Carolina García-Aguilera participates in the production of a genre of U.S. Latino/a detective fiction that explores Cuban American identity construction in the context of U.S.-Cuba geopolitics. García-Aguilera's novels—*Bloody Waters* (1996), *Bloody Shame* (1997), *Bloody Secrets* (1998), *A Miracle in Paradise* (1999), *Havana Heat* (2000), and *Bitter Sugar* (2001)—feature the glamorously beautiful and intelligent Guadalupe Solano as series protagonist and private investigator in Miami. García-Aguilera uses the mystery fiction genre to explore issues of Cuban (American) history, exile, memory, identity politics, homeland subjective relations, and cultural hybridity, and the materialization of these social dynamics in the body of Lupe Solano. The figure of Lupe Solano embodies not only the greater contradictions of representing Latinos/as within the mold of mystery fiction writing but also the Latina packaging of competing discourses on the body, gender, sexuality, excess, and consumption in the United States. In this symbolic economy, Latino/a images, particularly Cuban Americans ones, have greatly yet problematically appreciated in value, as the consumption of Latino-studded music, films, food, literature, and other products has shown.

In this chapter I examine how the fiction of U.S. Cubanidad is materialized in the Latina-styled body of the U.S.-born "Cubana from Havana," Lupe Solano. As we shall see, the body in question in García-Aguilera's novels is not so much the collective corpus delicti (the bodies of the crime victims strewn across the novels) but the sexed, classed, and geopoliticized body of Lupe Solano. Lupe's body materializes or incorporates larger ideologies, or, to use Judith Butler's words, "regulatory norms." Born in the aftermath and continued reiteration of U.S.-Cuban relations and cold war geopolitics, Lupe is not only the bodily effect (the child) of first-wave Cuban exiled parents who made their home in Miami in the 1960s, she is also the materialization of a larger body politic predicated on U.S.-made anticommunist and pro-capitalist ideologies. As Judith Butler (1993) suggests, the body—in this case, Lupe's body—is the "effect" of social norms and discourses situated within and reiterating elements of the larger context of U.S-Cuba geopolitics. Shaped by Cuban (American) history, entrenched in cold war rhetoric, and endowed with privileges of the U.S. "consumers' republic" (Cohen 2003), the character of Lupe Solano is the latest materialization of discourses on Cuban American identity as produced and mediated in the United States in the form of the detective novel.

Cuban American Success Story: Carolina García-Aguilera

In Carolina García-Aguilera's detective novels, Lupe Solano's family represents the Cuban American diaspora, particularly the so-called Cuban Golden Exiles, who made their first entry into the United States through Miami in the first years of the Cuban Revolution.[1] García-Aguilera's family emigrated, children in tow, from the island in the early 1960s. In the terms made famous by the Cuban American cultural critic, Gustavo Pérez-Firmat, García-Aguilera is part of the one-and-a-half generation of immigrants who, "[b]orn in Cuba but made in the U.S.A., . . . belong to an intermediate immigrant generation whose members spent their childhood or adolescence abroad but grew into adults in America" (Pérez-Firmat 1994, 4).[2] In an interview with the Mystery Guild, García-Aguilera confirms that she and Lupe Solano are products of that one-and-a-half generation experience. Born in Cuba, brought to the United States as a young child, and raised in New York until the age of fifteen, when she relocated to Miami, García-Aguilera explains, "I straddle both the Anglo world and the Latino world pretty easily—as Lupe does—so I see both sides of the equation. My books have been quite well received. I mean, the Cuban community is quite proud of me—because, you know, Cubans are very proud of anyone who's successful and has done well."[3]

In the circle of mainstream detective fiction, García-Aguilera has been recognized with various commendations and prizes, including the Shamus Award for the best P.I. novel of the year for *Havana Heat*, the Flamingo Award for the best Florida Mystery, and the Women of Mystery Fifth Dagger Award. Her novels have been translated into French, German, and Spanish, among other languages, and she is frequently invited to book fairs and promotional book readings. Like others of her generation—the writer Cristina García, the singer-entrepreneur Gloria Estefan, and the critic Gustavo Pérez-Firmat, to name only a few—García-Aguilera partici-pates in the construction of a larger narrative of Cuban (American) "life on the hyphen" in the United States. Her novels pay particular attention to specific identificatory processes of race, class, gender, and generational ideological positions as they are configured in her redeployment of detec-tive novels. In her mystery series, García-Aguilera proves once again that popular cultural forms such as the detective novel do matter, precisely because they bring to the fore competing ideologies in Latino/a identity formation in the United States.

An All-Americas Genre: The Latino/a Detective Novel

In 1998, *Hispanic* magazine celebrated the arrival of Hispanic mysteries and Latino detective fiction in an article titled "Latino Sleuths: Hispanic Mystery Writers Make Crime Pay," by Mary Helen Ponce. According to Ponce, "[w]hile each writer brings a unique perspective, landscape, and style to a [detective] work, all depict a particular aspect of Hispanic cul-ture"(46). A relatively new deployment of a favorite genre within popular culture, U.S. Latino detective fiction participates in the production of a larger Latino/a cultural body politic under critical inspection today. As Ponce suggests, "Hispanic literary critics have taken crime novels and mysteries to heart because they depict societal problems that in other genres are difficult to develop" (46). The formulaic and familiar structure of crime fiction, particularly the series model, allows Latino/a writers to engage in larger discussions of race, ethnicity, culture, class, gender, sexu-ality, transnational migration, community building, and identity construc-tion, which are examined by writers of color working in the detective genre (Pepper 2000). Moreover, the recent production of U.S. Latino mys-teries is situated within a Latin American genealogy of political fiction, or the *novela negra*, that has been widely read, written, and critiqued in Latin America and made popular by international writers such as Jorge Luis

Borges, Julio Cortázar, Ricardo Piglia, Paco Ignacio Taibo II, and Marcela Serrano. Detective fiction, thus, is far from new to Latin Americans or U.S. Latinos (Simpson 1992; Giardinelli 1996; Stavans 1997).

As many critics argue, crime fiction in Latin America has been at the vanguard of social protest and political critique, taking up thorny subjects such as corruption, dictatorship, torture, disappearance, war, drug trafficking, and the current state of impunity in Latin America. In *New Tales of Mystery and Crime from Latin America* (1992), Amelia Simpson asks readers to consider that "[t]o appropriate the genre and nationalize it by making it Brazilian, Argentine, Mexican, or Cuban is unwieldy because of a host of historical, social, political, cultural, and ideological differences" (12). Precisely because justice across Latin America is often a wayward practice, capable of inflicting great violence and repression on the national citizenry, the mystery genre has become a critical discursive site of contestation and interrogation of local judicial processes. It is precisely from that site of difference, contradiction, and interrogation that Latin American (and now U.S. Latino/a) writers of mystery fiction experiment with genre conventions and redeploy crime fiction in order to address historically specific, local and global issues of immediate concern to their communities. Produced within the sociopolitical context of Latinos in the United States, contemporary mystery fiction by Chicanos, Puerto Ricans, Cuban Americans, Salvadoran Americans, and other Latinos is thus situated within the dual genealogies of U.S. crime (pulp) fiction and Latin American political fiction.

Transculturating the mystery genre, U.S. Latino/a writers explore issues of family, community, (im)migration, memory, postwar trauma, border trouble, police brutality, hate crimes, environmental racism, and social, political, environmental, and economic (in)justice. Entering the mystery fiction market in the 1980s and 1990s, in the midst of the so-called Latino cultural boom, Latino/a writers of mystery fiction foray into a space of ethical contradictions, public expectations, and ethnic desires for incorporation into the popular, cultural, and political imaginary of the United States. Chicano writer Rolando Hinojosa brings new justice to the borderlands in his *Klail City Death Trip* series, while Alejandro Morales (*The Rag Doll Plagues*, 1992) and Lucha Corpi (*Black Widow's Wardrobe*, 1999) time-travel and revisit Chicano/Latino history. Michael Nava's lawyer-detective Henry Ríos defends the down-and-out while championing queer rights, AIDS activism, interracial relationships, and ethnic urban politics in his highly regarded series of novels set in Los Angeles. Partner-writers Charles LoPinto and Lidia Llamas cast EPA investigator Juliana Del Rio and narcotics agent Sean Ryan in a series of "envirocrime mysteries" (*Countdown in Alaska*, 2000, and *The Case of the Toxic Cruiseline*, 2000), while Marcos McPeek Villatoro with *Home Killings* (2001) initiated a series headed by Salvadoran American detective Romilia Chacón of the Nashville police force.

In *Detective Agency: Women Rewriting the Hard-Boiled Tradition* (1999), Priscilla L. Walton and Manina Jones duly note an increase in the market demand for mystery fiction representing women, gays and lesbians, and people of color as of the 1980s. This demand, or what Walton and Jones call heightened "reader expectations" in the mystery fiction market, calls for the incorporation of female, queer, ethnic, and nonwhite protagonists into a genre that has been traditionally dominated by white male protagonists in crime-solving roles, from Sherlock Holmes to more recent mystery fiction heroes. The inclusion of protagonists of color and women in mystery fiction invites the overhaul of a genre that, for the most part, has represented and supported racist social practices and ideologies of law enforcement in which the crime fighter, regardless of race, ethnicity, gender, or sexual identity, has been positioned to protect the larger interests of institutional and national power. Adversely, the criminal has represented questionable interests marked by race, ethnicity, gender, and sexual difference. Following a conventional crime-fighting logic, according to which hegemonic structures of power and the protection of private property are strictly enforced, the mystery genre has traditionally lined up crime fighters on one side and criminal factions on the other side. People of color in mystery fiction and crime media have usually made the lineup, but on the other side of the one-way mirror of the interrogation room. The new niche for mysteries calls for more diverse subjects, social actors, and plot narratives, and has opened a space for the production of detective fiction by writers of color. More important, it has presented an opportunity for writers of color to make incursions into and revisions of the mystery genre, principally by interrogating the Western critical I/Eye (investigator and field of vision) from other critically positioned knowledge schemata and problem (crime)-solving approaches.

In their brand of mystery fiction, Carolina García-Aguilera and other Latino/a writers have responded to the increased market demand for other protagonists (women, gay, ethnic, nonwhite) of mysteries by producing an impressive lineup of Latina/o private investigators, police detectives, criminal law lawyers, and expert, amateur, and sometimes renegade crime fighters. Often, Latino/a protagonists of crime fiction work in law enforcement while at the same time interrogating the inner workings of U.S.

political, judicial, and economic systems. At one end of the Latino crime fiction spectrum we find, for example, the ethically angst-ridden Henry Ríos—the lawyer protagonist of Michael Nava's series of detective novels (*How Town*, 1990; *The Hidden Law*, 1992; *The Death of Friends*, 1996; *The Burning Plain*, 1997). Uncovering the (mis)workings of the U.S. juridical apparatus, Ríos shows how impoverished, immigrant, ethnic, and divergently sexed subjects are systematically identified as the "criminal element" and how society participates in the production of delinquent subjects, as Michel Foucault taught us so long ago.

The Geopolitical Lupe Solano Detective Novels

Situated at the other end of Latino detective fiction, the Lupe Solano detective novels take readers to the world of Cuban Miami, where the palms are greener and the crimes are glitzier. García-Aguilera's crime fiction series is, moreover, embedded in the larger geopolitical history of Cuba and the United States and the transnational political agenda of the Cuban American exile community. In *Bloody Waters*, the first novel of García-Aguilera's series, a wealthy Cuban American couple contracts P.I. Lupe Solano to find the biological mother of their illegally adopted, chronically ill daughter. The mission takes Lupe on her first trip to Cuba, from which she secretly smuggles the birth mother out of the country under the surveillance of Cuban and U.S. high intelligence. In *Bloody Shame*, Lupe investigates a killing at a Cuban-owned jewelry story in Coral Gables, only to uncover a chain of family deceits and infidelities, resulting in the murder of the supposed thief and other unassuming accomplices. *Bloody Secrets* revolves around the stolen fortune and the tarnished honor of two divided Cuban families—one settled in Miami and the other remaining on the island—both of whom take equal advantage of the other's situation.

In *Miracle in Paradise*, the mother superior of the Order of the Holy Rosary sidelines Lupe into investigating an announced "miracle," or disguised hoax, to take place on October 10, 1999 (the Cuban independence day without Castro's revolution), in which the venerated Virgen de la Caridad del Cobre, the patron saint of Cubans, will shed public tears for the reunification of post-Elián González Cuba. The next book, *Havana Heat* returns Lupe to the island of her enchantment to recover for her client, Lucia Miranda, the lost eighth panel of the *The Hunt of the Unicorn* tapestries and other valuable art pieces confiscated by the Cuban government and claimed by wealthy Cuban exiles as their rightful property and cultural patrimony. For Lupe, the recovery of these art pieces signifies a trophy in her professional career and a victory in her personal war against Castro, for she will "liberate an important part of the country's heritage" (*Havana Heat*, 275).

In the last novel in the series, *Bitter Sugar*, Lupe comes to the aid of her father's best friend, tío Ramón Suárez, who stands accused of murdering his nephew over valuable property claims in Cuba. Faithful readers of the Lupe Solano series know full well that the end of the series is near when the Cuban family turns against itself, family blood is spilled, and family bonds are shattered in the novel. Up to now, Lupe has been convinced that "close friends, who, although not related by blood, were considered as close as family" (*Bitter Sugar*, 3) and that "blood held Cuban families together" (264). At the end of *Bitter Sugar*, when Tío Ramón is found to be guilty, something finally breaks in Lupe Solano. As she lies in a hospital recovering from a shotgun wound inflicted by Ramón's son, a near cousin and childhood playmate, she begins to fall in love with Detective Anderson, a most unassuming love interest in the impressive lineup of Lupe's boyfriends and lovers. As if to close a chapter in Lupe's liberated life by traditional standards and lost ideals, the "honest and moral" and respectful Anderson waits in the wings to make her feel "safe and secure" (*Bitter Sugar*, 93, 297), something that apparently the Cuban family can no longer accomplish. At the end of the novel, just as Lupe enters her thirties,[4] it is suggested that Lupe will end her private investigation practice and fall in love with and possibly marry Anderson ("a nice Anglo man"). With *Bitter Sugar*, Carolina García-Aguilera also publicly announces that she will write no more installments in the Lupe Solano series.

Lupe's work as a private investigator is put to the service of Cuba. Founder, president, and chief investigator of Solano Investigations, P.I. Solano is a self-identified "Cuban American princess." She is educated, rich, beautiful, sexy, independent, and highly admired by her family and friends, and desired as well by her clients and love interests. Intensely Cuban, completely bilingual, and fiercely committed to the cause of defeating Castro, Solano is the embodiment of the so-called Miami Cuban exile community. Each of the crimes she seeks to resolve is linked in some way to what she and her family consider the greater crime of Castro's revolution. Each text in the series is prefigured by an epigraph that calls for the demise of Castro and the return of Miami Cuban exiles to the island. In pursuit of the Cuban homeland, and under the banner of *familia*, the epigraph of *Bloody Waters* declares: "This book is dedicated to my three daughters, Sarah, Antonia, and Gabriella, the loves and passions of my life, and to Cuba, island of my dreams. ¡Volveremos!" Appropriating and redeploying the words of the nineteenth-century founder of the first Cuban Revolutionary Party, the epigraph of the final novel, *Bitter Sugar*, ends the Lupe Solano series with a (twisted) reiteration of José Martí's words: "Finally, and with integrity / Cuba breaks the hangman's noose / which oppressed her / And haughtily shakes her free head!" Serving as framing devices, the epigraphs ideologically situate the novels and position Lupe Solano as a self-styled Cuban liberator and executioner of justice for the Cuban American exile community who desires one thing—the return of and to Cuba. On the whole, the numerous crimes and bodies uncovered by Lupe serve as a trope for the larger preoccupations of the Cuban American exile community. On a culturally specific level, García-Aguilera's novels delve into the contradictions of Cuban exile, family separations, U.S.-born Cuban generations, and traditional values such as honor, faith, family, and community allegiances. García-Aguilera uses the genre of detective fiction to articulate the larger issues of the Cuban American diaspora, vis-à-vis the figure of Lupe Solano.

Coming to the Consumers' Republic in South Florida

Fleeing revolutionary Cuba after 1959, first-wave Cuban exiles such as those represented by the fictional Solano family began to arrive en masse in the United States at a significant moment, when the nation was becoming the premier "consumers' republic." In *A Consumers' Republic: The Politics of Mass Consumption in Postwar America* (2003), historian Lisbeth Cohen argues that between 1952 and the late 1970s, the United States went through great economic, social, and cultural transformations. During those years, the white middle class fled to the suburbs, shopping malls proliferated amid the new housing developments, purchasing on credit was generalized, the consumer lifestyle was popularized, and subtle forms of racial segregation and spatial containment in the cities became common practices. According to Cohen, since the world wars and the New Deal recovery programs of the Franklin Delano Roosevelt administration, the United States had begun the reconstruction of "an economy, culture, and politics built around the promises of mass consumption, both in terms of material life and more idealistic goals of greater freedom, democracy, and equality" (Cohen, 7). Consumerism and consumer power would be equated with the values of freedom, democracy, and equality in the United States. First-wave Cuban exiles, with some capital, entered the United

States just as the consumers' republic, in the cold war context, competed against what was perceived and propagandized as "the material depriva-tion of communism" (Cohen, 8). Within this larger economic and geo-political context, more wealthy Cuban exiles exploited opportunities per-mitted them in the United States, while the United States in turn fomented and exploited the anticommunist positions of relocated Cubans so as to validate and to enforce economic sanctions and foreign policies against Castro's Cuba.

A first-wave Cuban exile in the 1960s, García-Aguilera created the character of Miami-born Lupe Solano in the wake of cold war politics, the Cuban exile experience, and the capitalist expansion of (white) middle-class families to South Florida. Telling her family's story, early in *Bloody Waters*, Lupe Solano explains,

> Papi had been a contractor in Havana, building a sizable fortune in hotel construction during Batista's time, before he was forced into exile. He was educated in the United States, first at Choate in Connecticut, then at Prince-ton. He formed friendships with the kind of Americans who had traditionally invested in Cuba. When Cuba became too volatile and unsafe for business, Papi started to shift the family's investments to the states, with the help of his American friends. When Batista fell and Castro took over, Papi had already transferred most of his wealth out of the country. He and Mami had just married, and hated to leave their homeland, but after a few years of Castro's dictatorship they knew they had to leave while they could. Mami was three months pregnant with Fatima at the time. (*Bloody Waters*, 34)

Settling in Miami, Lupe's father established a lucrative construction busi-ness, installed his family in a "modest three bedroom home in Coral Gables," and in due time relocated them to a new building development in Cocoplum, where he constructed an impressive mansion. According to Lupe, it was "quite a home . . . the kind of house an immigrant who made piles of money in the land of golden opportunity would build . . . ten bed-rooms, all oversized, lots of living area, terraces, patios. Your basic capi-talist nightmare" (*Bloody Waters*, 34–35). Lupe's prehistory situates her in the specific migratory route of her family. This narrative of immigrant success also makes intelligible the body, the affectations, and the social positions that she materializes in the novels, for she is a child of privilege, one who explains that "I was a rich girl in my junior year at the University of Miami, majoring in advertising. I wasn't particularly ambitious—it's hard to agonize for long over your future when you live in a huge house in the exclusive Cocoplum section of Miami. If things ever got tight, I figured, I could always sell my Mercedes and live off the money for a while" (*Bloody Waters*, 10).

Lupe comes into her detective career almost by chance and circumstance, when, already bored of her advertising college major, she personally witnesses the infidelity of her older sister's husband with a caterer at his own wedding reception. Lupe interns in the office of the private investigator hired by the Solano family to investigate the husband in question. There Lupe's life takes another turn. She learns the trade of private investigation—a male-dominated field in any culture—in an all-male Miami office and crime-fighting profession. With a loan from her father and the secretarial assistance of her ambivalently sexed cousin, Leonardo, Lupe opens Solano Investigations at the age of twenty-one or so and establishes herself "as an independent and successful woman in a notoriously macho field of work" (*Bloody Waters*, 33). At every turn in her life, Lupe challenges the gender order of her conservative family, who hope that she will eventually grow out of her interests and marry a "nice Cuban man." Prospective clients, for the most part Miami Cubans, are skeptical of Lupe, but quickly learn that Lupe always gets her man, or woman, and restores the order they seek. In a Joe Friday-like soliloquy, P.I. Lupe Solano describes herself as she begins to work the first case of the first novel, *Bloody Waters*, explaining,

> They [her rich Cuban American clients] didn't expect an investigator who appeared as well off as they. Maybe they expected a big, tough bitch with a bad haircut, smoking a cigar—who knows? On a good day, I clear five feet. I've always thought I had too much figure for my height, but my boyfriends—and there have been plenty—never agree. I wear my long black hair in a very fifties French twist and keep my hands perfectly manicured with blood-red nails. My eyesight is lousy, so I like to experiment with colored contacts—the green ones are my favorite, even if they make me look like an alien who's lost her way. (*Bloody Waters*, 14–15)

By the age of twenty-eight, after eight years in the field, the beautiful and brash Lupe has gained the respect of Miami's crime-fighting community and the Cuban American exile community, which often hires her to solve increasingly complex local and transnational cases. Each case takes Lupe deeper into the heart of the Cuban American community and closer to their long-time opponent, Fidel Castro.

Corporeal Memories of Cuba

Lupe's connections to the island are anchored in the memories constantly recalled by her father, who keeps a gassed-up yacht ready to return any day to Havana as soon as Castro falls. In *Havana Heat*, she tells the reader, "I had spent my life in Miami, but I feel completely Cuban" (211), and again in *A Miracle in Paradise*, she reflects (on) the imaginary Cuba interpellated into her consciousness, not by direct experience but by reiterations of the exile memory. Echoing (citing) her father's memories of Cuba, Lupe explains a bit unconvincingly and at times ambivalently,

> Although I grew up and lived in America, it feels like an accident to me. I was Cuban. When asked where I was from I would say Miami, but in truth my soul was in Cuba. I had lived a full and rich life in Miami, like many other exiles, but I had always felt as though I was in a state of suspended animation — my "real" life would begin as soon as Castro fell from power and I was able to return to the island. But part of me also knew it might not be that simple. Cubans were a divided people and fractured by political acrimony. The days of el grito de Yara, when we were united, were a distant and almost imaginable past. (*A Miracle in Paradise*, 45)

In the same novel, Lupe repeats her community's often cited condemnation of Castro: "I oppose Castro like every other exile, and my every waking thought somehow always related back to Cuba, but the truth was that I had partied my way through college and had been pretty apolitical ever since" (*A Miracle in Paradise*, 100). At the same time, she recognizes that she is part of a "generation. . . . [that] wasn't as closely tied to Cuba," one that inherits Cuba as a "memory of a romance" (115) from previous generations. Reared on her father's stories of the lost Cuba, Lupe recites key moments in the history of Cuba, including the thwarted invasion at the Bay of Pigs, the rescue efforts at sea of the *Hermanos al Rescate*, and the so-called counterrevolutionary actions of exiled Cubans (*Bloody Secrets*, 89). As can be surmised from her account of Cuban exile history, Lupe's relationship to Cuba is based for the most part on second-hand memory bites as formulated in her father's oral histories.

To some degree, Cuba is also frozen in the family's deification of Lupe's deceased mother, whose "spirit, somehow, still permeated every inch of the place," that is, the luxurious family home built as Lupe's mother was dying of ovarian cancer (*Havana Heat*, 53). It is to this Cocoplum mother-house that Lupe, her father, her older sisters Lourdes and Fatima, and her young nieces retreat in the novels. Said to be the living image of her mother, Lupe admits, "I most resembled my mother. . . . I could honor her memory the best way I know how" (55)—by embodying her memory and by performing Cuban traditions. Metonymically, therefore, Lupe stands in for her mother, who symbolizes the motherland; thus, Lupe's body can be read as an embodiment of Cuban cultural identity. Indeed, an absent presence in the Solano household, Lupe's mother (Cuban identity) becomes a driving force behind Lupe's professional work and her personal effort to aid in the recovery of Cuba. Like many Cuban exiles, it was her mother's final and unfulfilled wish to return to Cuba, even if only to be interred. Cremated and kept as ashes in an urn on the family yacht facing Cuba, Lupe's mother's body-turned-to-ashes represents ultimately the family's intangible and almost immaterial ties to Cuba. Some day the family might return to keep the promise made to Lupe's mother, and Lupe (and her generation) might physically touch and be touched by a Cuba that lies "just beyond . . . reach," as Lupe puts it (*Bloody Waters*, 208). In the meantime, Lupe's father stores an archival memory of Cuba. In *A Miracle in Paradise* (1999), while engrossed in her father's account of Cuban national history, Lupe affirms, "What could be more Cuban, I asked myself, than drinking copious amounts of heart-stopping coffee while listening to my papi talk about our patria" (47). Repeatedly throughout the novels, she recognizes that she, like others of her generation, "had to rely on oral accounts of what life used to be like in our homeland" (*Bitter Sugar*, 104).

For Lupe Solano, then, Cuban identity is steeped in the stories she hears, the family photographs she sees, the memories she recites, the religious icons she hesitantly invokes, the music she listens to, the lovers she sleeps with, the food she eats, the Spanish language she speaks, and the Cubana body she revels in. In her daily life, Lupe practices her Cubanidad by speaking Spanish, wearing Cuban symbols, and ingesting Cuban food and mojitos by the gallons, for "though my sisters and I were born in Miami and had never been to Cuba, never for a day could we forget the island's impact on our lives" (*Bloody Waters*, 7). For Lupe, "Every bite of arroz con frijoles—black beans and rice—or ropa vieja—'old clothes,' or skirt meat in tomato sauce—or yucca, or flan, reinforce our lives to Cuba. Although we also know that, with the scarcity of food on the island, few people there ate nearly as plentifully as we did" (*Havana Heat*, 212). The Cuban national anthem plays on her cell-phone ringer (*Bitter Sugar*, 29), and medals of the Virgen de la Caridad del Cobre are pinned to her brassier. Her Cubanidad, thus, is visual, aural, tactile, and, on the whole, a physical and visceral experience. She reminds readers that being Cuban is not just a hyphenated state of mind, as many scholars of Cubanidad would argue, but a corporeal experience as well: "We spoke Spanish primarily at home and among our friends, which wasn't at all unusual. Cuba coursed through our blood and always would" (*Bloody Waters*, 8).

Upon visiting Cuba for a short time in her first investigation, she describes her experience in bodily terms: "I was in awe of this land and felt the blood of my ancestors moving through me, beckoning me home. I took a moment to experience it all—the air, the water, every detail—knowing that I would have to catalogue everything into my memory for when I returned to Miami" (*Bloody Waters*, 208). Cuba runs through her like the blood in her veins, explaining thus the titles of her first three novels— *Bloody Waters*, *Bloody Shame*, and *Bloody Secrets*—which serve as anatomical explorations of Cuban identity for Lupe Solano. Upon returning from her first visit to the island, only the fleeting bruises (blood imprints) on her skin give proof "that it was all real, that it hadn't been a dream or nightmare" (*Bloody Waters*, 273)—that, indeed, she had been physically in Cuba.

Excess, Food, and Body

By the last novel, Lupe has visited Cuba twice on job assignments, although only for a few hours at a time, thus giving no indication of how she, a self-identified "Cuban American Princess," bred on the excesses of U.S. consumption, would fare in the material scarcity of revolutionary Cuba. Self-admittingly "a creature of excess" (*A Miracle in Paradise*, 236), Lupe has a notable appetite for expensive food, fine wines, and male company. On all counts, she is a voracious consumer. In *The Anthropology of Food and Body: Gender, Meaning, and Power* (1999), Carole M. Counihan claims that "[d]ifferent consumption patterns are one of the ways the rich distinguish themselves from the poor" (8). On a local and global scale, privileged eating practices ensure the maintenance of "class, caste, race, and gender hierarchies" (8). Further, in many Western and non-Western cultures, food provisioning and consumption solidify patriarchal control over women's bodies. Women's rejection and consumption of food often serve as registers of women's assumed control over their own bodies (188), as well as the contradictions of weight control in a body-conscious society.[5] Lupe's prodigious and voracious consumption practices position her not only as an elite member of the "consumers' republic" but as a

Cuban American woman waging a personal war against communist Cuba. Lupe's indulgent eating habits analogize the "liberation" of Cuba and her body, for she has the power to challenge communism within the scope of her own body by readily consuming material goods and eating copious amounts of food, yet remaining ideally "thin" within the U.S. market economy of body images. Food consumption, in the Lupe Solano Mystery series, signifies a range of competing ideologies impinging on the representation of the female body. Only in her privileged world may Lupe Solano have her cake without gaining an ounce, affirming that, in the novels, food consumption serves as a trope for capitalist values—individuality, power, control, and the pursuit of desire.

Over the course of six novels, in fact, Lupe Solano, consumes a great number of meals and huge portions of food, while taunting her readers that "[n]ot many women today display their appetites in public" as she does (*Bloody Waters*, 51). Across the six novels, she consumes no less than forty-four meals, give or take a few, at some of the finest and most popular restaurants of Miami—Versailles, Cubantería, News Café, Caffé Abracci, Strand, Joe's, Christy's, Bice's, Monty Trainer's, Islas Canarias, China Grill, Pacific Time, East Coast Fisheries, Les Halles, Joe Allen, La Bussola, Smith and Wollensky's Restaurant, Claudius Italian Restaurant, Tuscan Steak Restaurant, Le Testival, Nemo's, Chart House, The Last Carrot, etc. She also takes many of her cocktails, snacks, and meals at her father's house, where Cuban food is always served abundantly. Typical of her eating habits, she describes a meal with her sister Lourdes at Versailles: "We ordered a traditional Cuban American hybrid breakfast—a bucket of scrambled eggs with burned bacon, Cuban bread slathered with butter, tumblers of orange juice, and café con leche so strong it could have been used to awaken coma patients" (*Bloody Secrets*, 257). In another meal with her colleague and long-time lover, criminal defense lawyer Tommy McDonald, Lupe proudly explains, "I had already polished off a burgeoning Caesar salad, half a loaf of homemade bread slathered with butter, and a basket of potato skins. I was on my third glass of Merlot, and working on my filet mignon. In other words, for the moment, I was at peace with the world" (*Bloody Secrets*, 183). At the same meal, McDonald could not help remarking, "Where the hell do you put it, Lupe. . . . Your capacity for food never ceases to amaze me" (185). Steaks, veal medallions, pork chops, salmon, pastas, potatoes, arroz con pollo, media noche sandwiches, chocolate mousse cakes, coconut flan, mango shakes, chilled wines and champagnes are all staples in Lupe's monumental diet.

Pumped into her petite figure (five feet in height, one hundred pounds), the volumes of food consumed by Lupe serve as the "fuel to run a high-energy machine" (*Bloody Secrets*, 185) used, in her estimation, to combat crime and to defeat communism. Waging a self-styled revolution of consumption, Lupe unabashedly declares in *Bitter Sugar*,

> I was waiting for the life of excess to come back into fashion. I would continue to indulge until then, but I relished the thought of all the repressed people around me finally letting their hair down and enjoying life as it should be lived. . . . (148)

In her declaration of consumer independence, Lupe equates excess and food consumption with the liberation of the repressed around the world. She transforms her body into a metabolizing machine running on capitalist ideologies and excess, and producing the energy to break down the fundamental tenets of Marxism in Castro's Cuba. Through her prodigious acts of eating, consuming, and desiring, García-Aguilera's detective novel series casts Lupe Solano as a Latina geopolitical crime fighter who, in the end, challenges the last vestiges of communism in the world.

The Material Girl

Arlene Dávila (2001) reminds us that in the "commodification of ethnicity" there is a "re-authentication of U.S. minorities in terms of the 'right' way of being an 'ethnic'" (98) and a production of the "ideal Latino" (234). Carolina García-Aguilera's materialization of Lupe Solano—young, beautiful, thin, affluent, cosmopolitan, desirous and desiring—comes close to reproducing the commodified "ideal" and "right" way of being Latina, as examined by Dávila in her book (234). Indeed, Dávila identifies this "ideal" as part of "the widespread dissemination of myths of affluence and upward mobility, or of the 'coming of age' of particular populations" such as that of Cuban Americans in the United States (235). This ideal Latina has a particular "look" and body type—precisely noted by one of Dávila's interviewees as having "'the long straight hair, olive skin, just enough oliveness to the skin to make them not ambiguous. To make them Hispanic" (Dávila, 110). The chic female and ethnic embodiment of those ideals as compiled in Dávila's research perhaps represents the capitalist production and consumption (through popular culture) of the Latina/o body at this moment in the U.S. consumers' republic. In this vein, Lupe reminds her reader, "I was small, dark, curvaceous: the typical Latina. Miami should have incorporated [me] into one of their advertising campaigns for cultural diversity" (*Bloody Secrets*, 67). College educated, wealthy, Catholic, Spanish speaking, mindful of her heritage, cultural traditions, and family ideals, Lupe is indeed the "typical" (normalized) Cuban Americana. Embedded in free market capitalist ideologies and practices of consumption, the Lupe Solano Mystery series thus participates in the selective marketing of ideal Latina/o bodies, such as those of Jennifer Lopez, Shakira, Ricky Martin, and other Latino/a popular icons. Lupe is the female embodiment of the desire for a Latino/a identity high in symbolic and cultural value on the competitive multicultural and multiethnic market of the United States. In this ethnic and geopolitical market of ideologies, some Latino/a bodies, such as those of Cuban Americans, carry more value.

As I have argued in this essay, the character of Lupe Solano represents the intersection of multiple discourses signified on the idealized Latina body within a late capitalist market economy, wherein Latinos/as are increasingly recognized as a potential political force and viable consumer market, contributing over $380 billion to the U.S. economy. The figure of Lupe Solano—always successful in crime solving and in love and wealth—embodies a range of normative values and ideals, from the conventional norms of Latina "beauty" to the free-trade market of the U.S. consumers' republic that I have delineated in this chapter. With each successive mystery novel in which she is the protagonist, Lupe assumes a greater degree of liberal feminist agency and diasporic mobility within a free market economy, flowing freely across racial, ethnic, gender, and national borders, at least twice entering and surreptitiously leaving the island of Cuba to do her crime-solving work. Moreover, she seems to become larger than her fictional character, as she takes on Fidel Castro, almost challenging the historical figure to a one-on-one fight over Cuba. She comes to embody what Donald M. Lowe, in *The Body in Late-Capitalist USA* (1995), has identified as the "subject-effect" of lived experiences as situated in particular political, economic, and discursive contexts.

In Lupe Solano's case, the Cuban Revolution of 1959 and its aftermath have produced her diasporic condition in the United States. Her bodily materialization is the "effect" of larger domestic and foreign politics in Cuba and the United States. As Lowe explains,

> The body, a historical materiality, is neither a body-in-itself nor a body-for-itself, but always an embodied being-in-the-world, constructed and realized within social practices to satisfy changing needs. There is no body as an entity prior to social codings and practices. The body in late-capitalist USA is con-

structed and realized in an expanded, accelerated whirlwind of exchangist practices. (174–175)

Lupe Solano's female body — eternally young, beautiful, thin, and wealthy — materializes a broad corpus of social, economic, and political discourses, all finding articulation in Carolina García-Aguilera's Lupe Solano Mystery series. In the figure of Lupe (the typical and normalized Latina image) foreign and local interests intersect, making Lupe's the body in question and the body through which we may interrogate contemporary constructions of Latinidad in the United States.

Notes

1. See María Cristina García, *Havana USA: Cuban Exiles and Cuban Americans in South Florida, 1959–1994* (Berkeley and Los Angeles: University of California Press, 1996). According to García, Cubans have migrated to the United States since the early nineteenth century, when they established communities in South Florida and New York. The 1959 Cuban Revolution set off the watershed exodus of Cubans, who fled Fidel Castro's governance and resettled in the United States. Between 1959 and 1962, more than 200,000 Cubans arrived in the United States. The "Golden Exiles," consisting of former government officials, members of the upper class, and other dissidents, were the first to leave Cuba and arrive in Miami, Florida. This group was for the most part white and upper class, and had some capital or preestablished contacts in the United States. They received much legal, financial, and other material aid to make the transition to living in the United States. They were followed by successive waves of Cuban emigrants "of different politics and more modest wealth." Between 1965 and 1973, "Freedom Flights" were allowed to depart from Cuba with the families of those who had already departed. Numbering approximately 200,000, this group was composed of 57 percent working class and 12 percent professionals. There was an effort in the United States to relocate Cubans outside the Miami area. In 1980, the Peruvian Embassy takeover (in March 1979) by Cuban nationals wishing to leave Cuba set off the Mariel boatlift. About 100,000 Cubans arrived in the United States. These immigrants included working-class people, people with families in the United States, political prisoners, and others. The boatlift emigration began as "*balseros*" threw themselves on rafts and set themselves adrift in the Florida Straits throughout the 1980s and 1990s, a period known in Cuba as the "Special Period," which was characterized by a great scarcity of material goods. The dire conditions were compounded by the breakup of the Soviet Union and the decline in Soviet support of Cuba.

2. In *Life on the Hyphen: The Cuban-American Way* (Austin: University of Texas Press, 1995), Gustavo Pérez-Firmat explains that one-and-a-half-generation Cubans are those "born in Cuba but made in the U.S.A." (4). Carolina García-Aguilera's protagonist, Lupe Solano, represents successive generations of U.S.-

born Cubans whose ties to the island are constructed second-hand from cultural materials relayed to them by those of earlier generations. Completely bilingual and seemingly comfortable in her hybrid "cultural habitat" (5), Solano possesses the hyphenated sensibilities that Pérez-Firmat extols in his book.

3. See "Mystery Guild: Author Interview," February 19, 2003 (http://www.mysteryguild.com).

4. Through *Bitter Sugar*, Lupe remains twenty-eight years old, although a slight slip of age occurs in *Havana Heat*, when readers are told that Lupe is thirty years old.

5. Naomi Wolf examines the relationship between food and power in *The Beauty Myth: How Images of Beauty Are Used Against Women* (New York: Harper Collins, 2002). She writes that "within the context of the intimate family, food is love, memory, and language. But in the public realm, food is status and honor" (189). Both food associations can be traced in Lupe Solano's consumption of food in her private and public spheres.

Bibliography

Butler, Judith. 1993. *Bodies That Matter: On the Discursive Limits of "Sex."* New York: Routledge.

Cohen, Lisbeth. 2003. *A Consumers' Republic: The Politics of Mass Consumption in Postwar America.* New York: Alfred A. Knopf.

Corpi, Lucha. 1999. *Black Widow's Wardrobe.* Houston: Arte Público Press.

Counihan, Carole M. 1999. *The Anthropology of Food and Body: Gender, Meaning, and Power.* New York: Routledge.

Dávila, Arlene. 2001. *Latinos, Inc.: The Marketing and Making of a People.* Berkeley and Los Angeles: University of California Press.

García, María Cristina. 1996. *Havana USA: Cuban Exiles and Cuban Americans in South Florida, 1959–1994.* Berkeley and Los Angeles: University of California Press.

García-Aguilera, Carolina. 1996. *Bloody Waters.* New York: G. P. Putnam's Sons.

———. 1997. *Bloody Shame.* New York: G. P. Putnam's Sons.

———. 1998. *Bloody Secrets.* New York: G. P. Putnam's Sons.

———. 1999. *A Miracle in Paradise.* New York: Avon Books/HarperCollins.

———. 2000. *Havana Heat.* New York: Avon Books/HarperCollins.

———. 2001. *Bitter Sugar.* New York: William Morrow.

Giardinelli, Mempo. 1996. *El género negro: Ensayos sobre literatura policial.* Córdoba, Argentina: Op Oloop Ediciones.

LoPinto, Charles, and Lidia Llamas. 2000. *Countdown in Alaska.* Yonkers, NY: Envirocrime Publishers.

———. 2000. *The Case of the Toxic Cruiseline.* Yonkers, NY: Envirocrime Publishers.

Lowe, Donald M. 1995. *The Body in Late-Capitalist USA.* Durham, NC: Duke University Press.

Morales, Alejandro. 1992. *The Rag Doll Plagues.* Houston: Arte Público Press.

"Mystery Guild: Author Interview." Interview with Carolina García-Aguilera. February 19, 2003 (http://www.mysteryguild.com).

Nava, Michael. 1986. *The Little Death*. New York: Alyson Publications.

———. 1990. *How Town*. New York: Harper and Row.

———. 1992. *The Hidden Law*. New York: Ballantine Books.

———. 1996. *Goldenboy: A Mystery*. New York: Alyson Publications.

———. 1996. *The Death of Friends*. New York: Ballantine Books.

———. 1997. *The Burning Plain*. New York: Bantam.

———. 2002. *Rag and Bone*. New York: Prime Crime.

Pepper, Andrew. 2000. *The Contemporary American Crime Novel: Race, Ethnicity, Gender, Class*. Chicago: Fitzroy Dearborn.

Pérez-Firmat, Gustavo. 1994. *Life on the Hyphen: The Cuban-American Way*. Austin: University of Texas Press.

Ponce, Mary Helen. 1998. "Latino Sleuths: Hispanic Mystery Writers Make Crime Pay." *Hispanic* (May): 44–59.

Simpson, Amelia. 1992. Introduction. *New Tales of Mystery and Crime from Latin America*, trans. and ed. Amelia Simpson. Cranbury, NJ: Associated University Presses.

Stavans, Ilán. 1997. *Antiheroes: Mexico and Its Detective Novel*, trans. Jesse H. Lytle and Jennifer A. Mattson. Cranbury, NJ: Associated University Presses.

Villatoro, Marcos McPeek. 2001. *Home Killings: A Romilia Chacón Mystery*. Houston: Arte Público Press.

Walton, Priscilla L., and Manina Jones. 1999. *Detective Agency: Women Rewriting the Hard-Boiled Tradition*. Berkeley: University of California Press.

Wolf, Naomi. 2002. *The Beauty Myth: How Images of Beauty Are Used Against Women*. New York: HarperCollins.

CHAPTER 13

La Princesa Plástica

Hegemonic and Oppositional Representations of *Latinidad* in Hispanic Barbie

KAREN GOLDMAN

No amount of human willpower can defy the might of the pink princess. Of all the forces against which resistance is futile, Barbie ranks right up near the top.

THE ECONOMIST (DECEMBER 21, 2002)

In the forty-some years since she emerged from her original mold, Mattel's Barbie doll has become, both as cultural icon and children's plaything, one of the world's most ubiquitous plastic objects. The doll's embodiment of a diversity of feminine images reflects Mattel's efforts to market to continuously changing and increasingly diverse groups of U.S. and international consumers. But is it true, as some observers have contended, that, given the preeminence and persistence of the image of "rich, blonde Barbie" worldwide, resistance, cultural or otherwise, to hegemonic Barbie culture is futile? Barbie scholar Erica Rand points out that there is often a wide gap between the contexts and narratives that are produced for Barbie by Mattel, which are far from monolithic themselves, and the meanings that are generated by her consumers, whether children at play, collectors, or those who find in Barbie's carefully constructed persona an irresistible target for parody and subversion (26–28).

This essay analyzes the narrowly circumscribed biographies and images of original Caucasian Barbie and then chronicles how Mattel, in attempting to capture a growing U.S. market in ethnic toys, projected its concept of Latina femininity onto the plastic body and the myriad accessories of Hispanic Barbie. My analysis examines how factory-produced images of (U.S.-marketed) Hispanic Barbie and Barbie in Latin America are countered, parodied, and contested by cultural actors occupying various non-hegemonic positions. These unofficial and resistant representations of

Hispanic/Latin American Barbie are generated and circulated beyond Mattel's closely held authorial control; they include readings of the dolls that extend or transcend the "official" narratives, as well as examples of cultural appropriation of the dolls' authorized meanings and identities for purposes of artistic experimentation, resistance, and parody. I consider, for example, some recent works that counter the official Barbie image, such as the 2001 animation *Barbie Can Also Be Sad,* by Argentine director Albertina Carri, in which the casting of Hispanic Barbie and Caucasian Barbie as servant and mistress offers a critical commentary on ethnicity, gender, and class as determinants of relative positions of power in Latin America.

The often quoted statistics on Barbie's global presence are staggering: more than one billion dolls sold in 150 countries, representing forty-five different nationalities (Barbie Collectibles). Although there is today a multitude of manifestations of Barbie culture, both hegemonic and oppositional, the point from which they all depart is the original, blue-eyed, blonde Barbie. Barbies are marked as "ethnic" or foreign only to the extent to which they differ from the original doll. In her "unauthorized biography," *Forever Barbie*, M. G. Lord begins a chapter on ethnic Barbie by drawing an analogy between the development of Ruth Handler's original doll and the creation of Caucasian, all-American Hollywood star icons by largely Jewish-run movie studios. Lord asserts that original Barbie's ethnic neutrality differs from and surpasses that of the flesh-and-blood female stars that she resembles because, unlike "real" actresses, Barbie had no biological heredity and was, in fact, better suited than a human actress to exemplify an impossible ideal: "There was no tribal taint in her plastic flesh, no baggage to betray an immigrant past. She had no navel; no parents; no heritage" (160). Barbie's plasticity afforded her creators the luxury of designing her from scratch and literally molding every aspect of her appearance.

Like Hollywood promoters, who need to "design" stars that will engage the identification of the largest number of viewers, Mattel strove to develop a Barbie that would appeal to the greatest number of the doll's target audience: white, middle-class American parents and their daughters. Thus, the company's marketing strategy involved stressing, above all else, the doll's "Americanness." She had to be, in the words of Barbie's admiring biographer, BillyBoy, "the personification of the all-round American girl" (28). In the social environment of the United States of the late 1950s, this meant she had to be Caucasian, blonde, light-skinned, and free of any obvious ethnic markers.

The original Barbie's ethnic neutrality not only served to emphasize the association of middle-class Caucasian femininity with "Americanness," it also served to bolster what Erica Rand refers to as Mattel's "language of infinite possibility" (28). Citing the need to allow children to project their own imagination onto the doll, Ruth Handler went to great lengths to expunge what she perceived as distinguishing characteristics that would give Barbie a distinct look or persona. In a 1990 interview she remarked, "the face was deliberately designed to be blank, without a personality, so that the projection of the child's dream could be on Barbie's face" (quoted in Rand, 40). But, like any cultural product, and despite the claims of her inventor, Barbie has indeed "always already" been inscribed in a manufactured narrative that is strictly circumscribed and defined by her producers. Clearly, within the rigid parameters of the doll's image as projected by Mattel, the possibilities for imagining a nonhegemonic Barbie were limited.

By 1961, Mattel had made the decision to allow Barbie to acquire a specific biography beyond her first name and the qualifier "teenage fashion model." During the early sixties, Barbie was appearing in books, records, and other texts as a blonde pony-tailed teenage fashion model with a personality, an address, a last name, and a boyfriend. While Barbie's and Ken's first names were taken from the real names of Ruth and Elliot Handler's two children, the other names are a veritable tribute to hyperbolic anglocentrism: Barbie's full name is Barbara Millicent Roberts. Ken's surname is Carson, and the two names together are, appropriately, an homage to Mattel's advertising firm: Carson/Roberts. Barbie's parents' names are identified as George and Margaret (only a minor variation of George and Martha, those archetypical grandparents of the nation). Barbie lives a glamorous but otherwise typical teenage life in a small American town called Willows.

Mattel has periodically adjusted Barbie's body, face, and hair in the interest of keeping up with styles and social realities of the day. But during the early years of her existence it was above all clothing and accessories that allowed her to (at least superficially) diversify her look. At first, the outfits marketed for Barbie fell into categories that emphasized her elegance ("Evening Splendor," "Silken Flame"), career aspirations ("Ballerina," "Registered Nurse"), leisure activities ("Ski Queen," "Movie Date"), or special occasions ("Easter Parade," "Bride's Dream"). None of these outfits departed in any substantial way from the standard of Barbie's (and later Ken's) middle-class Caucasian Americanness. By 1964, Barbie and Ken had already acquired many of the accoutrements of the American dream, for example, those appropriately named "dream" accessories: the "dream kitchen" (1964), the "dream house" (1964), and the sports car (1962). For members of the postwar American middle class who had already attained these assets, travel, particularly to an exotic location, became a status-bearing consumer item, akin to owning a nice house or car (Urry). In 1964, in a miniature reenactment of the U.S. middle-class's increasing tendency to dedicate capital and leisure time to long-distance travel, Mattel launched the Travel Costume series, and Barbie and Ken become tourists, visiting Japan, Switzerland, Holland, Hawaii, and Mexico. Each travel costume outfit included "charming traditional costumes" for Barbie and Ken, as well as a miniature storybook that narrated the pair's travel adventures.

Central to Barbie's Mexican travel experience is the fact that the dolls (with or without the storybook provided with the outfit) come with a ready-made Mattel-produced narrative that highlights the pair's status as Caucasian Americans enjoying leisure adventures, oblivious to the larger narrative that is the largely mestizo Mexican nation and its people. No images of other compete as meaning producer with the Mattel master narrative, for there are no traces of actual people (or doll personalities) in the narrative other than the costumed Caucasian Barbie and Ken. In the Travel Adventure set, the dolls are dressed in stereotypical folkloric Mexican fashion—Barbie wears a traditional tehuana skirt, and Ken is incongruently dressed in full *charro* attire, not unlike souvenir dolls typically sold in tourist shops and airports. But unlike the souvenir dolls, which one must presumably have crossed some national border to obtain, there is no suggestion that Barbie and Ken are in any way identified with real Mexicans. Rather, they engage in a kind of cultural masquerade, both through their clothing and through their participation in host culture activities—"Ken wears his costume to a fiesta!" Barbie and Ken's cultural cross-dressing metonymically invites the consumer to objectify the exotic other without ever actually invoking the image of the other's body.

Mexico is a backdrop for Barbie's and Ken's travel adventure, not unlike the stories of the Little Theatre Costume sets that were sold concurrently, featuring Barbie as a princess of the Arabian Knights, Little Red Riding Hood, Guinevere, and Cinderella. Like the memorable figure of Donald Duck wearing a sombrero and traveling through Mexico on a flying serape in the 1939 Disney cartoon film *The Three Caballeros*, Ken and Barbie perform their jovial masquerade against a background in which the totality of Mexico is represented as a storybook land. The story and the outfits depict folkloric or traditional elements of Mexican culture that, through caricature, are rendered no more unfamiliar or threatening to American cultural hegemony than the storybook characters. Thus, Ken's and Barbie's masquerading in the Mexico set functions more as an affirmation of the doll's implacable whiteness than any attempt to represent a multicultural opening. And, of course, in the history of colonial encounters between Americans and others, this dynamic in what Mary Louise Pratt calls the "contact zone" (6) is well established: "White appropriations of African-American culture, sentimentalizing images of disappearing Native Americans, condescending caricatures of inscrutable Asians or hot-blooded Mexicans have a long and disreputable history. . . . [I]dentification with otherness has become an essential element in the construction of whiteness" (Lipsitz, 53). Following a traditional pattern of imperialist penetration, Barbie's (and Mattel's) entry into an international, intercultural environment begins from the position of tourist, that of postcolonial traveler to exotic locations. However, and in spite of the Travel Collection's clear affirmation of the dolls as Anglo and American, even this limited acknowledgment of worlds beyond the United States points, however tenuously, to Barbie's (and Mattel's) imminent initial foray into global expansion. It marks the beginning of what would eventually become the breakup of the monolithic Barbie narrative in which nonwhite others are not only invisible, but their existence is never even an issue, for it simply does not come into play.

By the late sixties, Barbie's privileging of Caucasian femininity as the standard of American beauty, anachronistically silhouetted against a background of the civil rights movement and increasing ethnic and racial diversity in the United States, was becoming an encumbrance to Ruth Handler's notion that all girls must be able to identify with Barbie. Mattel decided to alter its master narrative in a reversal that reined in Barbie's biography and reintroduced the "language of infinite possibility." In 1967, Mattel launched a rather unconvincing Black Francie doll, followed, in 1968, by Barbie's black friend Christie. In 1980, Mattel introduced Black and Hispanic Barbie, as well as a "Dolls of the World" Collection. In 1988, Teresa, a Hispanic doll, was introduced, followed by a line of African American "friends of Barbie." In a 1990 interview for *Newsweek*, Mattel product manager Deborah Mitchell proudly announced, "now, ethnic Barbie lovers will be able to dream in their own image" (duCille, 554).

While it is clear that Mattel was intent on capturing the growing ethnic markets in the United States by developing dolls meant to allow identification by ethnic "others," there is much debate regarding how authentically the dolls actually represent diversity. The representation of Latinidad in the marketing of Hispanic Barbie dolls has followed the recent pattern of

many products aimed at Latino consumers. Media scholar Clara E. Rodríguez argues that in the popular media in the United States today, Latinos
are typically either absent or misrepresented. When they are represented,
it is often as negative stereotypes or as exotic foreigners (13–30). Behind
Mattel's portrayal of Latino/a identity lies a system of representation that
sells itself as authentic but that ultimately either depicts Latino/a culture
as homogeneous and exotic or repackages the doll's Latinidad in an assimilated form, whether to make her more attractive to more assimilated
Latinos or to market her more effectively in places where ethnic diversity
is not particularly marketable.

Until recently, and especially with the introduction of the unabashedly
curvy "My Scene" Barbies, the height and body measurements of all of
the dolls had remained steadfastly constant (Urla and Swedlund). The
use of the Spanish language, often combined with English/Spanish code-
switching, is typically a marker for products aimed at Latinos/as. This is
largely underplayed as a distinctive feature in marketing Hispanic Barbie,
despite the fact that the dolls' boxes are sometimes offered in bilingual
versions. The first Hispanic Barbie doll's bilingual box introduced her as
Barbie Hispanica (not the grammatically correct Hispana). Like the earlier
Mexico Travel Barbie, she is stereotypically dressed in a white peasant
blouse and a full red skirt, a lace mantilla over her shoulders and a red rose
tied around her neck. If the standard for Caucasian Barbie is light-skinned,
blonde, and blue-eyed, the U.S. Hispanic version presents those contrast-
ing physical attributes stereotypically associated with Latinas: dark hair,
dark eyes, and darker skin. However, in few of the dolls designed to represent Hispanic (or Latina) women is skin tone ever darker than the sun-
tanned Malibu Barbie dolls. Facial features never hint at indigenous or
African heritage. What most prominently distinguishes the original Hispanic Barbie from any of the brunette Caucasian Barbies is the doll's paratextual items: clothing and accessories, or, more accurately, her costume.
The original Hispanic Barbie, as well as subsequent special editions that
celebrate occasions culturally specific to Latinos, such as the Quinceañera
Barbie, all sport traditional folkloric clothing that is intended to mark
them very clearly as Latinas, and therefore as foreign, exotic other.

In her physical characteristics, posture, and dress, the original Hispanic
Barbie very closely resembles the international Hispanic (read: foreign)
Dolls of the World, which are designed to reflect "typical" national attributes and dress in folkloric clothing. To Caucasian Barbie's quintessen-
tial Americanness, the Dolls of the World represent a quintessentially foreign counterpoint. But, as Wendy Varney argues in her convincing analysis

of Australian Barbie, they are essentially American products and bear the stamp of U.S. cultural imperialism, no matter what the guise. With respect to Latina identity, the Dolls of the World tend to negotiate difference by representing those Latinas as either hyperbolically folkloric (Mexico, Peru) or splashy and exotic (Brazil). Mattel's stated goals in offering the Dolls of the World Collection is to foster international understanding and appreciation of cultural differences. Significantly, the Andalusian Barbie and Mexican Barbie, both of whom are included in the Dolls of the World Collection, differ only superficially from U.S. Hispanic Barbie. They all have fair complexions and long dark hair, each with a large red rose tucked behind one ear. They wear full skirts and blouses, and all three dolls' clothes feature bright red as the predominant color, a characteristic that persists in Mattel's representations of Hispanics. Cultural differences among diverse groups and nationalities are elided as Latinidad is reduced to one easily consumable, stereotypical identity-in-a-box.

The Peruvian doll, issued in 1999, provides a good example of how notions of Latin American class, race, and ethnicity play out in the real or implied narrative that frames the doll's paratextual positioning. For one thing, the doll is clearly meant to portray the identity of an indigenous Peruvian woman, with her long braids, round face, traditional woven shawl, and matching skirt. However, her facial features are wholly Caucasian, as is her rosy skin tone. In a clear and rather surprising break with standard Barbie design and Mattel's custom of representing racial differences only through what Ann duCille calls the "tint of the plastic," Peruvian Barbie carries a baby, who presumably is meant to be her own. One thing that has consistently defined the essence of Barbie has been her status as a single woman. While she is often depicted as a big sister or caring for children, and she has long been available as a bride, there has never been such a thing as a "Married Barbie," much less a maternal Barbie. Until the recent release of the "Happy Family" dolls, including a "Pregnant Midge" (not Barbie) that comes with a belly containing a removable baby, maternity has been wholly absent in the world of Barbie dolls. In the case of Midge, the issue of paternity is never in question, since, in a throwback to the early years of Mattel's use of heavy-handed biography, the doll wears a wedding ring, and her box provides a narrative identifying the father as Midge's husband, Alan.

The Peruvian doll comes with no such disclaimer. The baby is one more accessory, like Hispanic Barbie's lace mantilla, that identifies her as ethnically other. The representation of the Peruvian Barbie as mother is possible precisely because she is a Doll of the World, that is, she is foreign, and

Figure 13.1. U.S. "Hispanic" Barbie doll, 1980.
Figure 13.2. "Dolls of the World" Mexican Barbie Doll, 1995.
Figure 13.3. "Dolls of the World" Andalucía Barbie Doll, 1996.

Figure 13.6. Barbie (right) and her maid Teresa. From Albertina Carri, "Barbie Can Also Be Sad."

Figure 13.4. "Dolls of the World" Peruvian Barbie Doll, 1998.
Figure 13.5. "Dolls of the World" Brazilian Barbie Doll, 1989.

not subject to the rigid conventions of the "American" dolls. In addition, Peruvian Barbie's representation responds to principles of marketing and stereotypes that view Latinos as extremely family-oriented and conservative on the issue of nontraditional roles for women (Deanne et al.). The presence of the baby, with or without an implied father, is a much more important signifier of Mattel's notion of Latina femininity than any national costume or textual commentary might be.

Following the introduction of the first Hispanic Barbie in 1980, which differed little from the "foreign" Dolls of the World, Mattel favored more culturally assimilated Hispanic dolls that differed little from nonethnic Barbies beyond adjustments to physical characteristics such as hair color and skin tone. Hispanic Barbie and African-American Barbies were simply marketed as differently tinted versions of Caucasian Barbies. Such not-*too*-ethnic dolls were attractive to both ethnic minorities and majority Caucasian buyers, and thus served the dual purpose of appearing to foster diversity while increasing profits. In 1988, Mattel introduced Teresa, a bona fide Latina friend of Barbie. Like Barbie, Teresa has been produced with a multitude of physical characteristics over the years, morphing from a doll with consistently darker skin and hair to one that is often indistinguishable from nonethnic Barbie.

Today, all ethnic Barbie dolls vary in skin tone and hair color, but they typically wear the same clothes and accessories as Caucasian Barbie. It is tempting to consider that Teresa's changing looks signal Mattel's acknowledgment of the tremendous diversity among Latino populations worldwide. But beyond the dye that is used to tint her plastic body, it is hard to appreciate any substantial difference between Teresa and brunette Caucasian Barbies. What renders them similar is far more compelling than what sets them apart. Since recent issues of the Teresa doll don't even include Spanish text on the box, the only remaining link to Teresa's Latina identity is her name, Teresa (whose echo of the distant Spanish mystic Santa Teresa does not go unnoticed by many). Like the doll itself, the name is familiar enough to the Anglo public to be recognized as the Spanish translation of the name Theresa. And this is indeed the point: Teresa remains a kind of a translation, a "Barbified" version of a culturally exotic entity made familiar and thus consumable through her proximity to Barbie, that most American of icons. Even when Teresa is sold in a way that culturally marks her as Hispanic—for example, as Quinceañera Teresa—she more closely resembles Caucasian Barbie than the Latin American or Spanish Dolls of the World. The ultimate confirmation of her degree of assimilation is her marketing success in regions of the United States that do not have high concentrations of Latinos.

While Mattel has been congratulating itself for promoting diversity in the United States by including Hispanic Barbie and Teresa along with other dolls of color among its products, in Latin American countries where licensed Barbies are produced by regional subsidiaries they are nearly always modeled on the traditional Hollywood-inspired brands of American beauty: Caucasian and blonde. And although Caucasian blonde Barbie is certainly popular among Latina girls in the United States (Budge), it is unusual for a Hispanic doll to be marketed in the United States that does not possess those physical characteristics typically attributed to Latinas: darker skin, hair, and eyes. That Hispanic Barbies in the United States are not generally sold as blondes, whereas they very often are in Latin America, points to some of the complexities of racial and ethnic identification and marketing in both countries. As is evident in the success of female celebrities from Eva Perón to XuXa, in Latin American popular culture it is, ironically, the Hollywood-inspired ideal of blonde feminine beauty that prevails. And, given Barbie's relatively hefty price tag in Latin America (about $20), it is precisely the mostly white elite to whom Barbie dolls are marketed. The highest proportion of Barbie ownership in Latin America (outside of Puerto Rico, where a whopping 72 percent of girls own Barbies) is in Argentina (44 percent) and Chile (49 percent), nations that also have the lowest proportion of indigenous peoples, blacks, and mestizos and the highest proportion of European-descended Caucasians ("Barbie Dolls in Latin America"). Not surprisingly, the most popular Argentine Barbies tend to be those with the most Caucasian features. This is the backdrop for the 2001 Argentine film, *Barbie Can Also Be Sad* (*Barbie también puede estar triste*), by Albertina Carri. The film offers an alternative view and a biting criticism of those mostly invisible elements that underlie Barbie culture.

Barbie's hegemonic identity and her very ubiquity have always made her an attractive target for parodical representations of subversive intent. These counterhegemonic efforts include guerrilla tactics, such as the Barbie Liberation Organization, which sabotaged toys on store shelves. Other examples include works of criticism and literature that revisit and reinterpret the Barbie image, such as *Mondo Barbie* and *The Barbie Chronicles*, works of visual art, a multitude of Internet sites such as visiblebarbie .com and distortedbarbie.com, as well as the notable 1987 film *Superstar* by Todd Haynes. This film narrates the life of pop music star Karen Carpenter, who died of anorexia in 1983, using Barbie dolls to stand in for the human figures. Like Haynes's film, the majority of these counterhegemonic and often feminist-inspired criticisms target Barbie's absurd body proportions, her flawless physiognomy, her anachronistic femininity, and the culture of consumption she promotes. Few of them problematize the issues of race, ethnicity, class, and the privileging of U.S. perceptions of foreign others in their analyses.

Albertina Carri's 24-minute animation features (real) Barbie dolls involved in a series of relationships and encounters that include explicit scenes of sex between lesbian, gay, heterosexual, and transvestite characters. The protagonist Barbie is a neurotic blonde aristocrat who, in her ennui, enters into a lesbian relationship with Teresa, her darker Hispanic Barbie maid. Ken is cast as the patriarchal machista and the sadist to the film's masochistic secretaries. After its first screening at the Mexican Urban-Fest Festival, Mattel obtained a court order banning the film from being shown. The company argued that the film is pornographic and would damage Barbie's wholesome image. Mattel's Mexican lawyer Pablo Vásquez Rohde said, "This is a pornographic video and the company does not find it acceptable. We don't know what has happened in other countries but they won't be allowed to show it here" (Ananova). In a statement that points to the cultural differences between the United States and the Latin American nations, José Antonio Escalante, director of the Urban-

Fest, said that he was surprised at the company's reaction. "This film has been shown as a work of art in Argentina and in Brazil, where it was even shown on TV without any scandal" (Ananova). In the United States, the film has been screened mainly at gay and lesbian film festivals, most notably the San Francisco and New York International Lesbian and Gay Film Festivals.

The portrayal of Barbie as a lesbian is a problem for Mattel indeed, especially for a doll whose slogan remains, "We girls can do anything!" And although Mattel has unwittingly already released the first lesbian "friend of Barbie" (it happened when Mattel began marketing a Rosie O'Donnell doll, before the talk-show star came out as a lesbian), homosexuality—any mention of sexuality at all—has always been absent from the thoroughly sanitized world of Barbie. That is not to say that sex as an implicit subtext is not omnipresent in Barbie culture. Indeed, as Erica Rand argues, "The Handlers . . . pulled her out of a sexual arena in the first place and kept her there, even after the Barbie-hating mothers in their first market study confirmed that sex was the big message" (193). Carri's film follows a classic pornographic formula: it is technically uneven, sexually explicit, and highly melodramatic. It makes unequivocal what is only suggested through the ready-made narrative that invariably emerges from the fundamental aspects of Barbie's physical appearance and character. Moreover, it makes overt the homoerotic content that, as Rand points out, has always been implicit in Barbie culture.

Perhaps the most interesting aspect of the film is the unambiguous construction of class differences in the positioning of Caucasian Barbie and Ken (who stand in for the largely white Argentine middle class) vis-à-vis the mestiza servant. It exposes a postcolonial dynamic that underlies the whole of the Barbie–Hispanic Barbie relationship, and for that matter all social relationships involving disparate positions of power. In Argentina as in the rest of the Americas, darker-skinned sectors of the population are invariably less powerful in economic, social, and political arenas. As opposed to the superficially parallel positioning of blonde Barbie and her darker-skinned "friends" on the shelves of U.S. toy stores, Carri's film offers a view of the dolls that emphasizes the unequal relationships between First World and Third World, elite and subaltern, powerful and marginalized. At the same time, it exemplifies the essential cruelty and disregard for humanity that accompanies the dominant entity's (Ken and Barbie's) exercise of privilege and economic superiority over those who serve them (Teresa). What is so powerful about Carri's film, particularly for a U.S. audience accustomed to viewing Barbie as a thorn in the side of feminists but essentially innocuous on issues of social injustice, is that the servant, Teresa, like the original U.S. Latina Teresa, is also an oppressed minority in the context of Argentine society. Teresa is easily identifiable by her speech and her dark complexion as one of the many poorly paid, unskilled Paraguayan immigrants who, before the economic crisis that has paralyzed much of the Argentine economy, crossed into Argentina to find work, often living in miserable conditions in overcrowded slums. The film alternates between the affluent Barbie mansion (a new spin on the classic "dream house") and the drab working-class neighborhood where Teresa lives with a butcher, a transvestite, and her boyfriend. Racial and ethnic discrimination, a subject that is rarely spoken about in Argentina, in part due to the very small number of ethnic and racial minorities in the country, becomes an inextricable part of the ties that bind and separate the characters as they move about their lives, encountering (and exploiting) each other.

The film is a biting commentary on contemporary Argentina, but in addition, the use of a quintessentially American icon as protagonist allows the film to be read as a metaphorical commentary on the imperialist cultural politics of the United States vis-à-vis the nations of Latin America: Barbie is to Teresa as the United States is to Argentina. Carri's film represents a robust response to Ann duCille's commentary that "on the toystore shelf or in the collector's curio cabinet, maid and aristocrat enjoy an odd equality . . . but this seeming sameness denies the historical relation they bear to each other as the colonized and the colonizer" ("Barbie in Black and White," 127). In the end, power relationships turn out to be less rigid (more plastic) than they might at first appear, as it is Teresa who seduces her mistress, Barbie, and in doing so also undermines and emasculates the chauvinistic Ken.

A student-made short film (4 ½ minutes) that, like Carri's film, features animated Barbie and Ken dolls was shown recently at some festivals in Brazil. The short, entitled *Tudo que você quer ser* (All You Want to Be), also raises questions of gender and class, as well as that of national culture versus imported U.S. cultural products. It does this by presenting a conjugal argument between middle-class Barbie and Ken, who is jealous of Falcon, a G.I. Joe–style Brazilian doll. The competition between Ken and Falcon recreates, on a very small scale, the conflict that has hounded Latin American nations since their independence: how to preserve and protect national cultures in the face of the ubiquitous cultural imperialism of the United States. And while these small measures of agency represented by Carri's and Jovain's films may be minute against the backdrop of the totality of

Barbie culture, they do indeed offer remarkable alternative representations of (Latina) Barbie, ones that perhaps, given the ferociousness of the Mattel legal team, could never have been released in the United States.

The Internet has been a prodigious global source of Barbie resistance, parody, and criticism. Pocho.com is a Web site based on *Pocho Magazine*, which has been around since the late eighties. The site, subtitled "Aztlán's número uno source for satire y chingazos," features irreverent and biting satire, a longstanding tradition in Mexican journalism. Though *pocho* literally means faded, it is a disparaging term often used by Mexicans to describe U.S.-assimilated Mexican Americans. The magazine's and Web site's appropriation of the term reflects a sentiment that has grown consistently as people of Mexican heritage in the United States proudly embrace their identity as one of fluidity and hybridity. On the site, as in the lives and cultures of Chicanos and other Latinos in the United States, English and Spanish are mixed freely, and articles on Mexican president Vicente Fox are juxtaposed with ones on Ron Unz and Monica Lewinsky. The April 28, 2000, edition featured a satirical story titled "New Latina Barbies Unveiled," announcing that Mattel had launched a line of Barbies in the likeness of Latina celebrities Cameron Diaz, Christina Aguilera, and Jennifer Lopez, as well as a new "Hispanic Family."

The text says, in part, "These dolls accurately capture the cultural pride felt by all of these strong Latina women. . . . We hope little Latina girls feel validated each time they look at their realistic and culturally accurate Latina Barbie dolls" (Sanchez-McNulty). Of course, the joke, one that Mattel (and Hollywood) never gets, is that all of the dolls look the same; they are blonde, blue-eyed, and have perfectly symmetrical Caucasian features. Of course, this begs the question, posed by duCille with regard to black African American dolls: "What would it take to produce a line of dolls that more fully reflects the wide variety of sizes, shapes, colors, hair styles, occupations, abilities, and disabilities that African Americans—like all people—come in?" ("Dyes and Dolls," 559). Clearly, the answer to that question does not lie with Mattel, which proudly asserts that "Today, in her 43rd year, Barbie reflects the dreams, hopes and future realities of an entire generation of little girls who still see her as representing the same American dream and aspirations as when she was first introduced in 1959!" (Barbie.com).

Perhaps, as she straddles cultures, Hispanic Barbie must strive to (and be animated to) embody what Latina writer and critic Gloria Anzaldúa describes as "a tolerance for ambiguity" that characterizes the new mestiza: "She learns to juggle cultures. . . . Not only does she sustain contradictions, she turns ambivalence into something else" (101). Or perhaps, as Wendy Varney suggests, the Barbie phenomenon is itself inextricably, irrevocably bound up in a white, middle-class American context (3). As such, it is hard to resist the temptation to glimpse, behind each Barbie, regardless of her skin and hair color, facial characteristics and dress, or even the language that she speaks, a little blonde blue-eyed Barbie named Barbie Millicent Roberts from Willows.

Bibliography

Ananova. "Lesbian Barbie Film Banned in Mexico." http://www.ananova.com/news/story/sm_540282.html?menu=news.quirkies (accessed November 11, 2002).

Anzaldúa, Gloria. *Borderlands/La Frontera: The New Mestiza* (2nd ed.). San Francisco: Aunt Lute Books, 1999.

Barbie Collectibles. http://www.barbiecollectibles.com/index-home.asp (accessed November 12, 2002).

Barbie.com. Mattel Corporation. http://www.barbie.com/ (accessed October 10, 2002).

"The Barbie Doll Story." Mattel Corporation. http://www.shareholder.com/mattel/news/20020428 79139.cf (accessed October 22, 2002)

"Barbie Dolls in Latin America." Zona Latina. http//www.zonalatina com/Zldata37.htm (accessed December 22, 2002).

BillyBoy. *Barbie, Her Life and Times.* New York: Crown Trade Paperbacks, 1987.

Budge, David. "Barbie Is No Living Doll as a Role Model." *Times Education Supplement*, January 7, 2003.

Deanne, Claudia, et al. "Leaving Tradition Behind: Latinos in the Great American Melting Pot." *Public Perspectives* 11, no. 3 (May/June 2000): 5–7.

duCille, Ann. "Barbie in Black and White." In *The Barbie Chronicles: A Living Doll Turns Forty.* New York: Touchstone, 1999.

———. "Dyes and Dolls: Multicultural Barbie and the Merchandising of Difference." In *A Cultural Studies Reader*, ed. Jessica Rajan and Gita Rajan. London: Longman, 1995.

"Life in Plastic." *Economist*, December 21, 20–23, 2002.

Lipsitz, George. *Dangerous Crossroads: Popular Music, Postmodernism and the Poetics of Place.* Verso: London, 1994.

Lord, M. G. *'Forever Barbie' The Unauthorized Biography of a Real Doll.* New York: William Morrow, 1994.

Pratt, Mary Louise. *Imperial Eyes: Travel Writing and Transculturation.* London: Routledge, 1992.

Rand, Erica. *Barbie's Queer Accessories.* Durham, NC: Duke University Press, 1995.

Rodríguez, Clara, ed. *Latin Looks: Images of Latinas and Latinos in the U.S. Media.* Boulder, CO: Westview Press, 1997.

Sanchez-McNulty, Maria. "New Latina Barbies Unveiled." *Pocho.* http://www
.pocho.com/news/2000/barbies21200barbies31700.htm.
Urla, Jacqueline, and Alan Swedlund. "The Anthropometry of Barbie: Unsettling
Ideals of the Feminine in Popular Culture." In *Deviant Bodies,* ed. Jennifer
Terry and Jacqueline Urla. Bloomington: Indiana University Press, 1995.
Urry, John. *The Tourist Gaze* (2nd ed.). London: Sage, 2002.
Varney, Wendy. "Barbie Australis: The Commercial Reinvention of National
Culture." *Social Identities* 4 (June 1998): 161. http://search.epnet.com/direct
.asp?an=873697&db=aph (accessed October 2, 2002).

CHAPTER 14

Chusmas, Chismes, y Escándalos

Latinas Talk Back to *El Show de Cristina*
and *Laura en América*

VIVIANA ROJAS

The number of Spanish-language radio and television programs in the United States has grown rapidly over the past decade, raising concerns among Latino/Chicano scholars about the effects of this programming on immigrant and nonimmigrant Latina audiences (Noriega 2000, 2003; Subervi-Vélez et al. 2003). In particular, scant information is available on how the largest Spanish-language television networks, Univision and Telemundo, represent women and how Latina audiences interpret these representations. To date, it remains unclear whether the portrayal of Latinas in Spanish-language programming is empowering or whether it predisposes female viewers to accept subordinate roles. In addition, information on how Latinas decode, contest, or reproduce these representations is scarce. This lack of findings impedes efforts to develop a Latino media policy and to address issues of ownership, employment, and ethnic representation in the media (Noriega 2003; Subervi-Vélez et al. 2003).

The audience analysis presented here responds to these concerns. Applying a Latina feminist perspective to Pierre Bourdieu's (1999) theory of practice, I explore how a group of immigrant and nonimmigrant Latinas from Austin, Texas, evaluate their portrayal on Univision and Telemundo. Specifically, I analyze women's representations in the talk shows *El Show de Cristina* (The Cristina Show), broadcast by Univision, and *Laura en América*, broadcast by Telemundo.[1] Textual representations and audience evaluations are analyzed relationally in this study.

Literature Review

Three problems discussed by Latino scholars in recent years helped structure this study. First, researchers have identified the need to study issues of Hispanic representation and stereotyping in both English-language and Spanish-language media (Dávila 2002; Rodríguez 1999a; Subervi-Vélez et al. 1994). Second, Latino audiences have received little or no attention as research subjects for academic purposes (Delgado 2004; DeSipio 1998, 1999; Rodríguez 1999a; Valdivia 1998), and third, there is a lack of information on how Latinas consume popular culture in general, and on how they interact and respond to Spanish-language media in particular (Dávila 2000, 2001, 2002; Romero and Habell-Pallán 2002; Valdivia 1995, 1998, 2000).

Although there have been some studies on hegemonic representations of Latinidad[2] in mainstream English media and on how Latinos have contested what Aparicio and Chávez-Silverman (1997) call "tropicalized" discourse, these efforts have not addressed the content of the programming offered by Univision and Telemundo. As Spanish-language television networks expand, Univision and Telemundo would be expected to influence public opinion on a range of issues relevant to Latinos, and particularly the opinions of viewers who are primarily Spanish speakers relying exclusively on these media outlets.

In the realm of Latino popular culture, many questions of representation, audience, and production remain to be answered. Romero and Habell-Pallán (2002, 9) have formulated two questions that could provide direction to reception studies in the Latino community: (1) "Do Chicanas, Puerto Ricans, and Dominicans share similar views of racialized, gendered Latina and Latino images produced by Telemundo or Univisión?" and (2) "How do Latinos intervene, contest, or reproduce 'already' circulating representations?" A few years ago, some Latino scholars suggested that Hispanic television at times stereotyped and excluded Hispanics and others, "especially those of darker skin colors and/or lower social classes" (Subervi-Vélez et al. 1994, 351; see also Dávila 2002; Glascock and Ruggiero 2004; Noriega 2000; Rodríguez 1999a, 1999b, 1999c). More recently, other Latina scholars have begun talking about Latinas' racialization on Hispanic television (Dávila 2001, 170; 2002, 27–29). Thus, it appears relevant to ask the Latino audience if Hispanic television does provide more "corrective and valuable alternatives to Anglo-generated images," as Dávila (2001, 3) has suggested.

Latinas as an Active Audience

The relationship between women and television is a complex and conflicted one (D'Acci 1994; Press 1991; Press and Cole 1999). Similarly, the representation of Latinas is a contested terrain. Different social actors, such as production companies, production teams, and publicity firms, among others, participate in the struggle to define Latina identity. Spanish-language media and Latino-oriented English-language media actively participate in the process of Latinos' latinization, that is, "the consolidation of a common Latino/a identity among different Latino subgroups" (Dávila 2001, 15–17; 2002, 27).

Univision and Telemundo, the two largest Spanish-language television networks, are among the most visible definers of Latinos' presence and identity in the United States. With their access and degree of penetration into the Hispanic community, these networks enjoy a quasi-monopoly on the cultural representations of Latinos in the United States. A large number of Latinos regularly and loyally watch Spanish-language television. DeSipio (2003) estimates that 75 percent of adult Latino viewers watch television in both Spanish and English, and about 24 percent watch primarily or exclusively in Spanish. Researchers have already expressed concern over the concentrated ownership of Spanish-language television networks and the limited programming choices available to the audience. Subervi-Vélez and colleagues (2003, 6) argue that neither Univision nor Telemundo is "currently meeting the demands of the diversity of Hispanic Americans."

Latinas, in turn, participate in the "struggles over meanings," with the assets that they can mobilize in their everyday life and with their own power to differentiate and classify, as discussed by Bourdieu and Wacquant (1992). Latinas' evaluations of Spanish-language television content and depictions are considered part of their resources—cultural capital—used to negotiate with this social institution that shapes their lives to different degrees. The dialectical relationship between agency and structure, as developed by Pierre Bourdieu in his theory of practice (1980, 1999), is at the core of this research. This theory integrates the objective and subjective realms into a single framework to understand how individuals relate to and interact with the social world. The general assumption is that since agency and structure are inextricably linked in the individual's daily life, the understanding of social phenomena can equally include both subjective and objective explanations. As a corollary, an understanding of Latinas' opinions about Hispanic television necessarily requires placement of their subjective schemes and actions in relation to the institutional practices of main actors within the Hispanic television domain.

Cultural Capital

Bourdieu (1986, 242) conceives of society as a web of social institutions (fields) in which individuals, endowed with various kinds of capital, compete for positions of power and the accumulation of more and diverse types of capital. Bourdieu's definition of capital is very broad. It includes material things (which can have symbolic value), as well as intangible but culturally significant attributes such as prestige, status, and authority (referred to as symbolic capital), along with cultural capital (defined as culturally valued taste and consumption patterns) (Bourdieu 1986, 243–242). Researchers working within Bourdieu's framework have commonly discussed four types of capital: economic, cultural, symbolic, and social. To explain the structure and functioning of the social world, Bourdieu argues that "it is necessary to reintroduce 'capital' in all its forms and not solely in the one form recognized by economic theory" (243). He argues that immaterial forms of capital, as well as the material ones, should form part of a more general science of economic practices. His point is that, like economic capital, other forms of capital are also unequally distributed among social classes. Even though the different types of capital can be mutually convertible under certain circumstances, they cannot be reduced to each other. Possessing more economic capital does not necessarily mean possessing more cultural or symbolic capital, and vice versa.

Bourdieu considers symbolic and cultural capital particularly important in the field of cultural production. Symbolic capital refers to accumulated prestige, honors, status, and authority and is founded on a dialectics of knowledge (*connaissance*) and recognition (*reconnaissance*) (Johnson 1999, 7). Cultural capital, on the other hand, is a form of knowledge, "an internalized code or a cognitive acquisition which equips the social agent with empathy towards appreciation for, or competence in deciphering cultural relations and cultural artifacts" (Johnson 1999, 7). Possessing these types of knowledge and competence places the individual in a different location within the cultural field, compared with actors who do not have this accumulation of capital. Unlike from the economic field (in which agents use accumulated economic capital to compete for capital), the resources at stake in the cultural field are not always material. In the Latino television field, for example, the competition often relates to the authority and prestige of the networks and anchors, along with audience recognition of that authority (Bourdieu's *"reconnaissance"*). As Bourdieu has shown, actors' recognition or mis-recognition of this type of authority reflects a form of symbolic power that is crucial to processes of domination and subordination. The dialectic between material and symbolic power extends from the economic field, at one end, to the field of cultural production, at the other. Mass media systems fall at the cultural production end of the spectrum. Media are part of a symbolic system of power that works to legitimate a given state of material class relations by the subtle imposition of the correct and legitimate definition of the social world (Garnham 1986, 426; Mahar, Harker, and Wilkes 1990, 5).

Hispanic Talk Shows

Talk shows are the most popular programs on Univision and Telemundo, after the Latin American *telenovelas,* which have held programming primacy for decades. The number of talk shows increased from two in 1989 to eight in 2002 with the importation of Mexican, Venezuelan, and Peruvian productions. Although the Hispanic talk shows have some resemblance to daytime English-language talk shows in format and themes, they differ in their origin and in their declared philosophy of service. The most criticized elements of the U.S. talk shows, such as pseudo-intimacy, dramatic confession, and moral judgments, are also part of the discursive strategies used by *Cristina* and *Laura* and the rest of the Hispanic talk shows. However, the Hispanic talk shows have not been subjected to the cultural and ideological scrutiny that some U.S. talk shows have already gone through. The study presented here undertakes such an analysis from the perspective of Latina feminist cultural studies.

El Show de Cristina, produced in the United States and broadcast on Univision twice a day between 1989 and 2001, and *Laura en América*, one of the two Peruvian talk shows broadcast by Telemundo since 2000, are examined in this study as the initial step toward a more general evaluation of Latinas' representations in the Spanish-language television networks. These two shows reflect the hybrid nature of Hispanic television programming: about half the shows are produced in Latin America, which muddies a discussion of what a Hispanic show appropriate for U.S. Latino audiences would be like. Cristina Saralegui and Laura Bozzo, the hosts of *El Show de Cristina* and *Laura en América*, have declared that their aim is to improve the lives of Latinos living in the United States as well as in Latin America (Cristina Online, 1998; Telemundo.com, 2006). However, initial studies of *Cristina* have offered a more critical evaluation of the program (Ben Amor 1998; Calles 2001; Dávila 2001). Saralegui, a recognized anti-Castro television persona, has been accused of "debas[ing] her race with frank, nationally televised discussion of promiscuity, homosexuality and women's equality, still controversial subjects in many Latino homes" (Baxter 1998, 86) and "oversexualizing and ridiculing Dominicans" (Atanay 1998, cited in Dávila 2001, 170). A similar critique has been raised by some Puerto Rican residents, who perceive *Cristina* and other Univision programs as foreign products whose treatment of morality and sexuality "spoils the values of the Latino community" (Dávila 2001, 164). On the other hand, Laura Bozzo has been criticized in the Peruvian and Latin American media and on Internet Web sites for her racy topics, questionable tactics, and dubious taste (Garvin 2000, 2; Caspa TV, 2002).

Hispanic talk shows provide a place to study the articulation of race, class, and gender. Dávila's (2001) argument that Hispanic talk shows represent race more frequently than daytime or prime-time programming does provide the most substantive support for the study of these programs. However, Dávila (2002, 170) has also argued that Univision and Telemundo are involved in a strategy of whitening, with the intention of keeping the synergy between American and Latin American markets. Other scholars have also voiced their concerns that Hispanic talk shows seem to follow the "white model" of television talk show, claiming that this model co-opts the representation of African Americans and Hispanics either by "whiting them out or reducing them to stereotypes of oversexed Latinas, loud black women, and infantile black men" (Squire 1997, 243). Although Dávila does not analyze *Cristina*, she defines it as a paradigmatic case of inequality and white supremacy (2001, 169). Her claim that shows "that were initially devised to reflect a U.S. Latina sensibility, such as *Cristina*, end up showcasing and reproducing inequalities among and across Latinas subgroups" (2000, 170) is central to the arguments raised in this essay.

El Show de Cristina was broadcast for eleven years with consistently high ratings and virtually no competition. In 2000, as the show's ratings began to fall, in part because of the strong presence of the Peruvian show *Laura en América*, there was an increase in the more sexually audacious topics. However, neither an increase in sexualized elements—which Cristina Saralegui claimed to be based on her audience's taste and demands[3]— nor the more frequent appearances of Latina/o celebrities on the show could save *Cristina* from being canceled at the end of 2001. Reruns of the show are currently presented during late-night programming.

The increased body display and nudity did not go unnoticed by Latino audiences, as Cristina Online and Telemundo's chat rooms made clear. However, an increase in nudity, female and male, was occurring across the board in the network's programming, from the telenovelas to the variety shows and even the magazine news program, in an effort to increase ratings and attract more American advertisers (Associated Press Online 2002). This point is supported by newspaper columnist Diane Holloway, who asserts that in a good deal of Spanish-language TV, especially the prime-time shows, "sexy-looking women with lots of cleavage are the norm" (2002, K10).

The argument I present is that, contrary to their stated philosophy of serving and empowering Latinos, the talk shows *Cristina* and *Laura* do not help to promote Latinas' agency or tolerance for "difference" among the diverse Latino groups. More than a celebration of occasional transgressions permitted by the media or institutional authority, as it is theorized in some writings from the populist cultural studies perspective (McLaughlin 1993), these programs work under a very narrow definition of women's behavior; they are moralistic, conservative, and provide prescriptive endorsements of Latin American upper- and middle-class values. Work I did earlier found that topic treatment and co-optation of differences in *Cristina* and *Laura* discourage naming these cultural products a forum for resistance or a place for generating empowering discourses for U.S. Latina/os (Rojas 2003). At the textual level, the racialization and subordination of Latinas appear to be reinforced by "yet more images of whiteness" (Dávila 2001, 169). With that in mind, I turn to the consumption of such shows, investigating how Latinas decode and respond to images of Latinas on Hispanic television.

The Reception Study

My study was based on in-depth interviews with a group of first- and second-generation immigrant Latinas and Latin American women residing temporarily in the United States who watched Spanish-language television regularly and were familiar with Cristina's and Laura's talk shows. A total of twenty-seven women between twenty-two and sixty-four years old who resided in the city of Austin, Texas, participated in the study. Nine were born in the United States; the rest were immigrants or temporary residents who had lived in the country between three and twenty years. According to their own self-defined class location, fourteen women identified themselves as working class, ten as middle class, and three as upper-middle class. In terms of education, nine had finished high school and two held bachelor's degrees from their country of origin, while the rest had incomplete schooling and one was illiterate. With the exception of three interviewees, all the women had children and lived in a family setting, as married or single parents. Most of them could be considered "family women" according to the criteria of Reay (1995) and Coterill (1992).

The informants were contacted through different methods—by direct invitation, through referral from another informant, through acquaintances, or because they had been participants in previous research projects. The interviews with these women lasted between two and three hours, and in some cases we met a second or third time, depending on the particular situation. With only two exceptions, the interviews were conducted in the respondent's home, "a natural setting for women's conversations and discussions" (Press and Cole 1999; Reay 1995). In general, women were interviewed alone, without the husband or other adult family members present (young children were sometimes present). During the interviews, and depending on the respondent's time and the availability of VCRs in the home, we sometimes watched taped segments or complete programs from *Cristina* or *Laura*. Thematic coding, data triangulation, and authors' reflexivity were some of the techniques used in the analysis of the interviews and transcripts. Five bilingual graduate students revised English translations from Spanish-speaking respondents. The names of the interviewees have been changed to preserve confidentiality.

The interview protocol covered a wide array of issues relating to Latinas' perception of their place in U.S. society and corresponding media representations. This chapter is concerned only with the following questions: What is the relevance of Spanish-language television to Latinas' lives? What do Latinas think about representations of women on Hispanic television in general, and on *El Show de Cristina* and *Laura en América* in particular? The analysis presented here begins with the respondents' general evaluations of Univision and Telemundo's programming, continues with a section on Latinas' representation on the networks, and closes with women's opinions on the talk shows *El Show de Cristina* and *Laura en América*. In the analysis of the responses I provide some insights into how race, gender, and class are articulated in Latinas' discourses.

Univision and Telemundo

The majority of the respondents interviewed in this study perceived that Univision and Telemundo networks filled the role of providing "entertainment" rather than service for Latinos. They characterized the programming as having too many soap operas, providing little or almost no information about their countries of origin, presenting sensationalist programming mainly for commercial purposes, having a heavy emphasis on Mexican shows, and lacking children's programming. On the other hand, the interviewees recognized that the networks are for-profit business organizations. Four respondents elaborated on their criticism and indicated that the networks should seek more balance between entertainment and education, or at least offer more diverse programming. Other respondents indicated that the networks should promote the learning of English rather than simply carry advertising for it, such as the ad for *Inglés Sin Barreras* (English Without Barriers) presented on Univision. Respondents envisioned the existence of specific programs targeting Latino immigrants that could be broadcast on weekends. Some of them believed that if the networks really wanted to produce more educational or informative shows, they would have already done so. Informants said that the networks "would probably not enjoy such high ratings as they do with suggestive shows, but they would offer a different option for viewers." This desire for change suggests a need for alternatives from an industry that has adhered to the same formula for more than four decades.

Maritza (thirty-one, U.S.-born, self-identified as Puerto Rican, high school diploma, married, three children, a truck driver) indicated that the only serious programs on Univision and Telemundo "last only half an hour," and characterized the rest as "stupidity, soaps and more stupidity." Gardenia (thirty-seven, Spaniard, high school education, married, two daughters, domestic worker) said that Latinos cannot build Hispanic pride based on the programs they are presented by the networks. For her, Hispanic media in general do not act on Latinos' behalf because they are comfortable with the status quo. She explained this in Spanish, saying "porque todos están cómodos en el burro" (they are all comfortable on this mule).

Although Lidia (forty-two, Argentinean immigrant, college degree obtained in her home country, widowed, one daughter, domestic worker) claimed to watch a "great amount" of Hispanic television, she still criticized the programming because it hampered (*frena*) the Latinos' development. It was her belief that Univision and Telemundo "fulfill the function of orienting and helping the newcomer to adjust to their new situation." However, after Hispanics are settled, she felt that this reliance "keeps them stagnated because they do not watch other channels, and therefore do not learn English."

Corina (thirty-one, Argentinean immigrant, college degree, widowed, one daughter, baby sitter, occasionally worked as a movie extra) provided one of the harshest criticisms. She did not identify with any of the programming produced by either Telemundo or Univision. Even though she admitted that she was only interested in the newscasts, she still labeled them "yellow press." Corina said that on both television networks, sexist journalism and sexist programs predominated. In her view, talk shows and entertainment shows overlook too many offenses against other people.

The most educated U.S.-born and immigrant Latinas displayed a more sophisticated evaluation of the overall quality of the Spanish networks. For some women, the networks are targeting an audience "that does not have more than an elementary education" and offer only "cheap entertainment and nothing cultural" (Paula, thirty-one, Mexican immigrant, engineer, married, two children, worked for IBM). For others, Hispanic television is perceived as "low quality television with programs that sometimes border on vulgarity and promote certain Latino stereotypes" (Andrea, thirty, Chilean, temporary resident, psychologist, single, no children, graduate student). One respondent claimed a more ideological function for the networks because they contribute to the perpetuation of immigrants' lower status, keeping them from questioning their own situation (Lorena, thirty-two, Chilean, temporary resident, television producer, married, no children, graduate student). This last informant argued that the networks did not present programs that would encourage Latinos to think or question their place, as that could be "too dangerous" for Latinos' relationship with dominant U.S. society.

Some of the most educated Latinas also noted the absence of U.S.-born, college-educated Hispanics, particularly Mexican Americans, in the shows. Krystal (fifty-seven, U.S.-born Mexican American, PhD, married, one child, independent consultant) indicated that it is time to start lobbying and putting pressure on the mainstream and Hispanic networks for inclusion of U.S.-born Latinos in their programming. She said that over the years, she has been calling local English-language stations and some national networks to ask about the absence of Latino anchors in news programming. She is also concerned about Univision's and Telemundo's indifference to middle- and upper-class Latinos. According to Krystal, Hispanic television must include varied segments of the Latino population. Consider the class distinction this respondent establishes among Latinos:

> I would say the Hispanic television needs to grow. . . . Right now it is only projecting a need for a certain population. . . . I don't think the talk shows and other programs address the educated Hispanic or contain issues for the educated Hispanics, and I don't think the telenovelas do either. . . . As much

as I like the novelas, they are always fantasies. I think television is missing something. There are many Latinos around me who have done this and done that, [but] . . . they just represent people who come from the barrios . . . there are a lot of us who didn't grow up in the barrios. . . . We have Hispanic names, we speak Spanish, we have the background, the culture. . . . They don't target us. Right now . . . there is only space to represent the women and men who come from the barrios, but not for Latinos who do things and were not born in those conditions.

Krystal's comments can be interpreted from two perspectives. It appears to be an implicit acknowledgment that Hispanic television is constructed around the assumed tastes of a working-class immigrant audience, but it also operates as a critique of the dominant commercial representation of Latinos and Latina audiences, as discussed by Rodríguez (1999). The respondent refused to accept that the Hispanic audience "is racially non-white, linguistically Spanish speaking, and socioeconomically poor," as Rodríguez has suggested (47). Instead, she perceives Spanish-language television as a site of struggle for the inclusion of a different type of Latinidad, one that is not exclusively bound to Latin America and based on Spanish language usage. In sum, she seems to subscribe to and expect a Latinidad that is more assimilated into mainstream culture. Her activism in respect to English-language television and her requests for inclusion of middle-class college-educated Hispanics in Univision and Telemundo programming reveal the tensions existing among populations who are at different stages of the hybridization processes (García-Canclini 1995; Hall 1992).

The evaluations presented here do not necessarily mean that the respondents are against the existence of Spanish-language television networks or that all the programming is of poor quality. The newscasts and soap operas—which occupy most of the prime-time programming—were almost always exempted from the respondents' criticisms. With the exception of two English-speaking informants, the rest indicated that the afternoon and evening newscasts were most appreciated and watched on a regular basis. As mentioned before, only one respondent labeled these newscasts "yellow press." This favorable rating supports previous findings that more than 70 percent of bilingual Latino viewers watch news in Spanish, or a combination of English and Spanish news (DeSipio 1999, 2003; Suro 2004; see also Rincón and Associates 2004). Soap operas, which are pivotal to Hispanic television programming, were also exempted from strong criticism. The fact that more than half of the respondents, independent of economic status, watched novelas might have checked criticism of this cultural product. Although most indicated that the plots were formulaic and predictable, they liked the actors, the clothing, and the makeup, and generally, they enjoyed seeing something of Mexican or Latin American traditions. The main criticism of the novelas came from college-educated immigrant Latinas, who mostly targeted the class divisions and stereotypes presented in these productions.

Portrayals of Latinas

The respondents in this study agreed on the need to make changes to the programming offered by Univision and Telemundo. This agreement was even more pronounced when the discussion turned to representations of women. Latinas' bodies as portrayed by the networks become the place to enact cultural, political, race, and class struggles. The respondents indicated that prevailing portrayals of Latinas as "sexy" are superficial and disconnected from reality; in their view, these representations exclude other, more relevant characteristics of Latinas. For these women, Latinas are more than sexual objects for the male gaze (Latinos included) or for the social system and media system that define them in that way. Some of the women claimed that this image misrepresents the millions of hardworking Latinas who dress in conservative clothing and the many single mothers who support their families alone. Corina (thirty-one, Argentinean immigrant, college degree, widowed, one daughter, baby sitter and occasional movie extra) summarized this view:

> Latinas' image follows an ideological model of oppression . . . not only here, but also in Latin American countries. But, well, we come with this prototype to the U.S., where Latinas are hot, where they are the ones who f—k the best [la que mejor coge] . . . and Spanish programs take and use that. . . .

Some respondents realized that the commodification of Latinas' bodies on Hispanic television has serious implications for the development of their identity in U.S. society. Oversexualized portrayals disempower them and predispose them to ethnic subordination, and also serve to promote odious class and ethnic distinctions among different groups of Latinas. Many of the respondents criticized the scanty dresses of the models in variety shows, magazine programs, and telenovelas. Respondents included in these categories shows such as *Cristina*, *Don Francisco*, *El Gordo y la*

Flaca, and *Los Metiches*. They indicated that there have always been instances in which they felt "attacked," "insulted," "offended," or "embarrassed" by the networks' representations. Their reactions to these representations have ranged from asking their children to leave the room to discussing the issue with other members of the family or friends, switching channels, or simply turning off the TV set.

For Mariana (fifty-two, Cuban immigrant, high school diploma, married, two children, homemaker), the models on Univision are shameless ("tienen mucho descaro"), especially the ones who appear on *Don Francisco*, a variety program show. She said, "at any given moment the women will come out just like God brought them to earth, showing all their private parts." She apologized for sounding "old-fashioned," but regardless, she said, she dislikes it. Maritza (thirty-one, U.S.-born, self-identified as Puerto Rican, high school diploma, married, three children, truck driver) indicated that Hispanic television "totally forgets that women are watching, too." She considered that Univision and Telemundo "display nearly naked women just to capture the attention of male television viewers." To her, these television representations are in no way related to today's Latina, who is a "strong and hard-working woman." Consider the following quotation in support of this statement:

> They totally forget about women. Women in Telemundo, in the *Bienvenido* show, and in all the funny programs, have to come out in bikinis or thongs, so that guys can have something to watch. And it is not just guys who are watching. . . . And in the soap operas, women always have three boyfriends; they leave one and take another one. It seems to me that they represent women in a way that is definitely not true in today's Latino world. I think that there are many hard-working women who would never take off their clothes for any amount of money in the world. They just make others think that we are weak and that we like to carry ourselves just like that.

Nury (thirty-two, Mexican immigrant, middle school education, married, two children, school janitor, only watches Spanish television) distinguished between Latinas' sensuality and these representations of scantily dressed women. She said that "we all consider ourselves sexy at some point and I particularly consider myself sexy without having to walk around almost naked." These opinions contrast with those of Lidia (forty-two, Argentinean immigrant, college degree, widowed, one daughter, domestic worker), who believed that in the world of talk shows, Spanish television is still in its infancy ("a breast-feeding baby") compared to the amount of cleavage that is displayed on American networks. She said that if Univision and Telemundo "show too much," Jerry Springer or Howard Stern "show it all." Gardenia (thirty-seven, Spaniard, high school education, married, two daughters, house cleaner) felt that the problem is not in exhibiting bodies but in the situations in which women are portrayed:

> The models look really good. It doesn't bother me to see so much revealing clothing and short skirts, because, well, people do have legs, and here on American TV we never get to see the legs of half of the television hosts. What bothers me is when they do things like measure someone's derriere . . . like those strippers, those things that one doesn't really want to see, so you have to turn off the TV. What I mean is there should be a balance to what is shown.

Some respondents struggled with the contradictory representations of "Latinas as sexy" on television and the images of "Latinas as virtuous" promoted in the family and community. Respondents discussed how they cope with the feelings of embarrassment these representations provoke. Gina (twenty-seven, U.S.-born Mexican American, incomplete high school, single mother, two children, worked part-time in a shelter for battered women and lived in a subsidized apartment) felt the need to constantly clarify for her African American partner and her two African American children that Latinas "are not like that." She found herself in a constant struggle to justify the essence of "a Hispanic woman" or a "traditional identity," as expressed by Hall (1992, 1996), and to protect Latinas' bodies on Univision from a lascivious masculine gaze:

> All the women . . . are always wearing something small. . . . They are always showing everything. . . . Yeah, they are pretty . . . but it's like ridiculous. . . . They look like sluts. . . . Yeah. I mean they are pretty but Goddamn. . . . it's like overdoing it, especially on the soap operas.
> You can see [the effect] just going to people's houses. . . . My boyfriend had a white friend stay over and he just had the TV on mute on the Spanish station like the whole night, and I was . . . , "Why did you have it on there?" and he's like, "I don't know, the women are pretty. . . ." He don't understand what they are saying 'cause it's on mute, and he is not even listening to them. . . .

These feelings of collective embarrassment were also voiced by more educated and upper-middle-class Latinas:

Itzel (twenty-five, Mexican immigrant, college educated, worked in a newspaper):

My male friends say as a joke, but not always, "Ah, I flip to these channels to see the girls," like saying it's almost a skin show and they're not watching the news. That tells me, well it's clear that if the "low cuts" are very wide, it's too much stereotyping women as very sexy. And I would say that it's sensual when it is a little bit more covered; this is something normal, but sexy is too extreme. . . . I think these shows contribute to give a distorted picture to people who don't know or who do not belong to the culture. Whenever viewers flip to Hispanic channel, they see women dressed with provocative clothing and that's how stereotypes are created.

Krystal (fifty-seven, U.S.-born Mexican American, PhD, married, one child, independent consultant):

When my husband [who is Anglo] stops at a Spanish channel and sees one of these programs, he always comments to me: "They don't mind showing it."

The transcripts presented here support the perceptions conveyed in the English-language media that on Spanish-language television, sexy-looking women showing cleavage are the norm and that the dialogue on entertainment shows is "loaded with double entendre and sexual innuendo" (Holloway 2002, K10). On the other hand, respondents' opinions contradict essentialist assertions that the display of sexuality is "a reflection of the more sensual nature of the population" (Holloway 2002, K10).

Talk Shows: *El Show de Cristina* and *Laura en América*

Until 2000, Hispanic talk shows in the United States had been monopolized by *El Show de Cristina*. The arrival of *Laura en América* that year provided the interviewees with an opportunity to compare the content and style of the two shows. The difference in content between the shows was clear to the respondents. *El Show de Cristina* addresses family, sexuality, celebrity, and miscellaneous topics, whereas *Laura en América* focuses mainly on family problems.

Although the majority of the respondents disliked Laura's treatment of some of her guests and all the yelling and arguing she permitted on the set, most of them still preferred her over Cristina because they felt she was closer to "the people" and "their issues." Two of the interviewees considered her a defender of women's rights. However, for one Cuban immigrant, this assessment would last only "as long as her attitude remains genuine." (The respondent was alluding to the possibility that Laura Bozzo, by being politically involved with the government of ex-Peruvian president Alberto Fujimori, could have collaborated on "peoples' political oppression.")

For many of the immigrant and nonimmigrant women, Cristina Saralegui showed a great deal of shamelessness (*descaro*) on her show by displaying scantily clad people, homosexuals, lesbians, and others representing alternative lifestyles that "do not agree with the way many Latinos think." Perla (forty-two, Mexican immigrant, illiterate, married, three children, worked at a dry cleaner's) said that many times she had to tell her children to leave the room because the show was not appropriate for them. For her, *Cristina* was "filth, pure trash" (*"un mugrero, una pura porqueria"*). These epithets were shared by four other respondents. Maritza (thirty-one, U.S.-born, self-identified as Puerto Rican, high school diploma, married, three children, truck driver) indicated that the issues that *Cristina* deals with are "ridiculous" and "the most stupid ones are us, the Latinos who sit down to watch that trash." Lidia (forty-two, Argentinean immigrant, college degree obtained in her home country, widowed, one daughter, domestic worker) also disliked the shows that openly discussed Latino sexuality issues. She explained them as a hook to keep ratings up. For her, "people's private lives should not be showcased on television." Consider also the following evaluations:

> Leyla (age fifty-nine, Mexican-American, high school education, widowed, two children, security guard, watched the show once in a while due to her work schedule): I think that Cristina is of a slightly better rank than Laura is, but I don't like her either. I used to like watching her before because I saw her as a very pretty woman, but after some time, I felt that her programs had changed too much . . . it is pure filth what she shows us now.

> Angeles (age forty-two, Cuban, college educated in Cuba, pizza worker on a night shift, watched the 3 a.m. Cristina's show at least once a week and Laura's show every afternoon): Of course, Cristina discusses sexual taboos! . . . Cristina is a progressive woman, very liberal and I admire her. She's got a lot of merit. I have been watching her since 1996, but there are things that I don't like . . . and it's not that I am against that . . . but homosexuals dressed as women . . . I don't understand why, if she educates . . . why show that type of thing. If she is going to talk about homosexuality she doesn't have to go to the extreme of needing to show men dressed like women. I think Cristina needs the show for her own economic benefit and that distances her a little from what we are really interested in. For example, when she and her guests came out naked, I saw it. I saw it, and that is not called freedom, that is called

("*libertinaje*"). I am not interested in those topics; I don't find that they have any benefit, to the contrary.

Tete: (thirty-seven, Salvadorian immigrant, high school education, divorced, beauty parlor worker, watched Laura's show once a week): When I first arrived in Austin, I actually enjoyed Cristina's show. I used to watch it in El Salvador. Back then, her shows were more constructive, she would talk more about family, about reality, and suddenly she began to offer different types of shows and I wasn't as interested. It's like when she began to include too much pornography. In almost every show she uses sex, and that just doesn't draw me in.

Rosalia (twenty-four, Mexican-American, high school education, homemaker, mother of a two-year-old girl): No, we don't watch her [Cristina] anymore. . . . they were showing even naked people. . . . We saw this show, everyone sitting in the audience, men and women naked. . . . In three months, I think I have watched it once or twice, if that many times. We have seen *Cristina* a lot, but me, not anymore. . . .

One of the respondents considered Cristina's show a missed opportunity to empower Latinos living in the United States. Krystal (fifty-seven, U.S. born Mexican American, PhD, married, one children, independent consultant) believed that if there were ever going to be change in Spanish-language television, it should have started with *Cristina*, because she had already attracted an audience. According to her, the only thing *Cristina* needed was "to incorporate more education." Krystal believes that Cristina Saralegui has almost all the elements on her side to create a "good program," that is, a show that presents news of success and gives more presence to U.S.-born Latinos. She stated that it is about time for Spanish television to present new faces—local and national faces—instead of the foreign presenters. She asked, "Why we don't have someone like Oprah? Why did Cristina not follow Oprah's example when Oprah said 'enough is enough' and started having more talk shows about people's spirituality and achievements?" Krystal acknowledged Cristina Saralegui's potential for opening a space for women's issues in Spanish television and for succeeding in this endeavor. However, she argued that Cristina has not put much effort into changing her agenda and continues to talk about women's sexuality, machismo, and conflicts between couples. She thought that the constant portrayal of "deceived women is not a good example for young American girls." For this respondent, neither Cristina's show nor Laura's show is a feminist program. They mainly depict the Latin woman as weak, "because she either doesn't see it or doesn't get it . . . duhhh . . . that her husband is out with everybody else." Krystal believed that both hosts are just orchestrating the shows for profit. This evaluation contrasts with the latent assumption that the Spanish-language media should have a more informed and sensitive attitude regarding Latino portrayals as compared to their English-language counterparts.

On the other hand, Laura Bozzo's talk show, which tends to center on family and relationship issues, didn't have better luck when it came to interviewees' evaluations. Some interviewees liked the show because it "offers facts of real life that happen in every poor country" and because she is "more realistic" (Tete, age thirty-seven, Salvadorian immigrant, high school education, divorced, beauty parlor worker, watched Laura's show once a week). Other respondents liked Laura because she uncovers "heartbreaking situations" that otherwise would remain unknown (Gardenia, thirty-seven, Spaniard, high school education, married, two daughters, domestic worker) and because she is "more humanitarian, helps and instructs" (Angeles, forty-two, Cuban, college educated in Cuba, pizza worker on a night shift, watched the 3 a.m. *Cristina* at least once a week and *Laura* every afternoon). However, in all the cases, this support did not validate in any form "all the hitting and fighting" presented on the show. Only three women—Ramona (fifty, Cuban immigrant, high school education, married, three children, homemaker), Marina (fifty-two, Cuban immigrant, high school, married, two children) and Perla (forty-two, Mexican immigrant, illiterate, married, three children, worked in a cleaner's) supported Laura's aggressive style as necessary "to eradicate the problem that is being discussed there." Ramona believed that Laura needs to be loud and strong "for the truth to come out." For her, the best proof that the anchor defends women is that she is not afraid to show videotapes of men who are cheating on their partners, or vice versa. She conceded that sometimes "there are also women who cheat on their men." Laura's policing of her subjects' private life to prove their deviations is perceived as one of her main strengths. Ramona also approved Laura's use of the police on the set to arrest the men caught "committing crimes" such as cheating on loved ones or causing disturbances during the show. Ramona strongly believed in Laura's genuine efforts to help women because she provided some guests with scholarships and other tools, such as street vending carts, to help them make a living after a family break-up.

These more favorable opinions about Laura's show came from the same interviewees who had stopped watching *Cristina* because they were uncomfortable with the program showing "too much skin" (*"muchos desnudos"*). In general, all the interviewees liked Cristina's show when she offered "serious issues" such as helping Hispanics find a lost loved one or talking about teenagers and drugs. The interviewees highly valued the connection between topics and their everyday lives and/or previous experiences. However, more than half of the respondents disliked Laura's show for "commercializing the misery of Peru's poorest people" (Gloria, forty-five, Peruvian immigrant, high school education, secretary, married, one child; Lidia, forty-two, Argentinean immigrant, college degree obtained in her home country, widowed, one daughter, domestic worker). They didn't like her authoritarianism and the way she interferes in people's lives. Even though they felt that Cristina also gets involved with her guests, some interviewees believed that Laura is a lot more aggressive about it (Corina, thirty-one, Argentinean immigrant, college degree, widowed, one daughter, baby sitter and occasional movie extra).

For some of the women, Laura places too much emphasis on the clash between social classes in Peruvian society. The guests on the show are poor and look unruly in contrast to Laura herself, who represents Latin American upper-middle-class values and morality. Some interviewees refused to believe that the show presents real people, calling it just a *tongo* (a staged thing). Other respondents distanced themselves from the behaviors presented and claimed that in their country of origin, those things do not happen. In their view, the conflicts presented on the show correspond to the behavior of "people who lack education." The majority of Latina respondents emphatically agreed that they were different from the people presented in the shows. The process of marking the "difference" became intense, as the following excerpts show:

> Gardenia (thirty-seven, Spaniard, high school education, married, two daughters, domestic worker): The violence of poverty is evident. That is a psychic violence, a psychological violence; it is not just a physical violence. Laura defends women well; she helps them. The problem is poverty. Those people live in a sub-world. It's so sad what I see. She tries to educate people with her moral values, but they don't have ethics or morality. They survive at a basic level, almost at a beastly level, and maybe it has nothing to do with food; they are not starving to death. . . . The problem is one of values. The guests on *Laura* are on the level of a sub-world, where there are ugly things. It looks like you are watching Dante's Inferno. I can't describe it. Everything is so aggressive. I tell you these are people who don't have moral values, spiritual values, I don't know. That is typical of people who don't believe in anything;

it is typical of self-destruction. These people have a complete void, I don't know. They have no value; they don't value themselves. If they did they would not display themselves in these situations.

Tete (thirty-seven, Salvadorean immigrant, high school education, divorced, beauty parlor worker, watched Laura's show once a week): I believe this happens all over the world. However, I believe we Latinos make it more evident. These things happen in the lowliest barrios, you know?

Rosalia (twenty-four, Mexican-American, high school education, homemaker, mother of a two-year-old girl): The impression that I have is that the people she wants as guests . . . are people who are poor, that don't have much education. I don't know, you can't compare two lives, you see them, but they have nothing in common with us. . . . We have nothing in common with the panelists [Peruvian panelists] or with her [Laura], not even with the audience that you see before you. I feel a great difference between them and me. I don't relate to them at all . . . 'cause there are a lot of *gringos* that can watch that . . . They can flip between channels and say that these programs, *Laura* or *Cristina*, or the other shows . . . they are going to think that all Latinos are like that. . . . They get the impression . . . that the men are always messing around on all the women . . . that the women . . . are trashy, they are evil, that they are always fighting . . . They give you just a different script. . . . You are not at their same level, you always see the maid, stuff like that, you know. . . . If they would just change the channel and watch really quick . . . they would get a bad impression of all Latinos.

Lidia (forty-two, Argentinean immigrant, college degree obtained in her home country, widowed, one daughter, domestic worker) believed that social inequality permeates this show and it hurts her to see that people's poverty is used as entertainment for Latinos in the United States. She does not like the fact that Laura forcefully intrudes on her guest's private lives in order to uncover "their secrets" and use them to build a show. She was angry and felt sorry for the interviewees because it is clear to her that they are not really being helped. Corina (thirty-one, Argentinean immigrant, college degree, widowed, one daughter, baby sitter and occasional movie extra), in turn, defined Laura as "bossy and manipulative." To her, Laura represents "Hernan Cortes descending again upon the Aztecs, telling them what's right or wrong." In her analysis, the participants' ethnicity correlates with a class problem: "She is white . . . and in some way she personifies the values of the dominant class because her skin is lighter than others." Corina explained that Laura brings authoritarian and Catholic values to the program without really understanding people's social dynamics.

Laura's potential to defend women and provide a space for Latina agency is thus diminished by her characteristic aggressiveness. Many of the interviewees considered the host a tough, loud, and authoritarian woman who wanted to be famous "at others' expenses." Corina felt that Laura follows a rule that is very authoritarian by getting involved in her guests' problems, simplifying them, and then forcing solutions on them. This interviewee found that Laura pressures guests in many ways, by hurrying them, badgering them, hugging them, or even threatening some of the participants. Consider the following statements in support of these impressions:

> Lidia (forty-two, Argentinean immigrant, college degree obtained in her home country, widowed, one daughter, domestic worker): I do not like Laura. . . . I don't know her, people say that she helps other people, I wouldn't know, I'm not in Peru. . . . I don't like it when she sneaks into the life of other people to show how poor they are and how she puts her camera under their little stick-made bed with rags as blankets. . . . I don't like that and is not because I don't want to be aware of poverty, I don't want to ignore anything, I just don't like it. I think she, how can I put it, does not give them too much respect, she doesn't seem to respect her people.

> Corina (thirty-one, Argentinean immigrant, college degree, widowed, one daughter, baby sitter and occasional movie extra): Laura's show points to those Latinos that identify with those kinds of values. I do not identify with those values even though I am Hispanic and speak Spanish and I come from Latin America. I may come from a more educated class, I went to school, I may be more conscious about it . . . who knows . . . I had that experience and I chose to be like that, I consciously chose to be different and not let myself be carried by those values.

Perla (forty-two, Mexican immigrant, illiterate, married, three children, worked at a dry cleaner's) was the interviewee who provided the least critical viewpoint regarding the show *Laura en América*. She was also the one who showed most distress for not being able to watch the show more regularly due to her workload in and out of her home and her husband's negative view of the show. She said that she prefers this show to *Cristina* because "it is more different than *Cristina*." Although she had trouble explaining exactly what is wrong with *Cristina*, she summarized her feelings by saying, "it's complete garbage." On the other hand, the topics on *Laura* were more compelling to her. These topics included spousal infidelity and child abuse. She admitted that she sometimes cries along with the children on the screen and contemplates her own domestic situation. She wouldn't want anything to happen to her daughter at the hands of her new stepfather. She lives with the uncertainty about whether her decision to remarry was wise or not due to the toll it has taken on the children. For Perla, the problems faced over there (Peru) are the same ones that happen to "us," the Hispanics living here (Austin). Although she admitted that many people don't like the show, she said she liked it because Laura is very proper in what she says and because "she is on the side of women." In her view, this program is for women only, since she thinks "men don't like it when you say that type of things to them." Perla went on to explain that her husband feels that the show "is pure garbage, that it doesn't serve any purpose," and he simply won't allow her to watch it, insisting that they have to go to sleep. The husband's main argument is that the show serves to "wake women up [who] are already pretty smart." Perla said that the shows' topics, whether it's *Laura* or *Cristina*, always pop up as a topic of conversation with her co-workers at the cleaner's, whether it is because they liked it or because they disliked it. Sometimes, during breaks, they will discuss the programs, and if they don't have enough time, they will keep conversing as they hang the clothes when their manager is not watching. Television content is not something she usually discusses with her daughter, who is a high school student, nor with her husband, because she knows what he thinks of it. The show is important to her because she applies it to her daily life.

> Perla (regarding Laura's show): He doesn't want me to watch that. He says they're nothing but fantasies, that it's worthless, that we have to go to sleep, that *Laura* is not a good thing. That it is only there so women can mouth off, and blah blah blah. He says that women are smart enough already, and they're waking them up. No, he says. Let's go to sleep.

In contrast to this opinion, Corina (thirty-one, Argentinean immigrant, college degree, widowed, one daughter, baby sitter and occasional movie extra) once again provided the strongest critique of the show. Corina literally dissociated herself from both shows, proclaiming repeatedly that she did not identify with this type of program or with the stereotypes of Latinos in American society. This statement can be explained by the fact that she did not perceive herself to be a minority in this country, "although people keep telling me that I am." She asserted that she couldn't feel like a minority here because she came "with another background, with another experience." Corina did not see much difference between English and Spanish talk shows. She said that both "use the same confrontation techniques and use people that are vulnerable enough to talk about themselves." Nevertheless, one of the differences she saw between the two types of talk shows is that "among Hispanics, I have seen the least educated people overall." Another difference is in the confrontations on the screen, where she felt that American talk shows are not as explosive as Spanish talk shows and are more likely to discuss the problems presented. In contrast, on the Hispanic shows "there is more action than words."

Corina correlated this analogy about verbalization and passion with Cristina and Laura's behavior on their respective shows. In her opinion, Cristina does not scream like Laura; she does not "go down" to the level of the audience, but she does use other tools to "impose middle-class values." She believed that Cristina talks "from a less passionate place, a more rational place, and her personal life rises as an example to all." Corina did not think that Laura and Cristina represent anything or anyone, and least of all that they represent her. She said that the situation is more about whether or not the audience can identify with the shows. She also believed that the networks' only interest is to make money from other people's sufferings. This opinion was shared by at least six other interviewees. As far as Corina is concerned, those who watch these programs are working-class people who don't have much more to think about than going to work and being exploited. For her, immigrant and low-income workers are the ones who need entertainment. She expressed doubt that "anyone earning $20 an hour watches them." When Corina discussed the guests on Laura's show, she stated,

> When I say oppressed, it's because they are very alienated, they are not conscious of what's going on, that they go there for a particular reason which could be money, which I don't know for sure because they could indeed be paying them, I don't know . . . because they need the drama, they need the tradition because they cannot manage their lives in any other way.

Krystal (fifty-seven, U.S.-born Mexican American, PhD, married, one children, independent consultant) noted the passivity of the Latino audience regarding this type of show. She thinks that these programs are becoming popular because "they are catering to a lot of the immigrants" and because "this is all they have. . . . They are paying for programs they can understand." She considers that Hispanic immigrants cannot change the state of things for themselves and that they need the assistance of the more educated U.S.-born Hispanics, the policymakers, who do not watch these kinds of programs.

> Krystal (regarding immigrants): If they are here, are they going to be demanding? Are the people who are watching these programs be the kind that would go out and demand things? The ones that are out there, the ones that are politically demanding, are not sitting around watching that.

The previous statement reveals the class tensions among different groups of Latina/os. Although the informant acknowledges that Latinos are paying for this television, which is generally received through cable companies, she does not grant the immigrant viewers the agency to negotiate with the networks at any level.

Final Remarks

Latinas don't just watch television, they watch it in a personal and social context that shapes their consumption and interpretations of television texts. Their ethnic, gender, and class identity permeates their evaluations. Their social trajectories as immigrants, as U.S. Latinas, and as Texas residents also affect their interactions with the Latino media. The same occurs with their perceived location within the ethnic definitions for Latinas/os that are available in mainstream culture. That is why the interview protocol in this study went beyond television consumption and encompassed other social contextual variables, which are necessary to better understand Latinas' interaction with their ethnic television. Knowledge of the social context is an important part of a reception study. To that end, I closely followed the path delineated by other feminist researchers who have studied women and television (Ang 1996; Press 1991; Press and Cole 1999); my contribution is to examine some contextual variables such as ethnicity and class and the role they play in cultural consumption practices.

Latinas watch television while experiencing other life struggles, such as "becoming legal" or "keeping their children in school." In each of these "fields of struggles," to use Bourdieu's term (1993a, 1993b), they use different strategies, forms of capital (cultural, economic, social, symbolic), and negotiating skills. The interviews presented here provide some glimpses into their responses to and evaluations of the content and, more particularly, the representations of women in Univision and Telemundo programming. Their assessments, although critical, do not suggest that the respondents oppose the existence of Spanish-language television networks or feel that all the programming is of poor quality. Soap operas and news were exempted from criticism or received only a mild critique. The overall pattern of the responses indicates that Latinas have a contradictory relationship with Hispanic television that is informed by class, origin, and the perceived state of ethnic relations in U.S. society. Consistent with the initial findings of previous studies regarding Latinos' ambivalence toward Hispanic television (Dávila 2001; DeSipio 1998, 1999), these critiques confirm the complex expectations Latina/os have regarding the role of the Spanish-language networks in their community. As DeSipio's (1998, 1999) studies indicate, Latinos believe that Spanish-language television provides a more sensible portrayal of Latinos and presents less sexual and violent content than English-language television. However, like the Latinas interviewed in my study, the Latino respondents in DeSipio's studies were dissatisfied with the lack of children's programming and the scarcity of Latino role models for their children.

Other specific patterns emerged from the responses of the twenty-seven Latinas interviewed in this study. The first is a critique of the oversexualized representation of Latinas across the programming of Univision and Telemundo in general and on *El Show de Cristina* and *Laura en América* in particular. Contrary to Dávila's (2001) suggestion that U.S.-born Latinos and English-dominant Latinos would use their criticism of women's sexualization on Hispanic television as a strategy to escape the labels and stereotypes ascribed to Latinos by the majority group, the interviews conducted here indicate that immigrant Latinas also used their criticism with similar purposes. The majority of the respondents indicated that they did not relate to shows with highly suggestive portrayals of women. Even more, many of the respondents said they felt attacked, insulted, offended, and embarrassed by the images of models in scanty clothes, the sexual themes of certain entertainment shows, and the representation of sexuality on *Cristina*. Women expressed a sense of collective embarrassment over the gender representations in their own ethnic media. Many were concerned about the opinion of white Americans, particularly males, regarding Latinas and Latinos in general. They did not want them to get "the wrong impressions," because "not all Latina/os are like that."

Class as a marker of difference and distinction emerged as the second theme in this study. Educated and less educated Latinas with different immigration status used the category of class to differentiate themselves from the panelists presented on *Cristina* and *Laura* and also from the audience watching this type of show. U.S.-born Latinas, as well as professional and temporary resident Latinas, used a more material conception of class, such as educational level, to define the people being targeted by these shows. The shows were not for them, but for others—the poor and uneducated immigrants and the ones in the barrios. For the less educated and working-class Latinas, class differences were expressed from a less materialistic point of view. In this case, it is not the possession of economic, cultural, or symbolic capital but the possession of certain virtues or values that, according to Skeggs (1997), becomes a signifier of class. These working-class women used the concept of respectability as a class marker to differentiate between their own lives, the panelists' lives, and the lives of the audiences that watch these programs. The portrayal of sexually promiscuous and physically uninhibited women generates a symbolic class antagonism between Latina respondents and the panelists of the shows. The antagonism is even more dramatic when it takes place among people of similar working-class origin (see Ortner 1991).

The third emergent pattern reveals Latinas' disruption of the unified concept of Latinidad promoted by the networks. U.S.-born and more educated Latinas have a different conception of their Latinidad as compared with labor migrants or political refugees. The transcripts indicate that even though there is no single definition of Latinas, most of the immigrant and working-class women agreed that there are different levels of discrimination emerging from mainstream society and from other Latino subgroups that affect them and impact as well their ethnic identification (see Oboler 1996, 1999). The disruption of the discourse of cultural unity is also present in women's evaluation of the panelists presented on *Cristina* and *Laura*. For U.S.-born Latinas, the Peruvian panelists have nothing to do with the reality of Latinos living in the United States, and they do not relate to them. Immigrants of other nationalities might relate to the story but not to the people presented in the television programs because they are not like the people of their native countries. By disarticulating the unitary concept of Latinidad promoted by the networks, the respondents also convey an implicit criticism against the "foreignness" of Hispanic television and its power to define U.S. Latinos. Several questions deserve further examination, such as what is Latinidad for the networks, what programs best represent it, and how does the audience perceive and evaluate those programs.

The last emerging theme refers to the respondents' disagreement with

Cristina's and Laura's philosophy of empowering Latina/os. Even though the hosts of the shows have claimed over the past years that they work for the betterment of the Latino community, only three working-class immigrants felt that *Laura en América* contributes to educating and support Latina/os. The majority of the informants indicated there these are not educational but rather entertainment programs that do not help to change Latina/os' lives. Some of the respondents, working-class immigrants and professional Latinas included, considered *Cristina* a wasted opportunity to promote social change within the Latino community. Respondents felt that both shows display high levels of violence, offend women, perpetuate Latino stereotypes, and promote the Latin American patriarchal ideology according to which women are fully responsible for their virtue and deserve to be contained if they transgress the moral canon. Some informants believed that Cristina's and Laura's whiteness assist them in exerting their symbolic power over the participants in the shows.

The voices of the women interviewed in this study help to illustrate the power struggles between Latino audiences and Spanish-language networks, one of the most visible definers of Latina/os' identity in the United States. Latinas located in different social positions are able to use their cultural and symbolic capital to participate in a debate that shapes their ethnic, gender, and class identities. Bourdieu's (1980) theory of practice serves as a theoretical framework to understand Hispanic television as a field of forces where Latina/os, as well as other actors, compete for positions and the accumulation of diverse forms of capital, in this case, for the possibility to contest television classifications. Bourdieu's theory of practice, combined with a Latina feminist perspective, provides a strong theoretical framework for exploring the classification struggles that occur in relation to Latina television consumption practices, and for understanding the authoritarian discourse on talk shows as a particular case of symbolic violence.

Notes

1. The show is currently broadcast under the name *Laura* (http://www
.telemundo.com/laura/index.html).

2. Latinidad is an analytical concept that serves to identify the state of being Latino or Latina in a determined discursive space (Lao-Montes 2001, 3). The term embraces the multiplicity of intersecting discourses that define Latinos and locate them in U.S. society. From a structural perspective, the Hispanic media industry is part of a conflicted and contested symbolic domain in which many

actors, including Latinas and Latinos, participate in the struggle for the creation and reproduction of Latinos' identity. Univision and Telemundo are the most visible definers of Latinos' Latinidad. With their access to and penetration of the Hispanic community, these networks possess a quasi-monopoly on the cultural representation of Latinos in the United States.

3. At the end of the episode "Controversial Panelist" (May 27, 2002), Cristina Saralegui explained to the home audience that she is not crazy and that all the audacious topics she presents are based on people's requests, because it is "something you really enjoy" (*Porque a ustedes les encanta*).

Bibliography

Ang, I. 1996. *Living Room Wars: Rethinking Media Audiences for a Postmodern World*. New York: Routledge.

Aparicio, F., and S. Chávez-Silverman, eds. 1997. *Tropicalizations: Transcultural Representations of Latinidad*. Hanover, NH: University Press of New England.

Associated Press Online. 2002. "Univision Oks $3.5 B. radio deal." *Financial News*, June 12 (accessed June 12, 2002, from Lexis Nexis).

Baxter, K. 1998. "It's more than idle chat." *Los Angeles Times*, November 1, Section Calendar, 3.

Ben Amor, L. 1998. *La communauté inventée: La televisión hispanique dans l'espace public Américain*. Dissertation, Université de Toulouse Le-Mirail, France.

Bourdieu, P. 1980. *The Logic of Practice*. Stanford, CA: Stanford University Press.

———. 1984. *Distinction: A Social Critique of the Judgment of Taste*, trans. Richard Nice. Cambridge, MA: Harvard University Press.

———. 1986. "The Forms of Capital." In *Handbook of Theory and Research for the Sociology of Education*, ed. J. G. Richardson, pp. 241–258. Westport, CT: Greenwood Press.

———. 1993a. *Sociology in Question*. London: Sage.

———. 1993b. *The Field of Cultural Production*. New York: Columbia University Press.

———. 1999. *Outline of a Theory of Practice*, trans. Richard Nice. Cambridge, UK: Cambridge University Press.

Bourdieu, P., and Wacquant, L. J. D. 1992. *An Invitation to Reflexive Sociology*. Chicago: University of Chicago Press.

Calles, J. 2001. *El Show de Cristina*. Dissertation proposal, University of Iowa, School of Journalism and Mass Communication.

Caspa TV. 2002. Entrevista a TV chismes. http://www.caspa.tv/archives/000052 .html (accessed August 16, 2006).

Cotterill, P. 1992. "Interviewing Women: Issues of Friendship, Vulnerability and Power." *Women's Studies International Forum* 15, no. 5/6: 593–606.

Cristina Online. 1998. Univision official Web site. http://www.univision.net/ programacion/he-talk.htm (accessed December 15, 1998).

D'Acci, J. 1994. *Defining Women: Television and the Case of Cagney and Lacey*. Chapel Hill: University of North Carolina Press.

Dávila, A. 2000. "Mapping Latinidad: Language and Culture in the Spanish TV Battlefront." *Television and New Media* 1, no. 1: 75–94.

———. 2001. *Latinos, Inc.: The Marketing and Making of a People*. Berkeley and Los Angeles: University of California Press.

———. 2002. "Talking Back: Spanish Media and U.S." In *Latinidad in Latino/a Popular Culture*, ed. M. Habell-Pallon and M. Romero, 25–37. New York and London: New York University Press.

Delgado, F. 2004. "Beyond the Textual Paradigm: Latina/o Film and the Presence of Audiences." In *Ethnic Media in America: Images, Audiences and Transforming Sources*, ed. G. T. Meiss and A. A. Tait, 168–184. Dubuque, IA: Kendall/Hunt.

DeSipio, L. 1998. *Talking Back to Television: Latinos Discuss How Television Portrays Them and the Quality of Programming Options*. Claremont, CA: Tomas Rivera Policy Institute.

———. 1999. *Engaging Television in English y en Espanol*. Report. Claremont, CA: Tomas Rivera Policy Institute.

———. 2003. *Latino Viewing Choices: Bilingual Television Viewers and the Language Choices They Make*. Claremont, CA: Tomas Rivera Policy Institute.

García-Canclini, N. 1995. *Hybrid Cultures: Strategies for Entering and Leaving Modernity*. Minneapolis: University of Minnesota Press.

Garnham, N. 1986. "Bourdieu's Distinction." *Sociological Review* 34, no 2: 423–433.

Garvin, G. 2000. "Fujimori to critics: Stay out of Peru's politics." *Miami Herald*, April 3. On-line. Committee to Free Lori Berenson—A young woman held political prisoner in Peru. http://www.freelori.org/news/00apr03_miamiherald .html (accessed October 31, 2001).

Glascock, J., and Ruggiero, T. E. 2004. "Representation of Class and Gender on Primetime Spanish-Language Television in the United States." *Communication Quarterly*, 52, no. 4: 390–402.

Hall, S. 1992. "The Question of Cultural Identity." In *Modernity and Its Futures*, ed. S. Hall, D. Held, and T. McGrew, 273–325. Cambridge: Polity Press; Oxford: Blackwell.

———. 1996. "Introduction: Who Needs Identity?" In *Questions of Cultural Identity*, ed. S. Hall and P. DuGay, 1–17. New Delhi: Sage.

Holloway, D. 2002. "Viva la tele: As the audience grows, so does must-see television." *Austin American-Statesman*, June 23, K1, K10–K11.

Johnson, R. 1999. Editor's introduction. In P. Bourdieu, *The Field of Cultural Production*, 1–25. New York: Columbia University Press.

Lao-Montes, A. 2001. Introduction. In *Mambo Montage: The Latinization of New York*, ed. A. Lao-Montes and A. Dávila, 1–53. New York: Columbia University Press.

"Laura: Biografía." http://www.telemundo.com/laura/2579530 1/detail.html (accessed August 16, 2006).

Mahar, C., R. Harker, and C. Wilkes. 1990. "The Basic Theoretical Position." In *An Introduction to the Works of Pierre Bourdieu: The Practice of Theory*, ed. R. Harker, C. Mahar, and C. Wilkes, 1–25. London: Macmillan.

McLaughlin, L. 1993. "Chastity Criminals in the Age of Electronic Reproduction:

Re-viewing Talk Television and the Public Sphere." *Journal of Communication Inquiry* 17, no. 1: 41-55.

Noriega, C. A. 2000. *Shot in America: Television, the State and the Rise of Chicano Cinema.* Minneapolis: University of Minnesota Press.

———. 2003. "Strategies for Increasing Latinos' Media Access." *Harvard Journal of Hispanic Policy* 16:105-109.

Oboler, S. 1996. *Ethnic Labels, Latino Lives: Identity and the Politics of (Re)presentation in the United States.* Minneapolis and London: University of Minnesota Press.

———. 1999. "Racializing Latinos in the United States: Toward a New Research Paradigm." In *Identities on the Move: Transnational Processes in North America and the Caribbean Basin,* ed. L. Goldin. Vol. 7. *Studies on Culture and Society,* 45-68. New York: Institute for Mesoamerican Studies/State University of New York at Albany.

Ortner, S. 1991. "Reading America: Preliminary Notes on Class and Culture." In *Recapturing Ideology,* ed. R. G. Fox, 163-189. Santa Fe, NM: School of American Research Press.

Press, A. L. 1991. *Women Watching Television: Gender, Class, and Generation in the American Television Experience.* Philadelphia: University of Pennsylvania Press.

Press, A. L., and Cole, E. R. 1999. *Speaking of Abortion: Television and Authority in the Lives of Women.* Chicago: University of Chicago Press.

Reay, D. 1995. "Feminist Research: The Fallacy of Easy Access." *Women's Studies International Forum* 18, no. 2: 205-213.

Rincón and Associates. 2004. *Latino Television Study.* Report prepared for the National Latino Media Council. Dallas: Rincón and Associates.

Rodríguez, A. 1999a. *Making Latino News: Race, Language, Class.* Thousand Oaks, CA: Sage.

———. 1999b. "Making Latino News: Race, Language and Class." *Aztlán: A Journal of Chicano Studies* 24, no. 2: 15-24.

———. 1999c. "Creating an Audience and Remapping a Nation: A Brief History of US Spanish Language Broadcasting 1930-1980." *Quarterly Review of Film and Video* 16, no. 3/4: 357-374.

Rojas, V. 2003. *Latinas' Image on Spanish-Language Television: A Study of Women's Representation and Their Self-Perceptions.* Dissertation, School of Journalism, University of Texas at Austin.

Romero, M., and Habell-Pallan, M. 2002. Introduction. In *Latino/a Popular Culture,* ed. M. Romero and M. Habell-Pallan, 1-21. New York: New York University Press.

Skeggs, B. 1997. *Formations of Class and Gender: Becoming Respectable.* Thousand Oaks, CA: Sage.

Squire, C. 1997. "Who's White? Television Talk Shows and Representations of Whiteness." In *Off White: Readings on Race, Power and Society,* ed. M. Fine, L. Weis, L. Powell, and L. Mong, 242-250. New York: Routledge.

Subervi-Vélez, F., G. Gibens, T. Lopez-Pumarejo, D. Rios, O. Santa Ana, J. Schement, and G. Soruco. 2003. *Sociological Considerations Relevant to the Merger of Univision and HBC.* Report presented by Willkie Farr and Gallaher to the Federal Communications Commission.

Subervi-Vélez, F., C. Rámirez-Berg, P. Constantakis-Valdes, C. Noriega, D. Rios, and K. Wilkinson. 1994. "Mass Communication and Hispanics." In *Handbook of Hispanic Cultures in the United States*. Vol 4. *Sociology*, ed. N. Kanellos and C. Esteva-Fabregal, 304–357. Houston: Arte Público Press.

Suro, R. 2004. *Changing Channels and Crisscrossing Cultures: A Survey of Latinos on the News Media*. Washington, DC: Pew Hispanic Center.

Valdivia, A. 1995. "Rosie Goes to Hollywood: The Politics of Representation." *Education/Pedagogy/Cultural Studies*, 18, no. 2: 129–141.

———. 1998. "Stereotype or Transgression? Rosie Perez in Hollywood Film." *The Sociological Quarterly*, 39, no. 3: 393–408.

———. 2000. *A Latina in the Land of Hollywood and Other Essays on Media Culture*. Tucson: University of Arizona Press.

Contributors

Rosa Linda Fregoso is professor and chair of the Latin American/Latino Studies Department at the University of California–Santa Cruz. She writes in the areas of culture, transnational feminism, and human rights in the Americas. She is the author of *MeXicana Encounters: The Making of Social Identities on the Borderlands* (University of California Press, 2003), *The Bronze Screen: Chicana and Chicano Film Culture* (University of Minnesota Press, 1993), and *Lourdes Portillo:* The Devil Never Sleeps *and Other Films* (University of Texas Press, 2000), and co-editor with Norma Iglesias of *Miradas de mujer* (CLRC and COLEF, 1998). Her book, *MeXicana Encounters: The Making of Social Identities on the Borderlands* was recently awarded the Modern Language Association prize in United States Latino and Chicano Literary and Cultural Studies.

Cynthia Fuchs is director of George Mason University's Film and Media Studies Program, as well as a film, TV, and DVD editor for PopMatters .com and a film reviewer for *Philadelphia Citypaper* (citypaper.net) and Screenit.com. She has published articles on hip-hop, Prince, Michael Jackson, the Spice Girls, queer punks, "bad" kids in *Bully* and *George Washington,* and media coverage of the war against Iraq. She edited *Spike Lee: Interviews* (University of Mississippi Press, 2002) and co-edited *Between the Sheets, In the Streets: Queer, Lesbian, and Gay Documentary* (University of Minnesota Press, 1997).

Karen S. Goldman is associate professor of Spanish at Chatham College in Pittsburgh. She writes and speaks on contemporary Latin American literature and cinema.

Isabel Molina Guzmán is assistant professor of communications and Latina/o studies at the University of Illinois at Champaign-Urbana. Her research and publications examine the politics of gender, sexuality, race, and ethnicity in U.S. public discourse and popular media.

Tara Lockhart is a doctoral student at the University of Pittsburgh, where her teaching and scholarship focus on composition and literacy, in addition to film and cultural studies. She is also a practicing poet and has published several creative pieces.

Myra Mendible is associate professor in the English and Interdisciplinary Studies programs at Florida Gulf Coast University in Ft. Myers. She was co-founder of the English program at FGCU, where she has taught a range of courses in popular culture, ethnic and gender studies, and film and media analysis. She has presented her research at both national and international conferences and in a wide variety of peer-reviewed journals. Mendible is currently completing a book manuscript, *Putdowns and Showdowns: American Culture and the Politics of Humiliation*.

Frances Negrón-Muntaner is an award-winning filmmaker, writer, and scholar. She is the recipient of Ford, Truman, Scripps Howard, Rockefeller, and Pew fellowships; a founding board member and current chair of the National Association of Latino Independent Producers; and the founder of Miami Light Project's Filmmakers Workshop. Among her books are *Boricua Pop: Puerto Ricans and the Latinization of American Culture* (Choice Outstanding Book for 2004), *None of the Above: Contemporary Puerto Rican Culture and Politics,* and *Puerto Rican Jam: Rethinking Nationalism and Colonialism* (co-edited with Ramón Grosfoguel). Negrón-Muntaner is currently completing two documentaries, *For the Record: Guam and World War II* and *Regarding Vieques*. She teaches at Columbia University.

William A. Nericcio is associate professor of English and comparative literature at San Diego State University, where he is also on the staff of the Department of Chicana/o Studies and the Center for Latin American Studies. A graduate of Cornell University, where he studied with Carlos Fuentes, Gayatri Spivak, and Enrico Mario Santí, he numbers among his most recent published essays a rant on Rita Hayworth, electrolysis, and the existential in *Violence and the Body* (Indiana University Press) and a semiotic gloss on Gilbert Hernandez's illustrated biography of Frida Kahlo in *La-*

tina/o Popular Culture (New York University Press). His edited collection of photography, theory, and art, entitled *Bordered Sexualities: Bodies on the Verge of a Nation,* appeared in winter 2003 with Hyperbole Books.

Charla Ogaz is an assistant professor of liberal arts at Savannah State University. She received her doctorate in the history of consciousness from the University of California, Santa Cruz, in December 2000. She is interested in cultural and social issues revolving around what U.S. postcolonialism. Specifically, she studies theory as/and storytelling by U.S. women of color, women's participation in popular music, multiculturalism in education, and contemporary philosophy.

Ana Patricia Rodríguez is associate professor of U.S. Latino/a literature in the Department of Spanish and Portuguese at the University of Maryland, College Park. Her work focuses on Latino/a transnational identity construction and Central American cultural and literary production in the United States and the isthmus. Her published work includes articles in *Latino/a Popular Culture* (edited by Michelle Habell-Pallán and Mary Romero, New York University Press), *The Globalization of U.S.-Latin American Relations* (edited by Virginia M. Bouvier, Praeger Press), the journals *American Literature* and *Antípodas,* and numerous literary encyclopedias. Her forthcoming book is titled *Dividing the Isthmus: Central American Transnational Literatures and Cultures.*

Clara E. Rodríguez is professor of sociology at Fordham University's College at Lincoln Center. She is the author of nine books, including *Heroes, Lovers, and Others: The Story of Latinos in Hollywood* (Smithsonian Institution Press, 2004), *Changing Race: Latinos, the Census and the History of Ethnicity in the United States* (New York University Press, 2000), and *Latin Looks: Images of Latinas and Latinos in U.S. Media* (Westview Press, 1997); with E. Meléndez and Barry Figueroa, Jr., she has edited *Hispanics in the Labor Force: Issues and Policies* (Plenum Press, 1991). She is the recipient of numerous research and teaching awards, most recently, the American Sociological Association's 2001 Award for Distinguished Contributions to Research in the Field of Latina/o Studies and her university's Award for Distinguished Teaching in the Social Sciences in 2003. She is currently at work on an update of the classic Coser, Kadushin, and Powell text, *Books: The Culture and Commerce of Publishing,* which will be published by Stanford University Press.

Viviana Rojas is assistant professor at the University of Texas San Antonio. Her work focuses on Latino/as in the United States, Spanish-language television networks, American migration to Mexico, and immigrants and the digital divide. Her article, "The Gender of Latinidad: Latinas Speak about Hispanic Television," appeared in 2004 in *The Communication Review*, and she is the senior author of a book chapter, "Communities, Cultural Capital and the Digital Divide," which was published in *Media Access: Social and Psychological Dimensions of New Technology Use* (Lawrence Erlbaum Associates, 2004). She taught at the Universidad de Chile and Universidad Diego Portales in Santiago, Chile, between 1987 and 1997.

Karen R. Tolchin is assistant professor of English at Florida Gulf Coast University in Fort Myers, Florida and is the author of *Part Blood, Part Ketchup: Coming of Age in American Literature and Film* (Lexington, 2006). She teaches composition, creative writing, literature, film, and journalism.

Angharad Valdivia is a research professor at the Institute of Communications Research at the University of Illinois. She is the author of *A Latina in the Land of Hollywood* (University of Arizona Press, 2000) and editor of *Feminism, Multiculturalism and the Media* (Sage, 1995), the forthcoming *Blackwell Companion to Media Studies, Feminism, Multiculturalism, and the Media* (Sage), and co-editor of *Geographies of Latinidad* (Duke University Press). Her research focuses on transnational multiculturalist gender issues with a special emphasis on Latinas in popular culture.

Index